PROCEDURES FOR THE LEGAL SECRETARY

PROCEDURES FOR THE LEGAL SECRETARY

Elsie E. Swartz, CPS
*Humber College of Applied Arts and
Technology, Toronto*

Holt, Rinehart and Winston of Canada, Limited
Toronto   Montreal

Consultant:
Roger J. Smith M.A., LL.B.
Barrister and Solicitor
Toronto

ISBN 0-03-926600-1

Cover: Mike Yazzolino

Printed in Canada
1 2 3 4 5   74 73 72 71 70

FOREWORD

It will be at once apparent to anyone using this book that it is well written – clear in expression, as concise as the particular subject permits, as detailed as efficient exposition requires. It should be a treasure-house of information not only for students but for experienced secretaries to whom a "refresher course" has not been available.

The question one always asks concerning a "how-to-do-it" book is – does the author know what she's talking about? Elsie Swartz was my secretary, in a large and busy law office, for over eleven years. The high standards, the zeal for efficiency, the grasp of detail, the need for accuracy, set against a realization of the human elements of personality and good humour – all these are in the book, but they were first the hallmark of her own life and work. She knows, through actual and highly successful experience, how these things should be done.

When she resigned in 1967 to become a teacher of secretarial science, I was sure she had an invaluable contribution to make to her new profession. This book proves I was right.

John D. Arnup, Q.C., LL.D.

ACKNOWLEDGMENTS

p. 19. Reprinted by courtesy of Canada Law Book Limited, Law Publishers, Toronto.

pp. 23, 35, 37, 40, 42, 51, 53, 55 & 56, 66-70, 73-77, 78, 79-82, 89-93, 94, 95, 96, 98-102, 106-110, 111-114, 115-117, 118-120, 121-123, 126 & 127, 128, 142, 147-150, 154, 155 & 156, 157-160, 161-164, 165 & 166, 167 & 168, 183, 197-199, 200-203, 206 & 207, 208 & 209, 210-213, 214-217, 224 & 225, 226 & 227, 255, 256, 257, 262, 263, 265, 266, 267, 268, 269, 271, 272, 273, 277-289, 290 & 291, 318, 320, 322, 323, 328-334, 335-338. Reprinted by courtesy of Dye & Durham Company, Limited, Law and Commercial Stationers, Toronto.

pp. 84 & 85, 317. Reprinted by permission of The Royal Bank of Canada.

p. 97. Copyright © 1967 Setak Computer Services Corporation Limited. Published by courtesy of Setak Computer Services Corporation Limited, Toronto. Reproduction of this material in any form without prior written consent of Setak is prohibited.

p. 130. Reprinted by permission of the Finance Department, Borough of Etobicoke.

p. 221. Reprinted by permission of A. C. Devenport, Special Examiner.

PREFACE

This book is intended for students who wish to become legal secretaries, but perhaps it may also assist those who wish to return to legal secretarial work.

The contents cannot, of course, cover every practice or procedure which you may encounter during your legal secretarial career. Nor do the illustrations and instructions always outline the only way those procedures may be carried out. I have tried to keep the material basic and straightforward, to form a firm foundation upon which you may build as you encounter more detailed and complex legal secretarial work in the future. Many procedures must be followed exactly as outlined; they have been established by rules or Acts. Others are only illustrative of common and acceptable practice, and may be varied, of course, to conform to the preference of your law office.

The procedures outlined are intended to reflect those being followed in the spring of 1970. No doubt new procedures will be introduced in the future, or existing ones amended or revised. I hope that the basic principles shown in this book will assist you to understand and comply with any such changes.

Many of the law forms reproduced are now under process of minor revisions, but these revisions in no way alter the basic principles to be followed in completing the forms.

The completion of this book has been made possible with the assistance and interest not only of friends, colleagues, and members of the legal profession, who read all or part of the manuscript and offered comments and suggestions, but also of court and government officials, who provided much helpful information and advice. Their assistance is deeply appreciated, but the responsibility for what appears in this book is, of course, mine.

I should like to list individually all who assisted, but space does not permit. There are some, however, to whom I wish to extend my special thanks and gratitude.

To Gordon F. Beddis, Esq., Q.C., Registrar of the Supreme Court of Ontario;

J. Poag, Esq., Department of National Revenue; H. B. Ridout, Esq., Registrar of the Surrogate Court of the County of York; Charles R. B. Salter, Esq., Department of Financial and Commercial Affairs for Ontario; Stanley Sadinsky, Esq., LL.B.; I. Stephenson, Esq., Succession Duty Branch, Ontario Department of Revenue.

To my father, Harold Richards Swartz, who has patiently endured the clutter and clatter which of necessity have been part of this endeavour, and who on so many occasions made me a gift of time.

To Roger J. Smith, Esq., M.A., LL.B., my legal consultant, for his valuable advice, suggestions, and comments as the text progressed, and for his interest and constant encouragement.

To John D. Arnup, Esq., Q.C., LL.D., from whom I had the privilege of learning the wonderful heritage, integrity, and fascination of the legal profession, and its service to others.

And to the students I have been privileged to be associated with since September, 1967, whose interest in a legal secretarial career led to the writing of this book.

It is not unusual for a book to be dedicated. I should like, therefore, to dedicate this book to all legal secretaries — past, present, and future, and in particular to the memory of one, my mother, Edith Margaret Swartz.

Elsie E. Swartz, CPS
March, 1970

CONTENTS

Chapter 1   Lawyers and Law Firms   *2*
         2   The Legal Secretary   *5*
         3   Legal Correspondence   *7*
         4   Sources of Law and How to Refer to
              Them   *16*
         5   Memoranda   *20*
         6   Dockets, Entries, and Accounts   *22*
         7   Preparing Legal Papers   *33*
         8   Notarial Certificates, Affidavits, and
              Statutory Declarations   *49*
         9   Introduction to Real Estate
              Transactions   *57*
        10   Deeds and Transfers   *62*
        11   Mortgages and Charges   *83*
        12   Legal Instruments Relating to
              Mortgages and Charges   *103*
        13   Buying and Selling Real
              Property   *124*
        14   Statement of Adjustments   *136*
        15   Insurance and Reporting
              Letters   *141*
        16   Leases   *145*
        17   Powers of Attorney, Bills of Sale, and
              Chattel Mortgages   *151*
        18   Introduction to Civil Litigation   *169*
        19   Preparing Court Documents   *171*
        20   Types of Court Documents   *180*
        21   Steps in a Civil Lawsuit   *194*
        22   Bills of Costs and Taxation of
              Costs   *228*
        23   Appeals   *232*
        24   Wills   *244*
        25   Probate and Administration of
              Estates   *252*
        26   Succession Duty and Estate Tax   *274*
        27   Incorporating a Company   *298*
        28   Company Practice   *307*
        29   Separation Agreements and
              Divorce   *324*
              Summary of Provincial Courts   *344*
              Glossary   *346*
              Index   *357*

CHAPTER 1

Lawyers and Law Firms

The legal profession is one of the oldest in the world. Its terms and customs are a reflection of the fact that law itself is of great antiquity. With the adoption of English common law in most of the Canadian provinces, basic customs and traditions of the English legal profession were inherited, but with modifications to suit the particular circumstances of Canada.

Lawyers

In England a lawyer is either a *solicitor* engaged in transacting legal business on behalf of a client, or a *barrister* who appears in the courts. In Canada a lawyer is both a barrister and a solicitor. The term *counsel* is often used to describe a lawyer whose practice largely involves court work.

In addition, lawyers may be appointed a *Queen's Counsel (Q.C.)* as a mark of recognition. Such appointments are made annually on January 1 by the Attorney General or the Minister of Justice for each province, or by the Attorney General of Canada.

Lawyers practising in a province, or a city, are collectively referred to, for example, as "the bar of Ontario", "the bar of Toronto", "the bar of Vancouver". When a lawyer is admitted to the practice of law, he is said to be "called to the bar".

Each province has its own requirements for admission to its bar, and these are administered by the governing body for the legal profession of that province, examples of which are:

The Law Society of Alberta

The Law Society of Upper Canada (Ontario)

The Barristers Society of New Brunswick

Barreau de la Province de Québec

These societies are governed by lawyers who are elected at given intervals by the lawyers of the particular province. The head of the Society is the "President" in some provinces, the "Treasurer" in others (of which Ontario is one), and "Battonier" in Quebec. The members elected to govern the Society are called *Benchers* in most provinces. (See Figure 1.1.)

All practising lawyers of a province must be members of the provincial Society, paying annual dues, and following the rules of professional conduct laid down by the Society. These rules are very comprehensive and specify, for example, how money received from or for a client is to be treated, what information may appear on an office sign, or what size type may be used in advertising in the yellow pages of the telephone book. Breaches of the rules of professional conduct are considered by the Discipline Committee of each society; serious breaches may result in a lawyer being disbarred.

Many lawyers voluntarily belong to the Canadian Bar Association, which has provincial branches. The Association meets annually to discuss or explore pertinent matters relating to the legal profession.

In some provinces there are also County Law Associations which, among other areas of activity, maintain County Law Libraries for the use of the profession, and set the tariff (fee) which may be charged for performing certain types of legal work such as handling a real estate transaction.

Educational Background of Lawyers

An individual training to become a lawyer has many years of post high school education. In Ontario, for example, this would include at least two years at a university; three years at a law school to obtain the degree of Bachelor of Laws (LL.B.); twelve months working as a student in a law office, known as *articling;* six months at the *Bar Admission Course* at Osgoode Hall in Toronto. The would-be lawyer is then called to the bar.

There are many areas of service then open to the new lawyer. He may enter the employ of business or industry; he may join the legal

Governing Bodies of the Legal Profession in Canada

Province	Name of Society	Title of Chief Officer	Designation of Elected Representatives
Alberta	The Law Society of Alberta	President	Benchers
British Columbia	The Law Society of British Columbia	Treasurer	Benchers
Manitoba	The Law Society of Manitoba	President	Benchers
New Brunswick	The Barristers' Society of New Brunswick	President	Members of Council
Newfoundland	Law Society of Newfoundland	Treasurer	Benchers
Nova Scotia	Nova Scotia Barristers' Society	President	Members of Council
Ontario	The Law Society of Upper Canada	Treasurer	Benchers
Prince Edward Island	The Law Society of Prince Edward Island	President	Executive Committee
Quebec	Barreau de la Province de Quebec	Bâtonnier	Délégués
Saskatchewan	The Law Society of Saskatchewan	President	Benchers

Figure 1.1

staff at the municipal, provincial or federal level of government where lawyers are required in many departments. The vast majority of lawyers, however, enter what is known as private practice, either alone or with a law firm, to provide legal services to those persons known as *clients* who come to them for such assistance.

In any area of legal practice, a lawyer is automatically a *Commissioner* for the purpose of administering oaths to persons coming before him to swear to the truth of statements. He may be appointed a *Notary Public* to affirm under notarial seal the execution of certain legal writings or the authenticity of a copy of a document or writing, as well as administering oaths.

Law Firms

A law firm is not a company and that word or the word "limited" does not appear in its name. It is a partnership, composed of any number of lawyers, known as the partners, who have made an agreement to practise law together. The firm may consist only of those partners, or it may employ other lawyers to be associated with it.

The name of the law firm is determined by the partnership agreement and is usually composed of the last name of some or all of the partners arranged in agreed order; often by seniority of admission to the partnership. It may also include names of former partners who are now deceased. The firm name appears on its letterhead, usually with the full name of all partners and lawyers associated with the law firm (Figure 1.2).

Legal Directories

The names and addresses of Canadian law firms, and of individual lawyers, are published each year in THE CANADIAN LAW LIST (Canada Law Book Limited). This publication lists by province, and then alphabetically by city, town or village in that province, all law firms and practising lawyers.

Each year, in each major municipality, a publishing house also publishes a local legal directory which lists all lawyers and law firms in alphabetical order, giving addresses and telephone numbers.

TELEPHONE: 364-9999, AREA CODE 416

CABLE 3-1IL6 TORONTO

Suite 2501

17 Princess Street South

Toronto 560, Canada

Hill, Johnston & Grant

Barristers and Solicitors

Frank P. Hill, Q.C.
Edward N. Johnston, Q.C.
Peter T. Grant, Q.C.
John L. Craigmore

Henry Q. Winslow
Percy Y. McQuiller
Robert W. Burnsley

Counsel: P. B. Ranwood, Q.C.

Figure 1.2. Top of Legal Letterhead

CHAPTER 2

The Legal Secretary

Qualifications and Characteristics

Surveys of business executives indicate that in addition to excellent technical skills in shorthand and typing, employers want a secretary who is dependable, loyal, tactful, diplomatic, well organized, considerate, poised, personable and punctual.

To those qualifications and characteristics a legal secretary must add a sound knowledge of the principles, practices and procedures of legal office work, and the ethics by which it is bound. She must add one other very important ingredient: complete discretion.

All the work of a legal office is confidential and must never be discussed outside the office. In some offices it may not even be discussed with another secretary or others not directly concerned with the case or matter.

A lawyer is a *fiduciary*, a Latin word meaning "one who is entrusted". He receives information as privileged communication, to be held in strict confidence and used as necessary in the matter being handled for the client.

You are legally the agent, servant and employee of the law firm which employs you. Due to the nature of your secretarial responsibilities you may eventually know a great deal about the work being done in that office. You are bound by the same code of ethics as the lawyer. The lawyer must be able to rely on your discretion to keep confidential any information you may come by, and to resist any temptation to mention, even in passing, outside the office any details of a case or matter – whether it be an appointment, a major development, a conversation, a letter or document received, or simply a funny incident. Nothing may be discussed outside the office. There are no exceptions to this rule.

Performance

A legal **secretary** must be a highly competent and efficient stenographer. Even a simple error in typing may be both costly and embarrassing. Recently the newspapers reported a judgment of the courts which was largely based on an error in transcribing "a" instead of "the". The omission of one line of typing from a legal description of property which was being discussed at a hearing, resulted in the hearing being postponed at considerable expense to the parties who had travelled from another city, and the "typing error" was mentioned in the headline on the page on which the matter was reported in the press. Aim for complete accuracy in all your work, and use the following rules as a guide:

1. Check the spelling or division of any word about which you have any doubt. Never guess how to spell or divide a word; always check in the dictionary which should be part of the basic equipment on your desk.

2. Proofread and check all typed work. Never put any typed material on the lawyer's desk until you have proofread it for typing errors and misspelled words, and checked dates, amounts, and the spelling of names and places.

   Work which contains material copied from another source should be proofread or compared with someone else. Check your newly typed copy carefully as another person reads aloud from the original copy.

3. Be sure that what is typed makes sense. As material is typed it should read sensibly. A "metes and bounds" description is not a "leaps and bounds" description, for example.

   As a new legal secretary, some of the material you may type will initially not entirely make sense. Legal terminology is very formal and traditional, but conveys a precise meaning which has been developed over a great many years. As you progress in your work, this traditional phrasing will become very familiar.

4. Be sure that what is typed is grammatically correct. It is your responsibility to correct any error in grammar, provided that

when the correction is made it does not in any way alter the meaning of the sentence.

5. Maintain an index of unusual names and legal terms. If the lawyer dictates an unusual or unfamiliar legal phrase or name, at some convenient stopping point ask how it is spelled and, at the first opportunity, make a permanent note of it in a card index or in a special notebook maintained for the purpose.

6. Compile a set of precedents. Each time a new form or document is prepared for the first time, make an extra copy for a precedent file, to which you can refer when the form or document is prepared in the future.

7. Concentrate and do it right the first time. You should concentrate on doing each piece of work accurately on the first attempt. Check out any points about which you are uncertain before you begin; here, your set of precedents will prove very

useful. Both time and money are wasted when work must be redone.

Role of the Secretary

It is the lawyer's responsibility to practise law and to advise clients on what steps they should take to meet their specific problem or need. You assist the lawyer by anticipating his needs and relieving him of details and routine. Your scope is both large and interesting; there is great satisfaction to be gained from being part of a profession which serves others.

In fulfilling your duties, however, you must never under any circumstances offer legal advice to a client.

In a very real sense, a legal secretary contributes to the success of a law firm. To the telephone caller, to the office visitor, you set the atmosphere of your office. Your tact, courtesy and diplomacy create goodwill for your firm.

CHAPTER 3

Legal Correspondence

Lawyers in Canada are not permitted to advertise their services, and a letter may often be the first contact with a client. First impressions are important; receipt of an attractively typed and set-up letter will create the feeling of competence and high standard of performance of the sender. The lawyer is responsible for the content of the letter; the secretary, for its appearance.

Styles of Letter Set-up

Legal offices have been slow to adopt the more modern trends in letter set-up. Some offices still prefer the indented style, but the majority now prefer the semi-block style, with either closed or mixed punctuation.

Indented Style

Figure 3.1 illustrates this style. Each line of the inside address is indented five spaces, and each paragraph is indented ten spaces. Traditionally, closed punctuation is used with this style.

Semi-block Style

Figures 3.2 and 3.3 illustrate this style. Each new line of the inside address begins flush with the left-hand margin, but when a firm name is too long to appear on one line, the carry-over line is indented two or three spaces. Paragraphs are indented no more than ten spaces.

Punctuation

Closed

This form requires punctuation at the end of each line of the date, inside address, salutation, and complimentary close (Figures 3.1, 3.2).

Mixed

This form requires punctuation only after the salutation and complimentary close (Figure 3.3).

Date Line

Placement of the date line is governed by the format of the letterhead. Type it two or three lines beneath the letterhead, in a position where it will complement the letterhead.

A letter bears the date it was dictated, not the date it is transcribed, unless instructions are received to the contrary. In this event, correct any references to "today", "tomorrow", or "yesterday".

The ordinals "st", "nd", "rd" and "th" are omitted following the day of the month when typing the date.

Correct
October 28, 1970

Incorrect
October 28th, 1970

Inside Address

Messrs.

In addressing a firm of lawyers composed of men, or of men and women, the name of the firm is preceded by the word "Messrs."

Correct
Messrs. Rae & Brown

Incorrect
Rae & Brown

Mesdames

In addressing a firm of lawyers composed entirely of women, the name of the firm is preceded by the word "Mesdames".

Esquire or Esq.

In writing to an individual lawyer, or to a male client, omit the title "Mr." before the name, and use the title "Esquire" or "Esq." following the name.

Correct

John Smith, Esq.

Incorrect

Mr. John Smith, Esq.

Q.C. (Queen's Counsel)

If a lawyer holds the designation "Queen's Counsel", this is shown following the designation "Esq."

John Smith, Esq., Q.C.

Barristers and Solicitors

Law Firms

Whenever the name of a law firm is used in the inside address, the calling of that firm is shown by typing on the next line the words "Barristers and Solicitors", then continuing with the address.

Correct

Messrs. Rae & Brown
Barristers and Solicitors
27 Ringdate Blvd.
Malton, Ontario

Incorrect

Messrs. Rae & Brown
27 Ringdate Blvd.
Malton, Ontario.

Correct

John F. Brown, Esq.
Messrs. Rae & Brown
Barristers and Solicitors
27 Ringdate Blvd.
Malton, Ontario

Incorrect

John F. Brown, Esq.
Messrs. Rae & Brown
27 Ringdate Blvd.
Malton, Ontario

Individual Lawyer

When writing to a lawyer who is practising alone and who is not a Queen's Counsel, the designation "Barrister and Solicitor" appears on the second line of the inside address. These words do not follow the name of an individual lawyer who is a Queen's Counsel.

Correct

James Jones, Esq.
Barrister and Solicitor
17 Plateau Street
Calgary, Alberta

Incorrect

James Jones, Esq.
17 Plateau Street
Calgary, Alberta

Correct

James Jones, Esq., Q.C.
17 Plateau Street
Calgary, Alberta

Incorrect

James Jones, Esq., Q.C.
Barrister and Solicitor
17 Plateau Street
Calgary, Alberta

Salutations

Firms of Lawyers

When writing directly to a firm of lawyers, use the salutation "Dear Sirs" unless the firm is composed entirely of women, when "Mesdames" is used.

When a letter is addressed to the firm, but marked for the attention of a specific lawyer, the salutation is still to the firm, not to the individual lawyer.

Individual Lawyers

When writing directly to an individual lawyer, the salutation is either "Dear Sir", "Dear Mr. Grant" or "Dear Peter", depending on the tone of the letter, and relationship between the lawyer and the addressee.

Attention Line

Letters addressed to a firm of lawyers are frequently addressed to the attention of a specific lawyer by the use of an attention line. This procedure ensures that even if the lawyer is out of the office, the letter will be opened and any necessary action taken.

Type the attention line flush with the left-hand margin, two spaces below the inside address. The word "of" is not required, there is no special punctuation, and the line is not underscored. (See Figure 3.2.)

Subject Line

The subject line forms part of the body of the letter, and should appear on every outgoing letter in a law office in order to assist in filing correspondence. Type the subject line two spaces beneath the salutation, centred on the page and underscored.

If the subject line is long, divide it into logical groups, and type each on a separate line, in block style, and underscore the last line only. Carry the underscoring the length of the longest line in the subject. (See Figures 3.1, 3.2, 3.3.)

Body of Letter

Spacing

Letters are normally single spaced. Very short letters may be double spaced if the law firm does not have a short letterhead. Lengthy letters on legal questions, known as opinion letters are usually double spaced.

Punctuation

Regardless of the style of punctuation used for the date line, inside address, etc., normal punctuation is used in the body of the letter itself.

Capitalization

1. Capitalize the first letter of the proper nouns in such phrases as "City of Toronto", "Province of Manitoba", etc., but do not capitalize the first letter of the word "city", "borough", "province", "township" or "county" when it stands alone.

Province of Alberta	the province
County of Halton	the county
City of Halifax	the city

2. Do not capitalize the first letter of the names of legal papers such as a "will", "mortgage", "deed", "affidavit" or "statement of claim" when they appear in legal correspondence.

3. Capitalize the initial letters of phrases naming courts, but use lower case when the word "court" appears alone.

Supreme Court of Canada	the court

Complimentary Close and Signatures

The complimentary close preferred will frequently be dictated by the lawyer, but if this is not custom, use "Yours truly". A letter is then ended in one of two ways, which depends on the body of the letter.

Firm Name

If in the body of the letter it says: "we have ...", "in our opinion ...", "the writer believes ...", the firm name is typed in capital letters at the end of the letter, and the lawyer who dictated the letter will sign on behalf of the firm. (See also Figures 3.1, 3.2.)

```
        Yours truly,

        HILL, JOHNSTON & GRANT
```

```
        Per:
```

The word "Per" or "By" is used in the closing when the firm name is used, to indicate that the lawyer signing is doing so on behalf of the law firm, and not personally.

When the firm name is used in the closing, it does not contain the word "Messrs." but is typed exactly as it appears on the letterhead. Commas may be omitted if the name is long.

If the firm name is so long that it will extend beyond the right margin of the letter, commence it at a point on the page which will end it flush with the right margin. Use two lines to type the firm name only if that is the policy of the law firm.

```
Yours truly,

ARMSTRONG KELLY O'BRIEN & WHITE


Per:
```

Individual Name

If in the letter it says: "I have received...", "I am of the opinion..." or "My advice is..." then the letter is signed personally by the lawyer who dictated it. (See also Figure 3.3.)

```
                    Yours truly,



                    Peter T. Grant
```

The name of the lawyer is typed in the form in which he signs his name, omitting the designation "Esq." or "Q.C."

Since the names of all lawyers associated with the law firm usually appear on the letterhead, it is not always essential that the lawyer's name be typed in the closing. This is a matter of preference or firm policy, and the practice varies from office to office.

Reference Line

The reference line is not really required on the original of a letter; only on the carbon copies. However, it is usually typed on all copies to save time.

The standard location is flush with the left-hand margin, in line with, or one or two spaces beneath the last line of the signature. There are a variety of ways in which it may be typed, but perhaps the most common is the example shown below. (See also Figures 3.1, 3.2, 3.3.)

```
PTG:ees
```

Enclosure Notation

When a letter contains enclosures, type the word "Enclosure" or "Enc." flush with the left-hand margin, one or two spaces beneath the reference line. If there is more than one enclosure, indicate the number. (See also Figure 3.3.)

```
PTG:ees                    PTG:ees


Enc. 2                     Enclosure
```

If the letter is given to the lawyer for his signature before you have the enclosure ready, flag the letter with a coloured paper clip, or a small coloured clothespin as a reminder that the enclosure is not yet included, and, although signed, the letter should not be mailed.

Second or Continuation Pages

Many law firms have a printed second or continuation sheet, showing the name of the law firm, which is used when a letter runs to more than one page. If no such printed second sheet is available, use plain paper of the same quality as the letterhead.

Type the following information across the top of each additional page to a letter: name of addressee, page number, and the date. If it is not possible to begin a new page with a new paragraph, then at least two lines of a paragraph should be carried over. In addition, at least two lines of a carry-over paragraph must appear at the end of the previous page. The complimentary close and signature may never appear on a page alone.

Carbon Copies

When copies of outgoing letters are to be sent to other persons, use onionskin paper which will usually be marked in red with the word "C O P Y", and may also be printed with the firm name and address.

Carbon Copy Notation

When a carbon copy of a letter is to be sent to another person, type the abbreviation "cc." flush with the left-hand margin, two spaces beneath the last notation, on the original and all copies. (See also Figure 3.3.)

`PTG:ees`

`Enc. 2`

`cc. James Brown, Esq.`

Many secretaries now follow the practice of including in the notation the address of the person to whom the carbon is being sent.

Blind Carbon Copy Notation

When a carbon copy of a letter is to be sent to another person without the knowledge of the addressee, on the carbon copies only, type the abbreviation "bcc." in the upper left-hand portion, above the inside address, followed by the name of the person who is to receive the carbon copy.

Special Notations

Mailing Notations

On the original and all copies of a letter being sent by other than regular mail, show the method being used. Type the information in capital letters, underscored, two or preferably three spaces beneath the reference or enclosure notations on a letter (Figure 3.1), and beneath the space for postage on an envelope (Figure 3.4A) .

Personal Notations

Type the notations "Personal" or "Confidential" in capital letters, two or three spaces above the inside address on a letter, underscored.

While letters may show the notation "Personal" or "Confidential", envelopes are marked in both instances "Personal". Type this notation in capital letters, underscored, to the left of the address and two spaces above it (Figure 3.4B).

Without Prejudice Notation

The notation *without prejudice* indicates that the contents of the letter may not be used against the person writing it in any court proceedings. It is typed in capital letters, underscored, two or three spaces above the inside address on a letter. It never appears on an envelope. Many lawyers require that this notation appear on all letters written to any person concerned in a matter in which litigation is pending (Figure 3.3).

Number of Copies

The minimum number of copies prepared is the original and one file carbon. Many offices maintain a chronological file on all outgoing correspondence, known as a *Letter Book*, and an additional copy is made for this book. In some offices, an extra copy of an outgoing letter is used when recording the work done on behalf of a client, and another copy may be required for a reminder file.

The preference of the individual office determines how many copies are required; there is a wide variance in practice from office to office.

Hill, Johnston & Grant

Barristers and Solicitors

Frank P. Hill, Q.C. Henry Q. Winslow
Edward N. Johnston, Q.C. Percy Y. McQuiller
Peter T. Grant, Q.C. Robert W. Burnsley
John L. Craigmore

_____

Counsel: P. B. Ranwood, Q.C.

TELEPHONE: 364-9999, AREA CODE 416

CABLE 3-1IL6 TORONTO

Suite 2501
17 Princess Street South
Toronto 560, Canada

October 28, 1970

P E R S O N A L

Harold R. MacLeod, Esq.,
    Apartment 917A,
        139 Rossdale Blvd.,
            Newtondale, Ontario.

Dear Sir:

Roebuck

We act for Mr. Ben Roebuck with respect to the matter of an unpaid account owing by you in the amount of $387.56.

Please be advised that unless this account is paid by November 15, 1970 legal proceedings will be commenced immediately thereafter. All cheques should be made payable to this firm at par, and sent to this office at the above address.

In the event that it should become necessary to commence legal proceedings, you will of course be responsible for the costs.

Yours truly,

HILL, JOHNSTON & GRANT

PTG:ees   Per:

REGISTERED MAIL

Figure 3.1. Indented Style of Letter

Hill, Johnston & Grant

Barristers and Solicitors

TELEPHONE: 364-9999, AREA CODE 416
CABLE 3-1IL6 TORONTO

Suite 2501
17 Princess Street South
Toronto 560, Canada

Frank P. Hill, Q.C.   Henry Q. Winslow
Edward N. Johnston, Q.C. Percy Y. McQuilier
Peter T. Grant, Q.C.   Robert W. Burnsley
John L. Craigmore

Counsel: P. B. Ranwood, Q.C.

October 28, 1970

Messrs. Stuart, Thompson & Hall,
Barristers and Solicitors,
50 King Street North,
Toronto 595, Ontario.

Attention James R. McLelland, Esq.

Dear Sirs:

195 Halliday Blvd., Toronto

On October 15 we wrote at some length to the Commissioner of Property, pointing out several matters which
should be considered, and offering to accept $162,000.00,
plus interest from the date of possession. The letter concluded with this sentence:

"Failing agreement on this figure, our instructions
are to serve a submission to arbitration."

Mr. MacLeod of the Property Department telephoned
today to say that he and Mr. Carruthers had again reviewed the
entire file, and that the very best they could do was to increase their original offer by $5,000.00 to $150,000.00, plus
interest.

We confirm the opinion expressed earlier that this
is a reasonable settlement. Mr. Smithe's appraisal emphasizes
that the greatest weight should be given to the income approach to valuation, and on that approach his valuation is
$155,000.00, even though his final figure is $165,000.00.

Would you be good enough to take this up with Mr.
Williamson, and let us have your instructions.

Yours truly,

HILL, JOHNSTON & GRANT

PTG:ees   Per:

Figure 3.2. Semi-block Style of Letter with
Closed Punctuation   13

Hill, Johnston & Grant

Barristers and Solicitors

TELEPHONE: 364-9999, AREA CODE 416

CABLE 3-1IL6 TORONTO

Suite 2501
17 Princess Street South
Toronto 560, Canada

Frank P. Hill, Q.C.
Edward N. Johnston, Q.C.
Peter T. Grant, Q.C.
John L. Craigmore

Henry Q. Winslow
Percy Y. McQuiller
Robert W. Burnsley

Counsel: P. B. Ranwood, Q.C.

October 28, 1970

WITHOUT PREJUDICE

Gordon P. Williamson, Esq., Q.C.
Messrs. Carson, Stephenson & West
Barristers and Solicitors
250 King Street North
Toronto 591, Ontario

Dear Mr. Williamson:

O'Grady and Milne
Milgrady Fine Foods Ltd.

I have your letter of October 19. I do not think that Mr. Milne is prepared to make any proposal with respect to this case. He feels very strongly about this matter.

In addition, he has discovered that the accountant treated as receipts of the new firm (after O'Grady had been admitted) monies paid in respect of accounts rendered before there was such a firm. As you will recall from the partner-ship agreement, O'Grady did not acquire any interest in these accounts, and as a result received a good deal of money to which he was not entitled.

If Mr. O'Grady insists on the matter going to court, I am afraid there is nothing which we can do to prevent it. I am enclosing an extra copy of this letter which you might wish to send to your client.

Yours truly,

PTG:ees   Peter T. Grant

Enclosure

cc. J. L. Milne, Esq.
    19 Hillsdale Crescent
    Malton, Ontario

Figure 3.3. Semi-block Style of Letter with Mixed Punctuation

Hill, Johnston & Grant

17 PRINCESS STREET SOUTH
TORONTO 560, CANADA

SPECIAL DELIVERY

Messrs. Stuart, Thompson & Hall
Barristers and Solicitors
50 King Street North
Toronto 1, Ontario

Attention R. J. West, Esq., Q.C.

*Figure 3.4A. Envelope with Special Delivery
Notation and Attention Line*

Hill, Johnston & Grant

17 PRINCESS STREET SOUTH
TORONTO 560, CANADA

P E R S O N A L

Robert J. West, Esq., Q.C.
Messrs. Carson, Stephenson & West
Barristers and Solicitors
250 King Street North
Toronto 12, Ontario

Figure 3.4B. Envelope with Personal Notation

CHAPTER 4

Sources of Law and How to Refer to Them

In Canada all provinces but Quebec follow the English Common Law; that province follows the Civil Code, which closely resembles the Napoleonic Code of France.

The Canadian Parliament and the provincial legislatures have enacted legislation which has codified some of the common law in acts or statutes. We refer to this as written or *statute law*.

Much of the common law, however, is founded on the decision of judges, and is called *case* or *precedent law*.

Statute Law

Since Confederation the Parliament of Canada and the legislatures of the provinces have made laws under the provisions of the British North America Act. Sections 91 and 92 of that Act spell out the divisions of legislative power between Parliament and the provinces. Each province in turn grants power to municipalities and counties giving them the right to pass by-laws and ordinances. One of the most important powers given to municipalities by the province is the imposition and collection of realty or property taxes.

The courts have frequently been called upon to determine whether the Parliament of Canada or a province has the right to enact legislation on a certain matter. The disputes arising between the powers of the Parliament of Canada and the provinces is known as *constitutional law*.

Titles of Statutes

Each statute which is passed is called an *act* and is given a name which clearly identifies its main purpose. Practice varies from prov-

ince to province as to whether the article "the" is part of the proper name of an act; this article is not part of the proper name of any Dominion Act.

The printed statutes of a province will indicate the proper name of acts, but the following table outlines the current practice in connection with the article "the".

Part of Proper Name of Act

Alberta
Manitoba
Newfoundland
Ontario
Saskatchewan
Prince Edward Island

Not Part of Proper Name of Act

British Columbia
New Brunswick
Nova Scotia
Quebec
Northwest Territories
Yukon

Publication of Statutes

Each year the Dominion and each province publish volumes containing all new acts passed during the previous legislative year, as well as amendments to existing acts. These volumes of statutes are identified by year.

Name	Abbreviation
Statutes of Canada 1968-69	S.C. 1968-69
Statutes of Ontario	S.O. 1969

At stated intervals (for example, in Ontario, every ten years), all existing acts of the Dominion or province are published in a series of volumes known as the revised statutes and are also identified by year.

Name	Abbreviation
Revised Statutes of Ontario 1970	R.S.O. 1970
Revised Statutes of Canada 1952	R.S.C. 1952
Revised Statutes of Alberta 1962	R.S.A. 1962

In both publications of statutes and revised statutes, the acts appear in alphabetical order, and each is a numbered chapter. Copies of these publications are often maintained in the law office library.

Typing References to Acts

In the course of his legal practice a lawyer will frequently make reference to an act. The reference is shown by typing in the following order: the name of the act, the statutes or revised statutes where it may be found, the chapter number, and then possibly (but not necessarily), the particular section of the act. Each part of the reference is separated by a comma.

Income Tax, R.S.C. 1952, c. 148

The Succession Duty Act, R.S.O. 1960, c. 386, s.6(d)

Case Law

Much of our law is based on precedent, that is, something done before that established a pattern for similar cases. Under this principle, a judge hearing a case must reach the same decision as a judge of equal or higher rank who heard a case with similar facts. However, the facts and circumstances of one case will rarely be exactly the same as those of another, and these differences are said to *distinguish* one case from another. It is the responsibility of the judge to determine which precedent established in decided cases most closely fits the situation he is asked to decide, and to act accordingly.

Law Reports

Reference to earlier decided cases has been a feature of the English common law for centuries; regular reporting of cases of interest appears to have started in the thirteenth century.

Law reports are a published account of a legal proceeding, outlining a brief statement of the facts of the case, the arguments put forth on both sides, and the judgment given, as well as the reasons for arriving at that judgment. The more common Canadian law reports are:

Name of Series	Abbreviation
Canadian Criminal Cases	C.C.C.
Dominion Law Reports	D.L.R.
Ontario Law Reports	O.L.R.
Ontario Reports	O.R.

Ontario Weekly Notes	O.W.N.
Supreme Court Reports	S.C.R.
Western Weekly Report	W.W.R.
Western Law Reports	W.L.R.

Not all series shown are now published, but reference is still made to cases which they reported.

Reference may also be made to English reports, some of which are listed below. The abbreviation shown in brackets is the one used during the period 1875-90.

Name of Series	Abbreviation
All England Reports	All E.R.
Appeal Case	A.C. (App. Cas.)
Chancery Division	Ch. (Ch. D.)
King's Bench Division	K.B.
Queen's Bench Division	Q.B. (Q.B.D.)
Privy Council	P.C.
Probate	P.

When in doubt about the abbreviation of a law report, consult the list quoted on page 30 et seq. in Volume 1 of the third edition of HALSBURY'S LAWS OF ENGLAND, a summary of the rules of law.

Lawyers subscribe to the series of reports published in the province in which they practise, as well as to the reports dealing with cases decided in the Supreme Court of Canada. Many series come out weekly or monthly, and once a year are sent out and bound into hard-covered volumes. A copy of all bound volumes of law reports is often maintained in the office law library.

In order to facilitate references to these series of reports, each book is identified either by volume number, or by year. Some reports (e.g., the Ontario Reports) come out weekly and are so lengthy that they are bound in more than one book each year, and are identified by both year and volume number (e.g., 1970 2 O.R.).

Citing Cases from Law Reports

A lawyer will look for decided cases (also called *authorities*) which will support his client's position. His reference to these cases is known as *citing* and the actual reference is a *citation*.

A citation has two sections, which are separated by a comma:

1. The first section contains the name of the case or matter being referred to, and if the series in which it is reported is identified by volume number, then perhaps the year when the decision was made.
2. The second section contains the name of the series in which the case is reported, giving the year or volume number of the bound law reports, the page at which the case is first mentioned, and frequently the page or pages to which particular attention should be given. The parts of the second section of a citation are not separated by punctuation.

It is imperative that the citation indicate precisely which particular book of a series has been referred to. When the year must be known in order to locate the appropriate book, the date is said to be an essential part of the citation, and is typed in the second section of the citation.

When the volume number must be known in order to locate the appropriate book, the date is said to be nonessential. The volume number is typed in the second section, and the date may be shown following the name of the case or matter in the first section for information purposes only.

In printed material essential dates are shown in square brackets [1970]; nonessential, in round brackets (1970). Volume numbers are not enclosed in brackets.

Essential
  Jones v. Smith, [1933] A.C. 100
  Brown v. Black, [1969] 2 O.R. 1109 at 176
Nonessential
  Smith v. Green (1876), 18 App. Cas. 100

If your typewriter is not equipped with square brackets, and your office does not require that these be used when citing cases,

round brackets may be used for both essential and nonessential dates.

If your office requires that square brackets be used for essential dates, a special key can be fitted to your typewriter, or the brackets can be typed by using the underscore and oblique key, i.e., $\underline{/}$, or the brackets may be inserted in ink.

Guide for Essential Dates

Over the years some law reports have at one time been identified by volume number, at other times by year.

English Cases

So far as English cases are concerned, the year is not an essential part of any case having a date prior to 1891.

Canadian Cases

For Canadian cases, the date is an essential part of the citation for the following:

1. Dominion Reports
a. S.C.R. from 1923 to present
b. D.L.R. from 1923 to 1955 – This series ran numerically with the date not an essential part of the citation from Volume 1 to Volume 70, inclusive. From 1923 to 1955 inclusive, the year was an essential part of the citation. In 1955, the reports reverted to a straight numerical system, by volume number, with the addition of (2d) following the name of the report, to indicate the second numerical series, which ran until the end of 1968. The third numerical series (3d), commencing with Volume 1, began in 1969.
2. Ontario Reports
a. O.R. from 1931 to present
b. O.W.N. from 1933 to present
3. Western Reports
a. W.W.R. until 1955

Printed and Typed Citations – Extract from [1968] 2 O.R. 290-1

Printed Citations

In the instant case the fund was impressed with the trust. Neither the bank nor Asma had any power to pay or appropriate except for purposes of the trust and the rule in *Clayton's Case* is therefore inapplicable: *Agricultural Ins. Co. v. Sargeant* (1896), 26 S.C.R. 29.

Cory Bros. & Co. v. SS. "Mecca", [1897] A.C. 286, is also authority that *Clayton's Case* does not apply where from the circumstances it appears that the parties probably intended otherwise. It also contains a discussion of *Clayton's Case* and of the principles applicable to question of appropriation. In the course of his judgment Lord Macnaghten referred with approval to Blackburn, J.'s statement of the rule in *Henniker v. Wigg* (1843), 4 Q.B. 792, 114 E.R. 1095, referred to in *Agricultural Ins. Co. v. Sargeant, supra.*

Royal Bank of Canada v. Slack, [1958] O.R. 262, 11 D.L.R. (2d) 737, contains a helpful discussion of the principles applicable to appropriation. Schroeder, J.A., in delivering the

Typed Citations

Agricultural Ins. Co. v. Sargeant (1896), 26 S.C.R. 29

Cory Bros. & Co. v. SS. "Mecca", [1897] A.C. 286

Clayton's Case

Henniker v. Wigg (1843), 4 Q.B. 792, 114 E.R. 1095
(The above case was reported in two different series of law reports and both references are cited.)

Agricultural Ins. Co. v. Sargeant, supra
(The word "supra" indicates that the complete citation has been given earlier in the report.)

Royal Bank of Canada v. Slack, [1958] O.R. 262, 11 D.L.R. (2d) 737
(The above case was also reported in two series of law reports.)

Figure 4.1

CHAPTER 5

Memoranda

In legal offices inter-office or *file memoranda* are very important. They are used to convey to another lawyer developments in a case or matter, to ask that something be done, or to record details of a telephone conversation or conference with a client. Sometimes memoranda are very detailed. Such memoranda usually outline law bearing on certain disputed issues, and are known as *memoranda of law*.

Basic Form of Memoranda

Some offices have a pre-printed memorandum form; others use white or coloured paper with a typed heading. With either method the heading will include the following information, arranged in whatever way is preferred in the particular law office:

To (the name of the person or persons to whom it is going)
From (the name of the person who is sending it)
Date
Re or Subject (the subject of the memo)

Figure 5.1 illustrates one form of memorandum set-up. Initials are used instead of full names; there is no salutation, complimentary close or signature, although the initials of the sender are typed at the end. The text of the memorandum is double-spaced; quoted material, single-spaced.

Memoranda of Law

Frequently a lawyer will ask a junior lawyer or an articling student to "read law" on a certain question or point. This means that reference is made to decided cases on the point under review, and a memorandum

prepared outlining the information ascertained from reading the reports. This memorandum of law is usually many pages long, and contains citations of and quotations from decided cases.

Note these points in typing quotations:

1. Single space quotations, and indent five spaces from both the left and right-hand margins.
2. Show omissions from quoted material by three ellipsis dots (or periods) if the omission is from the body of the sentence, and by four ellipsis dots (the fourth is the period of the sentence) if the omission concludes a sentence.
3. Use quotation marks at the beginning of each paragraph in the quotation, and at the end of the last paragraph quoted.
4. Use single quotation marks for a quotation within a quotation, and if the second quotation comes at the end of the entire quotation, use both sets of quotation marks at the conclusion of the quotation.

   "... private park preserve.'"

5. Put only those punctuation marks which actually form part of the material being quoted inside quotation marks. Normally periods and commas which are not part of the quotation are typed inside quotation marks; in legal work, this might result in a major alteration of meaning.

Reference to Judges

The memorandum of law will usually indicate the last name of the judge or judges who gave the decision from which material is being quoted, followed by one of the abbreviations below, indicating the position of the person named:

Position	Abbreviation
Judge	J.
Judges	JJ.
Judge, Appeal Court	J.A.
Chief Justice, High Court	C.J.H.C.

Smith, Brown and Homer, JJ.
Smith, C.J.H.C.

Number of Copies

The number of copies of a memorandum prepared depends on its purpose, but a general guide is:

1. Type at least two copies of a memorandum of law; one for the person who prepared it, and one for the person to whom it is addressed.

2. Type a file copy of a memorandum addressed to another person only when it contains information which should permanently be in a file held by the lawyer sending it.

```
                    m e m o r a n d u m


TO:    J.J.A.                 DATE:  October 27, 1970

FROM:  P.T.G.                 RE:  Martin et al v. Crane


       The question upon which we have been asked to give our

opinion is:  What is the effect of s.76 of The Registry Act, R.S.O.

1960, c.348, as applied to the facts in this situation?

Ross v. Hunter (1889), 7 S.C.R. 289

    Per Strong J. at 321:


    "It is well settled that nothing short of actual notice
    ... is sufficient to disentitle a party to insist in
    equity on a legal priority acquired under the statute.

    "It is not sufficient....to find that from the state of
    the property purchased by the plaintiff, there was ocular
    proof that the wall of the house had been built upon....
    What we must find, in order to hold that the defendant
    is entitled to a verdict, is that he had knowledge of the
    deed conferring title to the easement...."


Ihde v. Starr (1909), 18 O.L.R. 471 (affirmed 21 O.L.R. 407)


       Briefly, this case concerned a dispute between adjoining

landowners, the plaintiff claiming that the defendant's buildings


                    *  *  *  *

    great difficulty in coming to the conclusion that the
    respondent had made out such a case.  Lord Thurlow's
    language is very strong on this subject:  'The evidence
    which goes to prove that the words taken down in writing
    were contrary to the concurrent intention of all parties
    must be strong evidence.' "


       I am checking on several other authorities, and will

furnish you with additional information in a day or two.


                    P.T.G.
```

Figure 5.1. Extract from a Memo of Law

CHAPTER 6

Dockets, Entries, and Accounts

The maintenance of proper records is a very necessary part of the office accounting operation, and most law offices employ a bookkeeper or accountant to do this. In small law offices, however, the maintenance of accounting records may be one of your responsibilities. The principles of accounting form a major area of study, and will not be considered here. We will consider only a part of your regular, daily routine which may be an important part of the overall accounting system of a law office.

Dockets

A lawyer is paid for his services, and one of the ways he knows the value of those services is by keeping a record of the time spent on looking after a matter for a client, and a record of any expenses incurred in doing so. Such records are known as *dockets*.

Contents of Dockets

Dockets are often kept in file folders measuring 4 by 8½ inches, on sheets attached to a heavy pressboard back by means of an accopress clip, or simply on a single sheet of paper. In each case, the docket will contain a day by day record, known as *entries* or *charges,* of the following items:
1. the amount of time, in hours or valued in dollars, spent in considering a particular case or matter
2. disbursements made on behalf of the client
3. payments made or monies received while the matter is in progress.

Docket Systems

The system of maintaining dockets is not standardized and varies from office to office. However, all systems fall within three broad classifications which are outlined below.

Lawyer's Docket Sheets

This is one of the simplest forms of maintaining records of work performed on behalf of a client. The docket sheet is stapled to the inside front cover of the file, and as services are rendered, or expenses incurred, either you or the lawyer will make a notation on the form (Figure 6.1).

Alphabetical System

This is a very straightforward docket system, which in most offices is maintained by the Accounting Department, but the contents of which come from you. Dockets are opened in the name of the client, and show the specific matter for which the firm is acting for him (Figure 6.4A). For example:

ANDERSON, Ronald re Chattel Mortgage to Peterson
ANDERSON, Ronald re Sale of 74 Prince William Avenue
ANDERSON, Ronald re Windfall Investments

Numerical System

This system is also maintained by the Accounting Department, and is more complex. When a new docket is opened, the Accounting Department assigns a number to it, and that number must be used on all subsequent docket entries (Figure 6.4B). An alphabetical cross-reference index, by name of client, is maintained by both the Accounting Department and the secretary concerned.

In some offices each specific client receives a docket number, to which a letter or number is added for any new dockets which may later be opened. For example:

15000   SMITH, John re Purchase of 9 Laurel Blvd.
15000/1 SMITH, John re Sale of 17 Kyle Road
15000/2 SMITH, John re Will

Instead of 15000/1 or 15000/2, in some offices you will see 15000/A or 15000/B.

LAWYER'S DOCKET

CLIENT	OPPOSITE PARTY
ANDERSON, Ronald Craig	Mrs. Elizabeth Peterson
ADDRESS **PHONE**	**ADDRESS** **PHONE**
34 Dawson Road, Etobicoke 233 5555	19 Hermain St., Toronto 999 9999
TYPE OF MATTER	**SOLICITOR**
Preparation of Chattel Mortgage	Smith, Webb & Hamilton
COURT **WRIT NO.**	**ADDRESS** **PHONE**
	75 Maryvale Cres., Toronto 364 0001

DATE		PARTICULARS	Time Spent	Charge	DR.	CR.
1970						
Nov.	19	Interview with you receiving instructions	1 hr	35.		35.00
"	22	Drafting mortgage + letter to client re bk	3 hr	70.		105.00
"	25	Attended at client's office to review draft	½ hr	20.		125.00
"	23	Post fare		1.05		126.05
"	28	Registration of mortgage; engrossing	1 hr	35.		161.05
"	30	Received payment on account		50.	50.00	

Figure 6.1. Lawyer's Docket Sheet

23

Entries

The records contained in a docket are known as *entries* and these may be either an entry recording time or money charges for the lawyer's services, or a record of a *disbursement* made. Most entry slips are pre-printed, and contain the following information set out in a way preferred by each office:

1. name or number of docket
2. initials or name of lawyer making the entry
3. date of service, or disbursement
4. nature of service performed, or disbursement incurred
5. value in time or money of work performed, or amount of disbursement.

First Entry

Under the alphabetical and numerical systems of dockets, the Accounting Department must be notified to open a docket. Many offices have a special new matter entry form; others require that these words be typed on the regular daily entry sheet (Figures 6.2, 6.3).

Once a docket has been opened, all subsequent entries must show the same name and matter, or the same docket number.

Typing Entries

Entries recording services are typed; disbursements are frequently written by hand. The number of copies varies. Some offices require only one copy which goes to the Accounting Department for filing in the docket. Other offices require two copies; one for the docket, and one for a chronological file you maintain in your office.

Where Information is Obtained For Entries

Many lawyers record in their diary the amount of time and the nature of the work performed on each matter during the day, and will either dictate the appropriate entries, or require you to type entries from the diary itself. You may be expected to make the appropriate entries to record all outgoing and incoming correspondence.

If you are required to type up entries independently, briefly record the work the lawyer performed, and show the time spent in quarter hours, half hours or hours. If the lawyer prefers his entries to show a dollar value for his services, ascertain from him what fee is to be shown. It is not your responsibility to determine a dollar value. In some offices if services are shown by dollar values, the Accounting Department will complete this portion of the entry.

In typing up entries keep the text brief and concise, giving just enough information to indicate the general nature of what was done.

> Attended by you to arrange meeting with creditors next week. Letter to you confirming arrangements.　　　½ hour

Monies Received

Frequently before a matter has been completed, monies are received which relate to it. A record of such monies must be included in the docket by means of a credit slip (Figure 6.5), which must show to whose docket it refers, the source of the money, the date, and to which bank account maintained by the firm the monies are to be deposited. A law firm has at least two bank accounts.

Firm or General Account

In the *firm* or *general account* are deposited all monies received by the firm in payment of services already rendered to a client. If an account has not yet been rendered to the client, the monies received are recorded in the docket by means of a credit slip. If an account has been rendered, no credit slip is required, since the Accounting Department has taken the appropriate steps to indicate this in the docket.

Trust Account

In the *trust account* are deposited all monies received by the lawyer to be held in trust for

NEW DOCKET MEMO

DATE: November 10, 1970

SOLICITOR: P.T. Grant

CLIENT'S NAME: ANDERSON, Ronald Craig

ADDRESS: 74 Prince William Avenue, Toronto

DOCKET DESIGNATION: Purchase of 984 Helena Avenue, Toronto

Nature of Service:	Reserved for Acctg. Department	
Attended by Mr. Anderson with accepted offer to purchase, and instructed to act on purchase.	Docket No. Assigned	✓
	Docket Prepared	✓
	Matter Indexed	✓

DOCKET NO. *10 978-70*

N E W   M A T T E R

Initials of
Lawyer   PTG

CLIENT: ANDERSON, Ronald Craig

ADDRESS: 74 Prince William Avenue, Toronto

CASE
OR MATTER: Purchase of 984 Helena Avenue, Toronto

DATE: November 10, 1970

NATURE OF SERVICES: TIME OR FEE

Attended by you with accepted offer to pur-

chase, and instructed to act on purchase.

Drawing direction as to title, and attending

upon execution   1/2 hour

Figure 6.2. Entries to Open Docket

DATE: November 15, 1970

DOCKET DESIGNATION: SMITH, Henry James re Bank of Hamilton

Signature of Lawyer

Peter T. Grant

TO BE COMPLETED BY DOCKET CLERK

DATE DOCKET OPENED *November 16, 1970*

DOCKET NUMBER *4981*

Mary J. Wallace

Figure 6.3. Opening Docket

	Initials of Lawyer	PTG

CLIENT: ANDERSON, Ronald Craig

ADDRESS:

CASE
OR MATTER: Purchase of 984 Helena Avenue

DATE: November 11, 1970

NATURE OF SERVICES:	TIME OR FEE
Wrote solicitors for vendor advising on how Andersons wish to take title, and requesting draft deed and a statement of adjustments.	
Instructed title searcher to search title as soon as possible.	1/2 hour

*Figure 6.4A. Regular Daily Entries –
Alphabetical System*

DOCKET NO. 10978-70 SOLICITOR P.T.Grant		Time or Fee		Sundry Disb.	
Nov.11/70	Wrote solicitors for vendor advising on how the Andersons wish to take title, and requesting draft deed and a statement of adjustments Instructed title searcher to search title as soon as possible	15.00			
		15.00			

Figure 6.4B. Regular Daily Entries –
Numerical System

PAY IN

Hill Johnston & Grant

Received by   ~~CASH~~ CHEQUE   the sum of $ 5,000.00 _____

To be credited to the TRUST ____xx____   FIRM _____   account.

FROM: __Ronald Craig Anderson_____

RE: __Balance due on closing real estate transaction_____

DOCKET: __ANDERSON, Ronald Craig re Purchase of 984 Helena Avenue_____

DATE: __November 25, 1970_____

Figure 6.5. Credit Slip

some purpose such as closing a real estate transaction. This money has not been earned by the law firm; it is not theirs. Money may be transferred from the trust account to the firm or general account only upon authorization of the lawyer.

The lawyer will indicate to you in which bank account money is to be deposited, and if a credit slip is required, you should prepare it and give both the slip and cheque or cash to the Accounting Department.

Disbursements

In addition to entries for fees, dockets will also contain entries relating to disbursements. These disbursement sheets are usually in different colours to distinguish them from service entry sheets, and normally will include cheque requisitions, telephone charges, and petty cash slips.

Cheque Requisitions

Cheques in payment of expenses incurred while acting for a client are secured through preparing a cheque requisition and presenting it, duly completed and signed, to the Accounting Department.

Cheque requisitions (Figure 6.6A) show the name of the person or firm to whom the cheque is to be made payable, the docket name or number, the amount of the cheque, whether it is to be a certified cheque, when it is required, the bank account on which it is to be drawn, the signature or name of the lawyer requesting it, and the date of the requisition.

When the cheque has been issued and signed, the Accounting Department either returns it to you for mailing, or takes the responsibility for mailing it themselves if they have been given the letter or invoice to which the cheque refers.

Cheque requisitions appearing in a docket cover a variety of expenses including travelling expenses, payment of fees to file, register or serve a document, purchase of a minute book, and printing of material.

Long Distance Telephone Calls

A charge slip is completed in duplicate in most large offices for all long distance tele-
phone calls made from the office (Figure 6.6B). One copy is filed in the appropriate docket, and the other is kept in a chronological file for use in verifying the telephone account each month.

Usually the switchboard operator completes these slips, checking with you to be sure of the proper name of the docket to which the call is to be charged.

Telegrams

The cost of a telegram is not known until the monthly telegram bill is received. A common practice is to give two copies of any outgoing telegram to the Accounting Department in order that the docket contains a record of this disbursement even if the account has not been received. One copy is placed in the appropriate docket, and the other is maintained in a chronological file to use in checking the account when it is received.

Petty Cash Expenditures

Small expenses incurred are paid for out of the Petty Cash Fund, maintained by the Accounting Department. Such expenses are recorded in the docket by means of a petty cash slip (Figure 6.6C), which is prepared in duplicate; the second copy is kept with the petty cash.

Accounts

An account is rendered to the client when a case or matter has been completed, or at intervals during its conduct if the case is a long one. Accounts are prepared on the basis of the docket entries and disbursements. Either the lawyer or the Accounting Department reviews the docket and determines the appropriate fee.

Accounts are typed on account paper, which may be short (about 7 inches in length), or a full 11-inch page. You should prepare a minimum of two copies; the original for the client, and one for the Accounting Department. In addition, the lawyer may wish a copy of the account placed in the file, and you may wish to maintain a chronological file of accounts rendered.

The following information appears on the account:

1. the lawyer's initials or name
2. the name of the person or firm to whom the account is rendered
3. the matter in which services were performed
4. the period covered by the account
5. the nature of the services rendered
6. the amount of fees and disbursements
7. the date of the account.

If an account is too long for one page, it may be continued on a second sheet, headed with the name of the client, the page number, and the date. Accounts of more than one page usually have a backing sheet, which identifies it as an account, and shows the date, the name of the client, and the name and address of the law firm (Figure 6.7).

If monies have been received to apply against fees and disbursements before the account is rendered, then one of two steps will be taken.

You will either send the client an account, marked "Paid in Full" if that is the case, or send the client the account together with a *ledger statement,* which shows the amount of the account, less the monies received, and the balance still owing (Figure 6.8).

Monies received in payment of rendered accounts do not require credit slips, but are handed to the Accounting Department, together with the rendered account so that it may be receipted.

CHEQUE REQUISITION   CHEQUE NO. _____

Hill Johnston & Grant

DATE: November 15, 1970

PAYABLE TO: SMITH, FRASER, HAMILTON & WEBB

RE: Balance due on closing real estate purchase   AMOUNT: $4,561.98

DOCKET: ANDERSON, Ronald Craig re Purchase of 984 Helena Avenue

Trust ___xx___   Certified ___xx___

Firm _____   Required by Nov. 17, 1970

P T Grant

Figure 6.6A. Disbursement Form – Cheque Requisition

TELEPHONE CALLS

Hill Johnston & Grant

DOCKET ___ANDERSON, Ronald Craig re Purchase of 984 Helena Avenue___

_____

Date of call: ___November 13, 1970___   To: ___Percival Quarrington___

At: ___Barrie___   By: ___P. T. Grant___

Time: ___3 minutes___

Charges: ___$0.55___

Figure 6.6B.   Disbursement Form – Telephone Calls

PETTY CASH VOUCHER

Hill Johnston & Grant

DATE: ___November 13, 1970___

PAID TO: ___Henry Jamieson___ $___6.50___

FOR: ___Disbursements re search of title___

_____

DOCKET: ___ANDERSON, Ronald Craig re Purchase of 984 Helena Avenue___

Received above amount

_____

Figure 6.6C.   Disbursement Form – Petty Cash Voucher

Ronald Anderson, Esq.,
34 Dawson Road,
ETOBICOKE, Ontario.

PTG

17 Princess Street,
TORONTO, Ontario.

- in account with -

Hill Johnston & Grant

Barristers & Solicitors

Chattel Mortgage to Peterson

1 9 6 8
December 17th

to

1 9 7 0
November 11th

Attended by you with instructions to prepare chattel mortgage for your execution in favour of Mrs. Elizabeth Peterson, conferences with you on several occasions in January, February, April and May, 1969 when it is decided to change the security; drafting, considering and engrossing further chattel mortgage and consideration of same with you at length, when it is agreed to withhold execution until the Fall; attended by you on several occasions by long distance from California with instructions to vary, and attendances upon Mrs. Peterson's solicitors to discuss the ramifications of the proposed alterations; conferences with you as to effect of changes on September 27th, 28th, and 29th, and again on October 2nd, when form of security is agreed upon; engrossing and arranging for execution of same, and instructing agents in regard to registration in the County

---

Ronald Anderson, Esq.   2.   November 26, 1970

Court of the County of York, and letter to you advising that the matter has been satisfactorily concluded.

Fees		$250.00
Disbursements:		
Paid account of agent	$25.00	
Long distance telephone	13.64	
Transportation	7.50	46.14
		$296.14

DATED at Toronto this 26th day of November, 1970

DATED: November 26, 1970

Ronald Anderson, Esq.
34 Dawson Road
ETOBICOKE, Ontario.

A C C O U N T

HILL, JOHNSTON & GRANT
17 Princess Street S.
Toronto, Ontario

Figure 6.7.   Two Page Account with Back

31

Ronald Anderson, Esq.,
34 Dawson Street,
ETOBICOKE, Ontario.

17 Princess Street,
TORONTO, Ontario.

~~- in account with -~~

LEDGER STATEMENT

Hill Johnston & Grant

Barristers & Solicitors

John Jones--Chattel Mortgage

November 26, 1970	To account herein	$160.70
July 15, 1970	To payment on account	150.00
	Balance due	$ 10.70

DATED at Toronto this 26th day of November, 1970

Ronald C. Anderson, Esq.,
34 Dawson Road,
ETOBICOKE, Ontario.

17 Princess Street,
TORONTO, Ontario.

- in account with -

Hill Johnston & Grant

Barristers & Solicitors

John Jones--Chattel Mortgage

1 9 7 0
October 1st   To fee for services drawing chattel mortgage
to John Jones; attending upon you and
instructed to change security; re-engrossing
    to   mortgage, and attended by you when mortgage
executed, letter to mortgagee with, and
October 31st   instructions for registration,

                                                      $150.00

Disbursements:
  Long distance telephone calls $5.35
  Paid account of Ottawa agent   5.00
  Miscellaneous   0.35   10.70

                                               $160.70

DATED at Toronto this 26th day of November, 1970

Figure 6.8. Account with Ledger Statement

CHAPTER 7

Preparing Legal Papers

Legal Papers

The tangible products of the lawyer are his carefully prepared legal papers. He is responsible for the content; the secretary, for the finished typed product – its appearance, set-up and quality.

All legal papers may be classified as either legal instruments or court papers. Legal instruments are formally written documents such as contracts, wills, deeds or mortgages, which give formal expression to a legal act or agreement, and which are properly signed, sealed and delivered, as evidence of the act or agreement.

Court papers are documents and pleadings prepared for use concerning matters brought before the courts.

Many common legal papers such as mortgages, powers of attorney, or writs of summons, are prepared by adding the appropriate content and clauses to printed forms. This is possible since certain legislation has prescribed the general form of these instruments, and standard clauses are contained in the printed forms.

Other legal papers such as contracts, agreements, court pleadings or wills, must be completely typed in accordance with established principles for preparing legal papers.

Types of Typing Paper

Traditionally legal paper meant paper of a size of 8½ by 14 inches. Legal instruments are still usually typed on this size of paper. The size to be used for court papers is prescribed by the court rules, and in Ontario, for example, is 8½ by 11 inches.

Many law firms type all legal papers on plain, good quality white bond paper of the correct length. Other firms use special legal paper which is ruled in red with a wide margin at the left, and a narrower margin at the

right. There are several ways of rulings, two of which are illustrated in Figure 7.1.

Number of Copies

The number of copies prepared varies, but is usually an original, a file copy, and a number of copies determined by the nature of the legal paper and the number of parties involved. Printed forms are used for all copies prepared on a standardized legal form. The same quality paper as used for the original is used for all copies of typed legal papers.

Frequently the first carbon copy of a legal instrument is treated as if it were also an original ribbon copy, and is signed just as if it were the original. It is then known as a *duplicate original* and the legal paper is then said to be made "in duplicate".

Heading of Legal Papers

All legal papers have four main parts: a heading, a body or text, an ending, and an endorsement or back.

The heading of a legal paper briefly identifies the nature of the paper, and sets out the party or parties to it. The heading of court papers is called the *style of cause* and is discussed in detail in a later chapter.

Introductory Words

The four main ways of heading legal instruments are:

THIS AGREEMENT made this   day of . . .

THIS INDENTURE made . . .

KNOW ALL MEN BY THESE PRESENTS THAT I . . .

THIS IS THE LAST WILL AND TESTAMENT of me . . .

Most legal papers are dated in the ending and the date shown is the date the document is executed. Some legal papers, however, are dated in the heading and the date shown is the date on which the instrument is prepared or made. Figures are used for the date and year unless a printed form is used showing the year in words, in which event the day of the month is also typed in words (Figure 7.2).

Figure 7.1. Margin Ruled Paper

Date in Figures

This Indenture

made (in duplicate) the   15th   day of November   19 70

Date in Words

This Indenture

made (in duplicate) the   fifteenth   day of November
one thousand nine hundred and   seventy.

No Date in Heading

Power of Attorney—Short.
Revised, July, 1964

Dye & Durham Limited, Toronto, Canada
Law and Commercial Stationers
Form No. 169

Know all Men by these Presents

THAT I   JOHN DOUGLAS WINTER

of the   City of Toronto, in the County of York, Merchant,

*Figure 7.2. Headings on Legal Instruments –
Introductory Words*

Parties

The party to a legal instrument may be shown following the introductory words (Figure 7.2). When there is more than one party, they are set out in a formal way, and identified by some general descriptive label which is used throughout the instrument whenever reference is made to the parties.

Figures 7.3 and 7.4 illustrate headings on both typed and printed legal instruments. Note that:

1. The recital of the parties is single-spaced.
2. The word "and" separates the last-named party in the recital from the other party or parties.
3. The names of the parties are shown in full. No initials are used.
4. For an individual, a general address of local municipality and the county, district, or regional municipality is shown; for a company, the jurisdiction under which it was incorporated.
5. For an individual, his occupation is shown; for a company, the location of its head office.
6. When a man and his wife, or two individuals, are parties with a similar interest, they appear as a single party.

Body of Legal Papers

Figures 7.5 and 7.6 illustrate extracts from the body of legal instruments, which have been prepared following these requirements:

Printed Forms

1. Line up the typed insertion exactly with the printed line.
2. Fill in any unrequired space on a line with dashes.
3. Fill in any large expanse of blank space with a Z ruling in ink.
4. Type amounts in words and then in figures in brackets.
5. Check to ensure that all required insertions in the printed form have been made.

Typed Legal Papers

1. Type only on one side of the paper.
2. Start the heading approximately one inch from the top of the page.

3. On plain, unruled paper, leave a left-hand margin of 1½ inches, and a right-hand margin of one inch.
4. On ruled margin paper, type within two spaces of the rulings. Do not type over the rulings.
5. Double space the body of the document, but single space legal descriptions, long quotations, and parties set out in the heading.
6. Leave a bottom margin of no more than one inch, and endeavour to end each page at approximately the same line.
7. Indent paragraphs ten spaces.
8. Number each paragraph, or capitalize the first word or group of words.
9. End each page with a minimum of two lines of a paragraph, and begin a new page with a minimum of two lines of a carry-over paragraph.
10. Type at least two lines of the body of the legal paper on the page with the ending.
11. Number each page after the first page. Centre the page number approximately three lines from the top of the page.
12. Type numbers in legal instruments first in words, and then in figures in brackets. Use only figures in court papers and in legal correspondence.

Ending of Legal Papers

Endings of legal instruments are illustrated in Figure 7.7. Endings for court papers and wills are discussed in detail in later chapters.

Testimonium Clause

The *testimonium clause* is the clause by which the body of a legal instrument concludes, and is followed by the signature (or attestation clause). The testimonium clause commences with the words "IN WITNESS WHEREOF" or "IN TESTIMONY WHEREOF", and indicates which parties to the instrument are to sign or execute it, if the instrument is to be witnessed, and whether legal seals are required. If the instrument is not dated in the heading, the date appears in the testimonium clause, and is the date of signing, not the date the document is prepared.

Attestation Clause and Signatures

Many legal instruments must be witnessed in order to make the instrument a valid document. This is known as *attesting* and the clause is called the *attestation clause*. The witness signs at the left-hand side of the page after he has actually seen the party or parties sign the instrument. The parties to an instrument sign at the right-hand side of the page in the same order as they are set out in the heading.

The by-laws of a company will indicate who may sign on its behalf. This will usually be any two of a given number of officers.

The testimonium clause and attestation clause may not appear on a page without at least two lines of the body of the instrument. In the unusual case where there are so many signatures that they require more than a full page, as many as possible appear on the same page as part of the body of the instrument, and the remainder are carried over to a following page.

Sealing

The testimonium clause indicates whether a legal instrument must bear a *legal seal*. For an individual this seal is a small red gummed seal, which is affixed following the name of the signing parties on signed copies only. For a company the legal seal is the company seal, which is impressed over the signatures of the officers signing on behalf of the company on the signed copies only.

In preparing instruments which must be sealed, type the abbreviation *L.S.* (*Locus Sigilii* meaning "the place of the seal") on all copies of the instrument, after the names of individual parties, so that all carbon copies will show that the instrument was sealed. Before submitting the instrument for signing, affix the red seal to the copies to be signed over the notation "L.S.". The abbreviation "L.S." is not used following the name of a company in the ending.

This Agreement

made in duplicate the   15th   day of   November   19 70,

Between:

PERCIVAL ANDREW PETERSON, of the City of Hamilton, in the County of Wentworth, Merchant,

hereinafter called the Party

of the First Part

and

RONALD CRAIG ANDERSON, of the Borough of Etobicoke, in the County of York, Physician,

hereinafter called the Party

of the Second Part.

Dye & Durham
Limited
Toronto, Canada

Forms 98 to 101

Figure 7.3. Heading of Parties in Printed Legal Instrument

THIS AGREEMENT made in duplicate the 15th day of October, 1970.

Approx. 1″ from top of page

Triple space

B E T W E E N :

Double space

        PERCIVAL ANDREW PETERSON, of the City
        of Toronto, in the County of York,
        Merchant, and ISOBEL MAUDE PETERSON,
        his wife, of the same place,

           hereinafter called the Parties of the First Part,

Triple space

              - and -

        RONALD CRAIG ANDERSON, Physician, and
        LUCILLE CAROLINE ANDERSON, his wife,
        both of the City of Toronto, in the
        County of York,

           hereinafter called the Parties of the Second Part.

Two alternate ways of listing a man and his wife as parties to a legal instrument are illustrated. In actual practice, however, if a man and wife were involved as parties of the first part, and also as parties of the second part, the headings for both listings would follow the same form.

Figure 7.4A. Heading Showing Married Couple as Parties in Typed Legal Instrument

THIS AGREEMENT made in duplicate this 15th day of November, 1970.

B E T W E E N :

        ARTHUR BLACKSTAR, of the City of
        Toronto, in the County of York,
        Restaurateur,

        hereinafter referred to as "Blackstar",

                    OF THE FIRST PART,

              - and -

        INDUSTRIAL DEVELOPMENT BANK, incor-
        porated by Special Act of the
        Parliament of Canada, and having its
        head office in the City of Ottawa, in
        the Province of Ontario,

        hereinafter referred to as "the Bank",

                    OF THE SECOND PART.

Figure 7.4B. Heading Showing Incorporated Company as a Party in Legal Instrument

THIS AGREEMENT made in duplicate the 12th day of
December, 1970.

B E T W E E N:

> NORMA MABEL EAST, of the City of
> Toronto, in the County of York,
> Married Woman,
>
> hereinafter called the Party
>
> OF THE FIRST PART,
>
>
> HENRY JOHN SMITH, of the City
> of Hamilton, in the County of
> Wentworth, Clerk,
>
> hereinafter called the Party
>
> OF THE SECOND PART,
>
>
> DAVID KENNETH HEBDON, of the
> Borough of Scarborough, in the
> County of York, Accountant,
>
> hereinafter called the Party
>
> OF THE THIRD PART,
>
>
> - and -
>
>
> GILBERT HECTOR GRAHAM, of the
> Borough of Etobicoke, in the
> County of York, Teacher,
>
> hereinafter called the Party
>
> OF THE FOURTH PART.

Figure 7.4C. Heading Showing a Number of
Parties in Legal Instrument

WHEREAS the Bargainor s are possessed of the goods, chattels and effects herein-after set forth, described and enumerated, and have contracted and agreed with the Bargainee for the absolute Sale to him thereof, for the sum of THIRTEEN THOUSAND FIVE HUNDRED-----------($13,500.00)-----------Dollars

NOW THIS INDENTURE WITNESSETH, that in pursuance of the said Agreement, and in consideration of the sum of THIRTEEN THOUSAND FIVE HUNDRED---------

-----------------($13,500.00)--------------------- Dollars of lawful money of Canada, paid by the said Bargainee to the said Bargainors at or before the sealing and delivery of these presents (the receipt whereof is hereby acknowledged), the said Bargainor s do bargain, sell, assign, transfer and set over unto the said Bar-gainee his executors, administrators, successors and assigns
ALL THOSE the said goods, chattels and effects

Ten (10) oak office desks and chairs

Five (5) Sunar four-drawer filing cabinets

Four (4) IBM Selectric typewriters, Serial Nos. 5947213-6

One (1) Ditto Machine, Serial No. 9531

One (1) National Cash adding machine, Serial No. 77749

Four (4) metal secretarial desks and chairs

Figure 7.5. *Extract from Printed Legal Instrument*

2.

agreement to the Bank and has or is about to execute a further
mortgage to the Bank to secure a further loan;

AND WHEREAS the Bank has requested that Blackstar assign to it as collateral security for the said mortgage his
rights under the said agreement dated October 28, 1969;

NOW THIS AGREEMENT WITNESSETH that in consideration of
the premises and the sum of One Dollar ($1.00) of lawful money
of Canada now paid to Blackstar (the receipt whereof is hereby
by him acknowledged) the parties hereto covenant and agree as
follows:

1.   Blackstar hereby grants and assigns to the Bank all
his rights under the said agreement as collateral security for
the said mortgages above referred to; provided that while there
is no default under either of the said mortgages, Blackstar and
those claiming under him shall be entitled to exercise all their
rights under the said agreement as if the same had not been
assigned as herein provided.

2.   Unless and until there is default under the said
mortgages and the said notice has been given to Blackstar as
aforesaid, the Bank will not register this agreement against
the title to any lands described in the said agreement or will

*Figure 7.6. Extract from Typed Legal
Instrument*

𝔍𝔫 𝔚𝔦𝔱𝔫𝔢𝔰𝔰 𝔚𝔥𝔢𝔯𝔢𝔬𝔣   the said parties hereto have hereunto set their hands and seals.

𝔖𝔦𝔤𝔫𝔢𝔡, 𝔖𝔢𝔞𝔩𝔢𝔡 𝔞𝔫𝔡 𝔇𝔢𝔩𝔦𝔳𝔢𝔯𝔢𝔡
IN THE PRESENCE OF

_____
Percival Andrew Peterson

_____
Ronald Craig Anderson

IN WITNESS WHEREOF, the said parties have hereunto set their hands and seals.

SIGNED, SEALED AND DELIVERED
In the presence of

DATED the   15th   **day of**   November   **A.D.** 1970

WITNESS:

Figure 7.7A. Endings in Printed Legal Instruments

IN WITNESS WHEREOF the parties hereto have hereunto set
their hands and seals.

```
SIGNED, SEALED AND DELIVERED )
       in the presence of     )
                              )
                              )
                              )
                              )   _____
                              )        Percival Andrew Peterson
                              )
                              )
                              )   _____
                              )        Ronald Craig Anderson
                              )
```

Company Signing

IN WITNESS WHEREOF the Party of the First Part has hereunto set his hand and seal, and the Party of the Second Part has
hereto affixed its corporate seal attested by the hands of its duly
authorized officers.

```
SIGNED, SEALED AND DELIVERED )
       in the presence of     )
                              )
                              )   _____
                              )        Ronald Craig Anderson
                              )
                              )   THE SMITH MANUFACTURING CO. LTD.
                              )
                              )   By:_____
                              )                  President
                              )
                              )
                              )   _____
                              )                  Secretary
                              )
```

*Figure 7.7B. Endings in Typed Legal
Instruments*

Endorsement or Back of Legal Papers

Legal instruments and papers have an identifying last page which is known as the *endorsement,* but more generally called the *back.* The nature of the document will determine what is typed but generally includes the date or name of the court, the name of the parties, a description of the paper, and the name and address of the law firm drawing the document.

Backs are also known as *long* (typed down the length of the paper) or *short* (typed across the length of the paper), depending on the nature of the legal paper. Court papers have a long back, which is discussed in a later chapter.

Backs for legal instruments are short backs; the paper is inserted horizontally into the typewriter, and the back is prepared across the length of the paper. The same quality paper as used for the instrument is used for the back. If ruled margin paper is used, type on the unruled side, checking that the wide left-hand margin is at the top as the paper is inserted, to ensure that the rulings on the pages of the instrument and the back will align when the copies are assembled.

Figures 7.8 and 7.9 illustrate the format of backs for legal instruments. Note the following:

1. On 14-inch paper the page is divided into quarters, and the endorsement is typed on the second quarter.
2. On 11-inch paper the page is divided into thirds, and the endorsement is typed on the middle third of the page.
3. The date of the instrument is typed one inch from the top of the page, and underscored.
4. The names of the parties are typed in capital letters approximately two inches from the top of the page. The names are separated by an "and" if all parties sign the instrument, and by a "to" if only the first party signs.
5. The name of the document is typed in capital letters approximately halfway down the page, centred between two horizontal lines.
6. The name and address of the law firm drawing the document is typed in capital letters approximately one inch from the bottom of the page.

Printed legal forms have a pre-printed back, which is filled in with the particular information required.

A Fully-Typed Instrument

Figure 7.10 illustrates an instrument which has been typed in full. Some offices use a printed form, but in others the instrument is typed as shown here. The example used here is a *release.* A release is a document in which the person signing it gives up all his rights or claims in a legal matter involving the party or parties to whom the release is given. Releases are used in court work, in estate work, and in any situation where it is necessary to have one party relinquish any rights he might have in a particular situation.

Since it is a legal instrument, a release has a short back. Usually a minimum of three copies is prepared: one signed copy, a copy for the person giving the release, and a copy for the lawyer's files.

In some instances a release is given to be held *in escrow* pending completion of some condition, for example, receipt of a cheque. To hold "in escrow" means that a third party will keep the release in safekeeping until the person to whom the release is to be given has met some condition.

What Usually Happens to Prepared Legal Instruments

When the instrument has been typed and checked, assemble complete sets, and staple each set in the upper left-hand corner. If there are a large number of pages in a set, insert the left-hand corner of the assembled pages in a diamond-shaped pocket, called a *corner* (which is usually blue in colour), and staple through the combined corner and pages. Check to be sure legal seals are affixed if required for individual parties. The instrument is then ready to be executed.

Execution of a document is doing what is required to give validity to the instrument. Properly this includes the signing, sealing, and delivering of the instrument. In practice, however, the term is used to refer to the signing and sealing only.

True Copies

When the instrument has been executed, you "conform" or make *true copies* of the unsigned copies, that is, you write in ink, and in quotation marks, the names of the signing parties exactly as they appear in the executed instrument. Also, write in any dates or other information which may have been inserted upon execution.

Registering

Many legal instruments are *registered* at an appropriate Registry Office or Land Titles Office, about which you will read more later. Registration is filing notice of an interest in real or personal property which is the subject matter of the particular legal instrument being filed.

Legal Offices Concerned with Legal Papers

There are many public offices which are concerned with legal papers, the names of which you should know.

Court House

Each county, group of counties, district, regional municipality, or judicial district in Ontario has a County Court House, where the offices of the County Court, the sheriff, and local court officials are located.

In Toronto, for example, the County Court House is the seat of the County Court for the County of York, and for the local sittings of the Supreme Court of Ontario. Osgoode Hall houses the Court of Appeal for Ontario, and other court offices which are discussed in a later chapter.

Land Titles Office

Land Titles Offices are offices where instruments giving notice of an interest in real property may be filed.

Registry Office

Registry Offices are offices where instruments may be registered or filed to give notice of an interest in real or personal property.

Office of Official Guardian

An Official Guardian is an officer who represents the interests of infants in legal matters.

Office of Public Trustee

A Public Trustee is an officer who administers the estates of individuals who are mentally incompetent to look after their own affairs.

Municipal Board

A Municipal Board is a tribunal composed of members appointed by the provincial government, and deals with municipal zoning by-laws, expropriations and matters within the jurisdiction of the municipalities in the province. For example, when the City of Toronto wished to change the boundaries of its electoral wards, its proposal was submitted to the Ontario Municipal Board for approval. In Ontario this board has its head office at 145 Queen St. in Toronto.

Upper left corner of back when instrument assembled

DATED: May 17,   1970

JOHN JAMES SMITH

- and -

WILLIAM RAY BROWN

A G R E E M E N T

HILL, JOHNSTON & GRANT
17 Princess Street S.
Toronto, Ontario

Date instrument dated or executed

Name of parties

Description of instrument

Name and address of law firm
drawing document

46

Figure 7.8.   Typed Short Back – 14-inch Paper

Date of instrument

DATED: October 28,   1970

Name of parties

RONALD CRAIG ANDERSON

to

PERCIVAL ANDREW PETERSON

Description of instrument

R E L E A S E

Name and address of law firm drawing document

HILL, JOHNSTON & GRANT
17 Princess Street S.
Toronto, Ontario

Figure 7.9.   Typed Short Back – 11-inch Paper   47

KNOW ALL MEN BY THESE PRESENTS that I, RONALD CRAIG ANDERSON, of the City of Toronto, in the County of York, in consideration of the settlement of the action brought by me in the Supreme Court of Ontario against Percival Andrew Peterson by writ number 3407 for 1969, and in consideration of the monies paid thereunder pursuant to such settlement (receipt whereof is hereby acknowledged), do hereby remise, release and forever discharge Percival Andrew Peterson, and his respective heirs, executors, administrators, successors and assigns, of and from all actions, causes of action, claims and demands which against Percival Andrew Peterson I or my respective heirs, executors, administrators, successors or assigns hereafter can, shall or may have for or by reason of any matter or thing existing up to the present time, and in particular but without limiting the generality of the foregoing of and from all actions, causes of action, claims and demands in any way arising out of or relating to services performed by us in connection with the construction of a private dwelling described municipally as Number 15 Lake Boulevard, in the Borough of Scarborough.

IN WITNESS WHEREOF I have hereto affixed my hand and seal this   day of   , 1970.

SIGNED, SEALED AND DELIVERED)
    in the presence of   )
)
)
)
)   LS
)
)
)

Figure 7.10. Typed Legal Instrument Called a
"Release" on Which Legal Seal is not yet
Affixed

CHAPTER 8

Notarial Certificates, Affidavits, Statutory Declarations

Certain office procedures are common in all law offices whether small or large, and regardless of the major area of law which may be practised. These procedures involve the necessity to verify the authenticity of an executed legal paper or other document, or to swear to the truth of certain statements of fact.

You will encounter such legal papers as *notarial certificates*, *affidavits* of all kinds, and *statutory declarations*.

Notarial Certificates

A notarial certificate is a legal instrument, signed by a Notary Public, which certifies the authenticity of the copy of the paper to which it is affixed. Individuals may have to prove that a copy of a paper is indeed an exact copy of the original paper. They come to a lawyer who is a Notary Public and present to him the original and a copy of the paper. The Notary Public will check the copy with the original, and if satisfied that the copy is in fact a copy of the original, will certify this by completing and signing a notarial certificate, which is then affixed to the front of the copy. The copy is then said to be a "notarial" copy, that is, it has been proved to be an authentic copy of the original.

In many offices a printed legal form is used to prepare notarial certificates (Figure 8.1); in other offices a short notarial certificate is completely typed (Figure 8.2). In either case, the basic wording and format are the same.

A separate certificate is prepared for each copy which is authenticated (notarized), and each certificate is individually signed by the Notary Public and his seal affixed.

A notarial certificate does not require a back, since the certificate is attached to the front of the paper being notarized.

Affidavits

One of the most common legal papers prepared is the affidavit. It forms part of the procedure in almost every area of legal practice.

An affidavit is a written statement in the name of an individual called the *deponent,* by whom it is voluntarily signed and sworn to before an authorized officer known as a Commissioner. The purpose of an affidavit is to establish or prove a fact, or facts.

An affidavit is usually made by only one person, although in some circumstances two people can join in a single affidavit.

Heading of an Affidavit

The heading of an affidavit is determined by the manner in which it is to be used. Affidavits used in court work have a very distinctive heading common to all court papers, and will be considered in a later chapter. At this time we will deal only with affidavits which form part of a legal instrument.

Affidavits which are part of a legal instrument are headed by the province and municipality (i.e., county, district, or regional municipality) in which they will be used. The heading also shows the name of the person making the affidavit, his general address, and occupation. (See Figure 8.3.)

Numbered paragraphs follow, outlining the facts that the person wishes to swear to. On signing the affidavit before a Commissioner, the deponent will place his hand on a Bible and swear that the contents of the affidavit are, to the best of his knowledge and belief, true.

Ending of an Affidavit

The ending of an affidavit is known as the *jurat.* It is the clause which attests that the affidavit was sworn to at a stated time before an authorized officer. The form of jurat is identical in every affidavit. It is typed at the left-hand side of the page, with room left beneath it for the signature of the authorized officer. The person swearing the affidavit signs on the right.

SWORN before me at the)
)
Borough of Etobicoke)
)
in the County of York)
)
this   day of August,)
)
197)
)
)
)
)
)

A COMMISSIONER, etc.

The jurat may not appear on a page alone; at least two lines of the body of the affidavit must appear on a page with it. Unless you know the exact date on which the affidavit will be sworn, leave the date blank in the jurat, to be filled in when the affidavit is being sworn before the Commissioner.

Affidavits in Legal Instruments

It is frequently necessary to include affidavits as part of legal instruments. These may concern the legal capacity of the persons involved to enter into a contract, information on marital status, and a sworn statement of a witness that he in fact saw the parties sign the instrument.

The three most common affidavits which are found as an integral part of other legal instruments are: *affidavit of execution, affidavit of legal age,* and *affidavit of marital status.* (The last two are usually combined into a single affidavit.)

In printed instruments, these affidavits are contained in the instrument and only require the appropriate blanks to be completed. In typed instruments, depending on the preference of your office, either the necessary affidavits are typed or printed affidavit forms are used.

Affidavit of Execution

This affidavit (Figure 8.3) is signed by the witness to the instrument, and is his sworn statement that he did see the document the affidavit is part of, signed by one or more of the parties.

You may be uncertain of the wording to use in paragraph 1 of this affidavit. Assuming that the same person witnesses the signing by all parties who must execute the instrument, the table below may be of assistance.

Affidavit of Legal Age and Affidavit of Marital Status

In most legal instruments these two affidavits are combined into a single affidavit (Figure 8.4).

Under Canadian law, a person may not legally enter into a contract (with the exception of necessities for minors), or hold title to land, unless he or she has reached the age of twenty-one.

A person who has executed a legal instrument dealing with title to land, usually completes an affidavit as to marital status.

The marital status of a man is an important factor when dealing with land and buildings. Under Ontario law, his wife has a one-third life-interest in real property owned by her husband. This is known as a wife's "dower interest", and is discussed in Chapter 9.

Number of Parties to Instrument	Number of Parties Signing	Wording
Two	Two	. . . both of the parties
Two or more	One	. . . one of the parties
Three	Three	. . . all of the parties
Three or more	Two	. . . two of the parties

Dye & Durham Limited, 76 Richmond Street East, Toronto
Law and Commercial Stationers
Form No. 164

CANADA

Province of Ontario

To Wit

To all whom these Presents

may come, be seen or known

I, PETER THOMAS GRANT,

a Notary Public, in and for the Province of Ontario, by Royal Authority duly appointed, residing

at the City of Toronto, in the County of York,

in said Province,

Do Certify and Attest that the paper-writing hereto annexed is a true copy of a document produced

and shown to me by Ronald Craig Anderson---------------------------------

and purporting to be the certificate of marriage between the said

Ronald Craig Anderson and Lucille Caroline Anderson

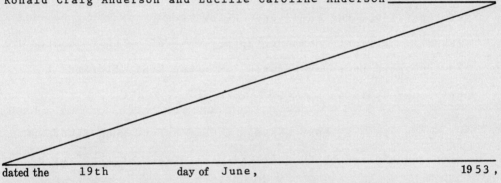

dated the 19th day of June, 1953,

the said copy having been compared by me with the said original document, an act whereof being

requested I have granted under my Notarial Form and Seal of Office to serve and avail as occasion

shall or may require.

In Testimony Whereof I have hereto subscribed my name and affixed my Notarial Seal of Office at

this 13th day of November, 1970.

SEAL

A Notary Public in and for the Province of Ontario.

Figure 8.1. Printed Notarial Certificate

```
C A N A D A            )
                       )    TO ALL WHOM THESE PRESENTS
PROVINCE OF ONTARIO    )
                       )        MAY COME, BE SEEN OR KNOWN
        To Wit        )
```

I, PETER THOMAS GRANT, a Notary Public, in and for the Province of Ontario, by Royal Authority duly appointed, residing at the City of Toronto, in the County of York, in said Province, DO CERTIFY AND ATTEST that the paper-writing hereto annexed is a true copy of a document produced and shown to me by Ronald Craig Anderson and purporting to be the certificate of marriage between the said Ronald Craig Anderson and Lucille Caroline Anderson, dated the 19th day of June, 1953, the said copy having been compared by me with the said original document, an act whereof being requested I have granted under my Notarial Form and Seal of Office to serve and avail as occasion shall or may require.

IN TESTIMONY WHEREOF I have hereto subscribed my name and affixed my Notarial Seal of Office at the City of Toronto, in the County of York, this 13th day of November, 1970.

A Notary Public
in and for the Province of Ontario

Figure 8.2. Typed Notarial Certificate

Affidavit of Execution of Documents

COUNTY
OF
YORK

To Wit:

J, ELSIE EDNA SWARTZ,

of the Borough of Etobicoke,

in the County of York, Secretary,

make oath and say

1. THAT I was personally present and did see the within or annexed Instrument and a Duplicate thereof duly signed, sealed and executed by Percival Andrew Peterson, and Ronald Craig Anderson,--

-- both of the parties thereto

2. That the said Instrument and Duplicate were executed by the said parties at the City of Toronto.

3. That I know the said parties.

4. That I am a subscribing witness to the said Instrument and Duplicate

SWORN before me at the City

of Toronto

in the County

of York

this 15th

day of November 1970

A Commissioner, etc.

Figure 8.3. Affidavit of Execution

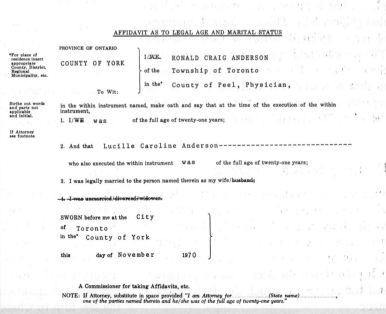

AFFIDAVIT AS TO LEGAL AGE AND MARITAL STATUS

*For place of residence insert appropriate County, District, Regional Municipality, etc.

PROVINCE OF ONTARIO

COUNTY OF YORK

To Wit:

I/WE RONALD CRAIG ANDERSON

of the Township of Toronto

in the* County of Peel, Physician,

Strike out words and parts not applicable and initial.

If Attorney see footnote.

in the within instrument named, make oath and say that at the time of the execution of the within instrument,

1. I/WE was of the full age of twenty-one years;

2. And that Lucille Caroline Anderson----------------------------------

who also executed the within instrument was of the full age of twenty-one years;

3. I was legally married to the person named therein as my wife/husband;

4. I was unmarried/divorced/widower.

SWORN before me at the City

of Toronto

in the* County of York

this day of November 1970

A Commissioner for taking Affidavits, etc.

NOTE: If Attorney, substitute in space provided "*I am Attorney for ....(State name), one of the parties named therein and he/she was of the full age of twenty-one years.*"

Figure 8.4. Affidavit of Legal Age and Marital Status Taken by Husband

The affidavit of legal age and marital status is completed by the party who executed the instrument. If two or more parties are executing, practice varies regarding completion of this affidavit. In some instances it may be completed by any one of the parties; in other instances each executing party must join in the affidavit. As we consider individual instruments, we will consider completion of this affidavit further.

In some instances it is also possible for an agent of the party to complete the affidavit, and the form indicates the wording to be used in these circumstances.

When a company is the party executing a legal instrument, no affidavit of execution or of legal age and marital status is required. A special affidavit outlining the authority of the officers executing the instrument may be required. This affidavit outlines the authority of the officers who executed the instrument, and is taken by an officer other than one of the officers who, in fact, executed the instrument. A form of this affidavit is considered in Chapter 10.

Statutory Declaration

Frequently an individual must provide proof of some facts when there is no action or matter in the courts, or when no legal instruments are involved. He will then complete what is known as a statutory declaration (Figure 8.5). This is a formal statement of facts, declared before a Commissioner. The person making the declaration is called the *declarant*. The form of jurat is identical to that of a standard affidavit, with the exception that instead of the word "Sworn", the word "Declared" is used.

Heading, Body and Ending

Statutory declarations are printed forms, which are completed from material provided by the lawyer. The heading is divided into two parts; the province and municipality (i.e., county, district, or regional municipality) in which the declaration is prepared, and the matter for which the declaration is made.

The name, address, and occupation of the declarant are then completed by filling in the spaces provided in the form.

Following the typed words on the form "DO SOLEMNLY DECLARE THAT", type numbered paragraphs setting forth the facts being declared. If the amount of material permits, you may double space the typing. If, however, a great many numbered paragraphs are involved, single space the material in order to ensure it will all be accommodated in the space available.

The statutory declaration is "declared" before a Commissioner. The declaration then requires the signature of first, the declarant, and second, the Commissioner. One copy only is signed, and it is your responsibility to conform all other copies of the declaration.

You will be instructed by your lawyer how many copies of the statutory declaration to prepare, this being determined by the use to which the declaration will be put.

Declarations by Two People

A statutory declaration is frequently made by two people simultaneously. In the printed forms, simply cross out references to "I", and substitute the word "WE". In the heading "DO SOLEMNLY DECLARE", the word "SEVERALLY" is inserted so that the heading reads:

/SEVERALLY
DO SOLEMNLY DECLARE

In the jurat the word "SEVERALLY" is typed immediately above the word "DECLARED", and both declarants sign in the right-hand portion of the jurat.

Backs

The printed form also has a printed back which must be completed with the information indicated; the date, the matter which is the subject of the declaration (the information for which appears in the heading of the statutory declaration), the name of the person whose declaration it is, and the name of the law firm in whose office it is prepared.

Dye & Durham Co. Limited, 76 Richmond Street East, Toron
Law and Commercial Stationers

Form No. 141

Canada
PROVINCE OF ONTARIO

COUNTY,
DISTRICT
or   OF (name)
REGIONAL
MUNICIPALITY
TO WIT:

In the Matter of --------------------------------

AND IN THE MATTER OF----------------------------

I, (name of person declaring the declaration)

of the (local municipality) of (name)   in the (County, District, or
Regional Municipality) of (name), (occupation of declarant),

DO SOLEMNLY DECLARE THAT

1.   ---

      ----

2.   ---

                              O R

1.   ---

----

2.   ---

AND I make this solemn Declaration conscientiously believing it to be true, and knowing
that it is of the same force and effect as if made under oath, and by virtue of "The Canada
Evidence Act."

DECLARED before me at the (local municipality)

of (name)

in the (County, District, or
Regional Municipality) of (name)   (Signed here by person(s)
                                            declarating the statutory
this   day of (month)   19--   declaration)

    (Signed here by Commissioner)

                A Commissioner, etc.

Figure 8.5.   First Page of Statutory Declaration   **55**

Dated (month) (day) 19 —

IN THE MATTER OF

AND IN THE MATTER OF-------------

Statutory Declaration

of

(NAME)

Dye & Durham Co. Limited, 76 Richmond Street East, Toronto
Law and Commercial Stationers

(NAME AND ADDRESS
OF LAW FIRM)

Figure 8.5. Back of Statutory Declaration

CHAPTER 9

Introduction to Real Estate Transactions

One of the most important areas of legal practice is known as *conveyancing*, the area of legal work dealing with real property.

Real property is immovable property such as lands, buildings and things attached to the land. *Personal property* generally includes movable property such as cars and clothing.

In his real estate practice the lawyer is involved in three main areas: (1) real property either bought or sold; (2) real property used as security for a loan, for example, a mortgage; (3) real property leased (rented) by the owner to another party.

Before considering what steps a lawyer takes in any of these areas, you should note some other points which play an important part in real estate practice.

Systems of Land Registration

All instruments relating to real estate may be registered to record the interest of the holder of the instrument in the real property. In Canada, there are two systems of land registration: the Registry Office system, and the Land Titles system.

Registry Office System

The Registry Office system is the older of the two systems, and in Ontario is governed by The Registry Act. The province is divided into Registry Divisions, each with a Registrar.

The Registrar is not responsible for checking the content of the instrument presented to him for registration; he is obliged only to satisfy himself as to its form, and to see that it is registered against the title of the real property which it describes. He has no responsibility to see that the person allegedly conveying title to real property has a good title to it. The responsibility to establish good title is that of the purchaser or his solicitor, and for this reason lawyers arrange to have titles "searched" when acting for a purchaser. Depending on the province, the search to establish good title may extend back as far as forty years, or in some cases, may go back to the root, that is, the first grant from the Crown. The lawyer can then guarantee title to the purchaser.

Land Titles System

In some provinces, including Ontario, the Torrens or Land Titles system of land registration is also used.

Land Titles Offices are administered by a *Master of Titles,* and no instrument relating to real property registered in that office is accepted until the Master of Titles is satisfied that it does what it purports to do.

For example, before the Master will accept for registration a transfer of land from A to Z, he first satisfies himself that A is shown in his records as the registered owner. He then checks to ensure that the transfer is correctly executed by A and is a proper transfer. Having done all this, he registers Z as the new owner, and upon payment of a fee, issues Z with a certificate of title, certifying Z to be the owner with an absolute title subject to any qualifications and restrictions he may make. Under the Land Titles system, the title is guaranteed by the government.

The advantages of this system are: it offers simplicity and security of title, and ease and economy in transferring and dealing with real property.

Figure 9.1 sets out the comparison of the two systems as they operate in Ontario.

Special Terms

In the area of real estate there are two special terms which are encountered frequently, and which you must clearly understand.

Dower

Dower is a life-interest of the widow in one-third of her late husband's real property, or the rents of profits therefrom, for her life.

Comparison of Land Registration Systems in Ontario

	Registry System	Land Titles System
Name of Office	The Registry Office for the Registry Division of the County of (Peel)	The Office of Land Title at (Toronto)
Official in Charge	Registrar	Master of Titles, or Local Master of Titles
Term Used for Registration	Registered	Filed
Principal Record Book	Abstract Index	Register
Classification of Land Entries	By reference to township lot in a concession of a county or municipality, or to a lot on a registered plan of subdivision	By parcel number
Documents	Not checked by Registrar before accepted for registration	Carefully checked by Master of Titles before being accepted for filing
Title Search	Forty-year chain of title searched	Outstanding entry on most recent parcel register
Certificate by Officials in Charge	Only a Registrar's Abstract certifying list of all entries on the abstract index affecting a particular piece of land	Certificate of Ownership, or Certificate of Ownership of Charge
Forms	Deed – grantor to grantee Mortgage – mortgagor to mortgagee Discharge of Mortgage Assignment of Mortgage	Transfer – transferor to transferee Charge – mortgagor to mortgagee Cessation of Charge Transfer of Charge
Legal Seals	Required on all instruments except Discharge of Mortgage	No seals required
Affidavits	Affidavit of Execution; Affidavit of Legal Age and Marital Status by one of executing parties; and on instruments conveying title, Land Transfer Tax Affidavit	Affidavit of Execution which requires witness to swear executing parties were of legal age; Affidavit of Legal Age and Marital Status taken by all executing parties; and on instruments conveying title, Land Transfer Tax Affidavit

Figure 9.1

While dower rights only arise on the husband's death, they are an important consideration when a married man in his own name is the sole owner of real property which he wishes to sell to another, or upon which he wishes to place a mortgage. Under these circumstances his wife must "join in", or be one of the parties to the conveyance to bar her dower, that is, to give up her one-third life-interest in the property. If she is not a party to the instrument, the purchaser or the mortgagee will acquire the real property subject to the right of dower of the wife.

Joint Tenants and Tenants in Common

More than one person may have an interest in the same real property. This is known as co-ownership, and may be held in either of the following ways: as *joint tenants* or as *tenants in common*.

Joint Tenants

Each tenant (i.e., owner) holds the same interest as the other, and the surviving co-owner acquires the interest of the deceased. The "right of survivorship" is the reason joint tenancy is so popular among married people as a means of holding title to real property.

Tenants in Common

Each tenant (i.e., owner) may dispose of his interest independently of the other, by deed or will. If real property is held as tenants in common, there is no right of survivorship.

Legal Descriptions of Real Property

In legal instruments dealing with real property a detailed legal description of the property is required. Accuracy in typing descriptions is imperative.

There are two methods of identifying real property:

By Township and Concession

This method is usually associated with rural areas. Land was surveyed and divided into areas known as Townships, which were divided by concessions and lines into a number of lots, each of which usually contain 200 acres. These lots, in turn, may be divided into smaller lots. An example of a description using township and concession is:

. . . in the Township of Pickering, in the County of Ontario, in the Province of Ontario, that part of Lot No. 15 in the 2nd Concession, East of Webb Street in the said Township, more particularly described as follows: . . . .

By Lot and Plan Number

This method is usually found in urban areas, that is, cities, villages and towns. Land is described by reference to a lot number on a plan of subdivision registered in the appropriate Registry Office. An example of such a description is:

. . . in the Borough of Scarborough, in the County of York, and being composed of the whole of Lot No. 154 according to a plan registered in the Registry Office for the Registry Division of the East and West Ridings of the County of York as No. 4888, more particularly described as follows: . . . .

When property has been identified by Township and Concession, or by Lot and Plan Number, it may be necessary to describe the "parcel" with some particularity, especially if any of the boundaries are irregular in shape. Then the property is "more particularly described" by indicating a determinable point of commencement, and proceeding to indicate a perimeter of the parcel by setting out directions and distances. This is known as a description by *metes and bounds,* and may be described in one of three ways:

a. by feet and inches (called a *distance*)
b. by minutes and degrees (called a *course*)
c. by chains and links. One chain equals 66 feet. In the County of York in Ontario, for example, most of the farm lots contained 200 acres, and measured 20 chains by 100 chains. Chains and links are not generally used alone; they are used in conjunction with foot and inch measurements.

Guide for Typing Legal Descriptions

1. Single space a description being typed into legal instruments, unless it is very short and there is sufficient space in the printed form to double space it.

2. Start a new paragraph for each distance and course. Do not indent paragraphs.

3. Capitalize the first word of each new paragraph.

4. Put a semicolon at the end of each paragraph, and a period after the words which end the description "more or less to the place of beginning" or "more or less to the point of commencement".

5. Capitalize the first letter of the points of the compass:

North	East	South
Northwest	West	Southwest
Northeast		Southeast

6. Do not capitalize the first letter of such words as:

northerly	easterly	southerly
northwesterly	westerly	southwesterly
northeasterly		southeasterly

7. Capitalize the first letter of such words as Borough, Township, Lot, County, Concession, Regional Municipality.

8. Write distances and courses first in words, then in figures in brackets:

   Distances: forty-two and sixty-three one-hundredths feet (42.63′); fifty-one feet seven and one-half inches (51′ 7½″)

   Courses: South twenty degrees, thirty-three minutes, forty-five seconds West (S 20° 33′ 45″ W)
   (° indicates degrees; ′ indicates minutes; ″ indicates seconds. Note that there is no punctuation in the above examples.)

Distances Using Chains and Links: 1,312 feet 4½ inches (19 chains 88⁴⁄₉ links) or 1,312′ 4½″ (19 chains, 88⁴⁄₉ links)

You will notice when copying legal descriptions that these guides have not always been followed. It will depend on the practice of your office whether you will copy legal descriptions exactly as they appear in another instrument, or whether you will do so in conformity with the above guides. However, whenever you must type a legal description from dictation, you should follow the principles outlined above.

How to Check Land Descriptions

A typographical error in the legal description of land can cause a great deal of trouble in the future. Unless great care is taken when copying the description, it is quite easy to be distracted. For example, if the expression "parallel to the southerly limit" appears several times in a few lines, it would be easy to omit the phrase once, and its omission would not necessarily be noticed when checking the typing by merely reading it over yourself. This omission, however, would affect the amount of land being conveyed by the deed, or subject to the mortgage.

Legal descriptions should always be compared with someone else reading the description to you from the original copy, while you check your newly typed copy. Some offices require that they be compared twice, with two persons alternating the reading and checking.

Proofreading is probably the most important single aspect of completing legal instruments accurately. Do not submit an instrument containing a legal description to the lawyer for execution until it has been thoroughly checked for accuracy.

ALL AND SINGULAR that certain parcel or tract of land and premises situate, lying and being in the Borough of Scarborough, the County of York, and Province of Ontario, said parcel being composed of part of Lot A according to a plan filed in the Registry Office for the Registry Division of Toronto as Number 1220, and which said parcel is more particularly described as follows:

BEGINNING at a point in the east limit of said Lot A distant 1,312' 4 1/2" (19 chains 88 4/9 links) measured northerly thereon from the Southeast angle of said Lot A;

THENCE westerly parallel to the southerly limit of said Lot A a distance of ten feet (10') more or less to a point in a line drawn parallel to and distant ten feet (10') measured westerly at right angles to the easterly limit of said Lot A, said point being the point of commencement;

THENCE northerly along said parallel line a distance of sixty feet (60') to a point;

THENCE westerly parallel to the southerly limit of said Lot A a distance of one hundred and fifty feet (150') to a point;

THENCE southerly parallel to the easterly limit of said Lot A, a distance of sixty feet (60') to a point;

THENCE easterly parallel to the southerly limit of said Lot A, a distance of one hundred and fifty feet (150') more or less to the point of commencement.

Figure 9.2. Extract from a Legal Description

CHAPTER 10

Deeds and Transfers

The legal instruments by which title is conveyed in a real estate transaction are *deeds* and *transfers*.

A deed is the instrument used under the Registry Office system; a transfer, the instrument used under the Land Titles system. The term *conveyance* is sometimes used for both deeds and transfers, since title to real estate is "conveyed" from one party to another.

There must be either a deed or a transfer to complete every real estate transaction. These instruments have been put on printed forms, and are completed with the specific details pursuant to the particular transaction.

Deeds

The parties to a deed are the *grantor(s)* – the person or persons who are giving title to the real estate (the vendors), and the *grantee(s)* – the person or persons who are receiving title to the real estate (the purchasers).

Deeds are prepared by the solicitors acting for the grantor. Usually a minimum of four copies of a deed is prepared, dating it the day it is typed. One copy of the deed is forwarded to the purchaser's solicitors for approval. When the deed is returned, approved, it is executed in duplicate by the grantor. Legal seals must be affixed, and affidavits completed. The affidavits include affidavit of legal age, affidavit of marital status, affidavit of execution, and a special affidavit concerning land transfer tax.

There are several types of deeds; the main ones are described below.

Deed Without Dower

A deed without dower is used when an unmarried man, a widower, a woman alone, a company, or a husband and wife jointly, are selling real property. The deed contains no printed clause relating to dower.

In the printed heading of a deed without dower, no words appear to refer to the parties to the deed as the party of the first part and so on. These words must be typed in when the deed is typed.

Many offices use this form of deed, and adapt it for use when the wife is a party to the deed to bar her dower. The necessary dower clause is then typed in on page 3, and the wife is shown in the heading as the party of the third part.

Figure 10.1 illustrates a completed deed prepared on a without dower form, in which the wife of the grantor is joining to bar her dower.

Deed With Dower

A deed with dower is used when a married man is himself the grantor (vendor) selling real property, and his wife is a party to the deed to give up her one-third life-interest in the real property. A printed clause in the deed appears before the testimonium and attestation clauses, to indicate that the wife of the grantor is a party to the deed to bar her dower in the real property which is covered by the deed.

In the printed heading of a deed with dower, the grantor is shown as the party of the first part, the grantee as the party of the second part, and the wife of the grantor as the party of the third part.

Joint Tenancy Deed

When title to property is being taken by the grantees as joint tenants, many law offices use a special joint tenancy deed which includes provisions as to joint tenancy in the printed portion of the form. Other firms use the without dower deed, and spell out the necessary joint tenancy requirements in the deed as illustrated in Figure 10.1.

Deed to Uses

A deed to uses is used by a married man who wishes to take title to real property in a manner which will permit him to dispose of the property without the necessity of having his wife a party to the subsequent deed to bar her dower.

Under such a deed a married man may later sell the property to anyone without his wife being a party to the deed at all. It should be noted, however, that under some circumstances a deed giving title to uses may not obviate his wife's dower interest.

Executor's Deed

When a deceased person in his lifetime was the sole owner of real estate, his interest in such real estate is transferred upon his death to the *executor* or *administrator* of his estate, to be disposed of under the terms of his will, or in accordance with the rules governing disposition of property under an *intestacy* (the state of dying without a will).

An *executor's deed* is the deed by which such real property is conveyed to the person inheriting it under a will, or under an intestacy. This deed is given by the executor or administrator in his capacity as executor or administrator of the deceased's estate. If the property had to be sold to settle the estate, an executor's deed is used to convey real property to the purchaser.

Quit Claim Deed

This form of deed is used to release interest in land, and is discussed at the end of this chapter.

Parts of a Deed

Heading

Deeds are executed in duplicate, and are dated the day on which they are typed. Naming of the parties in the heading follows the standard form of giving name, general address, and occupation. When more than one person is the grantor, it is required that the way in which they hold title also be shown in the heading:

JAMES JOSEPH SMITH, of the City of Toronto, in the County of York, Merchant, and MAY ANNE SMITH, his wife, of the same place, as joint tenants, and not as tenants in common

OR

JAMES JOSEPH SMITH, Merchant, and MAY ANNE SMITH, his wife, both of the City of Toronto, in the County of York, as joint tenants and not as tenants in common

The descriptive information for the parties is already included in most printed forms.

If the without dower deed is used, the descriptive information for each party must be typed in:

hereinafter called the Grantors,

OF THE FIRST PART

Some law offices indicate in the heading how the grantees are taking title. This information frequently appears in the body of the deed, however, and if a joint tenancy deed is used this information is part of the printed form.

If a married man himself is giving title under the deed, his wife is a party to the deed to relinquish her one-third life-interest in the property being conveyed. She is added as the party of the third part, and only her name need be shown.

Consideration

The *consideration* is the indication of what the purchaser is giving the vendor as payment for the real property. The usual practice in most law offices is simply to show the consideration as follows:

WITNESSETH that in consideration of other good and valuable consideration and the sum of TWO ——— ($2.00) ——— Dollars

This small amount is used since the law does not concern itself with the adequacy of consideration. As long as there is some consideration shown in the deed, this is sufficient to pass the title. The real consideration need not be shown except in the land transfer tax affidavit.

However, the consideration clause may be shown in other ways, varied in accordance with the circumstances of the sale:

All Cash

WITNESSETH that in consideration of the sum of FORTY THOUSAND————— ($40,000.00) ————————Dollars

Cash and Mortgage Assumed

WITNESSETH that in consideration of the assumption of an existing registered mortgage in favour of John Albert Doe for approximately SEVEN THOUSAND, TWO HUNDRED AND FOURTEEN——— ($7,214.00) ——————Dollars and the sum of TWENTY-FIVE THOUSAND———— ($25,000.00) ————————Dollars

Cash and a Mortgage Given Back

WITNESSETH that in consideration of the giving back of a mortgage for TWENTY THOUSAND———— ($20,000.00) ——— Dollars and the sum of FIFTEEN THOUSAND————— ($15,000.00) ————Dollars

Granting Clause and Legal Description

In the section of the deed containing the granting clause and legal description, it is necessary to insert information as to how the grantees, if there are more than one, are taking title.

In both a deed with dower, and a deed without dower, this information is typed in after the words "in fee simple" if two or more grantees are taking title.

. . . the said Grantor Doth Grant unto the said Grantees in fee simple as joint tenants and not as tenants in common.

The legal description of the property follows, copied very carefully from the deed given to the grantor when he took title to the property being conveyed. If the name of the municipality in which the property is located has altered through the creation of a regional municipality, for example, it is necessary to give both the current name of the local municipality and regional municipality, and the former name of the local municipality and county.

Habendum Clause

The clause on page 2 of the deed which commences "TO HAVE AND TO HOLD" is known as the *habendum clause*, that is, the clause in a legal instrument dealing with real property which indicates the estate to be taken by the grantee. Here again, when there are two or more grantees, it is necessary to indicate how they are taking title.

The provisions in this clause reading: "Subject Nevertheless to the reservations, limitations, provisos and conditions, expressed in the original grant thereof from the Crown" are the sources of (1) the authority to levy municipal real estate taxes against real property, and (2) the power given to expropriate property for use by the city, province, or Dominion.

Covenants and Release

The deed lists the *covenants* or promises which the grantor makes to the grantee in regard to title to the property, and a *release* gives up all the grantor's interest to the grantee.

If the consideration in the deed is expressed as "other good and valuable consideration and the sum of . . . ," or if payment is all cash, no revisions to covenants and release are required. Where there are mortgages involved in the transaction, however, the covenants and release are modified as set out below.

If there is a mortgage assumed by the grantee, add the words "save as aforesaid" to the end of the "quiet possession" and the "no act to encumber" covenants.

If there is a mortgage given back by grantee to grantor, add the words "save as aforesaid" to the end of the "quiet possession" covenant, and to the end of the release.

If there is a mortgage assumed and a mortgage given back, add the words "save as aforesaid" to the end of the "quiet possession" and "no act to encumber" covenants, and to the end of the release.

Ending

Deeds must be signed by the parties giving title to the real estate, the grantors, in the presence of a witness. Legal seals are required.

If the wife of the grantor is a party to the deed to bar her dower, she must also execute the deed.

Affidavit as to Legal Age and Marital Status

This affidavit is completed by one of the executing parties to the deed. In form it is suitable for use in any of the circumstances where land is conveyed; whether title was held as joint tenants or tenants in common, and conveyed by an unmarried person, a married man whose wife is joining to bar her dower, a married man and his wife, or two individuals.

When a married man and his wife are both grantors, either one may complete the affidavit. However, it is usual to have them swear it jointly. This is done by typing the names of both grantors in the heading and changing paragraph 1 of the affidavit so that the inappropriate wording is struck out and the following typed in:

1. We were each of the full age of twenty-one years, and were legally married to each other.

Paragraphs 2, 3 and 4 are then struck out, and the word "SEVERALLY" inserted in the jurat above the word "SWORN".

Land Transfer Tax Affidavit

The Land Transfer Act of Ontario provides that everyone registering an instrument conveying title to real property must pay a tax of $2.00 on every $1,000.00 of consideration up to $25,000.00, and $4.00 on every $1,000.00 over $25,000.00. The *land transfer tax affidavit* concerning the consideration for the sale must be filled in completely and exactly, and may be *deposed* (sworn) either by the grantor or grantee, or by their solicitor, who must indicate for which party he is acting.

The tax payable is paid by the purchaser, since it is on his behalf that the deed is registered, or the transfer filed. The fee must be paid before the registration will be made.

In the affidavit the consideration must be specified exactly, and the following points should be kept in mind:

"Monies paid in cash" represents the down payment and/or all cash that is paid on closing.

"Balance of existing encumbrances" refers to mortgages that may be in existence on the property when it is purchased and which the new owner (grantee) is assuming.

"Monies secured by mortgage under this transaction" refers to the amount of a mortgage when part of the purchase price is covered by a mortgage given back by the grantee to the grantor.

No item in paragraph 3 of the affidavit can be left blank; if there is no amount to be inserted, type in the word "nil".

Affidavit of Execution

The witness to the execution of the deed must swear an affidavit of execution. Most printed deeds provide two blank affidavits of execution, in the event that the same witness does not witness the signature of all parties to the instrument.

Back

A deed is given by the grantor to the grantee. If the grantor's wife is a party to a deed to bar her dower, she is not a grantor, and her name does not appear on the back.

The deed, prepared by the grantor's solicitors, gives their name and address, but the back also shows the name and address of the grantee's solicitors, since the executed deed is delivered to those solicitors upon closing the transaction, and will be registered by them. The address of the grantees is also shown on the back of the deed. Both copies of the deed delivered to the grantee's solicitors are left in the Registry Office and one copy is returned to the grantee's solicitors when the deed has in fact been registered. The registration number, date and time of registration will be stamped on the deed in the portion indicated on the back.

A brief description – lot, plan and municipal address – of the property conveyed by the deed is also shown on the back.

This Indenture

made (in duplicate) the   tenth   day of December,
one thousand nine hundred and seventy.

In Pursuance of The Short Forms of Conveyances Act

Between

Dye & Durham
Limited
Toronto, Canada

Form 1 to 4

       JOHN ALBERT DOE, of the City of Toronto,
       in the County of York, Merchant,
       hereinafter called the Grantor,

                              OF THE FIRST PART,

       JAMES JOSEPH SMITH, of the City of
       Toronto, in the County of York,
       Engineer, and MARGARET MARY SMITH,
       his wife, of the same place,
       hereinafter called the Grantees,

                            OF THE SECOND PART,

                 - and -

       ELIZABETH MARTHA DOE, wife of the
       said Grantor,

                            OF THE THIRD PART.

Witnesseth that in consideration of other good and valuable

consideration and the sum of TWO--------------------------

---------------------($2.00)----------------------------

--Dollars

of lawful money of Canada now paid by the said Grantees to the said
Grantor   (the receipt whereof is hereby by him   acknowledged),

the said Grantor   Do TH   Grant unto the said Grantees in fee simple,
as joint tenants and not as tenants in common.

All and Singular that   certain parcel   or tract   of land and premises
situate lying and being in the Township of Vaughan, in the County
of York, Province of Ontario, and being composed of Part of
Lot 15, Registered Plan No. 197Y, said parcel of land being
more particularly described as follows:

COMMENCING at the Southeast angle of the said Lot 15;

THENCE northerly along the easterly limit of the said Lot 15
a distance of one hundred and forty-one feet one and one-
half inch (141' 1 1/2");

THENCE westerly and parallel to the southerly limit of the
said Lot 15 a distance of seventy feet three and one-quarter
inches (70' 3 1/4"), more or less, to the westerly limit of
the said Lot 15;

THENCE southerly along the westerly limit of the said Lot 15
a distance of one hundred and forty-one feet one and one-
half inch (141' 1 1/2"), more or less, to the Southwest
angle of the said Lot 15;

Figure 10.1.   Completed Deed – Page 1

(Legal description continues in this space if

hecessary)

as joint tenants
and not as tenants
in common

𝕿𝖔 𝖍𝖆𝖛𝖊 𝖆𝖓𝖉 𝖙𝖔 𝖍𝖔𝖑𝖉   unto the said Grantee s ⁄ their heirs and
assigns, to and for   their sole and only use for ever.   𝕾𝖚𝖇𝖏𝖊𝖈𝖙
𝕹𝖊𝖛𝖊𝖗𝖙𝖍𝖊𝖑𝖊𝖘𝖘   to the reservations, limitations, provisoes and conditions,
expressed in the original grant thereof from the Crown.

Figure 10.1. Completed Deed – Page 2   67

𝕿𝖍𝖊 said Grantor 𝕮𝖔𝖛𝖊𝖓𝖆𝖓𝖙s with the said Grantee s 𝕿𝖍𝖆𝖙 he has the right to convey the said lands to the said Grantees notwithstanding any act of the said Grantor

𝕬𝖓𝖉 𝖙𝖍𝖆𝖙 the said Grantees shall have quiet possession of the said lands, free from all encumbrances.

𝕬𝖓𝖉 the said Grantor 𝕮𝖔𝖛𝖊𝖓𝖆𝖓𝖙s with the said Grantees that he will execute such further assurances of the said lands as may be requisite.

𝕬𝖓𝖉 the said Grantor 𝕮𝖔𝖛𝖊𝖓𝖆𝖓𝖙s with the said Grantees that he has done no act to encumber the said lands.

𝕬𝖓𝖉 the said Grantor 𝕽𝖊𝖑𝖊𝖆𝖘𝖊s to the said Grantees 𝕬𝖑𝖑 his claims upon the said lands.

Clause added to bar dower. This clause appears in With Dower Deed.

AND the said ELIZABETH MARTHA DOE, wife of the said Grantor, doth hereby bar her dower in the said lands.

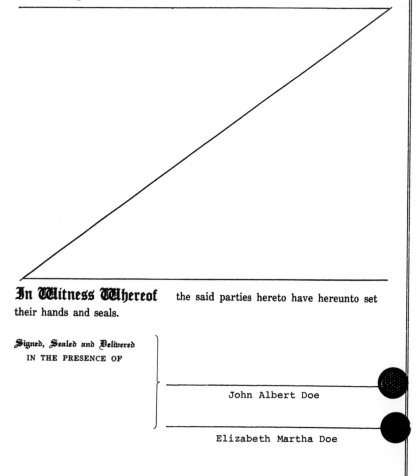

𝕴𝖓 𝖂𝖎𝖙𝖓𝖊𝖘𝖘 𝖂𝖍𝖊𝖗𝖊𝖔𝖋 the said parties hereto have hereunto set their hands and seals.

𝕾𝖎𝖌𝖓𝖊𝖉, 𝕾𝖊𝖆𝖑𝖊𝖉 𝖆𝖓𝖉 𝕯𝖊𝖑𝖎𝖛𝖊𝖗𝖊𝖉
IN THE PRESENCE OF

John Albert Doe

Elizabeth Martha Doe

Figure 10.1. Completed Deed – Page 3

AFFIDAVIT AS TO LEGAL AGE AND MARITAL STATUS

*For place of residence insert appropriate County, District, Regional Municipality, etc.

PROVINCE OF ONTARIO

COUNTY OF YORK

To Wit:

I/WE JOHN ALBERT DOE

of the City of Toronto

in the* County of York, Merchant,

Strike out words and parts not applicable and initial.

in the within instrument named, make oath and say that at the time of the execution of the within instrument,

1. I/WE was of the full age of twenty-one years;

If Attorney see footnote.

2. And that ELIZABETH MARTHA DOE

who also executed the within instrument was of the full age of twenty-one years;

3. I was legally married to the person named therein as my wife/husband;

4. I was unmarried/divorced/widower.

SWORN before me at the City
of Toronto
in the* County of York

this day of December 19 70

A Commissioner for taking Affidavits, etc.

NOTE: If Attorney, substitute in space provided "I am Attorney for...........................(State name)........................., one of the parties named therein and he/she was of the full age of twenty-one years."

Affidabit, Land Transfer Tax Act
IN THE MATTER OF THE LAND TRANSFER TAX ACT

PROVINCE OF ONTARIO

COUNTY OF YORK

To Wit:

I, JOHN ALBERT DOE

of the City of Toronto,

in the* County of York, Merchant,

for the

named in the within (or annexed) transfer make oath and say:

*For place of residence insert appropriate County, District, Regional Municipality, etc.

1. I am the Grantor named in the within (or annexed) transfer.

This affidavit may be made by the purchaser or vendor or by any one acting for them under power of attorney or by an agent accredited in writing by the purchaser or vendor or by the solicitor of either of them.

2. I have a personal knowledge of the facts stated in this affidavit.

3. The true amount of the monies in cash and the value of any property or security included in the consideration is as follows:

(a) Monies paid in cash		$10,000.00
(b) Property transferred in exchange; Equity value $...............	$...............	nil
Encumbrances $...............		nil
(c) Securities transferred to the value of...............	$...............	nil
(d) Balances of existing encumbrances with interest owing at date of transfer $...............		nil
(e) Monies secured by mortgage under this transaction		$15,000.00
(f) Liens, annuities and maintenance charges to which transfer is subject.....$...............		nil
Total consideration.......	$25,000.00	

all blanks must be filled in.

4. If consideration is nominal, is the transfer for natural love and affection? .... nil

5. If so, what is the relationship between Grantor and Grantee?............... nil

6. Other remarks and explanations, if necessary............... nil

SWORN before me at the City
of Toronto
in the* County of York

this day of December 1970

A Commissioner for taking Affidavits, etc.

Figure 10.1. Completed Deed – Page 4

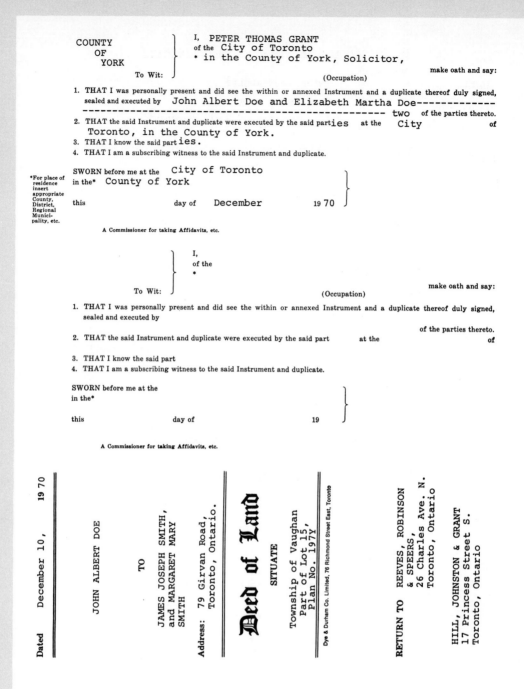

COUNTY
OF
YORK
To Wit:

I, PETER THOMAS GRANT
of the City of Toronto
* in the County of York, Solicitor,

(Occupation)

make oath and say:

1. THAT I was personally present and did see the within or annexed Instrument and a duplicate thereof duly signed, sealed and executed by John Albert Doe and Elizabeth Martha Doe-- two of the parties thereto.

2. THAT the said Instrument and duplicate were executed by the said parties at the City of Toronto, in the County of York.

3. THAT I know the said parties.

4. THAT I am a subscribing witness to the said Instrument and duplicate.

*For place of residence insert appropriate County, District, Regional Municipality, etc.

SWORN before me at the City of Toronto
in the* County of York

this   day of   December   19 70

A Commissioner for taking Affidavits, etc.

I,
of the
*
To Wit:

(Occupation)

make oath and say:

1. THAT I was personally present and did see the within or annexed Instrument and a duplicate thereof duly signed, sealed and executed by

of the parties thereto.

2. THAT the said Instrument and duplicate were executed by the said part   at the   of

3. THAT I know the said part

4. THAT I am a subscribing witness to the said Instrument and duplicate.

SWORN before me at the
in the*

this   day of   19

A Commissioner for taking Affidavits, etc.

Dated   December 10, 19 70

JOHN ALBERT DOE

TO

JAMES JOSEPH SMITH,
and MARGARET MARY
SMITH

Address: 79 Girvan Road,
Toronto, Ontario.

Deed of Land

SITUATE

Township of Vaughan
Part of Lot 15,
Plan No. 197Y

Dye & Durham Co. Limited, 76 Richmond Street East, Toronto

RETURN TO REEVES, ROBINSON
& SPEERS,
26 Charles Ave. N.
Toronto, Ontario

HILL, JOHNSTON & GRANT
17 Princess Street S.
Toronto, Ontario

THIS SPACE TO BE RESERVED FOR REGISTRY OFFICE CERTIFICATES

Figure 10.1. Completed Deed – Back

Transfers

A transfer (Figure 10.2) is the instrument transferring title to real property held under the Land Titles system of land registration. The parties to a transfer are the *transferor(s)* – the person or persons who are transferring title to the real estate (the vendors), and the *transferee(s)* – the person or persons who are taking title to the real estate (the purchasers).

Transfers are prepared by the solicitors acting for the transferor (vendor). Usually a minimum of four copies is prepared; one copy of the transfer is forwarded to the purchaser's solicitors for approval, and when approved, is executed in duplicate by the transferor.

Like a deed, a transfer can be either with dower or without dower.

Comparison of Deeds and Transfers

Date

A transfer is dated the day it is executed; therefore the date does not appear in the heading, only in the ending.

Legal Seals

Since a transfer is an instrument under the Land Titles system, no legal seals are required.

Listing of Parties, Consideration and Description

Only the name or names of the transferors appear in the heading, and no descriptive label such as "hereinafter called the Transferors" is used. If there are two transferors, then information is shown as to how they hold title to the property.

Information follows as to the general description of the lands being transferred, and the consideration, which is expressed usually as "other good and valuable consideration and the sum of . . ."

The name or names of the transferees are then shown; if there are two, it is necessary to show the way in which they are to take title.

If the wife of a transferor is a party to the transfer to bar her dower, the only reference to her appears on page three of the transfer.

Execution

A transfer is executed by the transferor(s), as well as the wife of any transferor when she is a party to the transfer to bar her dower.

Affidavit of Legal Age and Marital Status

The form of this affidavit differs only slightly to the form found in a deed.

If a man and his wife are the transferors, holding title as joint tenants, either of them may complete the affidavit, but frequently they swear it jointly. If a man alone is the transferor he, of course, completes the affidavit.

If two unmarried people are the transferors, or if any transferors hold title as tenants in common, each transferor must join in making the affidavit, each swearing that he is of the age of twenty-one.

Land Transfer Tax Affidavit

This affidavit is identical to that found in a deed.

Affidavit of Execution

The witness to a transfer is required to swear to more information than outlined in an affidavit of execution in a deed. However, the affidavit is self-explanatory, and only requires that the necessary blanks be appropriately completed.

Affidavit by an Officer of a Company

A great deal of land registered under the Land Titles system is owned by development companies, who build on it, and then sell it to individuals. It is, therefore, a company who is transferring title, and officers of the company sign the transfer on its behalf.

In these circumstances an officer of the company (other than one of the officers who signed the transfer) makes an affidavit of execution swearing as to the bona fides of the persons executing on behalf of the company. Figure 10.3 illustrates such an affidavit.

Back

The back of a transfer is completed in the same way as that of a deed. While the back does not require that the name and address of the solicitors for the transferees be shown, in practice this is frequently given.

Quit Claim Deed

To *quit claim* is to give up to a person any claim which you may have against him by reason of his prior ownership of real property. To be legally binding in the case of land, it must be relinquished by way of a deed known as a quit claim deed. This type of deed is most frequently found when the owner of land gives an *easement* (right of way) over his lands to someone like the Hydro or the Bell Telephone.

In quit claim deeds the dower provision of a wife is also important. Therefore, the wife of a man who is quitting claim must either be one of the parties who is giving the deed, or she must join in the deed to bar her dower, just as in other deeds.

Quit claim deeds are registered on title as are all deeds, and are an indication that the original grant of deed is subject to the grant made in the quit claim deed.

These deeds are very similar to ordinary deeds; they must contain affidavits of legal age and marital status, affidavit of execution, and an affidavit concerning land transfer tax.

Figure 10.4 illustrates a completed quit claim deed where the party of the first part is a widower.

𝔏𝔞𝔫𝔡 𝔗𝔦𝔱𝔩𝔢𝔰 𝔄𝔠𝔱

ℑ, WE, PERCIVAL ANDREW PETERSON, of the City of Toronto, in the County of York, Merchant, and ELIZABETH MAUDE PETERSON, his wife, of the same place, as joint tenants and not as tenants in common,

Dye & Durham
Limited
Toronto, Canada

the registered owners of the freehold   land   registered in the office

of Land Titles at Toronto

as Parcel 6620

in the register for the East Section, Borough of York,

in consideration of ~~the sum of~~ other good and valuable consideration

and the sum of TWO--

---------------($2.00)---------------------------------- **Dollars**

paid to   us   TRANSFER to RONALD CRAIG ANDERSON, Physician,

and LUCILLE CAROLINE ANDERSON, his wife, both------------------

of the   City   of Toronto   in the

County of York, as joint tenants and not as tenants in common,

the land hereinafter particularly described namely

(legal description)

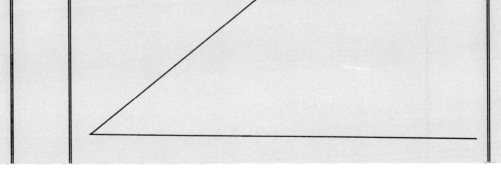

Figure 10.2. Completed Transfer – Page 1

Transfer, L.T.A.
Page 2—Dye & Durham

(legal description continued in this space

if necessary)

Insert here 'the whole' or 'a part' according to the fact. Where the whole parcel is transferred a particular description is unnecessary.

being   the whole   of the said Parcel.

(If only part of the parcel is being transferred,

description of that particular parcel included here.)

74

Figure 10.2. Completed Transfer – Page 2

(Legal description continued here from page 2

if necessary)

If wife of
Transferor
is barring
her dower
her name
appears here.

AND~I,~

~wife~of~the~said~

~hereby~bar~my~dower~in~the~said~land.~

DATED the   day of   December   A.D. 19 70

WITNESS:

> Percival Andrew Peterson
> _____
> Elizabeth Maude Peterson

═══════════════════════════════════════

Land Titles Act

I, PERCIVAL ANDREW PETERSON, one of

the transferors named in the above document, make oath and say:

That Elizabeth Maude Peterson

who executed the above instrument is my wife, and that we are both of the age
of twenty-one years or over.

SWORN before me at the City

of   Toronto

in the County

of   York

this

day of   December   A.D. 19 70

_____

A Commissioner, etc.

Figure 10.2. Completed Transfer – Page 3   75

Affidabit, Land Transfer Tax Act
IN THE MATTER OF THE LAND TRANSFER TAX ACT

PROVINCE OF ONTARIO

COUNTY
OF
YORK

To Wit:

*For place of residence insert appropriate County, District, Regional Municipality, etc.

I, PERCIVAL ANDREW PETERSON

of the City of Toronto,

in the* County of York,

Merchant,   for the

named in the within (or annexed) transfer make oath and say:

This affidavit may be made by the purchaser or vendor or by any one acting for them under power of attorney or by an agent accredited in writing by the purchaser or vendor or by the solicitor of either of them.

1. I am one of the grantors
named in the within (or annexed) transfer.

2. I have a personal knowledge of the facts stated in this affidavit.

3. The true amount of the monies in cash and the value of any property or security included in the consideration is as follows:

(a)	Monies paid in cash		$3,000.00
(b)	Property transferred in exchange; Equity value	$	$ nil
	Encumbrances	$	$ nil
(c)	Securities transferred to the value of		$ nil
(d)	Balances of existing encumbrances with interest owing at date of transfer		$ nil
(e)	Monies secured by mortgage under this transaction		$6,000.00
(f)	Liens, annuities and maintenance charges to which transfer is subject		$ nil
	Total consideration		$9,000.00

all blanks must be filled in.

4. If consideration is nominal, is the transfer for natural love and affection?   nil

5. If so, what is the relationship between Grantor and Grantee?   nil

6. Other remarks and explanations, if necessary   nil

SWORN before me at the City

of Toronto

in the* County of York

this   day of December   19 70

A Commissioner for taking Affidavits, etc.

AFFIDAVIT TO BE MADE BY AN OFFICER AS TO AUTHORITY OF PERSONS EXECUTING FOR A CORPORATION OR COMPANY
Land Titles Act

I,

of the   of

make oath and say:

(1) I am   of

(2)
whose signature is affixed to the annexed (or within) document is the
of the said company, and   whose signature
is also affixed thereto is the   thereof, and the seal
affixed thereto is the corporate seal of the said company.

(3) Under the by-laws of the said company the   and
are empowered to execute on behalf of the company
all deeds and other instruments requiring the seal of the company.
(If the officers executing are not authorized by by-laws then state how they are authorized).

(4) The said company is, I verily believe, the owner of the land (or charge) mentioned in the said document.

Sworn before me at

in the

this

day of   19

A Commissioner, etc.

Figure 10.2.   Completed Transfer – Page 4

Land Titles Act

J, PETER THOMAS GRANT,

of the City of Toronto

in the County of York, Solicitor,

make oath and say:

That I am well acquainted with Percival Andrew Peterson and Elizabeth Maude Peterson, named in the within document and saw them sign the said document, and the signatures purporting to be their signatures at the foot of the said document are in their handwriting.

The said Percival Andrew Peterson and Elizabeth Maude Peterson are as I verily believe the owners of the lands within mentioned, and the said Elizabeth Maude Peterson------------------------is reputed to be, and is, as I verily believe, his wife.

The said Percival Andrew Peterson and Elizabeth Maude Peterson are each of the age of twenty-one years or over, are each of sound mind, and signed the said document voluntarily at the City of Toronto in the County of York in the Province of Ontario

I am a subscribing witness to the said document

SWORN before me at the City

of Toronto

in the County

of York

this   day of December 1970

A Commissioner, etc.

Land Titles Act

Dated   day of December 1970

PERCIVAL ANDREW PETERSON and ELIZABETH MAUDE PETERSON,

TO

RONALD CRAIG ANDERSON and LUCILLE CAROLINE ANDERSON

Address: 74 William Avenue, Etobicoke, Ontario.

Transfer of Freehold Land ~~WITH DOWER~~

Dye & Durham Limited — Toronto, Canada
Printers to the Legal Profession

No.............

Received at the office of Land Titles,

....

at.............o'clock....m., of the

.............day of.............

A.D. 19....and entered in Folio.........

Volume.........Parcel.........

Master of Titles

SMITH, FRASER, HAMILTON & WEBB, 75 Maryvale Blvd., Toronto, Ontario.

Figure 10.2. Completed Transfer – Back

AFFIDAVIT TO BE MADE BY AN OFFICER AS TO AUTHORITY OF PERSONS EXECUTING FOR A CORPORATION OR COMPANY

𝕷𝖆𝖓𝖉 𝕿𝖎𝖙𝖑𝖊𝖘 𝕬𝖈𝖙

I,   JOHN JOSEPH JOHNSTON

of the   City   of   Toronto, in the County of York,

make oath and say:

(1) I am Vice-President   of Smith Bros. Company Limited.

(2) Howard Richards Williamson,
whose signature is affixed to the annexed (or within) document is the President
of the said company, and Robert Gary Henderson,   whose signature
is also affixed thereto is the   Secretary   thereof, and the seal
affixed thereto is the corporate seal of the said company.

(8) Under the by-laws of the said company the President, Secretary and
        Treasurer   are empowered to execute on behalf of the company
all deeds and other instruments requiring the seal of the company.
(If the officers executing are not authorized by by-laws then state how they are authorized).

(4) The said company is, I verily believe, the owner of the land (or charge) mentioned in
the said document.

Sworn before me at   Toronto

in the   County of York

this

day of   December   1970

A Commissioner, etc.

Figure 10.3. Completed Affidavit by an Officer of a Company

Quit Claim Deed.

This Indenture

made in duplicate the   seventh   day of   December,
one thousand nine hundred and seventy.

Between

> PERCIVAL ANDREW PETERSON, of the
> City of Toronto, in the County of
> York, Merchant,
>
> hereinafter called the Party

of the First Part

> - and -
>
> RONALD CRAIG ANDERSON, of the
> City of Toronto, in the County of
> York, Physician,
>
> hereinafter called the Party

of the Second Part

Dye & Durham
Limited
Toronto, Canada

Form No. 18-20

Witnesseth   that the said part y   of the first part for and in considera-
tion of   ONE HUNDRED--
--------------------($100.00)----------------------- Dollars of
lawful money of Canada, to   him   in hand paid by the said part y   of the
second   part, at or before the sealing and delivery of these presents (the receipt
whereof is hereby by   him   acknowledged)   ha s   granted, released and
quitted claim and by these presents Do t h   Grant, Release and   **Quit Claim**
unto the said part y   of the   second   part   his   heirs
and assigns for ever. All the estate, right, title, interest, claim and demand whatsoever
both at law and in equity or otherwise howsoever and whether in possession or expectancy
of   him   the said part y   of the first part of, in, to, or out of All and
Singular th a t   certain parcel   or tract   of land and premises situate,
lying and being.

(Legal description is typed here)

Figure 10.4.   Completed Quit Claim Deed –
Page 1   79

19–Quit Claim Deed
Page 2 – Dye & Durham

Legal description continues here if necessary

Together with the appurtenances thereunto belonging or appertaining TO HAVE and TO HOLD the aforesaid lands and premises with All and Singular the appurtenances thereto belonging or appertaining unto and to the use of the said party of the second part his heirs and assigns forever, subject nevertheless to the reservations, limitations, provisoes and conditions expressed in the original Grant thereof from the Crown.

Signed by Grantor or Grantors and by wife of Grantor if she is party only to bar her dower.

In Witness Whereof the said parties hereto have hereunto set their hands and seals.

Signed, Sealed and Delivered

IN THE PRESENCE OF

Figure 10.4. Completed Quit Claim Deed – Page 2

*For place of residence insert appropriate County, District, Regional Municipality, etc.

PROVINCE OF ONTARIO

COUNTY
OF
YORK

To Wit:

I/WE   PERCIVAL ANDREW PETERSON

of the City of Toronto

in the* County of York, Merchant,

Strike out words and parts not applicable and initial.

If Attorney see footnote.

in the within instrument named, make oath and say that at the time of the execution of the within instrument,

1. I/WE   was   of the full age of twenty-one years;

2. And that

who also executed the within instrument — — — — — — — — — of the full age of twenty-one years; —

3. I was legally married to the person named therein as my wife/husband;

4. I was unmarried/divorced/widower.

SWORN before me at the   City
of   Toronto
in the* County of York

this   day of   December   1970

A Commissioner for taking Affidavits, etc.

NOTE: If Attorney, substitute in space provided *"I am Attorney for.........................(State name)........................., one of the parties named therein and he/she was of the full age of twenty-one years."*

Affidavit, Land Transfer Tax Act
IN THE MATTER OF THE LAND TRANSFER TAX ACT

PROVINCE OF ONTARIO

COUNTY
OF
YORK

To Wit:

I, LORNE JAMES BLACK,

of the   City of Toronto,

in the* County of York,

Solicitor   for the Grantor

named in the within (or annexed) transfer make oath and say:

*For place of residence insert appropriate County, District, Regional Municipality, etc.

This affidavit may be made by the purchaser or vendor or by any one acting for them under power of attorney or by an agent accredited in writing by the purchaser or vendor or by the solicitor of either of them.

1. I am   solicitor for the grantor   named in the within (or annexed) transfer.

2. I have a personal knowledge of the facts stated in this affidavit.

3. The true amount of the monies in cash and the value of any property or security included in the consideration is as follows:

(a) Monies paid in cash .... $ 100.00

(b) Property transferred in exchange; Equity value $ .... $ nil

Encumbrances $ .... $ nil

(c) Securities transferred to the value of .... $ nil

(d) Balances of existing encumbrances with interest owing at date of transfer $ nil

(e) Monies secured by mortgage under this transaction .... $ nil

(f) Liens, annuities and maintenance charges to which transfer is subject.... $ nil

Total consideration...... $ 100.00

all blanks must be filled in.

4. If consideration is nominal, is the transfer for natural love and affection?............ nil

5. If so, what is the relationship between Grantor and Grantee?...................... nil

6. Other remarks and explanations, if necessary............................. nil

SWORN before me at the   City
of   Toronto
in the* County of York

this   day of   December   19 70

A Commissioner for taking Affidavits, etc.

Figure 10.4.   Completed Quit Claim Deed –
Page 3

81

COUNTY
OF
YORK

To Wit:

I,   MARGARET MARY MATTHEWS
of the   City of Toronto,
in the County of York, Secretary,
(Occupation)

make oath and say:

1. THAT I was personally present and did see the within or annexed Instrument and a duplicate thereof duly signed, sealed and executed by Percival Andrew Peterson-------------------------------- -- one of the parties thereto.

2. THAT the said Instrument and duplicate were executed by the said party   at the   City   of Toronto.

3. THAT I know the said part y .

4. THAT I am a subscribing witness to the said Instrument and duplicate.

SWORN before me at the City of Toronto
in the* County of York

this   day of   December   1970

A Commissioner for taking Affidavits, etc.

I,
of the
*

To Wit:

(Occupation)

make oath and say:

1. THAT I was personally present and did see the within or annexed Instrument and a duplicate thereof duly signed, sealed and executed by

of the parties thereto.

2. THAT the said Instrument and duplicate were executed by the said part   at the   of

3. THAT I know the said part

4. THAT I am a subscribing witness to the said Instrument and duplicate.

SWORN before me at the
in the*

this   day of

A Commissioner for taking Affidavits, etc.

Dated   December 7, 1970

PERCIVAL ANDREW PETERSON

TO

RONALD CRAIG ANDERSON

Address: 74 Lake Road, Toronto, Ontario.

Quit Claim Deed

Dye & Durham Co. Limited, 76 Richmond Street East, Toronto

SMITH, FRASER, HAMILTON, & WEBB
75 Maryvale Blvd.
Toronto, Ontario

Figure 10.4.   Completed Quit Claim Deed –
Back

CHAPTER 11

Mortgages and Charges

When a person borrows money using real property as collateral, the instrument completed to formalize the loan is known as a *mortgage*, under the Registry Office system, or a *charge*, under the Land Titles system.

Frequently in a real estate transaction, the purchaser will give the vendor a mortgage or charge instead of actual cash as part of the purchase price. The parties to a mortgage or charge are the *mortgagor(s)* – the person or persons giving the mortgage (borrower) and the *mortgagee(s)* – the person or persons receiving the mortgage (lender).

Mortgages and charges are prepared on printed forms, which are very similar in content, but there are two points which you should note: (1) By a mortgage the mortgagor gives (conveys) to the mortgagee actual legal title to the property, while the mortgage remains unpaid. When the mortgage has been fully paid, and the discharge of mortgage has been registered, title is reconveyed to the mortgagor. By a charge the mortgagor gives to the mortgagee only a claim against the property, not legal title to it. (2) Legal seals are required on mortgages. No legal seals are required on charges.

There are two types of mortgages and charges: without dower and with dower. The form which is used depends on whether the wife of a married man who is giving the mortgage is a party to the mortgage in her own right as an owner, or is merely joining in the mortgage to give up her dower rights.

Mortgages and charges are prepared by the solicitors acting for the mortgagor. Usually a minimum of four copies is prepared. One copy of the mortgage or charge is forwarded to the vendor's solicitors for approval if the vendor is taking a mortgage back, or to the party who is advancing mortgage funds, usually a mortgage company. When approved, the mortgagor will execute it in duplicate. Legal seals are required on mortgages, but not on charges, and both instruments require completion of affidavits of execution, and of legal age and marital status.

There may be more than one mortgage on real property; frequently there are two. The mortgage which is registered first is known as the first mortgage, and the other as the second mortgage. Should it become necessary to sell the property because of nonpayment by the mortgagor, the mortgagee under the first mortgage is entitled to have his claim paid in full before the mortgagee under the second mortgage receives anything. When the mortgagee enforces his right to prevent the mortgagor from recovering mortgaged property due to nonpayment, the mortgage is said to be *foreclosed*.

Application for Mortgage

If the purchaser wishes to raise part of the purchase price by means of a mortgage with someone other than the vendor, he may turn to a bank or trust company which deals in mortgages. He will then complete an application for mortgage. Figure 11.1 illustrates the application form used by The Royal Bank of Canada.

Parts of a Mortgage

The parts of a mortgage are illustrated in Figures 11.2 and 11.3.

Heading

Mortgages are dated the day they are typed.

The mortgagor is the party of the first part in a mortgage, and the mortgagee is the party of the second part.

If a married man is himself giving the mortgage, his wife must also be a party to it to bar her dower. She is added as the party of the third part, and as in a deed, only her name is given.

If a married man and his wife, or two or more individuals are co-owners of the property being mortgaged, or are taking the mortgage, in addition to the information required in the normal description of the parties, it is necessary to show how they hold or take title; that is, either as joint tenants, or as tenants in common.

THE ROYAL BANK OF CANADA

APPLICATION FOR MORTGAGE

_____ BRANCH

NAME OF APPLICANT(S) IN FULL	TELEPHONE
_____ _____	Business: _____ Residence: _____

PRESENT ADDRESS (Number, Street, City or Town, Province)

TITLE OF PROPERTY
WILL BE / IS IN NAME(S) OF:

DETAILS OF MORTGAGE REQUIRED

TYPE OF MORTGAGE	AMOUNT	INT. RATE	TERM	AMORTIZATION	DATE REQUIRED	PROGRESS ADVANCES
☐ Conventional	$	%	Years	Years		☐ Yes ☐ No
☐ Combined (with TanYor Ltd.) Amount of Mortgage includes Combined Mortgage Fee payable by Applicant(s).	PAYMENTS OF $		MONTHLY PRINCIPAL AND INTEREST PLUS ONE TWELFTH ESTIMATED ANNUAL TAXES		ESTIMATED ANNUAL TAXES $	

PURPOSE OF MORTGAGE (Complete only A or B or C)

A

PURCHASE

(ATTACH COPY OF OFFER TO PURCHASE)

FIRST MORTGAGE REQUIRED .... $ _____

SECOND MORTGAGE, IF ANY .... $ _____

CASH PAYMENT BY APPLICANT(S) .... $ _____

PURCHASE PRICE OF PROPERTY (Estimated date of closing.................19.........) $ _____

DETAILS OF SECOND MORTGAGE: LENDER (Name and address) _____

_____AMOUNT $_____ INT. RATE _____% MONTHLY PAYMENT $_____

B

CONSTRUCTION

(ATTACH COPY OF SITE PLAN BUILDING CONTRACT INCLUDING SPECIFICATIONS AND PLANS)

CONTRACT PRICE OF BUILDING (Estimated date of completion.................19.........) $ _____

LOT: YEAR PURCHASED 19_____ COST .... $ _____

CASH PAYMENT BY APPLICANT(S) $_____ TOTAL COST .... $ _____

DETAILS OF SECOND MORTGAGE, IF ANY: LENDER (Name and address)_____

_____AMOUNT $_____ INT. RATE _____% MONTHLY PAYMENT $_____

C

REFINANCING

PURPOSE OF REFINANCING_____

DATE PROPERTY PURCHASED_____19._____PURCHASE PRICE $ _____

NAME AND ADDRESS OF PRESENT FIRST MORTGAGEE (IF ANY)_____

_____ BALANCE OWING $ _____

NAME AND ADDRESS OF PRESENT SECOND MORTGAGEE (IF ANY)_____

_____ BALANCE OWING $ _____

SINCE PURCHASING $_____HAS BEEN SPENT ON THE FOLLOWING IMPROVEMENTS:
(Extra Bathroom, Garage, Recreation Room, etc.)

_____

APPLICANT'S ESTIMATED VALUE OF THE PROPERTY TODAY .... $ _____

PARTICULARS OF SECURITY

CIVIC ADDRESS	(NUMBER, STREET, CITY OR TOWN, PROVINCE)	
LEGAL DESCRIPTION	LOT OR BLOCK AND SUBDIVISION NUMBER(S)	PLAN
LOT	FRONTAGE FEET	DEPTH FEET	TOTAL AREA SQUARE FEET

BUILDING	NUMBER OF FAMILY UNITS ☐ Single ☐ Duplex ☐ Triplex	TYPE OF DWELLING ☐ Detached ☐ Semi-detached ☐ Attached

CONSTRUCTION

☐ Brick ☐ Stone ☐ Frame ☐ Other: Specify _____

No. OF STOREYS	BASEMENT ☐ Full ☐ Part ☐ None	AGE Years	No. OF ROOMS	No. OF BATHROOMS
TYPE OF HEATING	DRIVEWAY ☐ Yes ☐ No	GARAGE ☐ Yes ☐ No	GARAGE CONSTRUCTION: (SPECIFY)	

OTHER FEATURES (Fireplace, Recreation Room, etc.)

_____

SERVICES	DRAINAGE ☐ Sewer ☐ Septic	WATER ☐ Municipal ☐ Well

Figure 11.1. First Page of Mortgage Application

WITH RESPECT TO AN APPLICATION FROM A MARRIED WOMAN, THE FOLLOWING INFORMATION IS REQUIRED ON THE HUSBAND.

PERSONAL INFORMATION

EMPLOYER'S NAME AND ADDRESS		

POSITION	LENGTH OF SERVICE YEARS	ANNUAL INCOME $

IF EMPLOYED LESS THAN TWO YEARS, PREVIOUS EMPLOYER'S NAME AND ADDRESS	LENGTH OF SERVICE YEARS

WIFE'S EMPLOYER (IF ANY) AND ADDRESS	LENGTH OF SERVICE YEARS	WIFE'S ANNUAL INCOME $

SOURCE OF ANY OTHER INCOME (Rents, Stocks, Bonds, etc.)	ANNUAL AMOUNT $

IT WILL SPEED CONSIDERATION OF THE APPLICATION IF APPLICANTS WHO ARE:

EMPLOYED: Attach a letter from their employers confirming income or alternatively make available for confidential perusal a copy of last year's Income Tax T 4 Slip.

SELF-EMPLOYED: Attach audited current Financial Statement, or a copy of last year's Income Tax T 1 General. In either case, the document will be returned.

APPLICANT'S MARITAL STATUS ☐ Single ☐ Married ☐ Widow(er)	AGE years	AGES OF CHILDREN	(QUEBEC ONLY) ☐ Separate ☐ Community

BANK ACCOUNTS	NAME OF BANK(S)	BRANCH(ES)	ACCOUNT No. AND TYPE No. _____ ☐ Savings ☐ Chequing No. _____ ☐ Savings ☐ Chequing

LIST ALL PRESENT OBLIGATIONS OTHER THAN MORTGAGE INDEBTEDNESS: (Names and addresses)	BALANCE OWING	MONTHLY PAYMENT
	$	$
	$	$
	$	$
	$	$
	$	$
	$	$
TOTAL PRESENT OBLIGATIONS AND PAYMENTS	$	$

HAVE YOU ENDORSED NOTES OR GUARANTEED THE OBLIGATION OF ANY OTHER PERSON? ☐ NO ☐ YES IF "YES", AMOUNT $ _____
FOR WHOM? (Name and address)

STATEMENT OF ASSETS AND LIABILITIES

A S S E T S	DOLLARS	L I A B I L I T I E S	DOLLARS
Cash on hand and in Banks	$	Total Present Obligations	$
Bonds and Stocks	$	Present First Mortgage (if any)	$
Accounts Receivable	$	Present Second Mortgage (if any)	$
C.S.V. of Life Insurance	$	Other Liabilities:	$
Land and Buildings	$		$
	$		$
	$		$
	$		$
	$	NET WORTH	$
TOTAL	$	TOTAL	$

I/We hereby certify that the information given above is correct. If application is for a Combined mortgage this information may be disclosed to TanYor Ltd. It is understood that appraisal fees and legal expenses incidental to this application will be paid by me/us. It is also understood that if the applicant is a married woman, her husband will add his covenant to the mortgage.

....
DATE   SIGNATURE   SIGNATURE

Figure 11.1.   Reverse Side of Mortgage Application

Consideration

Unlike a deed, the full amount of money covered by the mortgage must be shown in the consideration clause.

Legal Description

The legal description of the property which is being mortgaged is copied from the draft deed provided by the vendor's solicitors. Here again you must be very careful in your typing, and the description should be proofread before the mortgage is put on the lawyer's desk.

Repayment Clauses

Page 2 of most mortgages sets out the repayment provisions and partially describes the covenants given under the mortgage.

It is in the completion of the repayment portion of a mortgage that you may experience some initial difficulties.

In order to facilitate completion of the repayment clause, note the following points:

The *principal* is the amount of the mortgage, upon payment of which (together with any accrued interest) the mortgage is discharged or cancelled.

The *terms* of the mortgage refer to the conditions of repayment that are typed in on a printed mortgage form, following the words "in lawful money of Canada with interest at . . . per centum per annum as follows".

The term *maturity* refers to the date on which all monies secured by the mortgage are due. A mortgage is said to "mature" a given number of years from the date on which it was given. For example, a mortgage commencing on December 1, 1970 and being for a period of five years, matures on December 1, 1975.

Repayment of a mortgage is usually made in one of two ways:

1. A set amount may be paid monthly, quarterly, or half-yearly, on account of principal, plus interest on the balance still outstanding on the mortgage. The set amount payable is said to be paid "on account of principal".

2. A fixed combined payment of principal and interest may be paid of the same amount each and every month during the term of the mortgage. This is called a *blended payment* since it includes both principal and interest, and is an amount calculated to completely *amortize* or pay off the mortgage over a certain period of time.

There are separate printed forms for mortgages containing different repayment clauses. To complete these forms you need to know the amount of the mortgage; the date it is to be effective; how long the mortgage is to run; the repayment terms, and any special provisions in regard to earlier repayment privileges; renewal of the mortgage upon maturity; and adjusted interest rates upon renewal.

Many mortgages are based on an amortized repayment schedule of twenty, twenty-five or thirty-five years, in order to keep the monthly payments as low as possible. Mortgages are usually for a term of five years, but are subject to renewal privileges, since the Federal Interest Act provides that in a mortgage which is for a term greater than five years, under certain conditions the mortgagor may pay off the principal outstanding at certain times by paying three months' interest as a bonus.

Repayments on Account of Principal Plus Interest

If a mortgage to run for five years is to be given as of November 1, 1970, and is to be repayable quarterly, payments will be due on the first days of February, May, August and November in each year, except the year in which the mortgage matures. Payments made on the first days of those months in each of the years 1971, 1972, 1973 and 1974 are on account.

In 1975 (the year in which the mortgage matures), the payment due on November 1, 1975 (the maturity date of the mortgage) is not on account, but is the total balance still unpaid that is due on that date. Therefore, if repayment is to be $500.00 quarterly on account of principal, the repayment clause in the mortgage reads:

The sum of FIVE HUNDRED———————
($500.00) ———————Dollars on account of
principal shall become due and payable
quarterly on the first days of February, May,
August and November in the years 1971,
1972, 1973, 1974 and on the first days of
February, May and August in the year 1975,
and the balance of . . . .

The date on which the balance of the mortgage will be due, that is, the maturity date,
is then filled in on the printed form.

The first payment on a mortgage is made
on the appropriate date following the giving
of the mortgage. This payment includes the
stipulated amount of principal, plus interest computed from the effective date of the
mortgage. If payments are made quarterly,
and the mortgage is given on November 1,
then the first payment on account of principal plus interest is made February 1, but
the interest is computed from November 1.

It is necessary to insert the dates outlined
above on the last two lines of the repayment
section of a mortgage: the date from which
interest is to be computed when determining
the amount of the first payment, and the
date on which the first payment of principal
and interest must be made.

In the first covenant which follows the
completion of the repayment provisions of a
mortgage, a blank must be filled in on the
fourth line. This covenant provides for payment of compound interest in the event of
default of payment. The number of months
allowed in which to pay outstanding interest
and compound interest coincides with the
term for which interest is calculated under
the mortgage. If interest is calculated half-
yearly, then a period of six months is allowed; if quarter-yearly, three months.
Figure 11.4 is a guide for completing the
repayment provisions of an unamortized
mortgage.

Amortized Payments

If a mortgage is to be repaid by a fixed
monthly payment of the same amount each
and every month during the term of the
mortgage, it is said to be *amortized,* and
page 2 of the standard mortgage form is re-

placed by a special amortized page (Figure
11.5).

Payments commence in the month following the giving of the mortgage, but interest
is, of course, computed from the date on/
which the loan secured by the mortgage is
advanced.

An amortized repayment clause also contains provisions for repayment of interest on
any mortgage monies which may have been
advanced prior to the drawing of the mortgage. This frequently happens when an individual is building a home, and secures a
mortgage to help finance construction. Advances are made from time to time, and
when the mortgage is drawn for the amount
of the mortgage loan, provision is made for
payment of interest on the amount advanced
prior to the execution of the mortgage. If no
monies have been advanced, then the first
three lines of the repayment clause are
crossed out.

The lawyer will usually have a booklet indicating a schedule of amortization payments for various interest rates (Figure 11.6).
If this is not available, amortization schedules may be obtained by writing a firm such
as Computing Services Company (Figure
11.7).

Special Clauses

Mortgages frequently contain special provisions such as giving the mortgagor the right
to pay additional amounts on the mortgage
without notice or bonus to the mortgagee, or
providing for renewal privileges.

These special clauses are typed on page 4
of the mortgage in the blank space provided.

Signature and Ending

A mortgage is signed by the mortgagor, and
any other person who is a party to the mortgage (e.g., the wife of a mortgagor) to relinquish any rights they may have in the
property in the event that the mortgage is
not repaid. Legal seals are required on mortgages.

Affidavits

Affidavits of execution, and of legal age and
marital status must be completed in order

that the mortgage may be registered in the Registry Office.

The Registry Act provides that one mortgagor may make the affidavit as to legal age and marital status, even if there are two mortgagors. However, in actual practice, many offices have both parties make a joint affidavit. As in a deed, this is done by striking out the "I" in the heading, typing in both mortgagors' names in the heading, and changing the wording of paragraph 1 to read:

1. We were each of the full age of twenty-one years, and were legally married to each other.

Paragraphs 2, 3 and 4 are then struck out, and the word "SEVERALLY" is inserted in the jurat.

Charge

Charges (Figure 11.8) are also prepared on printed legal forms, and like a mortgage, may either be with dower or without dower. The repayment and covenant portions of the forms are completed as in a mortgage, but the heading and ending of a charge differ.

Date

A charge is dated the day it is executed; therefore, the date appears in the ending.

Parties

The heading of a charge does not set out all the parties as does a mortgage. In the heading of a charge, you show only the name, general address, and occupation of the person or persons giving the charge. If two parties are giving it, the manner in which they hold title is shown following their names.

The name of the party or parties to whom the charge is given is shown on page 2. If the wife of a married man is a party to the charge to bar her dower, reference is made to her only on page 4 of the charge form.

Legal Seals

Since a charge is under the Land Titles system of land registration, no legal seals are required.

Affidavits

Each mortgagor must make an affidavit as to legal age and marital status, and if there are two mortgagors, they will then join to make this affidavit, which is similar in form to that in a transfer.

An affidavit of execution similar to that in a transfer is also made by the witness.

What Happens to Executed Mortgage or Charge

The original and duplicate of the mortgage or charge are given to the mortgagee. It is his responsibility to register or file the instrument in the appropriate office, since this step protects his interest in the property.

Both the original and duplicate are taken to the appropriate office, and the duplicate is returned to the mortgagee, with information endorsed on its back as to registration or filing, including registration number.

The mortgagee holds the duplicate original of the mortgage or charge until the mortgage or charge has been completely paid. At that time he will sign a discharge of mortgage or a cessation of charge (discussed in Chapter 12) and return his copy of the executed mortgage or charge to the mortgagor.

Mortgage Long

Dye & Durham Limited — Law and Commercial Stationers
76 Richmond Street E., Toronto
Form No. 46—49

This Indenture

made (in duplicate) the twenty-seventh day of November one thousand nine hundred and seventy.

In Pursuance of the Short Forms of Mortgages Act

Between

RONALD CRAIG ANDERSON, of the City of Toronto, in the County of York, Physician,

hereinafter called the Mortgagor   of the FIRST PART;

PERCIVAL ANDREW PETERSON, of the City of Hamilton, in the County of Wentworth, Merchant,

hereinafter called the Mortgagee   of the SECOND PART;

- and -

LUCILLE CAROLINE ANDERSON,

the wife of the said Mortgagor   of the THIRD PART;

Whereas the said Mortgagor at the time of the execution hereof is seized of an estate in fee simple in possession of the lands hereinafter mentioned, and has   applied to the Mortgagee for a loan upon mortgage thereof.

Now therefore this Indenture Witnesseth that in consideration of EIGHTEEN THOUSAND----- ----------------------- ($18,000.00) ----------------------------- dollars of lawful money of Canada now paid by the said Mortgagee to the said Mortgagor (the receipt whereof is hereby by   him   acknowledged) the said Mortgagor doth grant and mortgage unto the said Mortgagee   his   heirs, executors, administrators, successors and assigns forever.

All and Singular th at certain parcel   or tract   of land and premises situate, lying and being in the City of Toronto, in the County of York, and being composed of the easterly half of Lot No. 105 on the south side of Helena Avenue, according to plan registered in the Registry Office for the Registry Division of Toronto as No. 5948, being of uniform width of twenty feet (20') more or less from front to rear of said Lot.

SAVE AND EXCEPT the lands expropriated by the City of Toronto for lane purposes under and by virtue of by-law No. 13169 registered No.56129 W.B.

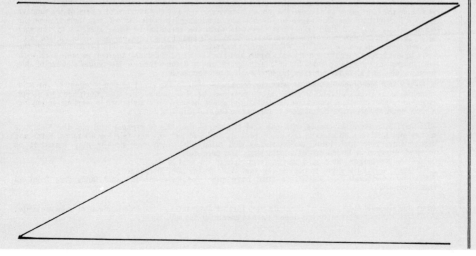

Figure 11.2. Mortgage with Dower –
Page 1

And the said wife of the said Mortgagor hereby bars her Dower in the said lands.

Provided this Mortgage to be Void upon payment of EIGHTEEN THOUSAND------------------
-------------------($18,000.00)--Dollars

of lawful money of Canada with interest at   ten--(10%)------- per centum per annum as follows:

The sum of FIVE HUNDRED---($500.00)---Dollars on account of principal
shall become due and be payable quarter-yearly on the first days of
March, June, September and December in the years 1971, 1972, 1973 and
1974, and March, June and September, 1975, and the balance of---------

the said principal sum of $ 18,000.00   shall become due and payable on the   1st   day of
December, 1975   and interest   quarter-yearly at the said rate as well after as before
maturity and both before and after default on such portion of the principal as remains from time to time
unpaid on the   1st   days of March, June, September and December
in each year until the principal is fully paid; the first payment of interest to be computed from the 1st
day of December   19 70 upon the whole amount of principal hereby secured, to become due
and payable on the   1st   day of March   next 19 71.

AND Taxes and performance of Statute Labor;   and observance and performance of all covenants, provisos and conditions herein contained.

AND it is hereby agreed that in case default shall be made in payment of any sum to become due for interest at any time appointed for payment thereof as aforesaid, compound interest shall be payable and the sum in arrear for interest from time to time, as well after as before maturity, shall bear interest at the rate aforesaid, and in case the interest and compound interest are not paid in three   months from the time of default a rest shall be made, and compound interest at the rate aforesaid shall be payable on the aggregate amount then due, as well after as before maturity, and so on from time to time, and all such interest and compound interest shall be a charge upon the said lands.

THE MORTGAGOR agrees that neither the preparation, execution nor registration of this Indenture shall bind the Mortgagee to advance the money hereby secured, nor the advance of a part of the moneys secured hereby bind the Mortgagee to advance any unadvanced portion thereof, but nevertheless the estate hereby conveyed shall take effect forthwith upon the execution of these presents by the said Mortgagor, and the expenses of the examination of the title and of this mortgage and valuation are to be secured hereby in the event of the whole or any balance of the principal sum not being advanced, the same to be charged hereby upon the said lands, and shall be without demand thereof, payable forthwith with interest at the rate provided for in this mortgage, and in default the said Mortgagee's power of sale hereby given, and all other remedies hereunder, shall be exercisable.

AND the said Mortgagor covenants with the Mortgagee that in the event of non-payment of the said principal moneys at the time or times above provided, he shall not require the Mortgagee to accept payment of said principal moneys without first giving six months' previous notice in writing, or paying a bonus equal to three months' interest in advance on the said principal moneys.

THE said Mortgagor covenants with the said Mortgagee that the Mortgagor will pay the Mortgage money and interest and observe the above proviso, and will pay as they fall due all taxes, rates and assessments, municipal, local, parliamentary and otherwise which now are or may hereafter be imposed, charged or levied upon the said lands and premises;
THAT the Mortgagor has a good title in fee simple to the said lands.
AND that he has the right to convey the said lands to the said Mortgagee;
AND that on default the Mortgagee shall have quiet possession of the said lands free from all encumbrances.

AND that the said Mortgagor will execute such further assurances of the said lands as may be requisite;
AND that the said Mortgagor has done no act to encumber the said lands;

*Figure 11.2. Mortgage with Dower –
Page 2*

AND that the said Mortgagor will insure the buildings on the said lands to the amount of not less than the principal money hereby secured in dollars of lawful money of Canada. Evidence of continuation of such insurance having been secured shall be produced to the Mortgagee at least three days before expiration thereof, otherwise the Mortgagee may provide therefor and charge the premium paid therefor and interest thereon to the Mortgagor and the same shall also be a charge upon the said land. It is further agreed that the Mortgagee may require any insurance on the said buildings to be cancelled and a new insurance effected in an office to be named by him, and also may of his own accord effect or maintain any insurance herein provided for, and any amount paid by him therefor shall be forthwith payable to him with interest at the rate aforesaid by the Mortgagor, and shall be a charge upon the said lands (without prejudice to the foregoing statutory clause).

AND the said Mortgagor doth release to the said Mortgagee all his claims upon the said lands subject to the said proviso.

PROVIDED that the said Mortgagee on default of payment for at least fifteen days may on at least thirty-five days' notice enter on and lease the said lands or on default of payment for at least fifteen days may on at least thirty-five days' notice sell the said lands. Such notice shall be given to such persons and in such manner and form and within such time as provided under Part II-A of The Mortgages Act, R.S.O. 1960, c. 245, as amended. In the event that the giving of such notice shall not be required by law or to the extent that such requirements shall not be applicable it is agreed that notice may be effectually given by leaving it with a grown-up person on the said lands, if occupied, or by placing it on the said lands if unoccupied, or at the option of the Mortgagee, by mailing it in a registered letter addressed to the Mortgagor at his last known address, or by publishing it once in a newspaper published in the county or district in which the lands are situate; and such notice shall be sufficient although not addressed to any person or persons by name or designation; and notwithstanding that any person to be affected thereby may be unknown, unascertained, or under disability. PROVIDED FURTHER, without prejudice to the statutory powers of the Mortgagee under the foregoing proviso, that in case default be made in the payment of the said principal or interest or any part thereof and such default continue for two months after any payment of either falls due then the Mortgagee may exercise the foregoing powers of entering, leasing or selling or any of them without any notice, it being understood and agreed, however, that if the giving of notice by the Mortgagee shall be required by law then notice shall be given to such persons and in such manner and form and within such time as so required by law. AND it is hereby further agreed that the whole or any part or parts of the said lands may be sold by public auction or private contract, or partly one or partly the other; and that the proceeds of any sale hereunder may be applied in payment of any costs, charges and expenses incurred in taking, recovering or keeping possession of the said lands or by reason of non-payment or procuring payment of moneys, secured hereby or otherwise, and that the Mortgagee may sell any of the said lands on such terms as to credit and otherwise as shall appear to him most advantageous and for such prices as can reasonably be obtained therefor and may make any stipulations as to title or evidence or commencement of title or otherwise which he shall deem proper, and may buy in or rescind or vary any contract for the sale of the whole or any part of the said lands and resell without being answerable for loss occasioned thereby, and in the case of a sale on credit the Mortgagee shall be bound to pay the Mortgagor only such moneys as have been actually received from purchasers after the satisfaction of the claims of the Mortgagee and for any of said purposes may make and execute all agreements and assurances as he shall think fit. Any purchaser or lessee shall not be bound to see to the propriety or regularity of any sale or lease or be affected by express notice that any sale or lease is improper and no want of notice or publication when required hereby shall invalidate any sale or lease hereunder. AND the Mortgagor hereby attorns and becomes a tenant of the said lands to the Mortgagee from year to year from the day of the execution hereof during the term of this Mortgage and any renewal or renewals thereof at a rental, equivalent to, applicable in satisfaction of, and payable at the same times as the payments of interest hereinbefore provided to be paid; the legal relation of landlord and tenant being hereby constituted between the Mortgagee and Mortgagor; but it is agreed that neither the existence of this clause nor anything done by virtue hereof shall render the Mortgagee a Mortgagee in possession, or accountable for any moneys except those actually received by him, and the Mortgagee may in default of payment or on breach of any of the covenants in this Mortgage contained, enter on the said lands and determine the tenancy hereby created without notice. PROVIDED that the Mortgagee may distrain for arrears of interest. PROVIDED that the Mortgagee may distrain for arrears of principal in the same manner as if the same were arrears of interest. PROVIDED that in default of the payment of the interest hereby secured the principal hereby secured shall become payable at the option of the Mortgagee. PROVIDED that upon default of payment of instalments of principal promptly as the same mature, the balance of the principal and interest shall immediately become due and payable at the option of the Mortgagee. PROVIDED that the Mortgagee may in writing at any time or times after default waive such default and upon such waiver the time or times for payment of said principal shall be as set out in the above proviso for redemption. PROVIDED further that any such waiver shall apply only to the particular default waived and shall not operate as a waiver of any other or future default. AND it is further agreed by and between the parties that the Mortgagee may at his discretion at all times release any part or parts of the said lands or any other security or any surety for the money hereby secured either with or without any sufficient consideration therefor, without responsibility therefor, and without thereby releasing any other part of the said lands or any person from this Mortgage or from any of the convenants herein contained, it being especially agreed that every part or lot into which the mortgaged lands are or may hereafter be divided does and shall stand charged with the whole money hereby secured and no person shall have the right to require the mortgage moneys to be apportioned; and without being accountable to the Mortgagor for the value thereof, or for any moneys except those actually received by the Mortgagee. PROVIDED further that no sale or other dealing by the Mortgagor with the equity of redemption in the said lands or any part thereof shall in any way change the liability of the Mortgagor or in any way alter the rights of the Mortgagee as against the Mortgagor or any other person liable for payment of the moneys hereby secured. THE said Mortgagor covenants with the said Mortgagee that he will keep the said lands and the buildings, erections and improvements thereon in good condition and repair according to the nature and description thereof respectively, and that the Mortgagee may, whenever he deems necessary, by his surveyor or agent enter upon and inspect the said mortgaged lands, and the reasonable cost of such inspection shall be added to the Mortgage debt, and that if the Mortgagor neglects to keep the said premises in good condition and repair, or commit or permit any act of waste on the said lands (as to which the Mortgagee shall be sole judge) or make default as to any of the covenants or provisos herein contained, the principal hereby secured shall at the option of the Mortgagee forthwith become due and payable, and in default of payment of same with interest as in the case of payment before maturity, the powers of entering upon and leasing or selling hereby given may be exercised and the Mortgagee may make such repairs as he deems necessary, and the cost thereof with interest thereon shall be a charge upon the land prior to all claims thereon subsequent to these presents.

*Figure 11.2. Mortgage with Dower –
Page 3*   91

AND it is hereby agreed between the parties hereto that the Mortgagee may pay all premiums of insurance and all taxes and rates which shall from time to time fall due and be unpaid in respect of the mortgaged premises, and that such payments together with all costs, charges and expenses (between solicitor and client), which may be incurred in taking, recovering and keeping possession of the said lands, and of negotiating this loan, investigating title, and registering the mortgage and other necessary deeds, and generally in any other proceedings taken, in connection with or to realize this security, shall be with interest at the rate aforesaid, a charge upon the said lands in favor of the Mortgagee and that the Mortgagee may pay or satisfy any lien, charge or encumbrance now existing or hereafter created or claimed upon the said lands, and that any amount paid by the Mortgagee shall be added to the debt hereby secured and shall be payable forthwith with interest at the rate aforesaid, and in default this Mortgage shall immediately become due and payable at the option of the Mortgagee, and all powers by this Mortgage conferred shall become exercisable.

PROVIDED that until default of payment the Mortgagor shall have quiet possession of the said lands.

PROVIDED and it is hereby agreed, that the taking of a judgment or judgments on any of the covenants herein contained shall not operate as a merger of the said covenants or affect the Mortgagee's right to interest at the rate and times herein provided; and further that said judgment shall provide that interest thereon shall be computed at the same rate and in the same manner as herein provided until the said judgment shall have been fully paid and satisfied.

PROVIDED and it is hereby further agreed by and between the Mortgagor and the Mortgagee that should default be made by the Mortgagor in the observance or performance of any of the covenants, provisos, agreements or conditions contained in any mortgage to which this mortgage is subject, then and in that event the moneys hereby secured shall forthwith become due and be payable, at the option of the Mortgagee, and all the powers in and by this mortgage conferred shall become exercisable, and the powers of sale therein contained may be exercised forthwith without any notice, unless the giving of notice shall be required by law in which event notice shall be given to such persons and in such manner and form and within such time as required by law.

PROVIDED also that the covenant for insurance hereinbefore contained shall apply to all buildings whether now or hereafter erected on the said lands.

PROVIDED also that on default of payment of any of the moneys hereby secured or payable or on any proceedings being taken by the Mortgagee under this Mortgage, he shall be entitled to require payment, in addition to all other moneys hereby secured or payable hereunder, of a bonus equal to three months' interest in advance at the rate aforesaid upon the principal money hereby secured, and the Mortgagor shall not be entitled to require a discharge of this Mortgage without such payment.

The mortgagor, when not in default, shall have the privilege of paying an additional One Thousand---($1,000.00)---Dollars or any sum in multiples thereof on account of principal on any interest date without notice or bonus.

The mortgagor if not in default shall have the privilege of renewing this mortgage upon its maturity for a further period of five years on the same terms and conditions as are herein contained but with no right of further renewal.

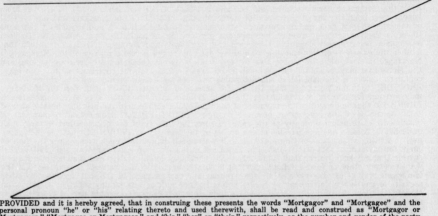

PROVIDED and it is hereby agreed, that in construing these presents the words "Mortgagor" and "Mortgagee" and the personal pronoun "he" or "his" relating thereto and used therewith, shall be read and construed as "Mortgagor or Mortgagors," "Mortgagee or Mortgagees," and "his," "her" or "their," respectively, as the number and gender of the party or parties referred to in each case require and the number of the verb agreeing therewith shall be construed as agreeing with the said word or pronoun so substituted. And that all rights, advantages, privileges, immunities, powers and things hereby secured to the Mortgagee or Mortgagees shall be equally secured to and exercisable by his, her, or their heirs, executors, administrators and assigns, or successors and assigns as the case may be. And that all covenants, liabilities and obligations entered into or imposed hereunder upon the Mortgagor or Mortgagors shall be equally binding upon his, her or their heirs, executors, administrators and assigns, or successors and assigns as the case may be, and that all such covenants and liabilities and obligations shall be joint and several.

The undersigned being the Mortgagor   named in the within Mortgage, acknowledge   having received a true copy of the said Mortgage.

𝕴𝕟 𝕸𝕚𝕥𝕟𝖊𝖘𝖘 𝕸𝖍𝖊𝖗𝖊𝖔𝖋 the said parties hereto have hereunto set their hands and seals.

SIGNED, SEALED AND DELIVERED
In the presence of

Ronald Craig Anderson

Lucille Caroline Anderson

Figure 11.2. Mortgage with Dower —
Page 4

COUNTY
OF
YORK   To Wit: I, RONALD CRAIG ANDERSON
of the City of Toronto,
•in the County of York, Physician,

Strike out words and parts not applicable and initial

in the within instrument named, make oath and say that at the time of the execution of the within instrument,

1. I was of the full age of twenty-one years;

2. And that Lucille Caroline Anderson---------------------------------------

If Attorney use separate affidavit.

   who also executed the within instrument   was   of the full age of twenty-one years;

3. I was legally married to the person named therein as my wife/husband;   4. I was unmarried/divorced/widow/widower.

•For place of residence insert appropriate County, District, Regional Municipality, etc.

SWORN before me at the   City of Toronto
in the*   County of York

this   day of   November   19 70

A Commissioner for taking Affidavits, etc.

COUNTY
OF
YORK   To Wit: I, PETER THOMAS GRANT,
of the City of Toronto,
•in the County of York, Solicitor,
            (Occupation)   make oath and say:

1. THAT I was personally present and did see the within or annexed Instrument and a duplicate thereof duly signed, sealed and executed by Ronald Craig Anderson and Lucille Caroline Anderson, --two of the parties thereto.

2. THAT the said Instrument and duplicate were executed by the said part ies at the   City   of Toronto.

3. THAT I know the said part ies.

4. THAT I am a subscribing witness to the said Instrument and duplicate.

SWORN before me at the   City of Toronto
in the*   County of York

this   day of   November   19 70

A Commissioner for taking Affidavits, etc.

DATED November 27 1970

RONALD CRAIG ANDERSON

TO

PERCIVAL ANDREW PETERSON

Address: 2497 Primrose Ave.
Toronto, Ontario

Mortgage

East Half of Lot No. 105,
Plan M5948, Toronto

Dye & Durham Co. Limited, 76 Richmond Street East, Toronto

Not to be recorded in full.

SMITH, FRASER, HAMILTON
& WEBB,
75 Maryvale Blvd.,
Toronto, Ontario.

Solicitors for the Mortgagee.

HILL, JOHNSTON & GRANT
17 Princess Street S.
Toronto, Ontario.

THIS SPACE TO BE RESERVED FOR REGISTRY OFFICE CERTIFICATES

Figure 11.2. Mortgage with Dower –
Back

Dye & Durham Limited — Law and Commercial Stationers
76 Richmond Street E., Toronto
FORM NO. 190-193

𝕿𝖍𝖎𝖘 𝕴𝖓𝖉𝖊𝖓𝖙𝖚𝖗𝖊

made (in duplicate) the twenty-eighth day of November
one thousand nine hundred and seventy.

𝕴𝖓 𝕻𝖚𝖗𝖘𝖚𝖆𝖓𝖈𝖊 𝖔𝖋 𝖙𝖍𝖊 𝕾𝖍𝖔𝖗𝖙 𝕱𝖔𝖗𝖒𝖘 𝖔𝖋 𝕸𝖔𝖗𝖙𝖌𝖆𝖌𝖊𝖘 𝕬𝖈𝖙

𝕭𝖊𝖙𝖜𝖊𝖊𝖓

HAROLD WILLIAM MARTIN, of the Borough of Etobicoke, in the
County of York, Merchant, and PAULINE GRACE MARTIN, his
wife, of the same place, as joint tenants and not as
tenants in common,

hereinafter called the Mortgagors   of the FIRST PART;

- and -

TRAILER COMPANY LIMITED EMPLOYEES' CREDIT UNION, a
company incorporated under the laws of the Province
of Ontario, having its head office at the City of
Toronto, in the County of York,

hereinafter called the Mortgagee   of the SECOND PART;

𝖂𝖍𝖊𝖗𝖊𝖆𝖘 the said Mortgagor at the time of the execution hereof is seized of an estate in fee simple in possession of the lands hereinafter mentioned, and have   applied to the Mortgagee for a loan upon mortgage thereof.

𝕹𝖔𝖜 𝖙𝖍𝖊𝖗𝖊𝖋𝖔𝖗𝖊 𝖙𝖍𝖎𝖘 𝕴𝖓𝖉𝖊𝖓𝖙𝖚𝖗𝖊 𝖂𝖎𝖙𝖓𝖊𝖘𝖘𝖊𝖙𝖍 that in consideration of EIGHTEEN THOUSAND THREE

HUNDRED---------------($18,300.00)-------------------------------- dollars
of lawful money of Canada now paid by the said Mortgagee to the said Mortgagor (the receipt whereof is hereby by them   acknowledged) the said Mortgagor doth grant and mortgage unto the said Mortgagee its   ~~heirs, executors, administrators,~~ successors and assigns forever.

𝕬𝖑𝖑 𝖆𝖓𝖉 𝕾𝖎𝖓𝖌𝖚𝖑𝖆𝖗 that certain parcel   or tract   of land and premises situate, lying and being in the Township of East Gwillimbury, in the County of York, and Province of Ontario, being composed of the whole of Lot Number 13 according to Plan 393, registered in the Registry Office for the Registry Division of the North Riding of the County of York.

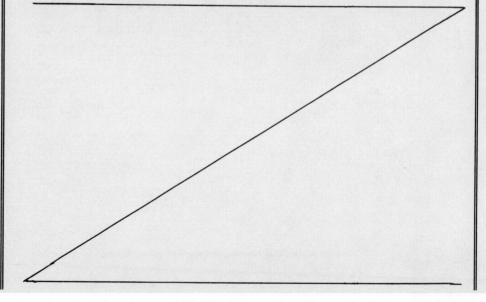

*Figure 11.3. First Page of Mortgage, Married
Couple as Mortgagors*

Provided this Mortgage to be Void upon payment of _Amount of Mortgage_ **Dollars**

in lawful money of Canada with interest at _Rate of Interest_ **per centum per annum as follows:**

Terms of Repayment

the said principal sum of $ _Full Amount of Mortgage_ shall become due and payable on the _Maturity Date of Mortgage_ **day of**

19 and interest yearly at the said rate as well after as before

maturity and both before and after default on such portion of the principal as remains from time to time

unpaid on the _Date of Payment_ **days of** _Months When Payment Due_

in each year until the principal is fully paid; the first payment of interest to be computed from the

day of _Beginning Date of Mortgage_ 19 upon the whole amount of principal hereby secured, to become due

and payable on the _Date of First Payment on Mortgage_ **day of** next 19

AND Taxes and performance of Statute Labor; and observance and performance of all covenants,
provisos and conditions herein contained.

AND it is hereby agreed that in case default shall be made in payment of any sum to become due for
interest at any time appointed for payment thereof as aforesaid, compound interest shall be payable and
the sum in arrear for interest from time to time, as well after as before maturity, shall bear interest
at the rate aforesaid, and in case the interest and compound interest are not paid in _Same Basis as Interest_ months
from the time of default a rest shall be made, and compound interest at the rate aforesaid shall be
payable on the aggregate amount then due, as well after as before maturity, and so on from time to time,
and all such interest and compound interest shall be a charge upon the said lands.

_Figure 11.4. Guide for Completing the
Repayment Provisions of an Unamortized
Mortgage_

(NO ADVANCE PAYMENTS)

And the said wife of the said Mortgagor hereby bars her Dower in the said lands. (X this out if not applicable)

The amount of principal money secured by this Mortgage is TWELVE THOUSAND------------------
----------------------($12,000.00)--------------------------DOLLARS

and the rate of interest chargeable thereon is nine and one-half (9 ½) per centum per annum calculated half -yearly not in advance.

Provided This Mortgage to be Void on payment of TWELVE THOUSAND----------------------
--------------------------($12,000.00)-----------------------DOLLARS

of lawful money of Canada with interest at nine and one-half (9 ½)--per centum per annum calculated half-yearly, not in advance, as well after as before maturity and both before and after default, as follows:—

~~Interest at the aforesaid rate on the amounts advanced from time to time, com-~~ (X out if no ~~puted from the respective dates of such advances, shall become due and be paid~~ advances) ~~on the --------------day of-------------19--; and, thereafter,~~ the sum of TWELVE THOUSAND------($12,000.00)------DOLLARS with interest thereon at the aforesaid rate computed from the first day of December 1970, shall become due and be paid in instalments of ------$amount-------- each, on the first day of each and every month in each and every year from and including the first day of January 1971, to and including the first day of November 19 75, (such instalments to be applied FIRST in payment of the interest due from time to time, calculated at the said rate of -9 1/2 per centum per annum, and the BALANCE to be applied in reduction of the principal sum) and the BA-LANCE of the said principal sum of TWELVE THOUSAND----------- -------------------($12,000.00)---------------- DOLLARS with interest thereon as aforesaid shall become due and payable on the first day of December 19 75 .

AND Taxes and performance of Statute Labor; and observance and performance of all covenants, provisos and conditions herein contained.

AND it is hereby agreed that in case default shall be made in payment of any sum to become due for interest at any time appointed for payment thereof as aforesaid, compound interest shall be payable and the sum in arrear for interest from time to time, as well after as before maturity, shall bear interest at the rate aforesaid, and in case the interest and compound interest are not paid in six months from the time of default a rest shall be made, and compound interest at the rate aforesaid shall be payable on the aggregate amount then due, as well after as before maturity, and so on from time to time, and all such interest and compound interest shall be a charge upon the said lands.

THE MORTGAGOR agrees that neither the preparation, execution nor registration of this Indenture shall bind the Mortgagee to advance the money hereby secured, nor the advance of a part of the moneys secured hereby bind the Mortgagee to advance any unadvanced portion thereof, but nevertheless the estate hereby conveyed shall take effect forthwith upon the execution of these presents by the said Mortgagor, and the expenses of the examination of the title and of this mortgage and valuation are to be secured hereby in the event of the whole or any balance of the principal sum not being advanced, the same to be charged hereby upon the said lands, and shall be without demand thereof, payable forthwith with interest at the rate provided for in this mortgage, and in default the said Mortgagee's power of sale hereby given, and all other remedies hereunder, shall be exercisable.

AND the said Mortgagor covenants with the Mortgagee that in the event of non-payment of the said principal moneys at the time or times above provided, he shall not require the Mortgagee to accept payment of said principal moneys without first giving six months' previous notice in writing, or paying a bonus equal to three months' interest in advance on the said principal moneys.

THE said Mortgagor covenants with the said Mortgagee that the Mortgagor will pay the Mortgage money and interest and observe the above proviso, and will pay as they fall due all taxes, rates and assessments, municipal, local, parliamentary and otherwise which now are or may hereafter be imposed, charged or levied upon the said lands and premises;
THAT the Mortgagor has a good title in fee simple to the said lands.
AND that he has the right to convey the said lands to the said Mortgagee;
AND that on default the Mortgagee shall have quiet possession of the said lands free from all encumbrances.

AND that the said Mortgagor will execute such further assurances of the said lands as may be requisite;
AND that the said Mortgagor has done no act to encumber the said lands;

Figure 11.5. Amortized Payment Sheet of Mortgage

COMPUTING SERVICES COMPANY
20 SPADINA ROAD, TORONTO 4, ONTARIO

LOAN $	18000.00	PAYMENT $	157.99	PAYABLE	MONTHLY	TERM	25 YEARS	MTHS
RATE %	9.750	COMPOUNDED	SEMI-ANNL			INTEREST PAYMENT FACTOR	0796471400	

PAYMENT NUMBER	INTEREST PAYMENT	PRINCIPAL PAYMENT	BALANCE OF LOAN	PAYMENT NUMBER	INTEREST PAYMENT	PRINCIPAL PAYMENT	BALANCE OF LOAN
1	143.36	14.63	17985.37	61	134.45	23.54	16857.06
2	143.25	14.74	17970.63	62	134.26	23.73	16833.35
3	143.13	14.86	17955.77	63	134.07	23.92	16809.43
4	143.01	14.98	17940.79	64	133.88	24.11	16765.32
5	142.89	15.10	17925.69	65	133.69	24.30	16761.02
6	142.77	15.22	17910.47	66	133.50	24.49	16736.53
7	142.65	15.34	17895.13	67	133.30	24.69	16711.64
8	142.53	15.46	17879.67	68	133.11	24.88	16686.96
9	142.41	15.58	17864.09	69	132.91	25.08	16661.88
10	142.28	15.71	17848.38	70	132.71	25.28	16636.60
11	142.16	15.83	17832.55	71	132.51	25.48	16611.12
12	142.03	15.96	17816.59	72	132.30	25.69	16585.43
13	141.90	16.09	17800.50	73	132.10	25.89	16559.54
14	141.78	16.21	17784.29	74	131.89	26.10	16533.44
15	141.65	16.34	17767.95	75	131.68	26.31	16507.13
16	141.52	16.47	17751.48	76	131.47	26.52	16480.61
17	141.39	16.60	17734.88	77	131.26	26.73	16453.88
18	141.25	16.74	17718.14	78	131.05	26.94	16426.94
19	141.12	16.87	17701.27	79	130.84	27.15	16399.79
20	140.99	17.00	17684.27	80	130.62	27.37	16372.42
21	140.85	17.14	17667.13	81	130.40	27.59	16344.83
22	140.71	17.28	17649.85	82	130.18	27.81	16317.02
23	140.58	17.41	17632.44	83	129.96	28.03	16288.99
24	140.44	17.55	17614.89	84	129.74	28.25	16260.74
25	140.30	17.69	17597.20	85	129.51	28.48	16232.26
26	140.16	17.83	17579.37	86	129.29	28.70	16203.56

Figure 11.6.   Extract from Printed
Amortization Schedule

---

csc

COMPUTING SERVICES COMPANY
20 Spadina Road, Toronto 4, Ontario/927-1633

LOAN AMOUNT	INTEREST RATE CALCULATED	PAYMENT TYPE AND FREQUENCY
$	% ☐ MONTHLY ☐ QUARTERLY ☐ SEMI-ANNUALLY ☐ ANNUALLY	☐ INTEREST & PRINCIPAL BLENDED ☐ MONTHLY ☐ QUARTERLY ☐ SEMI-ANNUALLY ☐ ANNUALLY

DATE.................................. RE:..................................

NAME..................................
PLEASE PRINT

ADDRESS..................................

CITY..................................

SHADED ITEMS WILL APPLY UNLESS OTHERWISE MARKED

PDC 4426-30

SPECIFY ONE OR BOTH OF
PAYMENT AMOUNT and/or TERM

PAYMENT AMOUNT	TERM
$	AND/OR _____ YEARS _____ MONTHS

PAYMENT MUST BE INCLUDED WITH THIS ORDER:
$1.00 FOR ONE SCHEDULE IN DUPLICATE
$ .35 FOR EACH ADDITIONAL SET

NO. OF EXTRA SETS

PLEASE INCLUDE EXCHANGE ON OUT-OF-TOWN CHEQUES

Figure 11.7.   Request Form for Amortization
Schedule

Charge or Mortgage, Long

Dye & Durham Limited — Toronto, Canada
Printers to the Legal Profession
Form No. 195 to 198

Land Titles Act

I, WE, RONALD CRAIG ANDERSON, of the City of Toronto, in the County of York, Physician, and LUCILLE CAROLINE ANDERSON, his wife, of the same place, as joint tenants and not as tenants in common,

(hereinafter called the Mortgagors   ),

the registered owner s   of the land entered in the office of Land Titles, at Toronto

as Parcel 122345 WB   in the Register for the East Section

In consideration of the sum of   TEN THOUSAND--
----------------------($10,000.00)----------------------------- Dollars

paid to us, charge the land hereinafter particularly described, namely, Lot 59, on the North side of Humber Crescent in the Borough of East York as shown on Plan M659 filed in the Office of Land Titles at Toronto;

TOGETHER with a right-of-way in, over, along and upon the westerly ten inches (10") of the southerly seventy feet (70') of the lands immediately adjoining the lands herein described on the East.

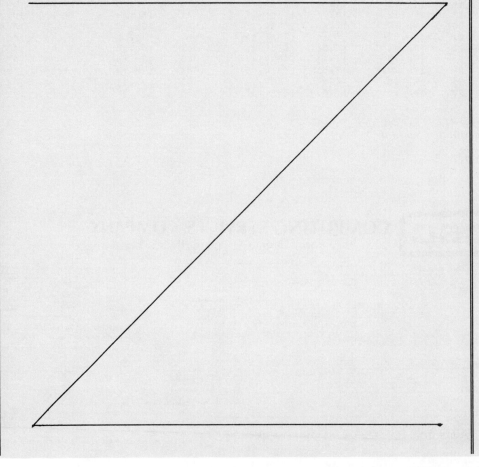

Figure 11.8.   Charge – Page 1

Charge or Mortgage, Long — p. 2
Dye & Durham

being   the whole   of the said parcel with the payment to

PERCIVAL ANDREW PETERSON,

of the   City   of Toronto   in the   County of York, Merchant

(hereinafter called the Mortgagee   ) of the principal sum of   TEN THOUSAND-----------------
------------($10,000.00)----------------------- Dollars, with interest at the rate
of nine (9%)----- per centum per annum, payable as hereinafter provided, and with the powers
of sale hereinafter expressed.

Provided this Mortgage to be Void upon payment of TEN THOUSAND----------------------
------------------($10,000.00)------------------------------------Dollars.
in lawful money of Canada with interest at nine (9%)-----------------------------
per centum per annum as follows:

FIVE HUNDRED---($500.00)---Dollars on account of principal

shall become due and payable quarterly on the 15th days of February,

May, August and November in the years 1971, 1972, 1973, 1974, and

February, May and August in the year 1975, and the balance of_____

the said principal sum of $10,000.00   shall become due and payable on the   15th   day of
November   1975 and interest   quarter~half-yearly at the said rate as well after as before
maturity and both before and after default on such portion of the principal as remains from time to time
unpaid on the   15th   days of February, May,   and August and November
in each year until the principal is fully paid; the first payment of interest to be computed from the 15th
day of November   19 70 upon the whole amount of principal hereby secured, to become due and
payable on the   15th   day of   February   next 19 71.

AND Taxes and performance of Statute Labor;   And observance and performance of all covenants,
provisos and conditions herein contained.

AND it is hereby agreed that in case default shall be made in payment of any sum to become due for
interest at any time appointed for payment thereof as aforesaid, compound interest shall be payable and
the sum in arrear for interest from time to time, as well after as before maturity, shall bear interest
at the rate aforesaid, and in case the interest and compound interest are not paid in   three
months from the time of default a rest shall be made, and compound interest at the rate aforesaid shall
be payable on the aggregate amount then due, as well after as before maturity, and so on from time to
time, and all such interest and compound interest shall be a charge upon the said lands.

THE MORTGAGOR agrees that neither the preparation, execution nor registration of this Indenture
shall bind the Mortgagee to advance the money hereby secured, nor the advance of a part of the moneys
secured hereby bind the Mortgagee to advance any unadvanced portion thereof, but nevertheless the
estate hereby conveyed shall take effect forthwith upon the execution of these presents by the said
Mortgagor, and the expenses of the examination of the title and of this mortgage and valuation are to be
secured hereby in the event of the whole or any balance of the principal sum not being advanced, the
same to be charged hereby upon the said lands, and shall be without demand thereof, payable forthwith
with interest at the rate provided for in this mortgage, and in default the said Mortgagee's power of sale
hereby given, and all other remedies hereunder shall be exercisable.

AND the said Mortgagor covenants with the Mortgagee that in the event of non-payment of the said
principal moneys at the time or times above provided, then he shall not require the Mortgagee to accept
payment of said principal moneys without first giving six months' previous notice in writing, or paying
a bonus equal to three months' interest in advance on the said principal moneys.

THE said Mortgagor covenants with the said Mortgagee that the Mortgagor will pay the Mortgage
money and interest and observe the above proviso, and will pay as they fall due all taxes, rates and
assessments, municipal, local, parliamentary and otherwise which now are or may hereafter be
imposed, charged or levied upon the said lands and premises;
THAT the Mortgagor has a good title in fee simple to the said lands.
AND that he has the right to convey the said lands to the said Mortgagee;
AND that on default the Mortgagee shall have quiet possession of the said lands free from all
encumbrances.

AND that the said Mortgagor will execute such further assurances of the said lands as may be requisite;
AND that the said Mortgagor has done no act to encumber the said lands;

Figure 11.8. Charge – Page 2

AND that the said Mortgagor will insure the buildings on the said lands to the amount of not less than the principal money hereby secured in dollars of lawful money of Canada. Evidence of continuation of such insurance having been secured shall be produced to the Mortgagee at least three days before expiration thereof, otherwise the Mortgagee may provide therefor and charge the premium paid therefor and interest thereon to the Mortgagor and the same shall also be a charge upon the said land. It is further agreed that the Mortgagee may require any insurance on the said buildings to be cancelled and a new insurance effected in an office to be named by him, and also may of his own accord effect or maintain any insurance herein provided for, and any amount paid by him therefor shall be forthwith payable to him with interest at the rate aforesaid by the Mortgagor, and shall be a charge upon the said lands (without prejudice to the foregoing statutory clause).

PROVIDED that the said Mortgagee on default of payment for at least fifteen days may on at least thirty-five days' notice enter on and lease the said lands or on default of payment for at least fifteen days may on at least thirty-five days' notice sell the said lands. Such notice shall be given to such persons and in such manner and form and within such time as provided under Part II-A of The Mortgages Act, R.S.O. 1960, c. 245, as amended. In the event that the giving of such notice shall not be required by law or to the extent that such requirements shall not be applicable it is agreed that notice may be effectually given by leaving it with a grown-up person on the said lands, if occupied, or by placing it on the said lands if unoccupied, or at the option of the Mortgagee, by mailing it in a registered letter addressed to the Mortgagor at his last known address, or by publishing it once in a newspaper published in the county or district in which the lands are situate; and such notice shall be sufficient although not addressed to any person or persons by name or designation; and notwithstanding that any person to be affected thereby may be unknown, unascertained, or under disability. PROVIDED FURTHER, without prejudice to the statutory powers of the Mortgagee under the foregoing proviso, that in case default be made in the payment of the said principal or interest or any part thereof and such default continue for two months after any payment of either falls due then the Mortgagee may exercise the foregoing powers of entering, leasing or selling or any of them without any notice, it being understood and agreed, however, that if the giving of notice by the Mortgagee shall be required by law then notice shall be given to such persons and in such manner and form and within such time as so required by law. AND it is hereby further agreed that the whole or any part or parts of the said lands may be sold by public auction or private contract, or partly one or partly the other; and that the proceeds of any sale hereunder may be applied in payment of any costs, charges and expenses incurred in taking, recovering or keeping possession of the said lands or by reason of non-payment or procuring payment of moneys, secured hereby or otherwise, and that the Mortgagee may sell any of the said lands on such terms as to credit and otherwise as shall appear to him most advantageous and for such prices as can reasonably be obtained therefor and may make any stipulations as to title or evidence or commencement of title or otherwise which he shall deem proper, and may buy in or rescind or vary any contract for the sale of the whole or any part of the said lands and resell without being answerable for loss occasioned thereby, and in the case of a sale on credit the Mortgagee shall be bound to pay the Mortgagor only such moneys as have been actually received from purchasers after the satisfaction of the claims of the Mortgagee and for any of said purposes may make and execute all agreements and assurances as he shall think fit. Any purchaser or lessee shall not be bound to see to the propriety or regularity of any sale or lease or be affected by express notice that any sale or lease is improper and no want of notice or publication when required hereby shall invalidate any sale or lease hereunder. PROVIDED that the Mortgagee may distrain for arrears of interest. PROVIDED that the Mortgagee may distrain for arrears of principal in the same manner as if the same were arrears of interest. PROVIDED that in default of the payment of the interest hereby secured the principal hereby secured shall become payable at the option of the Mortgagee. PROVIDED that upon default of payment of instalments of principal promptly as the same mature, the balance of the principal and interest shall immediately become due and payable at the option of the Mortgagee. PROVIDED that the Mortgagee may in writing at any time or times after default waive such default and upon such waiver the time or times for payment of said principal shall be as set out in the above proviso for redemption. PROVIDED further that any such waiver shall apply only to the particular default waived and shall not operate as a waiver of any other or future default. AND it is further agreed by and between the parties that the Mortgagee may at his discretion at all times release any part or parts of the said lands or any other security or any surety for the money hereby secured either with or without any sufficient consideration therefor, without responsibility therefor, and without thereby releasing any other part of the said lands or any person from this Mortgage or from any of the covenants herein contained, it being especially agreed that every part or lot into which the mortgaged lands are or may hereafter be divided does and shall stand charged with the whole money hereby secured and no person shall have the right to require the mortgage moneys to be apportioned; and without being accountable to the Mortgagor for the value thereof, or for any moneys except those actually received by the Mortgagee. PROVIDED further that no sale or other dealing by the Mortgagor with the equity of redemption in the said lands or any part thereof shall in any way change the liability of the Mortgagor or in any way alter the rights of the Mortgagee as against the Mortgagor or any other person liable for payment of the moneys hereby secured. THE said Mortgagor covenants with the said Mortgagee that he will keep the said lands and the buildings, erections and improvements thereon in good condition and repair according to the nature and description thereof respectively, and that the Mortgagee may, whenever he deems necessary, by his surveyor or agent enter upon and inspect the said mortgaged lands, and the reasonable cost of such inspection shall be added to the Mortgage debt, and that if the Mortgagor neglects to keep the said premises in good condition and repair, or commit or permit any act of waste on the said lands (as to which the Mortgagee shall be sole judge) or make default as to any of the covenants or provisos herein contained, the principal hereby secured shall at the option of the Mortgagee forthwith become due and payable, and in default of payment of same with interest as in the case of payment before maturity, the powers of entering upon and leasing or selling hereby given may be exercised and the Mortgagee may make such repairs as he deems necessary, and the cost thereof with interest thereon shall be a charge upon the land prior to all claims thereon subsequent to these presents.

PROVIDED that until default of payment the Mortgagor shall have quiet possession of the said lands. PROVIDED and it is hereby agreed, that the taking of a judgment or judgments on any of the covenants herein contained shall not operate as a merger of the said covenants or affect the Mortgagee's right to interest at the rate and times herein provided; and further that said judgment shall provide that interest thereon shall be computed at the same rate and in the same manner as herein provided until the said judgment shall have been fully paid and satisfied.

PROVIDED and it is hereby further agreed by and between the Mortgagor and the Mortgagee that should default be made by the Mortgagor in the observance or performance of any of the covenants, provisos, agreements or conditions contained in any mortgage to which this mortgage is subject, then and in that event the moneys hereby secured shall forthwith become due and be payable, at the option of the Mortgagee, and all the powers in and by this mortgage conferred shall become exercisable, and the powers of sale therein contained may be exercised forthwith without any notice, unless the giving of notice shall be required by law in which event notice shall be given to such persons and in such manner and form and within such time as required by law.

Figure 11.8. Charge – Page 3

PROVIDED also that the covenant for insurance hereinbefore contained shall apply to all buildings whether now or hereafter erected on the said lands.

PROVIDED also that on default of payment of any of the moneys hereby secured or payable or on any proceedings being taken by the Mortgagee under this Mortgage, he shall be entitled to require payment, in addition to all other moneys hereby secured or payable hereunder, of a bonus equal to three months' interest in advance at the rate aforesaid upon the principal money hereby secured, and the Mortgagor shall not be entitled to require a discharge of this Mortgage without such payment.

AND it is hereby agreed between the parties hereto that the Mortgagee may pay all premiums of insurance and all taxes and rates which shall from time to time fall due and be unpaid in respect of the mortgaged premises, and that such payments together with all costs, charges and expenses (between solicitor and client), which may be incurred in taking, recovering and keeping possession of the said lands, and of negotiating this loan, investigating title, and registering the mortgage and other necessary deeds, and generally in any other proceedings taken, in connection with or to realize this security, shall be with interest at the rate aforesaid, a charge upon the said lands in favor of the Mortgagee and that the Mortgagee may pay or satisfy any lien, charge or encumbrance now existing or hereafter created or claimed upon the said lands, and that any amount paid by the Mortgagee shall be added to the debt hereby secured and shall be payable forthwith with interest at the rate aforesaid, and in default this Mortgage shall immediately become due and payable at the option of the Mortgagee, and all powers by this Mortgage conferred shall become exercisable.

PROVIDED and it is hereby agreed, that in construing these presents the words "Mortgagor" and "Mortgagee" and the personal pronoun "he" or "his" relating thereto and used therewith, shall be read and construed as "Mortgagor or Mortgagors," "Mortgagee or Mortgagees," and "his," "her" or "their," respectively, as the number and gender of the party or parties referred to in each case require and the number of the verb agreeing therewith shall be construed as agreeing with the said word or pronoun so substituted. And that all rights, advantages, privileges, immunities, powers and things hereby secured to the Mortgagee or Mortgagees shall be equally secured to and exercisable by his, her, or their heirs. executors, administrators and assigns, or successors and assigns as the case may be. And that all covenants, liabilities and obligations entered into or imposed hereunder upon the Mortgagor or Mortgagors shall be equally binding upon his, her or their heirs, executors, administrators and assigns, or successors and assigns as the case may be, and that all such covenants and liabilities and obligations shall be joint and several.

~AND I,~

~wife of the said Mortgagor hereby bar my Dower in the said lands~

The undersigned being the Mortgagor s named in the within Mortgage, acknowledge   having received a true copy of the said Mortgage.

THIS CHARGE is made in pursuance of The Short Forms of Mortgages Act.

DATED the   day of   November   19 70

WITNESS

_____
                    Ronald Craig Anderson

_____
                    Lucille Caroline Anderson

LAND TITLES ACT.

~I~, WE, RONALD CRAIG ANDERSON, and LUCILLE CAROLINE ANDERSON,

the Mortgagor s named in the above Charge, make oath and say:

    That we are legally married to each other and

~who executed the above Charge is my wife and we~ are both of the age of twenty-one years or over.

SEVERALLY

SWORN before me at the   City

of   Toronto

in the   County

of   York

this

day of   November   1970

                    A Commissioner, etc.

Land Titles Act

I, ELSIE EDNA SWARTZ,

of the   Borough of Etobicoke,   of

in the   County of York, Secretary,

make oath and say:

That I am well acquainted with   Ronald Craig Anderson and Lucille Caroline Anderson-- named in the within document and saw   them   sign the said document, and the signatures   purporting to be   their   signatures at the foot of the said document   are in their handwriting.

The said   Ronald Craig Anderson and Lucille Caroline Anderson are   as I verily believe the owners   of the lands within mentioned, and the said Lucille Caroline Anderson---------------- is reputed to be, and is, as I verily believe, his wife.

The said Ronald Craig Anderson and Lucille Caroline Anderson are   of the age of twenty-one years or over, are each of sound mind, and signed the said document voluntarily at the   City   of   Toronto   in the   County of York,   in the Province of Ontario.

I am a subscribing witness to the said document

SWORN before me at the   City

of   Toronto

in the   County

of York

this   day of November 1970

A Commissioner, etc.

Land Titles Act

Dated   day of November 1970

RONALD CRAIG ANDERSON and LUCILLE CAROLINE ANDERSON

TO

PERCIVAL ANDREW PETERSON

Address: 2497 Queenston Heights Blvd., Toronto

LONG SPECIAL

Charge or Mortgage

WITH DOWER

Dye & Durham Limited — Toronto, Canada
Printers to the Legal Profession

HILL, JOHNSTON & GRANT
17 Princess Street
Toronto, Ontario

Figure 11.8.   Charge – Back

CHAPTER 12

Legal Instruments Relating To Mortgages and Charges

Once executed and in existence, mortgages and charges may be the subject of other legal instruments. As well as being taken over by another party from the existing mortgagor, they may be assigned, renewed, or discharged.

The procedures in both the Registry Office and Land Titles Office are quite similar, and we will limit our consideration to those instruments which relate to a mortgage, with the exception of instruments used to cancel charges.

Assignment of Mortgage

Frequently the mortgagee may find it necessary to obtain money, and will decide to sell a mortgage he holds for as much money as possible. When he does this, he is said to assign the mortgage to a new party who becomes the mortgagee (Figure 12.1). The mortgage may be a good investment, in which case the original mortgagee may be able to sell it for its actual worth. It may be a poor investment, and he may have to sell it for much less than it would seem to be worth; this is known as discounting a mortgage.

The parties to an assignment of mortgage are the *assignor(s)* – the person or persons assigning (selling) the mortgage, that is, the original mortgagee, and the *assignee(s)* – the person or persons purchasing the mortgage, and becoming the new mortgagee.

In some assignments the assignor guarantees payment of the mortgage, so that if the mortgagor fails to pay the mortgage, the original mortgagee can be required to pay off the mortgage. However, in most assignments the original mortgagee sells the mortgage outright, and the purchaser (assignee or new mortgagee), is then in the same position as the original mortgagee.

Four copies of an assignment are prepared in the office of the solicitors for the assignor; the instrument is dated the day it is typed. The assignor will execute the assignment in duplicate, and legal seals are required. The usual affidavits of legal age, marital status, and execution are completed.

Two executed copies of the assignment are given to the assignee, who arranges to have a copy registered in the Registry Office, so that the records will indicate the transfer of the mortgage from the original mortgagee. The assignee then holds the second executed copy of the mortgage, together with the executed copy of the original mortgage, which the assignor provides to him.

The following information or material is required to complete an assignment of mortgage:

1. a duplicate copy of the mortgage, from which can be ascertained the date of the mortgage, and particulars of registration
2. the names of the original mortgagor and mortgagee, and the name and address of the new mortgagee
3. the amount of the original mortgage, and the amount still owing
4. the consideration given for the assignment. This usually appears as "other good and valuable consideration and the sum of TWO——($2.00)——Dollars..." The actual amount paid for the assignment of mortgage is not shown.
5. the legal description of the property which is the subject matter of the mortgage taken from the mortgage itself
6. an acknowledgement from the mortgagor as to the amount outstanding on the mortgage. This statement also indicates that the mortgagor has no claims against the mortgagee that would affect the mortgage.
7. a direction from the mortgagee to the mortgagor directing that all future payments on the mortgage be made to the assignee.

Renewal of Mortgage

Mortgages are generally for a period of five years, but may contain a special clause providing for renewal upon maturity.

A mortgage is renewed by having the parties sign an instrument known as an agreement extending mortgage (Figure 12.2).

A minimum of four copies is prepared, and the instrument is executed in duplicate by all parties. It is dated the day it is typed. It may be prepared by the solicitors for either party, but usually is prepared by the solicitors for the mortgagor, since the extension benefits the mortgagor.

The agreement is sealed, and requires only an affidavit of execution. The original mortgage established the legal age and marital status of the mortgagor.

Each party to the extension agreement receives an executed copy. If the agreement is to be registered, the mortgagor will arrange for this.

To complete the agreement extending a mortgage, the following information or material is required:

1. a copy of the original mortgage, from which can be ascertained the date of the mortgage, and particulars of registration
2. a copy of any assignment of mortgage
3. the names of the original mortgagor and mortgagee
4. the names of the present mortgagor and mortgagee if the mortgage has been assumed, or assigned
5. the amount of the original mortgage, and the amount still owing
6. the legal description of the property which is the subject matter of the mortgage.

An agreement extending mortgage requires that a new repayment clause be included. This is done in the same manner as the repayment clause of a mortgage, but shows the new maturity date, and any new terms which may be agreed upon, such as a new rate of interest.

Discharge of Mortgage and Cessation of Charge

When a mortgage or charge has been paid in full, the mortgagee then gives to the mortgagor an instrument stating this fact. This is necessary since the mortgage or charge has been registered as a claim against the property. In order to cancel such a claim, another instrument showing that the claim no longer exists must also be registered. Such instruments are a discharge of mortgage (Figure 12.3) or a cessation of charge (Figure 12.4).

Preparation

A discharge or cessation is prepared by the solicitors for the mortgagee holding the mortgage or charge at the time of its payment in full. Two copies are prepared. One copy is executed and then given to the mortgagor so that it can be registered.

Both a discharge and a cessation are dated the day of execution. Legal seals are not required on either instrument; a discharge of mortgage is one of the very few instruments registered under the Registry Office system which does not require a seal.

In order to complete a discharge or cessation, you require the following material or information:

1. a duplicate copy of the original mortgage, and a copy of any assignments of mortgage
2. the names of the original mortgagor and mortgagee
3. the names of the present mortgagor and mortgagee if different from item 2 above
4. the details of registration of the mortgage, which can be obtained from the duplicate copy.

Special Points

In preparing these instruments, the following points should be noted:

1. The discharge of mortgage requires that certain additional information be given on page 2:
   a. a statement in regard to creation of lots on the mortgaged property. You will be instructed by the lawyer on the completion of this portion of the discharge.
   b. a statement that the person giving the discharge is in fact the person entitled to have received the money under the mortgage.
2. On the back of the cessation, only the name of the mortgagee appears; on the back of the discharge, the name of the mortgagee and the mortgagor.

3. If the original mortgage cannot be produced, the mortgagee must complete a declaration giving the reason.
4. Only affidavits of legal age, and of execution are required. If two mortgagees are giving the discharge or cessation, then both must join in a joint affidavit as to legal age.

Partial Discharge

Both a discharge and a cessation can be provided whereby part of the real property subject to the original mortgage or charge can be released.

This situation often arises when a large development company owns many lots on which it has built houses. When the company sells one of these houses, it must give a deed or transfer to the new owner. The development company will arrange a discharge of mortgage (or cessation of charge) from the mortgage company from which it borrowed mortgage monies, covering only the lot to be sold.

For a partial cessation the same form as used for a full cessation of charge is used, but indicates exactly what real property is being released.

For a partial discharge a separate instrument (Figure 12.5) is used. It is similar in content to the full discharge but requires a description of that part of the lands being discharged from the mortgage.

Registration of Discharges and Cessations

The mortgagor will register the discharge or cessation in the appropriate office, and must produce the instrument to which the discharge or cessation refers. When the appropriate office has made the necessary entry or check, the mortgagor will receive the duplicate copy of the instrument if it has been fully discharged. In the case of a completely discharged mortgage, for example, the word "DISCHARGED" is stamped on the duplicate mortgage, in a manner which perforates that word through all pages of the instrument.

This Indenture

made (in duplicate) the   10th   day of   December   1970

Between

PERCIVAL ANDREW PETERSON, of the City
of Toronto, in the County of York,
Merchant,

hereinafter called the Assignor
of the First Part

- and -

PETER JAMES CORMACK, of the City
of Toronto, in the County of York,
Broker,

hereinafter called the Assignee
of the SECOND Part

Whereas by a Mortgage dated on the   1st   day of   October   1969
and registered in the Registry Office for the Registry Division of the County of
Halton

as No. 25907 for Trafalgar,

RONALD CRAIG ANDERSON, of the City of
Toronto, in the County of York,
Physician,

Did Grant and Mortgage   the land   and premises therein and hereinafter described
to   the said PERCIVAL ANDREW PETERSON, his--------------------

heirs, executors, administrators, successors and assigns, for securing the payment of
TWELVE THOUSAND-----------($12,000.00)-------------DOLLARS

And Whereas   there is now owing upon the said Mortgage for principal money the
sum of ELEVEN THOUSAND FIVE HUNDRED---($11,500.00)---DOLLARS
together with interest thereon from the   6th   day of December,
1970,

And Whereas The Assignor   has   agreed to Sell and Assign the said
Mortgage to the Assignee.

*Figure 12.1. Assignment of Mortgage –
Page 1*

𝕹𝖔𝖜 𝕿𝖍𝖎𝖘 𝕴𝖓𝖉𝖊𝖓𝖙𝖚𝖗𝖊 𝖂𝖎𝖙𝖓𝖊𝖘𝖘𝖊𝖙𝖍 that in consideration of other good and

valuable consideration and the sum of TWO--($2.00)---- Dollars
of lawful money of Canada now paid by the said Assignee   to the said Assignor   (the
receipt whereof is hereby acknowledged,) the said Assignor   𝕯𝖔 TH 𝖍𝖊𝖗𝖊𝖇𝖞 𝕬𝖘𝖘𝖎𝖌𝖓
and set over unto the said Assignee,   his   heirs, executors, administrators, successors and assigns, 𝕬𝖑𝖑 𝖙𝖍𝖆𝖙   the said before in part recited Mortgage and
also the said sum of   ELEVEN THOUSAND FIVE HUNDRED----------------
-------------($11,500.00)---------------------------DOLLARS

now owing as aforesaid, together with all moneys that may hereafter become due or
owing in respect of the said Mortgage, and the full benefit of all powers and of all covenants
and provisos contained in said Mortgage, and also full power and authority to use the
name or names of the said Assignor   his   heirs, executors, administrators, successors and assigns, for enforcing the performance of the covenants and other
matters and things contained in the said Mortgage.

𝕬𝖓𝖉   the said Assignor   DoTH   hereby Grant and Convey unto the said Assignee,
        his   heirs, executors, administrators, successors and assigns,
𝕬𝖑𝖑 𝖆𝖓𝖉 𝕾𝖎𝖓𝖌𝖚𝖑𝖆𝖗 that   certain parcel   or tract   of land   and premises
situate, lying and being

(legal description of mortgaged premises)

Figure 12.1. Assignment of Mortgage –
Page 2

107

To have and to hold   the said Mortgage and all moneys arising in respect of the same and to accrue thereon, and also the said land   and premises thereby granted and mortgaged unto and to the use of the said Assignee ,   his   heirs, executors, administrators, successors and assigns absolutely forever, but subject to the terms contained in such Mortgage.

And the said Assignor   for himself, his   heirs, executors, administrators, successors and assigns, do th hereby covenant with said Assignee   his heirs, executors, administrators, successors and assigns, THAT the said Mortgage hereby assigned is a good and valid security, and that the sum of ELEVEN THOUSAND FIVE

HUNDRED----------($11,500.00)------------------------DOLLARS

is now owing and unpaid and that   he   has   not done or permitted any act, matter or thing whereby the said Mortgage has been released or discharged either partly or in entirety; And that   he   will upon request do, perform and execute every act necessary to enforce the full performance of the covenants and other matters contained therein

In Witness Whereof   the   said parties hereto have hereunto set their hands and seals.

Signed, Sealed and Delivered
   IN THE PRESENCE OF

(Executed by Assignor only)

Figure 12.1. Assignment of Mortgage – Page 3

AFFIDAVIT AS TO LEGAL AGE AND MARITAL STATUS

*For place of
residence insert
appropriate
County, District,
Regional
Municipality, etc.

PROVINCE OF ONTARIO

COUNTY OF YORK

To Wit:

I/~~WE~~ PERCIVAL ANDREW PETERSON

of the City of Toronto

in the* County of York, Merchant,

Strike out words
and parts not
applicable
and initial.

If Attorney
see footnote.

in the within instrument named, make oath and say that at the time of the execution of the within instrument,

1. I/~~WE~~ was   of the full age of twenty-one years;

2. ~~And that~~

~~who also executed the within instrument~~ – – – – – – – – ~~of the full age of twenty-one years;~~

3. ~~I was legally married to the person named therein as my wife/husband;~~

4. I was unmarried/~~divorced/widower.~~

SWORN before me at the   City
of   Toronto
in the* County of York

this   day of December   197 0

_____
A Commissioner for taking Affidavits, etc.

NOTE: If Attorney, substitute in space provided *"I am Attorney for*........................*(State name)*......................,
one of the parties named therein and he/she was of the full age of twenty-one years."

Figure 12.1. Assignment of Mortgage –
Page 4

109

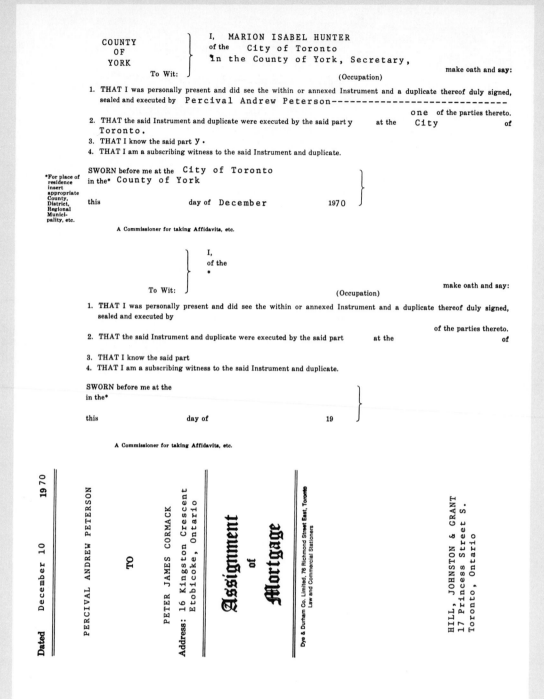

COUNTY
OF
YORK
To Wit:

I, MARION ISABEL HUNTER
of the   City of Toronto
in the County of York, Secretary,
(Occupation)
make oath and say:

1. THAT I was personally present and did see the within or annexed Instrument and a duplicate thereof duly signed, sealed and executed by Percival Andrew Peterson------------------------------
one of the parties thereto.

2. THAT the said Instrument and duplicate were executed by the said part y   at the   City   of Toronto.

3. THAT I know the said part y .

4. THAT I am a subscribing witness to the said Instrument and duplicate.

*For place of residence insert appropriate County, District, Regional Municipality, etc.

SWORN before me at the City of Toronto
in the* County of York

this   day of December   1970

A Commissioner for taking Affidavits, etc.

I,
of the
*
To Wit:
(Occupation)
make oath and say:

1. THAT I was personally present and did see the within or annexed Instrument and a duplicate thereof duly signed, sealed and executed by
of the parties thereto.

2. THAT the said Instrument and duplicate were executed by the said part   at the   of

3. THAT I know the said part

4. THAT I am a subscribing witness to the said Instrument and duplicate.

SWORN before me at the
in the*

this   day of   19

A Commissioner for taking Affidavits, etc.

Dated   December 10   19 70

PERCIVAL ANDREW PETERSON

TO

PETER JAMES CORMACK
Address: 16 Kingston Crescent
Etobicoke, Ontario

Assignment
of
Mortgage

Dye & Durham Co. Limited, 76 Richmond Street East, Toronto
Law and Commercial Stationers

HILL, JOHNSTON & GRANT
17 Princess Street S.
Toronto, Ontario

Figure 12.1. Assignment of Mortgage –
Back

This Agreement

made in duplicate the 12th   day of April   19 70

Between:

> NORMA MARGRET DARKE, of the City of
> Toronto, in the County of York,
> Married Woman,
>
> hereinafter called the Party

of the First Part

and

> WALTER KING, of the City of Toronto in
> the County of York, Clerk, and JANE MABEL
> KING, his wife, of the same place, as joint
> tenants and not as tenants in common,
>
> hereinafter called the Parties

of the Second Part.

Dye & Durham
Limited
Toronto, Canada
Forms 98 to 101

WHEREAS by Indenture dated the 25th   day of May   19 65,

and registered in the Registry Office for the Registry Division of Toronto

on the   29th   day of

May,   ,1965 as No. 89869 W.T.

WALTER KING, of the City of Toronto, in the County of York, Clerk,

and JANE MABEL KING, of the same place, his wife, as joint tenants

and not as tenants in common,

did grant and mortgage ALL AND SINGULAR that certain parcel or tract of land

and premises situate, lying and being in the City of Toronto, in the County

of York, and being composed of the northerly forty-five feet (45')

in width throughout from front to rear of Lot Number 43 on the

east side of Princess Avenue, according to Registered Plan

Number 1112;

TOGETHER with a right-of-way in, over, along and upon the

northerly three feet five inches (3' 5") of the westerly sixty-

seven feet (67') of the lands immediately adjoining to the south

of the lands hereinbefore described and reserving and subject to

a right-of-way in, over, along and upon the southerly three feet

five inches (3' 5") of the westerly sixty-seven feet (67') of

the lands hereinbefore described.

Figure 12.2. Agreement Extending Mortgage –
Page 1

UNTO   NORMA MARGRET DARKE, her-------------------------------------

heirs and assigns for securing the payment of   THIRTEEN THOUSAND, FIVE HUNDRED
-----($13,500.00)------dollars and interest at the times and in the manner therein
set forth _____

AND WHEREAS the time for payment of the said principal moneys has elapsed and the sum of
TEN THOUSAND FIVE HUNDRED--
----------($10,500.00)--------------------DOLLARS still remains unpaid

AND WHEREAS the said part ies hereto of the Second Part have   applied for an
extension of time for payment of said sum upon the terms and conditions hereinafter set forth,
and the said part y   hereto of the First Part ha s   agreed thereto.

NOW THIS INDENTURE WITNESSETH that in consideration of the premises and of the sum
of one dollar to her paid by the said part ies of the Second Part she   the said party
of the First Part doth ,subject to terms hereinafter set forth, GRANT AND EXTEND to the
said Parties of the Second Part time for payment of the said principal money;

The sum of ONE HUNDRED---($100.00)---Dollars on account of
principal shall become due and payable on the 15th days of
August and November, 1970; and February, May, August and November
in each of the years 1971, 1972, 1973, 1974,   and February,
1975, and the balance of the said principal sum shall become due
and payable on the--

until the-   15th   day of   May,
19 75 , the said part ies of the Second Part in the meantime and until final payment of
the principal money paying interest on the unpaid principal quarter   half-yearly on the
       15th   day of February,   xxxk May, August and
November--
in each year at   eight-------(8%)---------- per cent. per annum, as well after as
before maturity.
The first of such quarter half-yearly payments of interest to be made on the
    15th   day of   August   1970, to be computed from the
15th day of May, 1970.

*Figure 12.2. Agreement Extending Mortgage –
Page 2*

THE SAID parties of the Second Part do hereby covenant with the said party of the First Part to pay said principal money and interest at the rate and in manner hereinbefore mentioned, and to well and truly keep, observe, perform and fulfil all the covenants, provisos and agreements in said mortgage contained, and to keep the said principal money until the expiration of the said extended term.

AND it is expressly declared and agreed that if at any time during the said term the said party of the Second Part shall make default in payment of the interest secured by the said Mortgage, or any part thereof, or in the performance of any of the covenants contained in said mortgage, the extension hereby given shall, if the said party of the First Part so elect, become void, and the said principal money and every part thereof shall become due and payable, and the said part of the First Part shall be at liberty to take any proceedings she may see fit for the purpose of enforcing payment of the said principal and interest, or of the interest only, and performance of the said covenants in like manner as if these presents had not been executed.

IT IS HEREBY AGREED AND DECLARED that nothing herein contained shall in any way affect or prejudice the rights of the said party of the First Part as against the said parties of the Second Part, her heirs, executors, administrators and assigns, or as against any party to the said mortgage or as against any surety or other person whomsoever for the said mortgage debt or any part thereof or as against any collateral which the said party of the First Part may now or hereafter hold against the said mortgage debt or any part thereof.

PROVIDED that the mortgagors shall have the privilege of prepaying the whole or any part of the principal sum secured at any time without notice or bonus.

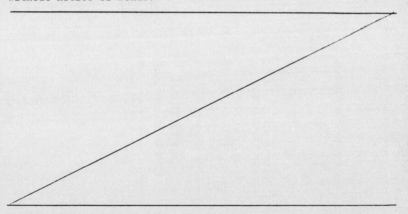

AND it is further agreed and declared and these presents shall extend to, be binding upon, and enure to the benefit of their heirs, executors, administrators, successors and assigns of each of the parties hereto respectively.

IN WITNESS WHEREOF the parties hereto have hereunto set their hands and seals.

SIGNED, SEALED AND DELIVERED
    In the Presence of

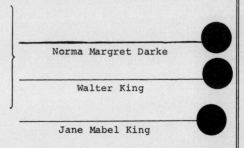

Norma Margret Darke

Walter King

Jane Mabel King

Figure 12.2. Agreement Extending Mortgage –
Page 3

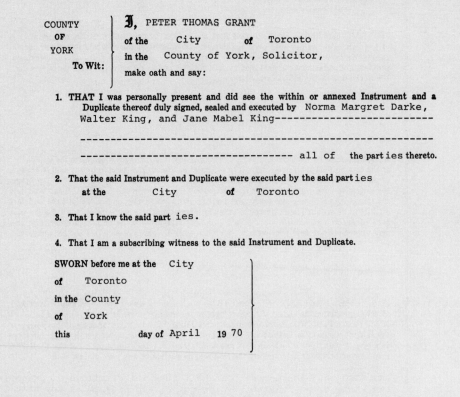

COUNTY
OF
YORK
To Wit:

I, PETER THOMAS GRANT

of the   City   of   Toronto

in the   County of York, Solicitor,

make oath and say:

1. **THAT I was personally present and did see the within or annexed Instrument and a Duplicate thereof duly signed, sealed and executed by** Norma Margret Darke, Walter King, and Jane Mabel King-------------------------

----

----------------------------------- all of   the parties thereto.

2. **That the said Instrument and Duplicate were executed by the said part**ies

at the   City   of   Toronto

3. **That I know the said part** ies.

4. **That I am a subscribing witness to the said Instrument and Duplicate.**

SWORN before me at the   City

of   Toronto

in the County

of   York

this   day of April   19 70

Dated   April 12   19 70

NORMA MARGRET DARKE

TO

WALTER KING, and
JANE MABEL KING

Address: 472 Lawn Blvd.,
Toronto.

Agreement
EXTENDING MORTGAGE

Dye & Durham Limited — Toronto, Canada
Printers to the Legal Profession

HILL, JOHNSTON & GRANT
17 Princess Street,
Toronto, Ontario.

*Figure 12.2. Agreement Extending Mortgage –
Back*

Discharge of Mortgage
Revised January, 1970

Dye & Durham Co. Limited, 76 Richmond Street East, Toronto
Form 137

To the Registrar of the Registry Division of TORONTO

I/~~We~~   FREDERICK GEORGE KINGSTON

of the   City of Toronto   in the   County of York

Do Certify that   LEWIS JAMES McKENZIE and RUTH JANE McKENZIE

ha ve satisfied all money due on, or to grow due on *

*Where applicable, substitute "has satisfied the sum of $ mentioned in" etc.

a certain mortgage made by   them

~~of~~

to me

which mortgage bears date the 15th   day of   April   1967 ,

and was registered in the Registry Office for the Registry Division of Toronto

on the   18th   day of   April   1967 , at   ten minutes past

Here mention the date and the date of registration and registered No. of each Assignment of the Mortgage and the names of the parties, or mention that such Mortgage has not been assigned according to the fact

ten   o'clock   a.m.   as No. 41141
                    (a.m. or p.m.)

and that such mortgage has   not   been assigned

Figure 12.3. Discharge of Mortgage –
Page 1

AND THAT I am

the person   entitled by law to receive the money,

AND THAT such mortgage*

*Where applicable substitute, "such sum of money as aforesaid"

is therefore discharged.

Where applicable insert: "Since the date of registration of the mortgage (part of) the land hereby discharged has been designated as Lots (numbers) by a plan registered in the said Registry Office as Plan No."

Witness my hand this   day of   December   1970

Witness

CAUTION

THE REGISTRY ACT provides that "where Land is mortgaged and subsequently subdivided by a registered plan of subdivision, a judge's plan, registrar's compiled plan, or any other registered plan by which lots are created, any certificate of discharge of the mortgage shall contain a description of the affected land with reference to the plan".

AFFIDAVIT AS TO LEGAL AGE

PROVINCE OF ONTARIO   I/WE   FREDERICK GEORGE KINGSTON

* COUNTY   of the   City of Toronto

OF   *in the   County of York
                    Fireman

YORK   To Wit:

NOTE: If Attorney, substitute in space provided "I am Attorney for (State name), one of the parties named therein and at the time of the Execution of the Power of Attorney he/she was of the full age of twenty-one years."

named in the within instrument, make oath and say that at the time of the execution of the within instrument, I/WE   was   of the full age of twenty-one years.

(SEVERALLY) SWORN before me at the   City

of   Toronto

in the*   County of York

this   day of   December   1970

A Commissioner for taking Affidavits, etc.

*In describing the Municipality; Insert County, United Counties, Provisional County, District or Regional Municipality, and the appropriate name in each case.

Figure 12.3. Discharge of Mortgage – Page 2

COUNTY
OF
YORK

To Wit:

I, PERCY YORK McQUILLER,

of the   City of Toronto,

in the*   County of York, Solicitor,

make oath and say:

1. That I was personally present and did see the within discharge of mortgage duly signed and executed by

Frederick George Kingston--
--one of the part!es thereto.

2. That the said discharge was executed by the said party   at the City   of   Toronto.

3. That I know the said party

4. That I am a subscribing witness to the said discharge of mortgage.

*For place of
residence insert
appropriate County,
District, Regional
Municipality, etc.

SWORN before me at the   City of Toronto

in the* County of York

this   day of   December   19 70 .

A Commissioner, etc.

I,

of the

in the*

To Wit:

do solemnly declare:

Declaration when
Duplicate Mortgage
or Duplicate
Assignment cannot
be produced.

1. That   the person   who signed the within discharge of mortgage.

2. That the registered duplicate,   mortgage No.
    made by

as mentioned in the within discharge of mortgage, cannot be produced for the reason that

And I make this solemn declaration conscientiously believing it to be true, and knowing that it is of the same force and
effect as if made under oath, and by virtue of the Canada Evidence Act.

DECLARED before me at the

in the*

this   day of   19

A Commissioner, etc.

Dated December 19 70

FREDERICK GEORGE KINGSTON

TO

LEWIS JAMES McKENZIE, and
RUTH JANE McKENZIE,

Address: 73 Monk Road,
         Toronto, Ontario.

Discharge of Mortgage

Dye & Durham Co. Limited, 76 Richmond Street East, Toronto

HILL, JOHNSTON & GRANT
17 Princess Street S.
Toronto, Ontario.

This Space is reserved for Registry Office Certificates.

*Figure 12.3. Discharge of Mortgage –
Back*

Dye & Durham
Limited
Toronto, Canada
Form 205 to 207

Cessation of Charge

𝕷𝖆𝖓𝖉 𝕿𝖎𝖙𝖑𝖊𝖘 𝕬𝖈𝖙

Authority by Owner of Charge to Notify Cessation of Charge

To the Master of Titles:

I,   HENRY JOHN CAMPBELL,

of the   City   of   Toronto

the registered owner of the Charge made by   SYDNEY JOHN GILBERT,

to (¹)   me

1. If the Charge has not been transferred insert "me". If it has been transferred insert the name of original Mortgagee and add "and transferred to me."

dated the   15th   day of   November   , 1962 , and
registered as No.   543211   on the Land registered in the Office of Land
Titles at   Toronto   as Parcel   2151   in the
Register for   Sec. P. Toronto   hereby
authorize the Master of Titles to notify on the Register the CESSATION of the said
Charge (²). _____

2. When only part of the land covered by the Charge is to be released, insert here, "as to the following land," and add a description of the land to be released.

Dated this   day of   December   , 1970

Witness

Figure 12.4.   Cessation of Charge – Page 1

Land Titles Act

I,   HENRY QUENTIN WINSLOW,

of the   Borough   of   Etobicoke

in the   County of York, Solicitor,

make oath and say:

I am well acquainted with   Henry John Campbell

named in the annexed document authorizing the Master of Titles to notify the Cessation of the Charge therein mentioned, and saw   him sign the said document and the signature   purporting to be   his signature   at the foot of the said document is in   h is   handwriting. The said   Henry John Campbell

is as I verily believe the owner of the said Charge;   he   is   of the

age   of 21 years or over,   is of sound mind and signed the said document voluntarily

at the   City   of   Toronto

in the   County of York   in the Province of Ontario.

I am a subscribing witness to the said document.

Sworn before me at the City of
Toronto
in the County

of York

this

day of   December   1970

A Commissioner, etc.

AFFIDAVIT TO BE MADE BY AN OFFICER AS TO AUTHORITY OF PERSONS EXECUTING FOR A CORPORATION OR COMPANY

Land Titles Act

I,

of the   in the

make oath and say:

(1) I am   of

(2)
whose signature is affixed to the annexed (or within) document is the
of the said company, and   whose signature
is also affixed thereto is the   thereof, and the seal
affixed thereto is the corporate seal of the said company.

(3) Under the by-laws of the said company the   and
are empowered to execute on behalf of the company
all deeds and other instruments requiring the seal of the company.
(If the officers executing are not authorized by by-laws then state how they are authorized).

(4) The said company is, I verily believe, the owner of the land (or charge) mentioned in the said document.

Sworn before me at

in the

of

this

day of   19

A Commissioner, etc.

Figure 12.4.   Cessation of Charge – Page 2   119

AFFIDAVIT AS TO LEGAL AGE

PROVINCE OF ONTARIO

* **COUNTY OF YORK**

To Wit:

I/~~WE~~ HENRY JOHN CAMPBELL

of the City of Toronto

*in the County of York,

Clerk

NOTE: If Attorney, substitute in space provided "I am Attorney for (State name), one of the parties named therein and at the time of the Execution of the Power of Attorney he/she was of the full age of twenty-one years."

named in the within instrument, make oath and say that at the time of the execution of the within instrument, I/WE was of the full age of twenty-one years.

(~~SEVERALLY~~) SWORN before me at the City

of Toronto

in the* County of York

this day of December 1970

A Commissioner for taking Affidavits, etc.

*In describing the Municipality, Insert County, United Counties, Provisional County, District or Regional Municipality, and the appropriate name in each case.

Application
—BY—

HENRY JOHN CAMPBELL

FOR ENTRY OF
𝕮essation of 𝕮harge
CREATED BY
𝕷and 𝕿itles 𝕬ct

Dye & Durham Limited — Toronto, Canada

SMITH, FRASER, HAMILTON
& WEBB
75 Maryvale Boulevard,
Toronto, Ontario.

Figure 12.4. Cessation of Charge – Back

Dye & Durham Co. Limited, 76 Richmond Street East, Toronto

Form 138

To the Registrar of the Registry Division of TORONTO

I/We   FREDERICK GEORGE KINGSTON, and DORIS RUTH KINGSTON,

of the   City of Toronto   in the   County of York

Do Certify that WAYSON ARNOLD LIGHT and SYLVIA DENISE LIGHT

*Where applicable substitute "has satisfied all money due on, or to grow due on a certain mortgage"

have satisfied the sum of $ 7,500.00----------mentioned in a certain mortgage

*

made by   them

~~of~~

to   HUMBER CONSTRUCTION LIMITED

which mortgage bears date the 17th   day of   June   1967,

and was registered in the Registry Office for the Registry Division of Toronto

on the 26th   day of   June   1967 , at six minutes past

three   o'clock p.m. as No. 54678
             (a.m. or p.m.)

Here mention the date and the date of registration and registered No. of each Assignment of the Mortgage and the names of the parties, or mention that such Mortgage has not been assigned according to the fact

and that such mortgage has   been assigned by assignment of mortgage dated the 20th of August, 1968, and registered in the Registry Office for the Registry Division of Toronto on the 25th day of August, 1968, at four minutes past eleven o'clock in the morning, as Number 3957, wherein Humber Construction Limited assigned its interest to Frederick George Kingston and Doris Ruth Kingston.

AND THAT we are

the person**s** entitled by law to receive the money,

AND THAT such part of the land as hereinafter particularly described, that is to say

(Legal description)

is therefore discharged.

W̶i̶t̶n̶e̶s̶s̶ our hand**s** this day of December 1970

W̶i̶t̶n̶e̶s̶s̶

_____
Frederick George Kingston

_____
Doris Ruth Kingston

CAUTION

THE REGISTRY ACT *provides that "where Land is mortgaged and subsequently subdivided by a registered plan of subdivision, a judge's plan, registrar's compiled plan, or any other registered plan by which lots are created, any certificate of discharge of the mortgage shall contain a description of the affected land with reference to the plan".*

AFFIDAVIT AS TO LEGAL AGE

PROVINCE OF ONTARIO

. COUNTY OF YORK

To Wit:

I/WE FREDERICK GEORGE KINGSTON and DORIS RUTH KINGSTON,

of the City of Toronto

*in the County of York

NOTE: If Attorney, substitute in space provided "I am Attorney for (State name), one of the parties named therein and at the time of the Execution of the Power of Attorney he/she was of the full age of twenty-one years."

named in the within instrument, make oath and say that at the time of the execution of the within instrument, I̶/WE were each of the full age of twenty-one years.

(SEVERALLY) SWORN before me at the City

of Toronto

in the* County of York

this day of December 19 70

A Commissioner for taking Affidavits, etc.

*In describing the Municipality, insert County, United Counties, Provisional County, District or Regional Municipality, and the appropriate name in each case.

*Figure 12.5. Partial Discharge of Mortgage –
Page 2*

COUNTY
OF
YORK

To Wit:

I,   JOHN ERNEST CRAIGMORE
of the   City of Toronto
in the*   County of York, Solicitor

make oath and say:

1. That I was personally present and did see the within discharge of mortgage duly signed and executed by
    Frederick George Kingston and Doris Ruth Kingston——————————
                                                  two of the   parties thereto.
2. That the said discharge was executed by the said parties at the   City   of   Toronto.   .
3. That I know the said parties.
4. That I am a subscribing witness to the said discharge of mortgage.

*For place of residence insert appropriate County, District, Regional Municipality, etc.

SWORN before me at the City of Toronto
in the*   County of York

this   day of   December   1970 .

A Commissioner, etc.

To Wit:

I,
of the
in the*

do solemnly declare:

Declaration when Duplicate Mortgage or Duplicate Assignment cannot be produced.

1. That   the person   who signed the within discharge of mortgage.

2. That the registered duplicate,   mortgage No.
made by

as mentioned in the within discharge of mortgage, cannot be produced for the reason that

And I make this solemn declaration conscientiously believing it to be true, and knowing that it is of the same force and effect as if made under oath, and by virtue of the Canada Evidence Act.

DECLARED before me at the
in the*

this   day of   19   .

A Commissioner, etc.

Dated   December   19 70

FREDERICK GEORGE KINGSTON, and DORIS RUTH KINGSTON,

TO

WAYSON ARNOLD LIGHT, and SYLVIA DENISE LIGHT,

Address: 135 Adorne Road, Toronto, Ontario.

Discharge
OF PART OF MORTGAGED LANDS

Dye & Durham Co. Limited, 76 Richmond Street East, Toronto

HILL, JOHNSTON & GRANT
17 Princess Street S.
Toronto, Ontario

This Space is reserved for Registry Office Certificates.

Figure 12.5. Partial Discharge of Mortgage – Back

CHAPTER 13

Buying and Selling Real Property

Agreement of Purchase and Sale

The first step in a real estate transaction is the execution of an *offer to purchase* (Figure 13.1). This printed form is usually completed by a real estate agent, and calls for information as to the name and address of the solicitors for both the purchaser and the vendor.

If Brown wishes to purchase a house owned by White, and which White is offering for sale, Brown will sign an offer to purchase and submit it to White for his consideration. If White accepts the offer, he signs his name and the completed agreement is known as an *agreement of purchase and sale*.

This agreement sets out the property involved, states the price, the terms of payment, the date on which the sale is to close, and other special terms and conditions. In addition, the agreement of purchase and sale provides that the purchaser may search title and submit any requisitions (questions as to the validity of title to the property) within a stated number of days. If there are claims or questions which the vendor cannot answer or satisfy, the agreement may be null and void, and any deposit money may be returned to the purchaser.

In all parts of Canada there are provincial government offices where instruments of title, that is, deeds or mortgages, may be deposited. There is no law compelling property owners to register their instruments of title, but registration constitutes notice to all the world of an interest in the property, and it is therefore common practice to have instruments relating to land registered. In this way the record of ownership is preserved and protected.

Frequently the first indication a lawyer has that a client is buying or selling real property is receipt of an agreement of purchase and sale. Upon receipt of this agreement, a file is opened for the client. A special folder (Figure 13.2) is sometimes used, and provides a handy check list of the routine required to complete the transaction. In some offices a coloured file folder may be used to identify all files concerned with real estate transactions, and a list similar to that in Figure 13.2 is often stapled into the inside file cover.

Following receipt of an agreement of purchase and sale, the handling of the transaction depends on whether the lawyer acts for the purchaser or vendor. In our consideration of those steps we shall assume the transaction involves land under the Registry Office system.

Acting for the Purchaser

In a real estate transaction the solicitors for the purchaser have a great deal of responsibility to protect the client's interest, and to ensure that he acquires everything he is entitled to receive. In order to accomplish this, his solicitor takes the steps outlined below.

Diary Entries

In his diary entries are made of the following dates, ascertained from the agreement of purchase and sale: (1) expiry date for making requisitions as to any questions concerning the validity of the title, (2) closing date for the transaction.

Direction

A direction (Figure 13.3) is obtained from the purchaser indicating how title is to be taken to the property. If a man is married, this direction indicates if title is to be held in the name of the man and his wife, and if so, whether as join tenants or as tenants in common.

Letter to Vendor's Solicitors

A letter is sent to the solicitors for the vendor advising that the law firm is acting for the purchaser and indicating how the purchaser wishes to take title. A draft deed and a statement of adjustments are requested. The vendor's solicitors are also asked to provide a copy of a survey of the property being sold. This is important, since the purchaser's solicitor must ensure that the property being purchased is exactly as described. The purchaser's solicitors must also check with the municipality to ensure that no municipal by-laws are being breached.

Searches

Of all the steps taken by the solicitor for the purchaser, searches are perhaps the most important. It is the function of the solicitor to ensure that his client gets a valid title to the real property. In order to do this there are a number of steps that he must take.

Title

If the property is registered under the Registry Office system, the lawyer attends at that office to search the title to the property and prepare an *abstract of title,* that is, a chronological history of all instruments and events affecting title to the real property. This abstract commences with the present owner, lists all instruments registered in connection with title to the property, and shows all registered sales and mortgages. This search goes back for a period of forty years. (If the property is under the Land Titles system, the government guarantees title, and only the most recent entries must be searched.)

The offices dealing with registration of instruments in connection with real property, charge a fee for searching a title. This fee is a disbursement charged to the client when the account is rendered following the close of the transaction.

The title searcher also checks with the sheriff of the appropriate county to ensure that there are no unpaid judgments registered against the owner of the property. Court judgments are *liens* (claims) against the property. There are also other searches which must be completed to ensure there are no unregistered liens against the property, such as retail sales tax or corporation tax

liens, to name only a few. These liens attach to the property and a purchaser takes the property subject to these liens.

Sometimes the search reveals what is known as an *encumbrance,* for example, an undischarged mortgage, or an execution (registration of an unpaid judgment against previous owners of the property, or a lien for unpaid corporation tax). If this was not referred to in the agreement of purchase and sale, a letter of requisition is written to the vendor's solicitors requesting that the encumbrance be removed prior to closing. In the event that the encumbrance is not removed, the purchaser does not have to complete the transaction.

Tax Certificates

Realty Taxes

The Tax Department of the municipality in which the property is located is requested by letter to provide a certificate showing the amount of paid and unpaid realty taxes on the property outstanding as of the closing date of the transaction (Figure 13.4). There is usually a fee of $1.00 payable to the municipality for this certificate.

It is important to know the state of the realty taxes, since this is one area in which an adjustment is made on closing the transaction.

Corporation Taxes

The Office of the Provincial Secretary is requested to provide a certificate showing the amount of paid or unpaid corporation taxes affecting the property as of the closing date of the transaction. This certificate (usually a letter) is only requested if any of the previous owners of the property were companies.

Retail Sales Taxes

The local office of the Retail Sales Tax Department, in provinces which levy such a tax, is requested to provide a certificate showing any claim for unpaid retail sales taxes owing by previous owners of the property.

OFFER TO PURCHASE

Dye & Durham Limited Toronto
Printers to the Legal Profession
Form No. 116

I/WE, RONALD CRAIG ANDERSON and LUCILLE CAROLINE ANDERSON

of the ....City........ of ....Toronto........ (as purchaserS), hereby agree to and with

JOHN SMITH and MARY SMITH

(as vendorS), through ..BROWN REAL ESTATE LIMITED.. Agent ....

to purchase all and singular the premises situate on the ....south........ side of ..Helena Avenue..

in the ....City........ of ....Toronto........ known as ..984 Helena Avenue..,

--- (herein called "the real property")

having frontage of about ....twenty---(20)---.... more or less, by a depth of about ..eighty--(80)--feet..

being ..easterly half.. Lot No. ..105.. according to Plan No. ..5948..

Registered in the Registry Office ..for the Registry Division of Toronto..

at the price or sum of ..Twenty-Eight Thousand Nine Hundred--------.. Dollars ($..28,900..)

as follows: ..One Thousand--------------------------------------..Dollars ($..1,000..)

cash or certified cheque to the said Agent/Vendor on this date as a deposit, and covenant, promise and agree to pay

a further sum of Nine Thousand Six Hundred--($9,600.00)--Dollars to the vendor
by cash or by certified cheque on date of closing subject to the usual
adjustments.

Vendor agrees to take back a first mortgage for the balance of the purchase
price, namely $18,300.00, repayable $500.00 quarter-yearly off principal
plus interest at the rate of ten per centum per annum, and having five
years to run, said mortgage to contain the privilege of renewing for a
further period of five years on the same terms and conditions, save only
for the proviso for renewal and providing payments are not in default.
Said mortgage being open after the first five years and remaining open for
the further period of five years, giving the purchaser the privilege of
paying a greater amount or all at any time or times without notice or bonus.

The following items, the property of the Vendor, shall be included in this sale for the price above mentioned:— Storm and
all screen doors; aluminium doors and storm windows; electric light fixtures;
T.V. antennae, oil burner and equipment; runners on stairs and halls; drapery
tracks. The hot water heater is on rental basis from the Hydro.
PROVIDED the title is good and free from all encumbrances, except local rates, and except as aforesaid; said title to be examined
by me at my own expense, and the Purchaser is not to call for the production of any title Deeds or Abstracts of Title, Proof or
Evidence of Title, or to have furnished any copies thereof, other than those in Vendor's possession or under his control. The
Purchaser accepts the property subject to the restrictions and covenants that run with the land providing the same have been
complied with. The Purchaser to be allowed thirty (30) days from the date of acceptance hereof to investigate the title
at his own expense, and if within that time he shall furnish the Vendor in writing with any valid objection to the title which the
Vendor shall be unable or unwilling to remove, and which Purchaser will not waive, this agreement shall be null and void and the
deposit money returned to the Purchaser without interest.
This offer to be accepted by November 14th 19 70, otherwise void; and sale to be completed on or before the
15th day of December 1970 , on which date possession of the said premises is to be given to the
Purchaser, or he is to accept the present tenancies and to be entitled to the receipt of the rents and profits thereafter. This offer,
when accepted, shall constitute a binding contract of purchase and sale and time in all respects shall be the essence of this agreement.
It is agreed that there is no representation, warranty, collateral agreement or condition affecting this agreement or the real property
or supported hereby other than as expressed herein in writing.
Until completion of sale, all buildings and equipment on the property shall be and remain at the risk of the Vendor until closing
and the Vendor will hold all policies of insurance effected on the property and the proceeds thereof in trust for the parties hereto, as
their interests may appear. In the event of damage to the said buildings and equipment before the completion of this transaction,
the Purchaser shall have the right to elect to take such proceeds and complete the purchase, or cancel this agreement, whereupon the
Purchaser shall be entitled to the return without interest of all monies theretofore paid on account of this purchase.
Unearned Fire Insurance Premiums, Fuel, Taxes, Interest, Rentals and all Local Improvements and Water Rates to be proportioned
and allowed to date of completion of sale; Deed or Transfer to contain covenant on part of the Purchaser to pay off any Mortgage
that by the terms of this instrument is to be assumed and prepared at the expense of Vendor on form acceptable to the Purchaser's
solicitor and if mortgage is to be given back, same to be prepared at the expense of the Purchaser on a form acceptable to Vendor and
drawn pursuant to The Short Forms of Mortgages Act, Ontario.
Any tender of documents or money hereunder may be made upon the solicitor acting for the party on whom tender is desired and
it shall be sufficient that a negotiable certified cheque may be tendered instead of cash.
Each party is to pay the costs for registration and taxes on his own documents.
Whenever the singular or masculine are used in this Offer, they shall mean and include the plural and feminine if the context or the parties hereto so require.

Dated at ..Toronto.. this ..12th.. day of ..November.. 19 70

SIGNED, SEALED AND DELIVERED IN WITNESS whereof we have hereunto set our hand s and seal s,

in the presence of:

Herman G. Roberts   *Ronald C. Anderson*
Ronald Craig Anderson

Lucille Caroline Anderson
Lucille Caroline Anderson

I/WE, hereby accept the above offer and its terms, and covenant, promise and agree to and with the said above-named purchaser to
duly carry out the same on the terms and conditions above mentioned, and I hereby accept the deposit of $1,000 out of which
the agent hereby authorized to retain its commission of 5 per cent of an amount equal to
the above mentioned sale price. Commission is only payable if the transaction is duly closed.
Dated at Toronto this 13th day of November, 1970.
Witness:

Herman G. Roberts   *John Smith*
Mary Smith

Figure 13.1. Offer to Purchase

COUNTY | 𝕵, HERMAN GEORGE ROBERTO

OF | of the   City   of   Toronto

YORK | in the   County of York

To Wit: | make oath and say

1. That I was personally present and did see the within or annexed Instrument and a Dup-
    licate thereof duly signed, sealed and executed by Ronald Craig Anderson,

    Lucille Caroline Anderson, John Smith and Mary Smith--------

                                        all of the parties   thereto

2. That the said Instrument and Duplicate were executed by the said parties

        at the   City   of   Toronto.

3. That I know the said parties.

4. That I am a subscribing witness to the said Instrument and Duplicate

SWORN before me at the   City

of Toronto

in the   County of York

of-

this

day of   November   1970

A Commissioner, etc.

Dated   November 12,   1970

RONALD CRAIG ANDERSON
and LUCILLE CAROLINE
ANDERSON

TO

JOHN SMITH and
MARY SMITH

Offer to Purchase

Dye & Durham Co. Limited, 76 Richmond Street East, Toronto
Law and Commercial Stationers

Vendor's Solicitor Smith, Fraser, Hamilton & Webb, 75 Maryvale Boulevard,
                                                        Toronto 4
Wife's Name   Mary Smith

Purchaser's Solicitor Hill, Johnston & Grant, 17 Princess Street S., Toronto

Wife's Name   Lucille Caroline Anderson

Deed or Transfer to be made to Ronald Craig Anderson and Lucille Caroline
                        Anderson, as joint tenants

Figure 13.1. Offer to Purchase – Back

Sale or Purchase of

To Close

CLIENT .... Add. ....Ph...............

OTHER PARTY .... New Add. ....Ph...............

    Solicitor .... Add. ....Ph...............

PRE CLOSING ROUTINE
ORDER

( ) Tax Cert. ....

( ) Corp. Tax Cert. ....

( ) Survey ....

( ) Draft deed or mtge. ....

TITLE:

....

....

( ) 1st mtge. state ....

( ) 2nd mtge. state ....

PREPARE

( ) State. of Adjust. ....

( ) Insurance transfers ....

( ) Increase Insurance to ....

( ) Deed ....

( ) Mortgage ....

( ) Direction re Proceeds ....

( ) Direction re Grantees ....

( ) Notice to Tenants ....

( ) Acknowledgement by Tenants ....

REQUISITIONS

    Last Date ....

    Sent ....

    Answered ....

MISCELL.

    Key at ....

    Oil .... Gas ....

REPORTING

    Mortgagee Advised ....

    Deposit Forwarded ....

    Ins. Transferred ....

    Ins. Forwarded ....

    Treasurer Notified ....

    Report Done ....

GENERAL INFORMATION

1st mtgee - Name..

    Address..

    Pr. $..................... + int. at ....%

    Repayable $..

2nd mtgee - Name...

    Address..

    Pr. $..................... + int. at ....%

    Repayable $..

Grantee or mtgee ....

....

....

....

....

Search Executions

....

....

....

....

....

Undertaking given or received

....

....

....

....

Cheques Required ....

$ ....

$ ....

$ ....

$ ....

Date deal Closed ....

SPECIAL NOTES

Date Received .... Given Title Searcher .... Fee........................

DYE & DURHAM LTD. NO. 80 REAL ESTATE R.T.

Figure 13.2. Front Cover of Special File
Folder for Real Estate Transactions

D I R E C T I O N

TO: John Smith and Mary Smith

AND TO: Messrs. Smith, Fraser, Hamilton
              & Webb
           Barristers and Solicitors
           75 Maryvale Boulevard
           Toronto 514, Ontario

           Anderson and Smith
           Purchase of 984 Helena Avenue, Toronto

I, the undersigned Ronald Craig Anderson, the purchaser of the above lands by way of an agreement of purchase and sale, hereby authorize and direct you to make the deed in the above transaction as hereinafter set out, and this shall be your good and sufficient authority for so doing.

> RONALD CRAIG ANDERSON, of the City of Toronto,
> in the County of York, Physician, and LUCILLE
> CAROLINE ANDERSON, his wife, of the same place,
> as joint tenants and not as tenants in common.

        DATED at Toronto this   day of December, 1970.

WITNESS:

_____   _____

Figure 13.3. Direction on Taking Title   129

SPECIMEN ONLY

ISSUED TO:

BOROUGH OF ETOBICOKE   **5127**

TREASURER'S CERTIFICATE OF TAX STANDING
(WATER AND HYDRO RATES ARE NOT INCLUDED)

Date Issued _____ **JULY 18th, 1969**

LOT: **27**

TAX ROLL No... **00-123**

PLAN OR CONCESSION: **FTH**

PROPERTY ADDRESS: **69 Alder Road**   **Etobicoke, Ontario**   FEE $ **1.00**

ASSESSED OWNER: **John Doe**

STATEMENT OF TAX ARREARS

Years: 19 ____   Taxes $ _____

Under Section 146   Interest $ _____
of the
Assessment Act.   Total $ _____

TAXES PAID TO: DECEMBER 31   19 **68**

I hereby certify that other than shown above there are no arrears of taxes unpaid against the above lands and that no part of the said lands have been sold, nor has a vesting certificate been registered within the last 18 months.

STATEMENT OF CURRENT TAXES

Interim Bill Only ☐
Total Current Year ☒
Year: 19 **69**   Taxes Levied $ **500.00**

Under Section   Taxes Payable $ _____
119 of the
Assessment Act.   Taxes Owing $ **500.00**

Penalty $ **nil**

TOTAL $ **500.00**

I hereby certify that other than shown above there are no current taxes unpaid against the above lands and that no part of the said lands have been sold, nor has a vesting certificate been registered within the last 18 months. Subsequent supplementary taxes are not included.

_____
For Treasurer

Figure 13.4. Specimen Tax Certificate

Other Liens

There are also searches which must be completed to ensure that there are no outstanding chattel mortgages, conditional sales, public utility or Workmen's Compensation Board liens which affect the property.

After all these searches have been completed and the lawyer is satisfied that there are no encumbrances against the property, the *pro rata* (proportionate) amount owing by the vendor for realty taxes is calculated as of the date of closing, and either the vendor or the purchaser is credited with an amount on the statement of adjustments (see Chapter 14), depending on whether the vendor has paid all, part, or none of the realty taxes for that year. If there are arrears in realty taxes, these are shown as a credit to the purchaser against the purchase price of the property, since the purchaser will have to pay the municipality any such arrears.

Building Restrictions

The Building Department of the municipality in which the property is located is requested to indicate what zoning restrictions might affect the property; for example, size and type of construction, distance from street and side lot lines, minimum floor and lot areas. This request is made by letter, and a copy of the survey of the property should also be forwarded with the letter to assist the Department in determining whether or not the survey shows any transgressions of existing or proposed municipal by-laws. Copies of the by-laws affecting the property should be purchased and checked against any existing use or uses the purchaser intends to make of the property. The by-laws will also reveal any limitations or prohibitions concerning additions or improvements the purchaser may intend to make to the property.

Deed and Statement of Adjustments

It is necessary to check and approve the draft deed and statement of adjustments prepared by the vendor's solicitors.

Mortgages

In most real estate transactions part of the purchase price is covered by a mortgage.

This mortgage may be (1) a mortgage taken back by the vendor, (2) an existing mortgage on the property which the purchaser is assuming, or (3) a mortgage with a third party, usually a mortgage company who will advance funds to the purchaser to be used to pay the balance due on closing the transaction.

Mortgage Back

If the vendor is taking back part of the purchase price by way of a mortgage (i.e., the purchaser is giving the vendor a mortgage on the property), the solicitors for the purchaser draft that instrument, and forward one copy to the vendor's solicitors for approval. When it is approved, the purchaser executes it in duplicate, and the executed mortgage is held in the file until the date for closing the transaction.

Mortgage Assumed

If the purchaser is taking over a mortgage already existing on the property, a mortgage statement should be obtained from the mortgagee certifying the exact amount owing on the mortgage the day of closing. The lawyer will ensure that the mortgage does not contain any special clauses which adversely affect the purchaser.

Mortgage with Mortgage Company

If the purchaser is arranging a mortgage with a mortgage company, the vendor is not involved. An application for the mortgage is completed by the purchaser, and when the application is approved, the purchaser's solicitors prepare the necessary mortgage for approval by the mortgage company.

When approved, the mortgagor executes it in duplicate, the executed mortgage is forwarded to the company, and arrangements are made to provide the money covered by the mortgage.

In many cases where an individual is building a home, a mortgage is arranged quite early and monies are advanced as construction proceeds.

Cheques to Close

Cheque for Vendor

The vendor's solicitors will indicate by means of a signed direction from the vendor how the cheque on closing is to be made payable: whether to the vendor, or to his solicitors. With this direction it is necessary to request from the purchaser either a certified cheque for the balance due on closing (set out in the statement of adjustments), or a cheque payable to your law firm for the balance due and the fees and disbursements.

If the cheque is made payable to the purchaser's law firm, it is deposited in the trust account, and a certified, trust cheque is drawn for the balance due on closing, payable as directed by the vendor. The amount remaining in the trust account is transferred to the firm account when the transaction has been completed, in payment of the account for services rendered.

Cheques for Registration Fee and Tax

When making the final arrangements to close the transaction, the purchaser's solicitors also require cheques to pay the land transfer tax and the fee to register the deed.

Closing

A time is arranged to close the transaction on the day set out in the agreement of purchase and sale and the necessary cheques are obtained.

When we have considered what steps the solicitors for the vendor must take before closing the transaction, we will discuss what happens on closing a real estate transaction.

Acting for the Vendor

In a real estate transaction the vendor's solicitors are responsible to ensure that he gives good title, and receives in return the purchase price and all adjustments to which he is entitled. In order to accomplish this, the solicitor for the vendor takes the steps outlined below.

Diary Entries

In his diary the following dates are entered: (1) expiry date for making requisitions as to any encumbrance on title, (2) closing date for the transaction.

Material from Vendor

The vendor is requested to furnish the following:
1. his copy of the deed to property, and a copy of any mortgage on the property
2. a survey of the property
3. the tax bill for the current year
4. the insurance policies on the property
5. copies of leases (if any) and names of tenants
6. water bills
7. hydro bills
8. fuel bills.

Mortgages

Existing Mortgage on Property

If there is an existing mortgage on the property which the purchaser is to assume, the vendor furnishes full particulars of this mortgage. A letter is written to the mortgage company requesting a mortgage statement, showing the balance outstanding on the mortgage, plus interest, as of the date of closing the sale. This information is required for preparing the statement of adjustments.

If there is an existing mortgage on the property which the purchaser is not going to assume, the vendor's solicitors arrange to discharge the mortgage by having it paid off before the transaction is closed. In these circumstances the monies paid on closing the transaction are made payable to the vendor's solicitors so that they will have funds to discharge the mortgage.

Mortgage Back

If the vendor is taking back a mortgage as part of the purchase price, the purchaser's solicitors are requested to prepare and submit a draft mortgage for approval.

Insurance on Mortgage Back

If there is an existing first mortgage which the purchaser is assuming, and the vendor is also taking back a second mortgage, the two mortgages are added together and the insurance agent is asked (often by telephone) to increase the insurance coverage as of the date of closing. The cost for this increased protection is ascertained, and this amount is included as a credit to the vendor on the statement of adjustments.

Deed

A draft deed is prepared, and one copy forwarded to the solicitor for the purchaser for approval, along with the survey of the property.

When the draft deed has been approved, the vendor will execute it in duplicate. The executed deed is retained in the file until the date for closing the transaction.

Statement of Adjustments

A statement setting out the purchase price and all adjustments for realty taxes, fire insurance, mortgages and public utilities, is prepared and two copies are sent to the purchaser's solicitor. If a mortgage is being assumed, the mortgage statement is also sent with the statement of adjustments.

Direction

The vendor signs a direction (Figure 13.5) stating how he wishes the cheque for the balance due on closing to be payable. The usual practice is for this cheque to be made payable to his firm of solicitors, for deposit in its trust account. Subsequently there is a payment to him of the amount to which he is entitled. Deductions are made in order to pay off any outstanding mortgages which must be discharged, and to pay the account of his solicitors.

Insurance Transfers

The transfers of insurance forms are completed.

Closing

The time for closing the transaction is arranged.

Closing the Real Estate Transaction

At the agreed time on the date scheduled close the real estate transaction, lawyers for the purchaser and the vendor meet at the appropriate Registry Office.

Immediately before the time for closing the purchaser's lawyer checks with the Sheriff's Office to search for executions (judgments or liens) against the property, and brings the search of title up to date to ensure that no additional instruments have been registered against the property since the date of the original search.

The purchaser's lawyer delivers to the vendor's lawyer the duly executed mortgage in duplicate, and the certified cheque for the balance due on closing.

The vendor's lawyer delivers to the purchaser's lawyer the duly executed deed in duplicate, the keys to the property, a certified copy of the insurance policy on the building, and completed assignments of the policy, noting the interest of the purchaser as the new insured, subject to the interests of any mortgages.

With the exchange completed, the real estate closing is completed.

Acting for the Purchaser after Closing

Registry of Deed

Immediately upon receipt of the deed from the vendor, it is registered in the Registry Office, and the required registration fee paid. If a tax is levied on the transfer of title, this tax must be paid before the instrument is registered.

After the fee and any tax applicable is paid, both copies of the deed are left in the Registry Office. One copy is returned with the registration details completed; the other copy remains permanently on file in the Registry Office.

Mortgage Assumed

If a mortgage has been assumed, the mortgagee is requested to send all further notices to the purchaser.

Taxes

The appropriate tax department is requested to send all further tax notices to the purchaser.

Insurance

The insurance company with which the property is insured is sent the copy of the insurance policy and the completed assignment, and requested to return the policy with an endorsement noting the change of ownership.

Reporting Letter

A reporting letter is written to the purchaser giving full details of the transaction, and enclosing all documents which were received on his behalf when the transaction was closed.

Account

If monies were received in advance to pay the account for services rendered, the purchaser will usually be sent a receipted account showing payment has been made. If no monies were received, an account covering services rendered is sent to the client.

Acting for the Vendor after Closing

Mortgage Back

If the vendor is taking a mortgage back, it is registered immediately after the transaction is closed. Both copies of the mortgage are left at the Registry Office, and one copy is subsequently returned endorsed with the registration information.

Mortgage Assumed

The mortgagee is informed of the sale, and given the name of the purchaser.

Tax Office

The appropriate tax department is notified of the change in ownership.

Reporting Letter

A reporting letter is sent to the vendor giving particulars of the transaction, enclosing all documents which were received on his behalf when the transaction was closed, together with a cheque for the monies to which he is entitled.

Account

The client is sent the firm's account for services rendered if no monies were received on closing to cover payment of these fees and disbursements.

In Chapters 14 and 15 we will consider in detail those aspects of a real estate transaction not previously discussed.

DIRECTION

TO: Ronald Anderson and Lucille Anderson

AND TO: Messrs. Hill, Johnston & Grant
          Barristers and Solicitors
          17 Princess Street South
          Toronto 560, Ontario

                Smith and Anderson
                Sale of 984 Helene Avenue, Toronto

We, the undersigned John Smith and Mary Smith,
the vendors of the above lands by way of an agreement of
purchase and sale, hereby authorize and direct you to
make the proceeds of the above sale to our solicitors,
Messrs. Smith, Fraser, Hamilton & Webb, and this shall
be your good and sufficient authority for so doing.

                DATED at Toronto this   day of December, 1970.

WITNESS:)
)
)
)
) _____
)   John Smith
)
)
) _____
)   Mary Smith

Figure 13.5. Direction as to Payment of
Proceeds

135

CHAPTER 14

Statement of Adjustments

It is the responsibility of the solicitor for the vendor to prepare and submit a detailed statement outlining the exact amount of money which the purchaser must pay when a real estate transaction is closed. Included in this amount are adjustments which must be made because of realty taxes paid or unpaid on the property for a period before and after the closing date, or for prepaid premiums on a policy of fire insurance covering a period when the vendor will no longer be the owner of the property. These and other items are set out in the *statement of adjustments*. Information on adjustments required on closing is included in the agreement of purchase and sale. Other required information is provided by the vendor to his solicitor from realty tax bills, insurance policies, water, hydro and fuel bills.

Preparation and Set-up

The statement of adjustments is prepared in the office of the solicitor for the vendor, and two copies are sent to the solicitor for the purchaser for approval. The secretary is often asked to calculate the adjustments. Printed forms are available for presenting the statement, but frequently the statement is completely typed. The style of set-up varies from office to office, and Figures 14.1 and 14.2 illustrate one style you may use.

Heading

There are various ways of heading a statement of adjustments, and there is no one correct way. While the arrangement of information varies, the same basic information appears in all headings:
1. the name of the paper, i.e., Statement of Adjustments
2. the date as of which the adjustments are made (i.e., the date on which the transaction is to close)
3. the name of the parties to the transaction
4. a brief description of the property which is the subject of the transaction.

Body

The body of the statement sets out the amounts due to the vendor, and the amounts which the purchaser has already paid or will pay to close the transaction. A simple formula is: prepaid expenses – allowance to the vendor; unpaid expenses – allowance to the purchaser.

Allowances to the vendor appear in the right-hand column of figures; allowances to the purchaser, in the left-hand column. Sufficient detail is provided for all items to allow the computations to be checked by the purchaser's solicitor.

The amounts shown on a statement as payable to the vendor include the purchase price of the property, allowances for prepaid expenses such as realty taxes, insurance, and fuel oil left in the tank if the building is heated by oil.

The amounts which the purchaser has paid, or which he may be given an allowance for, include the deposit paid, any mortgages which may have been assumed by the purchaser, any mortgages which the vendor is taking back, and any payments made on behalf of the vendor.

The difference between the amounts due to the vendor, and the amounts paid by or allowed to the purchaser, is the balance due on closing.

Ending

The abbreviation "E. & O. E." (errors and omissions excepted) is typed in the lower left-hand portion of the statement.

How to Compute Statements of Adjustments

Sale Price and Deposits

The amounts of the sale price and any deposits made are ascertained by reference to the agreement of purchase and sale.

Mortgages

In real estate transactions mortgages are often used in lieu of money to finance part of the purchase price. The purchaser may arrange a mortgage with a mortgage company or an individual, assume an existing mortgage, or give back to the vendor a mortgage on the property.

A statement of adjustments is concerned only with a mortgage assumed or a mortgage back.

Mortgage Assumed

If the purchaser is to assume an existing mortgage, the vendor's solicitor will have written to the mortgagee requesting a mortgage statement which indicates the amount of principal and accrued interest outstanding as of the closing date. The purchaser is credited for the total amount of the principal and accrued interest outstanding as of the day of closing, since this is a liability he is assuming from the vendor, and is therefore to be deducted from the amount to be paid to the vendor.

Mortgage Back

If the vendor is taking back a mortgage, the amount of such mortgage is shown as if the vendor had in fact already received the money, that is, as a credit to the purchaser.

Taxes

The vendor will frequently have paid all or part of the realty taxes for the current year. Since he will no longer be the owner of the house after the transaction is closed, the vendor is only responsible for taxes from January 1 to the date of closing, and is therefore given credit for any taxes he may have paid for a period *after* the closing date.

If the vendor has not paid the taxes for the year, these will have to be paid by the purchaser. The purchaser is allowed credit for the portion of the realty taxes covering the period *up to* the date of closing, since this is a liability the purchaser is assuming

from the vendor, and is therefore to be deducted from the amount to be paid to the vendor.

If the tax rate has not been determined at the date of closing, the lawyers for the two parties will estimate the taxes to determine the allowance to be made, and readjust any difference when the tax rate is determined later on in the year.

One of the first steps of the solicitor for the purchaser is to write to the appropriate Tax Department requesting a tax certificate to ascertain whether any realty taxes are outstanding on the property for past years or the current year.

To compute the tax allowance, divide the amount of realty taxes by 365 (366 if the year is a leap year), and determine the tax rate per day. Then determine the number of days for which an allowance is to be made, and multiply that number by the tax rate per day. This will give the allowance due to the appropriate party.

For example, if a transaction is to close on September 22 in a year which is not a leap year, and realty taxes of $730.00 have been paid, the allowance to the vendor will be $200.00. This figure is arrived at as shown below.

$$\text{Tax Rate: } \frac{\$730.00}{365} = \$2.00 \text{ per day}$$

Number of Days Prepaid by Vendor:	September	8
	October	31
	November	30
	December	31
		100 days

Allowance to Vendor: 100 x $2.00 = $200.00

If, however, the realty taxes had not been paid at the date of closing, and were to be paid by the purchaser, the purchaser would be allowed $530.00 for the 265 days the vendor was the owner of the property and therefore responsible for paying the taxes.

Insurance

Generally the vendor will carry a policy of fire insurance on the buildings, and this policy is transferred to the new owner on the day of closing, subject to the interests of any mortgagees. The vendor is entitled to be repaid for the amount of premiums covering the period after the date of closing to the expiry date of the policy.

Most fire insurance policies are for a period of three years; there are 1095 days in that period unless one of the years is a leap year.

To compute the allowance to the vendor, determine the number of days from the date of closing to the expiry date of the policy. Divide the number of days in the life of the policy into the total premium paid, and determine the rate per day. Multiply the number of days allowed to the vendor by the rate per day, and show the result as an allowance to the vendor.

Oil Tank

The vendor is expected to leave his oil tank completely full on the date of closing the transaction; most oil tanks hold 200 gallons of fuel. Therefore, on closing, the vendor is given an allowance for 200 gallons at the current per gallon rate.

Water Rates, Hydro, Telephone and Gas

It is not usually necessary to make any provisions in the statement of adjustments to cover these services. On closing, the vendor informs the Water Department, the Hydro, the Telephone Company, and the Gas Company (if the building is heated by gas) that he is selling and giving up possession on a particular day. The vendor requests them to attend on that day to read the appropriate meters, or disconnect the telephone, so that he may be billed up to and including the day of closing.

Rent

If any part of the property is rented to another party or parties, an adjustment of prepaid rent must be included in the statement of adjustments.

The vendor usually receives rent in advance, and is only entitled to it up to the day of closing. Any rent received for a period after that date is shown as a credit to the purchaser.

Balance Due

The amount of money which must be paid by the purchaser on closing is the total of all amounts due to the vendor, less all amounts already paid by or allowed to the purchaser. The amount due on closing is shown on the statement of adjustments.

If the purchaser's solicitor is satisfied that the statement of adjustments is correct, he will then request the purchaser to pay the balance due.

The balance due on closing is usually paid by a certified cheque made payable to the vendor or his solicitors in accordance with the vendor's written directions.

STATEMENT OF ADJUSTMENTS

as of January 15, 1970

Knight Sale to Cowley
1391 Chrisden Avenue
Township of Toronto

Sale Price		$31,900.00
Deposit	$ 1,000.00	

Mortgage to be assumed:
  The Canadian Bank of Commerce
  Principal:
	$9,053.14	

Plus: Interest at 5 1/2%
          from Dec. 26 to
          Jan. 15, 1970
	12.94	

Allow Purchaser	9,066.08	
Second Mortgage back to Vendor	13,000.00	

Municipal Taxes for 1970 estimated
  at $380.99.
  Allow Purchaser 15 days at
  $1.04 per day
	15.60	

Insurance: London and Midland
  General Insurance Company
  Policy No. 410747 for $20,000.00,
  expiring December 30, 1970.
  Three year premium $90.20
  Allow Vendor 349 days at 8¢ per day
		27.92

Second mortgage costs borne by Purchaser as per agreement		150.00
Fuel Oil: 200 gallons at 19.1¢		38.20
Balance due on closing	9,034.44	
	$32,116.12	$32,116.12

E. & O. E.

Figure 14.1. Statement of Adjustments   139

STATEMENT OF ADJUSTMENTS

as of December 15, 1970

Smith Sale to Anderson
984 Helena Avenue
City of Toronto

Sale Price		$28,900.00
Deposit	$ 1,000.00	
Mortgage Back	18,300.00	
Municipal Taxes for 1970 --$689.55 Allow Vendor 16 days at $1.89 per day		30.24
Insurance: Henderson and Loon General Insurance Company, Policy No. 12356 for $15,000 expiring January 31, 1971. Three year premium, $71.18. Allow Vendor 47 days at 6.5¢ per day		3.06
Fuel Oil: 200 gallons at 19.1¢		38.20
Balance due on closing	9,671.50	
	$28,971.50	$28,971.50

E. & O. E.

Figure 14.2. Statement of Adjustments – 2

CHAPTER 15

Insurance and Reporting Letters

Insurance

A policy of fire insurance held upon real property is usually transferred to the purchaser when the real estate transaction is closed. If the property is subject to a mortgage, it is a condition of the mortgage that fire insurance be carried, with any loss payable to the mortgagees as their interests may be in the property.

Therefore, as soon as the real estate transaction is closed, the purchaser's solicitors immediately formally notify the insurance company of the change of ownership.

Figure 15.1 illustrates the form which is completed by the solicitors for the vendor to arrange for this transfer. Three copies are prepared in advance of closing, and given to the purchaser's lawyer on closing. Two executed copies are sent, following closing, to the insurance company for its consent to the transfer.

Before completing the form, the solicitors for the vendor will check the coverage of the policy. Some policies cover contents or personal liability along with fire insurance on the building, but it is to the building fire insurance that reference is made when the item 1(a) is inserted in Figure 15.1. This item number is illustrative only, and is not necessarily the applicable item of any actual policy which may be transferred.

Signing of Transfer

Usually the solicitors for the vendor sign the request for transfer or assignment of insurance. In Figure 15.1, Thomas A. Beadle is a solicitor who practises alone. If he had been with a law firm, this section would appear as follows:

JOHN DAVID SMITH and
MARY JANE SMITH

by HILL, JOHNSTON & GRANT
Per: _____

The transfer requires that the application portion for transfer of insurance be signed, sealed, and delivered.

Return of Consent

The solicitors for the purchaser send two copies of the executed transfer to the insurance company whose policy is being transferred for the consent of that company to the transfer. The insurance company completes the consent section of the form, and returns a certified copy of the insurance policy with the consent attached. In addition, the insurance company will attach a printed form known as a mortgage clause, which sets out in detail the rights of the mortgagee.

The solicitors for the purchaser then forward the certified copy of the policy to the purchaser.

Reporting Letters

When the details of the transaction have all been completed, the solicitors for both parties write letters to their respective clients, reporting on all aspects of the transaction.

Reporting Letter of Solicitor for Purchaser

A reporting letter to the purchaser is much more detailed than the reporting letter to the vendor. The purchaser's solicitors give their client exact details of all facts of the transaction, and most important, certify that the purchaser has a good, marketable title to the property purchased.

Details are also given of any mortgages assumed or given back, the realty taxes, insurance coverage, conformity to local by-laws, and registered documents. The purchaser is sent copies of the important documents relating to the purchase including:
1. an executed copy of the registered deed
2. a copy of mortgages assumed or given

3. a survey of the property
4. certificates re realty and other taxes
5. a certified copy of the insurance policy
6. a copy of the statement of adjustments
7. a copy of the sheriff's certificate re executions.

In some offices a printed form is sometimes used to draft reporting letters to a purchaser. Figure 15.2 illustrates the first page of such a form. In other offices each reporting letter is individually dictated. Figure 15.3 illustrates the first page of an individually dictated reporting letter.

Reporting Letter of Solicitor for Vendor

A reporting letter to the vendor is not as detailed as that to the purchaser. The vendor is given details of the sale, and the following documents are returned to him: a copy of the statement of adjustments, an executed copy of any mortgage he may have taken back, any other material he may have furnished which was not forwarded to the purchaser's solicitors.

You will recall that, on closing, the vendor usually signs a direction indicating how the proceeds are to be made payable. Usually the proceeds are made payable to his solicitors so that their fees and disbursements may be paid, and the balance is then paid over to the vendor. Normally the vendor has received these monies before the reporting letter is forwarded. If he has not, a cheque for the appropriate amount is also enclosed with the letter.

DYE AND DURHAM LIMITED — FORM NO. 647

TRANSFER AND CONSENT

COMPANY___THE BROWN & GREEN INSURANCE COMPANY___POLICY No.___329465-10-D___

INSURED___JOHN DAVID SMITH & MARY JANE SMITH___DATE OF EXPIRY_July 10, 1972___

For value received___we___hereby transfer, assign and set over unto___RONALD CRAIG ANDERSON and LUCILLE CAROLINE ANDERSON_____of_Toronto, Ontario___

the Purchasers___all___our___right, title and interest in Item(s)_1(a)_of this Policy of Insurance
(Insert the words—the Purchaser or the Mortgagee of the Property or as Collateral Security as the case may be)

and all benefits and advantages to be derived therefrom_with loss, if any, payable to Stephen___
(Insert name of Mortgagee or other Payee, if any)

Trust Company, 1st mortgagee, and John David Smith and Mary Jane Smith, 2nd mortgagees, as their interests may appear.

Witness_our_hand and seal at_Toronto___this_10th_day of_December___1970

Signed, sealed and delivered in presence of

JOHN DAVID SMITH and MARY JANE SMIT
by___Thomas A. Beadle___
their Solicitors herein

CONSENT

_____, hereby consents
(Name of Company)
to the above assignment, subject, however, to all the provisos, conditions and stipulations contained in said Policy, or endorsed thereon, it being understood that if the assignment be made in favor of a mortgagee, or for collateral security, the insurance under said Policy shall continue in the name of the Insured, whose loss, if any, shall be payable to the Assignee, as the interest of such Assignee may appear.

Date_____   _____
Authorised Representative

Figure 15.1. Transfer of Insurance

Dear

Purchase From

_____

       The above transaction of purchase and sale having now been completed, I am pleased to enclose herein the following items:

1. Deed of Land
2. Statement of Adjustments
3. First Mortgage
4. First Mortgage Statement
5. Second Mortgage
6. Second Mortgage Statement
7. Account
8. Ledger Statement
9. Insurance
10. Amortization Schedules
11. Tax Bill
12. Water Bill

TITLE

       Title was taken in the names of
and   as joint tenants. The law of survivorship applies to joint tenancies and therefore if either of you should die, the survivor is the automatic owner of the whole.

DEED OR TRANSFER

       Gives you ownership to part of Lot   Plan
Registered as Instrument #   at   o'clock
on the   day of   197 .

STATEMENT OF ADJUSTMENTS

       Adjusted as of   197 . Amounts in the right-hand column are credited to the Vendor(s) and in the left-hand column are your credits.

Figure 15.2. First Page of Form
Reporting Letter Used to Draft Contents

Hill, Johnston & Grant

Barristers and Solicitors

TELEPHONE: 364-9999, AREA CODE 416
CABLE 3-1IL6 TORONTO

Suite 2501
17 Princess Street South
Toronto 560, Canada

Frank P. Hill, Q.C.   Henry Q. Winslow
Edward N. Johnston, Q.C. Percy Y. McQuiller
Peter T. Grant, Q.C.   Robert W. Burnsley
John L. Craigmore

Counsel: P. B. Ranwood, Q.C.

January 19, 1971

Mr. and Mrs. Ronald Anderson,
174 Prince William Avenue,
Toronto 560, Ontario.

Dear Mr. and Mrs. Anderson:

> Anderson Purchase from Peterson
> 174 Prince William Avenue

The purchase of the above property was closed at the Land Titles Office on January 15 last. The vendor was Mr. Percival Peterson, and the transfer is made to you as joint tenants.

We therefore now enclose the following material:

1. Duplicate original of transfer

2. File copy of mortgage

3. Certificate as to Title

4. Copy of Statement of Adjustments

5. Our account and ledger statement

The policy of insurance will be forwarded to you as soon as we have received it.

This property is subject to a first mortgage held by the Humber Life Insurance Company. Payments on account of principal in the amount of $300.00 with interest at nine per cent per annum are payable quarterly on the first days of February, May, August and November each year, and the balance of the principal falls due on the 1st day of February, 1976.

The taxes for 1970 have been paid in full. Taxes for 1971 were estimated at $730.00, and you have been allowed $30.00 as set out in the statement of adjustments.

The property is insured for $10,000.00 by the Moon Life Insurance Company. This is a three-year policy, for which the premium is $109.50. You are responsible for the payment of the premium for the unexpired term of this policy, as set out

Figure 15.3. First Page of Typed
Reporting Letter

CHAPTER 16

Leases

When the owner of real property agrees with another party to allow the second party to occupy and use that property, such an agreement is frequently put in writing. This agreement is called a *lease*.

A lease may be defined as an instrument proving the exchange of the right of possession of real property from the owner to another party in exchange for the payment of rent.

The parties to a lease are the *lessor* – the person who owns the property, and who gives the lease (also known as the "landlord"), and the *lessee* – the person who rents the property, and who receives the lease (also known as the "tenant").

Forms of Leases

Many leases are not in writing, but are simply oral agreements; for example, when one rents a room by the week. Other leases are in writing, and are usually prepared on printed forms which have been drawn up in accordance with the relevant provincial legislation governing leases. In Ontario this is The Short Forms of Leases Act.

A minimum of three copies of a lease is prepared; two are executed, and the third retained in the file. A lease is dated the day it is typed, and the body of the lease indicates the date from which it is to be effective. Figure 16.1 illustrates a completed lease.

Preparing a Lease

Information Required

The following information is required to prepare a lease:
1. the names of lessor and lessee
2. a description of the property being leased
3. the term of the lease
4. the amount of rent and the terms of payment
5. any special clauses.

Heading

The parties to the lease are described in the standard way showing name, general address, and occupation.

Body

The term of the lease is shown. This is the exact period of time during which the lease is to run or be effective. A lease usually starts on the first day of a stated month, and if it runs for twelve months is for one calendar year. For example, a lease which runs for one year, and which begins on December 1, 1971, terminates November 30, 1972.

The amount of rent is spelled out by stating the amount of rent to be paid during the term of the lease, and indicating how this is to be paid – usually monthly in advance, commencing with the month in which the lease begins. In a one-year lease commencing December 1, 1971, the first month's rent is due December 1, 1971, and the last month's rent, November 1, 1972.

Ending

Leases are executed by all parties to it; legal seals are required.

Affidavits

Leases require the lessor to complete an affidavit of legal age and marital status, and require the witness to complete an affidavit of execution.

Back

The back of a printed lease requires information as to the date it is made, the names of the parties, the term of the lease, and the yearly rental.

Typed Leases

Frequently special leasing arrangements are drawn up, and are typed out in their entirety in the law office. This often happens when a company constructing a new building obtains a short term loan to finance construction. When the building is completed, it may be sold to another company (often an insurance company), and "leased back" to the company which originally built it. Such leasebacks are quite detailed legal agreements, and are typed out in full on 14-inch conveyance paper.

Many copies may be required of this type of lease. It is usual to prepare drafts first, and then to *engross* (copy) the lease in final form, and duplicate (usually by Xerox) the necessary copies. If the lease contains many pages, it is usual to use a corner when assembling the sets.

Style of Typing

The style of typing follows standard requirements for typing legal instruments. However, in long leasing agreements the lease may be divided into sections, and the various paragraphs within that section numbered. Each section is frequently started on a new page. An illustration of this type of set-up is shown below.

Numbering the Pages

When a lengthy instrument such as a lease is being typed, the numbering of pages is frequently governed as follows:

1. In one continuous self-contained document, pages after the initial page are numbered consecutively from 2 to the end of the given number of pages. The first page is not numbered. Numbers are centred at the top of the page.
2. In a document which consists of a number of individual sections, each of which is started on a new page, each section is treated as a self-contained document for purposes of page numbering. For example, the first page of Section III would be 1, the second 2, and so on. Pages in self-contained sections are also frequently identified by the section to which they refer, with Arabic numbering used to refer to sections instead of Roman numerals. Each page is then identified by section number *and* the appropriate page number; that is, 3-1 represents the first page in Section III; 3-2, the second page in Section III, and so on. The next section, Section IV, is then paged as 4-1, 4-2, and so on.

    When the whole document is completed, overall consecutive page numbers are then typed in the bottom right-hand corner of each page starting with the figure 1, and proceeding progressively until the last page has been reached.

    Each page in the instrument then bears *two* page numbers; one in the bottom right-hand corner, which is the consecutive page number in the completed document, and one centred on the top line of type on the page, which is the section and page number within that section.

ARTICLE I
DEFINITIONS

1. ....
....

   (a) ....
....

      (i) ....
....

      (ii) ....

Dye & Durham Limited, 76 Richmond Street East, Toronto
Form No. 90-93

This Indenture

made (in duplicate) the   fourteenth   day of   November
one thousand nine hundred and   seventy.

In pursuance of The Short Forms of Leases Act, The Landlord and Tenant Act and amendments.

Between

RONALD CRAIG ANDERSON, of the
Township of Toronto, in the County
of Peel, Physician, and LUCILLE
CAROLINE ANDERSON, his wife, of the
same place,

hereinafter called the LESSOR S , of the FIRST PART

and

ELIZABETH MAUD PETERSON, of the
City of Toronto, in the County
of York, Secretary,

hereinafter called the LESSEE   , of the SECOND PART

Witnesseth, that in consideration of the rents, covenants and agreements hereinafter reserved

and contained on the part of the Lessee   , the Lessor s   DO   demise and LEASE unto the

Lessee   , h e r executors, administrators, successors and assigns, all that messuage or tenement

situate, lying and being in the Borough of Etobicoke, in the County of

York, municipally known as 277 Lakeshore Drive North,

Etobicoke.

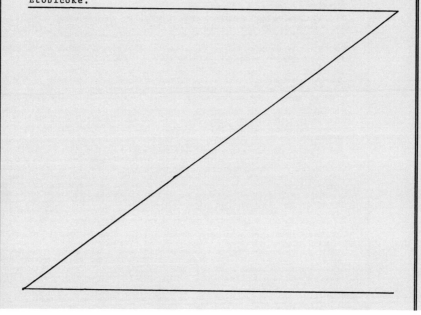

Figure 16.1. Completed House Lease – Page 1   147

TO HAVE AND TO HOLD the said demised premises for and during the term of two----(2)
years   to be computed from the   first   day of   December,
one thousand nine hundred and   seventy   and from thenceforth next ensuing and fully to be
complete and ended.

YIELDING AND PAYING therefor ~~yearly and every~~ year during the said term unto the Lessor,
his heirs, executors, administrators, or assigns, the sum of   THREE THOUSAND SEVEN HUNDRED AND
TWENTY ($3,720.00') – Dollars (of lawful money of Canada), to be payable on the following
days and times, that is to say, on   the first day of each month as follows:
ONE HUNDRED AND FIFTY-FIVE------($155.00)------DOLLARS on the
first days of December, 1970, January to December, inclusive, 1971
and January to November, inclusive, 1972,------------------------

the first of such payment to become due and be made on the   1st   day of   December, 1970.

The Lessee covenants with the Lessor to pay rent, to keep the premises in an ordinary state of
cleanliness, and to repair damage caused by his wilful or negligent conduct or that of persons permitted
on the premises by him; and will not assign or sublet without leave, such leave not to be arbitrarily or
unreasonably withheld.

The Lessee shall prepay to the Lessor the sum of $ ----------------which payment shall be
applied in payment of rent for the last month under this lease, and the Lessor shall pay to the Lessee
interest at the rate of 6% per annum on such prepayment.

PROVIDED that the Lessee may remove his fixtures, if such removal may be and is done without injury
to the said premises.

PROVIDED that in the event of damage by fire, lightning or tempest, rent shall cease until the premises
are rebuilt, and The Frustrated Contracts Act shall apply to this lease.

AND ALSO that if the term hereby granted shall be at any time seized or taken in execution or attachment,
by any creditor of the Lessee, or if the Lessee shall make an assignment for the benefit of creditors, or
becoming bankrupt or insolvent shall take the benefit of any Act that may be in force for bankrupt or
insolvent debtors, the then current rent, together with the rent for three months thereafter, shall immediately become due and payable, all subject to the provisions of The Landlord and Tenant Act, as amended.

THE Lessor covenants with the Lessee for quiet enjoyment.

THE Lessor shall maintain the demised premises in a good state of repair, fit for habitation during the
term of the lease, and complying with health and safety standards, including any housing standards
required by law, notwithstanding that any state of non-repair existed to the knowledge of the Lessee before
the lease was entered into. Subject to the provisions of The Landlord and Tenant Act, as amended, the
Lessor shall be entitled to enter the demised premises and view the state of repair and make such
alterations and repairs as necessary.

THE Lessor covenants with the Lessee that the Lessor will pay all taxes, rates, duties and assessments
whatsoever whether municipal, parliamentary or otherwise, including water rates for the supply of water
to the said building, which during the said term may be charged upon the demised premises or upon the
Lessor or Lessee in respect thereof. The Lessee covenants with the Lessor that the Lessee will pay all gas
and electric charges in connection with the demised premises and shall heat the said premises at his own
expense.

PROVIDED that the Lessee will not do anything or permit to be done on the said premises anything which
may be annoying to the Lessor or which the Lessor may deem to be a nuisance on the said premises or
by which the insurance on the building or buildings on said premises may be increased.

PROVIDED that the Lessee shall use and occupy the said premises as a private dwelling house only,
and will not carry on or permit to be carried on therein any trade or business.

PROVIDED that the Lessee shall not allow any ashes, refuse, garbage or other loose or objectionable
material to accumulate in or about the building, yards or passages of such premises and will at all times
keep the said premises in clean and wholesome condition, and shall, immediately before the termination
of the term hereby created, wash the floors, windows and woodwork of the premises hereby demised.

PROVIDED that the Lessee shall keep the lawns in good condition and shall not, during the said term,
injure or remove the shade trees, shrubbery, hedges or any other tree or plant which may be in, upon or
about the said premises, and shall keep the sidewalks in front and at the sides of the said premises free of
snow and ice.

THE Lessee covenants and agrees with the Lessor that he will not without the written consent of the Lessor
erect or cause to be erected on the said building or any part thereof any television or radio antenna or any
other device or apparatus whatsoever, and if any such television or radio antenna, device or apparatus is
erected without such written consent, to immediately remove the same upon request of the Lessor or his
agent or representative. The Lessee further agrees that if any such television or radio antenna, device or
apparatus is erected on the said building he (whether with or without the consent of the Lessor) will at his
own expense repair any damage done to the building or premises by reason of the erection, maintenance
or removal thereof and will indemnify and save harmless the Lessor, his servants or agents from all liability
for damages to persons or property as a result of the erection, maintenance or removal thereof.

THE Lessee further covenants and agrees with the Lessor that in case the said leased premises shall be
vacated or abandoned, the Lessor in addition to all other rights hereby reserved to him, shall have the
right to enter the same either by force or otherwise without being liable for any prosecution therefor, and
to re-let the said premises and to receive the rent therefor. PROVIDED that if the rent hereunder is overdue
and the premises are vacant, it shall be presumed that the Lessee has vacated or abandoned the said
premises and the Lessor shall be entitled to take immediate possession thereof.

Figure 16.1. Completed House Lease – Page 2

Dye & Durham Limited

Nothing in this lease contained and no entry made by the Lessor hereunder shall in any way release the Lessee from payment of the rent hereby reserved during the term hereof beyond such sum as may be realized by the Lessor by the re-letting hereinbefore allowed.

THE Lessor shall not be liable for any damage to any property at any time in the said premises or building from gas, water, steam, waterworks, rain or snow, which may leak into, issue or flow from any part of the said building of which the premises hereby leased are a part or from the pipes or plumbing works of the same, or from any other place or quarter.

THE Lessee shall give the Lessor prompt written notice of any accident or other defect in the water pipes, gas pipes or heating apparatus, telephone, electric light or other wires.

THE Lessee shall be liable for any damage done by reason of water being left running from the taps in the demised premises or from gas permitted to escape therein.

PROVIDED that if the Lessee be assessed as a Separate School Supporter, he will pay to the Lessor a sum sufficient to cover the excess of the Separate School tax, over the public school tax, if any, for a full calendar year and the Lessee shall pay to the Lessor on demand, as additional rent, any increase in real property taxes and local improvements assessed against the said premises over and above those levied for the said calendar year.

PROVIDED that if the Lessee remain in occupation of the demised premises after the expiration of the term hereby granted without a written agreement to the contrary, he shall not be deemed to be a tenant from year to year, but shall be a monthly tenant at a rental equivalent to the monthly payment of rent herein provided for, payable in advance, and all the terms and conditions hereof, so far as applicable, shall apply to such monthly tenancy.

THE acceptance by the Lessor of arrears of rent or compensation for use or occupation of the premises after notice of termination of the lease has been given shall not operate as a waiver of the notice or as a reinstatement of the lease or as a creation of a new lease unless the parties so agree.

PROVIDED that upon notice of termination of the lease being given, the Lessor shall have the right, at reasonable times during daylight, to enter and show the demised premises to prospective tenants; otherwise, except in cases of emergency, the Lessor shall not exercise a right to enter the rented premises unless he has first given written notice to the Lessee at least twenty-four hours before the time of entry, which shall be during daylight and specified in the notice.

IF the Lessee is obliged to vacate the demised premises on or before a certain date and the Lessor has entered into a lease with a third party to rent the said premises after such date and the Lessee fails to vacate the said premises thereby causing the Lessor to be liable to such third party, then the Lessee shall, in addition to any other liability hereunder, indemnify the Lessor for all losses suffered by reason of his failure to vacate.

Additional clauses may be typed in.

IT IS agreed between the parties hereto that every covenant, proviso and agreement herein contained shall enure to the benefit of and be binding upon the parties hereto, and their respective heirs, executors, administrators, successors and assigns, and that all covenants herein contained shall be construed as being joint and several, and that when the context so requires or permits the singular number shall be read as if the plural were expressed, and the masculine gender as if the feminine or neuter, as the case may be, were expressed.

𝔍𝔫 𝔚𝔦𝔱𝔫𝔢𝔰𝔰 𝔚𝔥𝔢𝔯𝔢𝔬𝔣 the parties hereto have hereunto set their hands and seals.

SIGNED, SEALED AND DELIVERED

in the presence of

Ronald Craig Anderson

Lucille Caroline Anderson

Elizabeth Maud Peterson

The Lessee acknowledges receipt of a fully executed duplicate original of this lease on the _____ day of

November   19 70

Figure 16.1. Completed House Lease – Page 3

Dye & Durham Limited — Toronto, Canada
Printers to the Legal Profession
Form No. 71

AFFIDAVIT AS TO LEGAL AGE AND MARITAL STATUS

PROVINCE OF ONTARIO   I/WE   RONALD CRAIG ANDERSON

COUNTY OF   YORK   of the   Borough   of   Etobicoke

To Wit: in the County of   York, Physician

Strike out words and parts not applicable and initial.

in the within instrument named, make oath and say that at the time of the execution of the within instrument,

1. I was of the full age of twenty-one years;

If Attorney see footnote.

2. And that   Lucille Caroline Anderson---------------------------

    who also executed the within instrument   was   of the full age of twenty-one years

3. I was legally married to the person named therein as my wife/husband;

~~4. I was unmarried/divorced/widower.~~

SWORN before me at the   City

of   Toronto

in the   County of York

this   15th   day of November

A.D. 19 70

A Commissioner for taking Affidavits, etc.

NOTE: If Attorney, substitute in space provided "I am Attorney for_____(State name)_____, one of the parties named therein and he/she was of the full age of twenty-one years."

Figure 16.1. Completed House Lease – Affidavit on Page 4

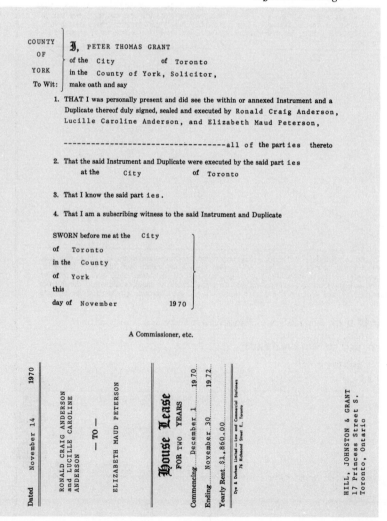

COUNTY

OF

YORK

To Wit:

I, PETER THOMAS GRANT

of the   City   of   Toronto

in the   County of York, Solicitor,

make oath and say

1. THAT I was personally present and did see the within or annexed Instrument and a Duplicate thereof duly signed, sealed and executed by Ronald Craig Anderson, Lucille Caroline Anderson, and Elizabeth Maud Peterson,

    -------------------------------------all of the parties   thereto

2. That the said Instrument and Duplicate were executed by the said parties
    at the   City   of   Toronto

3. That I know the said parties.

4. That I am a subscribing witness to the said Instrument and Duplicate

SWORN before me at the   City

of   Toronto

in the   County

of   York

this

day of   November   1970

A Commissioner, etc.

Dated   November 14   1970

RONALD CRAIG ANDERSON and LUCILLE CAROLINE ANDERSON

— TO —

ELIZABETH MAUD PETERSON

House Lease

FOR TWO YEARS

Commencing....December..1....19.70..

Ending....November..30....19.72..

Yearly Rent. $1,860.00.

Dye & Durham Limited — Law and Commercial Stationers
74 Richmond Street E., Toronto

HILL, JOHNSTON & GRANT
17 Princess Street S.
Toronto, Ontario

Figure 16.1. Completed House Lease – Back

CHAPTER 17

Powers of Attorney, Bills of Sale, and Chattel Mortgages

Although frequently lawyers restrict their legal practice to some particular aspect of law such as estate work, conveyancing, litigation, expropriation, constitutional law, criminal law or corporate law, many lawyers also engage in general practice, and are involved in some measure in all areas and fields of legal practice. A good legal secretary, therefore, must be acquainted with a fundamental knowledge of a wide spectrum of legal secretarial work.

In this chapter we will consider three legal instruments which you will encounter if you are working for a lawyer in general practice.

Power of Attorney

A *power of attorney* is a formal legal instrument by which one person empowers another to represent him, or to act in his place. The persons so empowered may be given certain specified powers or, alternatively, wide general powers. It may be given by one or more persons, to one or more individuals at the same time.

The party who gives the power is the *donor* or principal. The party who gets the power is the *donee*, or agent, also called an *attorney*. The term "attorney" does not mean a lawyer, but is a term naming a person appointed by another to act in his place or to represent him.

A power of attorney is made in duplicate, and is dated the day of execution. It is signed by the party or parties giving it, and requires legal seals. Affidavits of execution and of legal age are required.

There are many printed forms of Power of Attorney, the most common being:
1. Power of Attorney – General – gives the attorney or agent wide general powers.
2. Power of Attorney – Short – gives only specific authority.

Power of Attorney – General

Power of attorney – general is a four-page, printed form, simple to complete. It commences with the words "KNOW ALL MEN BY THESE PRESENTS", followed by the description of the party or parties giving the power, and the name of the person who is being appointed. The balance of the form then requires only the insertion of the proper pronoun, that is, "my", "me", "our", or "we", in blanks left in the printed form. If two parties are granting the power, use "our" and "we". In this way the printed form is adapted to fit the particular circumstances.

Figure 17.1 illustrates an extract from a printed general power of attorney. You can see that the powers given under it are very wide in scope.

Power of Attorney – Short

Power of attorney – short is a one-page form with the back printed on the reverse side (Figure 17.2). It is simple to complete, and requires only information as to the name of the donor, the name of the attorney or agent, and exact details of the specific powers being granted. It is made in duplicate, dated the day of execution, and is given under seal. Affidavits of legal age and execution are required.

Bills of Sale and Chattel Mortgages

These commercial instruments deal with personal property, as distinguished from real property. They are considered at the same time, since in some transactions you cannot have a chattel mortgage without a bill of sale.

Bill of Sale

A *bill of sale* (Figure 17.3) is a written legal instrument covering the sale of personal property, where title to the property passes to the purchaser. Either the purchaser or the vendor may hold the property, depending on the circumstances. The parties to a bill of sale are formally known as the *bargainor(s)* – the person or persons selling (vendors), and the *bargainee(s)* – the person or persons buying (purchasers).

Preparing a Bill of Sale

A bill of sale is prepared by the solicitors for the bargainor. It is dated the day it is typed, and a minimum of four copies is prepared. A bill of sale is executed in duplicate by the bargainor, and both executed copies given to the bargainee.

Information Required

The following information is required to complete a bill of sale:
1. the name of parties with general address and occupation
2. the consideration
3. the description and locations of goods being sold.

Affidavits

In the affidavit of execution, the witness must swear to the date on which the bill of sale was executed. The bargainee must complete an *affidavit of bona fides,* swearing that the sale is an honest and genuine one, and not made to enable the bargainee to hold the goods so that a creditor of the bargainor cannot claim them in payment of a debt.

In order to protect his title to the property, particularly if the property remains in the hands of the vendor, the bargainee registers an executed copy of the bill of sale. We will discuss registration when we have considered chattel mortgages.

Chattel Mortgage

A *chattel mortgage* (Figure 17.4) is a mortgage of personal property as security for a loan or debt. The parties to a chattel mortgage are the *mortgagor(s)* – the person or

persons giving the mortgage, and the *mortgagee(s)* – the person or persons taking the mortgage.

Chattel mortgages are used in two ways:
1. Personal property is used as security for a loan. With the advent of *conditional sales agreements,* however, chattel mortgages are less frequently used in this way.
2. Personal property is sold, and the vendor transfers title to the purchaser. The purchaser gives the vendor a chattel mortgage as security for part or all of the purchase price.

In this instance the sale would be by way of a bill of sale, and the bargainee in the bill of sale becomes the mortgagor in the chattel mortgage.

Preparing a Chattel Mortgage

A chattel mortgage is prepared by the solicitors for the mortgagor. It is dated the day it is typed, and a minimum of four copies is prepared. The mortgage is executed in duplicate by the mortgagor, and both executed copies are given to the mortgagee.

Information Required

The following information is required to complete a chattel mortgage:
1. the name of parties, with *full* (not general) address and occupation
2. actual consideration
3. the description and location of the personal property being mortgaged.

Affidavits

Affidavit of Execution

In a chattel mortgage, the witness must complete an affidavit of execution, which includes an additional clause relating to the date of execution of the mortgage.

Affidavit of Bona Fides

In the affidavit of bona fides, the mortgagee must verify the consideration shown in the mortgage, as well as swearing to the genuineness of the mortgage.

In order to protect his interest in the property which is the subject of the mortgage, the mortgagee will register the chattel mortgage.

Registration of Bills of Sale and Chattel Mortgages

To protect his interest in the property, a bargainee or mortgagee must usually register the bill of sale or chattel mortgage within five days from the date of execution of the instrument. The document is registered in the office of the clerk of the County or District Court of the county or district in which the property mortgaged or sold is located at the time of execution of the mortgage or bill of sale.

By registration, the bargainee or mortgagee protects his title against any future attempts of the bargainor or mortgagor to endeavour to sell or mortgage the property to another party.

Renewal of Chattel Mortgage

Every chattel mortgage which has been registered must be renewed each year (Figure 17.5).

Within thirty days of the anniversary date of the original registration, the mortgagee must file a renewal statement showing the amount still due for principal and interest under the mortgage.

Preparing a Renewal

The mortgagee need only execute one copy of the renewal, and will usually want to have a copy for his file. The renewal is not under seal, and is not witnessed.

No affidavit of execution is required, but the mortgagee must complete an affidavit as to the bona fides of the mortgage.

Information Required

The following information is required to complete a renewal:

1. the name and full address of parties to original chattel mortgage
2. the details of registration of the chattel mortgage
3. information as to present mortgagee, and details of any assignment of mortgage
4. the amount of the mortgage still outstanding
5. a description of the mortgaged property.

Discharge of Chattel Mortgage

When the debt for which the personal property was used as security has been paid in full, the mortgagee gives to the mortgagor a discharge of chattel mortgage (Figure 17.6), which is registered in the appropriate county court office as proof that the mortgage has been paid. The clerk of the appropriate court office will mark in the appropriate court records "Discharged", and the word "Discharged" will also be endorsed on the back of the original mortgage.

Preparing Discharge of Chattel Mortgage

A discharge is prepared by the solicitors for the mortgagee. A minimum of two copies is typed, and an executed copy given to the mortgagor who arranges to have it registered.

Only an affidavit of execution is required in a discharge of chattel mortgage, and indicates what date the discharge was executed by the mortgagee.

Information Required

The following information is required to complete a discharge of chattel mortgage:

1. the name of present mortgagee
2. the name of original mortgagor and mortgagee
3. the details of date of mortgage and registration.

and in   my   name to make such claims and demands, arrests, seizures, levies, attachments, distraints and sequestrations, or to commence, institute, sue and prosecute to judgment and execution such actions, ejectments and suits at law or in equity as   my   said attorney or attorneys shall think fit; ALSO to appear before all or any Judges, Magistrates or other officers of the Courts of Law or equity, and then and there to sue, plead, answer and defend in all matters and causes concerning the premises; AND ALSO to exercise and execute all Powers of Sale or Foreclosures and all other powers and authorities vested in me
by any mortgage or mortgages belonging to   me
as mortgagee or assignee thereof.

AND ALSO, in case of any difference or dispute with any person or persons concerning any of the matters aforesaid, to submit any such differences and disputes to arbitration or umpirage in such manner as   my   said attorney or attorneys shall see fit; AND to compound, compromise and to accept part in satisfaction for the payment of the whole of any debt or sum of money payable to   me   or to grant an extension of time for the payment of the same, either with or without taking security, or otherwise to act in respect of the same, as to   my   said attorney or attorneys shall appear most expedient.

AND ALSO, for   me   and in   my   name, or otherwise on   my   behalf, to take possession of and to let, sell, manage and improve   my   real estate, lands, messuages, and hereditaments whatsoever or wheresoever, and to mortgage or raise money upon   my   real estate, and to repay the same, and to purchase and sell, pledge, hypothecate and assign mortgages and to fully discharge or partly discharge the same; and from time to time to appoint any agents or servants to assist him or them in managing the same, and to displace or remove such agents or servants, and appoint others, using therein the same power and discretion as   I   might do.

AND ALSO, as and when   my   said attorney or attorneys shall think fit to sell and absolutely dispose of   my   said real estate, lands and hereditaments, and also such shares, stooks, bonds, mortgages and other securities for money as hereinbefore mentioned either together or in parcel, for such price or prices, and by public auction or private contract, as to   my   said attorney or attorneys shall seem reasonable and expedient; AND to convey, assign, transfer, and make over the same respectively to the purchaser or purchasers thereof, with power to give credit for the whole or any part of the purchase money thereof; AND to permit the same to remain unpaid for whatever time and upon whatever security, real or personal, either comprehending the purchased property or not as   my   said attorney or attorneys shall think safe and proper.

Figure 17.1. Extract from Power of Attorney, General

Power of Attorney—Short.
Revised, July, 1964

Dye & Durham Limited, Toronto, Canada
Law and Commercial Stationers
Form No. 169

Know all Men by these Presents

THAT I   JOHN DOUGLAS WINTER

of the   City of Toronto, in the County of York, Merchant,

do hereby make, nominate, constitute and appoint MARY ELIZABETH SPRING
my true and lawful Attorney for me and in my name, place and stead and for my sole use and benefit to
endorse cheques for deposit to and issue cheques drawn on Savings
Account No. 456, The Bank of Montreal, University and Queen Street
Branch, in the City of Toronto.

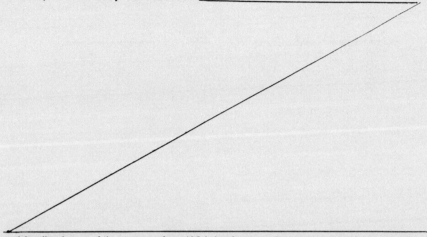

and for all and every of the purposes aforesaid I do hereby give and grant unto my said Attorney full and
absolute power and authority to do and execute all acts, deeds, matters and things necessary to be done in
and about the premises, also to commence, institute and prosecute all actions, suits and other proceedings
which may be necessary or expedient in and about the premises, as fully and effectually to all intents and
purposes as I myself could do if personally present and acting therein; also to appoint a substitute or
substitutes and such substitution at pleasure to revoke, I hereby ratifying and confirming and agreeing to
ratify and confirm and allow all and whatsoever my said Attorney or such substitute or substitutes shall
lawfully do or cause to be done in the premises by virtue hereof.

IN WITNESS WHEREOF I have hereunto set my hand and seal this   23rd

day of   October   1970

SIGNED, SEALED AND DELIVERED
    in the Presence of

PETER THOMAS GRANT

I, ...

COUNTY OF YORK   of the ......City.................. of .....Toronto.......... in the

TO WIT: ....County...................... of ......York..................

                          ....Solicitor....................... make oath and say:
                                          (Occupation)

1. THAT I was personally present and did see the within or annexed Instrument and a duplicate thereof duly signed,
sealed and executed by ......John Douglas Winter...

.... one ......of the parties thereto.

2. THAT the said Instrument and duplicate were executed by the said part y   at the.........City............of
    Toronto, in the County of York.

3. THAT I know the said part y .

4. THAT I am a subscribing witness to the said Instrument and duplicate.

SWORN before me at the ....City...
of ....Toronto....................................... in the County
of ....York................. this ....23rd.................
day of ....October................. A.D. 1970

    A Commissioner for taking Affidavits, etc.

Figure 17.2.   Short Power of Attorney   155

AFFIDAVIT AS TO LEGAL AGE

PROVINCE OF ONTARIO
COUNTY OF YORK

To Wit:

I̶ We,   JOHN DOUGLAS WINTER

of the   City of Toronto   in the   County

of   York, Merchant,

in the within instrument named, make oath and say:

Strike out words and parts not applicable and initial.

If Attorney see footnote.

(1) THAT at the time of the execution and delivery by me of the within instrument I was of the full age of twenty-one years.

~~(2) And that~~

~~who also executed the within instrument - - - - - of the full age of twenty-one years.~~

SWORN before me at the   City

of   Toronto

in the   County of York

this   23rd   day of   October

A.D. 19 70

A Commissioner for taking Affidavits, etc.

NOTE: If Attorney, substitute in space provided "I am Attorney for..................(State name)..................., one of the parties named therein and he/she was of the full age of twenty-one years."

Dated   October 23   19 70

JOHN DOUGLAS WINTER

—TO—

MARY ELIZABETH SPRING

SHORT

Power of Attorney

Dye & Durham Limited, Toronto, Canada
Law and Commercial Stationers

HILL, JOHNSTON & GRANT
17 Princess Street
Toronto, Ontario

Figure 17.2.   Short Power of Attorney – Back

This Indenture

made the 20th day of October 1970

Between

RONALD CRAIG ANDERSON, of the
City of Toronto, in the County of
York, Physician,

hereinafter called the Bargainor
of the First Part

and

ELIZABETH MAUD PETERSON, of the
City of Toronto, in the County
of York, Secretary,

hereinafter called the Bargainee
of the Second Part

WHEREAS the Bargainor is possessed of the goods, chattels and effects hereinafter set forth, described and enumerated, and h a s contracted and agreed with the Bargainee for the absolute Sale to her thereof, for the sum of FIVE HUNDRED AND SEVENTY-FIVE---------($575.00)--------------------- Dollars

NOW THIS INDENTURE WITNESSETH, that in pursuance of the said Agreement, and in consideration of the sum of FIVE HUNDRED AND SEVENTY-FIVE---------

-----------------($575.00)---------------------- Dollars of lawful money of Canada, paid by the said Bargainee to the said Bargainor at or before the sealing and delivery of these presents (the receipt whereof is hereby acknowledged), the said Bargainor do t h bargain, sell, assign, transfer and set over unto the said Bargainee her executors, administrators, successors and assigns
ALL THOSE the said goods, chattels and effects

One oak office desk and chair

One IBM electric typewriter, Model 142, Serial No. 5947213986

One walnut bookcase

Dye & Durham
Limited
Toronto, Canada
Form No. 132-135

Figure 17.3. Bill of Sale – Page 1

157

all of which goods, chattels and effects are contained in an office
situate and being Room 423, 2 Prince William Avenue, in the City of
Toronto, in the County of York, known municipally as lot
number 1234, Plan 623.

AND all the right, title, interest, property, claim and demand whatsoever of the said Bargainor of, in, to, and out of the same, and every part thereof:

TO HOLD the said hereinbefore assigned goods, chattels and effects and every of them and every part thereof, and all the right, title and interest of the said Bargainor therein and thereto, unto and to the use of the said Bargainee

AND the said Bargainor doth hereby, for himself, his executors, administrators, successors and assigns, covenant, promise and agree with the said Bargainee herself, her executors, administrators, successors and assigns, in manner following, that is to say: THAT the said Bargainor is now rightfully and absolutely possessed of and entitled to the said hereby assigned goods, chattels and effects and every of them, and every part thereof:

AND that the said Bargainor now has in himself good right to assign the same unto the said Bargainee her executors, administrators, successors and assigns, in manner aforesaid, and according to the true intent and meaning of these presents; AND that the said Bargainee her executors, administrators, successors and assigns, shall and may from time to time, and at all times hereafter, peaceably and quietly have, hold, possess, and enjoy the said hereby assigned goods, chattels and effects and every of them, and every part thereof, to and for her own use and benefit, without any manner of hindrance, interruption, molestation, claim or demand whatsoever of, from or by him the said Bargainor or any person or persons whomsoever; AND that free and clear and freely and absolutely released and discharged, or otherwise, at the cost of the said Bargainor is effectually indemnified from and against all former and other bargains, sales, gifts, grants, titles, charges and incumbrances whatsoever:

Figure 17.3. Bill of Sale – Page 2

AND, moreover, that   he   the said Bargainor   and all persons rightfully claiming, or to claim any estate, right, title or interest of, in, or to the said hereby assigned goods, chattels and effects and every of them and every part thereof, shall and will from time to time, and at all times hereafter upon every reasonable request of the said Bargainee   her   executors, administrators, successors and assigns, but at the cost and charges of the said Bargainee   make, do and execute, or cause or procure to be made, done and executed, all such further acts, deeds and assurances for the more effectually assigning and assuring the said hereby assigned goods, chattels and effects unto the said Bargainee   her   executors, administrators, successors and assigns, in manner aforesaid, and according to the true intent and meaning of these presents, as by the said Bargainee   her   executors, administrators, successors and assigns, or his or their Counsel in the law shall be reasonably advised or required.

IN WITNESS WHEREOF, the said parties have hereunto set their hands and seals.

SIGNED, SEALED AND DELIVERED
    In the presence of

ONTARIO:

County of York

To Wit:

I,   ELIZABETH MAUD PETERSON

of the City of Toronto

in the County of York

the Bargainee   in the foregoing Bill of Sale named, make oath and say:

THAT the sale therein made is bona fide, and for good consideration, namely the sum of $575.00 as set forth in the said conveyance and is not for the purpose of holding or enabling the Bargainee therein named, to hold the goods mentioned therein against the creditors of the Bargainor   therein named.

~~I am aware of the circumstances connected with the said Bill of Sale by way of Mortgage, and have personal knowledge of the facts herein deposed to.~~

SWORN at the City

of   Toronto

in the County of York

this   day of October   1970

before me,

If the affidavit is made by an agent, or by the officer of a Corporation.

A Commissioner, etc.

Figure 17.3. Bill of Sale – Page 3

Ontario:

County of YORK

To Wit:

I, PETER THOMAS GRANT
of the Borough of Etobicoke
in the County of York, Solicitor,
make oath and say:

1. THAT I was personally present and did see the within Bill of Sale duly signed, sealed and executed by ---RONALD CRAIG ANDERSON---one of the parties thereto.

2. THAT I know the said party and that the name Peter T. Grant

set and subscribed as a witness to the execution thereof, is of the proper handwriting of me this deponent.

3. THAT the said Bill of Sale was executed at the City of Toronto in the County of York on the day of October 1970 .

Sworn before me at the City
of Toronto
in the County
of York
this day of October 1970

A Commissioner for taking Affidavits, etc.

Dated October 20 1970

RONALD CRAIG ANDERSON

AND

ELIZABETH MAUD PETERSON

Bill of Sale

Dye & Durham Limited — Toronto, Canada
Printers to the Legal Profession

HILL, JOHNSTON & GRANT,
17 Princess Street,
Toronto, Ontario.

Figure 17.3. Bill of Sale – Back

Chattel Mortgage

Dye & Durham Limited — Toronto, Canada
Printers to the Legal Profession
Form No. 63-66

This Indenture

made in duplicate the   10th   day of   October   19 70

Between

RONALD CRAIG ANDERSON, Physician, of
32 Dawson Street,

of the   Borough   of   Etobicoke   in the County of York,
hereinafter called the MORTGAGOR of the FIRST PART; and

ELIZABETH MAUD PETERSON, Secretary,
of 401 Canmotor Boulevard,

of the   Borough   of   Etobicoke   in the County of York,
hereinafter called the MORTGAGEE of the SECOND PART

Witnesseth that the Mortgagor for and in consideration of EIGHT THOUSAND--------------
-----------------($8,000.00)--------------------Dollars of lawful money of Canada
to him in hand well and truly paid by the Mortgagee at or before the sealing and delivery of these Presents (the
receipt whereof is hereby acknowledged) HATH granted, bargained, sold and assigned, and by these Presents
DOTH GRANT, bargain, sell and assign unto the Mortgagee, his executors, administrators and assigns.

ALL AND SINGULAR the goods and chattels, particularly mentioned and set forth in Schedule endorsed hereon
(or hereunto annexed) and marked with the letter "A", all of which said goods and chattels are now the property
of the said Mortgagor and are situated in, around and upon the premises known as 32 Dawson Street,
in the Borough of Etobicoke in the County of York, in the Province of Ontario.

AND it is hereby further understood and agreed by and between the parties hereto that all goods and chattels of
a like or similar description to or different from those hereinbefore mentioned which shall hereafter be taken or
brought into stock or possession by the Mortgagor during the currency of these Presents or any renewal thereof,
either in addition to or in substitution for the said goods and chattels or any of them, either upon the said premises
or upon any other premises to which he may remove his business, or a substantial part of his business, or upon which
he now carries on or may hereafter carry on, commence or start any branch of his business, shall at once upon being
so brought into stock or possession, become mortgaged hereby without a fresh instrument being executed for that
purpose, and all such goods are hereby mortgaged.

AND it is hereby further understood and agreed by and between the parties hereto that in case the Mortgagor
shall take in any party or parties with him in said business or any branch thereof then these Presents shall cover his
or their interests in all goods and chattels thereafter purchased by said partnership and brought into stock or
possession as aforesaid.

TO HAVE AND TO HOLD all and singular the said goods and chattels unto the Mortgagee, his executors, administrators and assigns, to the only proper use and behoof of the Mortgagee, his executors, administrators and assigns
forever. PROVIDED ALWAYS and these presents are upon this express condition that if the Mortgagor do and
shall well and truly pay or cause to be paid to the Mortgagee the full sum of EIGHT THOUSAND------
--------------------($8,000.00)-----------------------------Dollars
with interest on the same at the rate of six (6%)--per centum per annum on the days and times following,
that is to say:

The said principal sum of EIGHT THOUSAND---($8,000.00)---Dollars
together with interest at the aforesaid rate of six (6%) per centum
per annum calculated half-yearly not in advance as well after as
before maturity shall become due and payable on demand by the
mortgagee; interest at the aforesaid rate to be computed from the
first day of October, 1970.

Figure 17.4. Chattel Mortgage – Page 1   161

THEN THESE PRESENTS and every matter and thing herein contained shall cease, determine and be utterly void to all intents and purposes, anything herein contained to the contrary notwithstanding:

AND the Mortgagor doth hereby COVENANT, PROMISE and AGREE to and with the Mortgagee that the Mortgagor shall and will warrant and forever defend ALL and SINGULAR the said goods and chattels unto the Mortgagee against the Mortgagor and against all and every other person or persons whomsoever; And also that the Mortgagor shall and will well and truly pay or cause to be paid unto the Mortgagee the said sum of money in the above proviso mentioned with interest on the same as aforesaid on the day and time and in the manner hereinbefore provided for the payment thereof; AND ALSO THAT IN CASE DEFAULT SHALL BE MADE IN THE PAYMENT of the said sum of money in the said proviso mentioned or of the interest thereon or any part thereof as hereinbefore provided, or the Mortgagor shall attempt to or shall sell or dispose of or in any way part with the possession of the said goods and chattels or any of them or to remove the same or any part thereof out of the Borough of Etobicoke--or suffer or permit the same to be seized or taken in execution without the consent of the Mortgagee to such sale, removal or disposal thereof first had and obtained in writing or in case the Mortgagee feels unsafe or insecure or deems said goods and chattels in danger of being sold or removed, THEN and in every such case the whole of the money secured by this Indenture shall immediately thereon become due and payable and it shall and may be lawful for the Mortgagee or his servant or servants and with such other assistant or assistants as he or they may require at any time during the day or night to enter in or upon any lands, tenements, houses and premises wheresoever and whatsoever where the said goods and chattels or any part thereof may be and for such persons to break and force open doors, locks, bolts, fastenings, hinges, gates, fences, houses, buildings, enclosures and places for the purpose of taking possession of and removing said goods and chattels; and upon and from and after the taking possession of said goods and chattels as aforesaid it shall and may be lawful for the Mortgagee and he is hereby authorized and empowered to sell the said goods and chattels or any of them or any part thereof at public auction or private sale as to him may seem meet; and from and out of the proceeds of such sale in the first place to pay and reimburse himself all such sum and sums of money as may be secured by virtue of these Presents and all such expenses as may have been incurred by the Mortgagee in consequence of the action, default, neglect, failure or attempt of the Mortgagor as aforesaid or in consequence of such action of the Mortgagee, and in the next place to pay unto the Mortgagor all such surplus as may remain after such sale and after payment of all such sum or sums of money and interest thereon as may be secured by these Presents at the time of such seizure, and after payment of the costs, charges, and expenses incurred by such seizure and sale as aforesaid; AND IT IS HEREBY UNDERSTOOD AND AGREED that in case default shall be made in the payment of any of the said sums of principal or interest, then interest shall continue to be payable at the rate aforesaid thereon from the maturity thereof until the same shall be fully paid; PROVIDED ALWAYS nevertheless that it shall not be incumbent on the Mortgagee to sell and dispose of the said goods and chattels, but that in case of default of payment of the said sum of money or the interest thereon as aforesaid or any part thereof or in case the said Mortgagor shall attempt to sell, remove or dispose of the said chattels without the consent (in writing) of the said Mortgagee it shall and may be lawful for the Mortgagee peaceably and quietly to take hold, use, occupy, possess and enjoy the said goods and chattels without the let, molestation, eviction, hindrance or interruption of the said Mortgagor or any other person or persons whomsoever; AND FURTHER that in case the sum of money realized under any such sale as above mentioned shall not be sufficient to pay the whole amount of principal, interest, costs, charges and expenses according to the provisions of his Indenture, that the Mortgagor shall and will forthwith pay or cause to be paid unto the Mortgagee all such deficiency.

AND FURTHER that the Mortgagor will during the continuation of this Mortgage and any and every renewal thereof INSURE and keep insured the goods and chattels hereinbefore mentioned against loss and damage by fire in some Insurance Company authorized to transact business in Canada and approved of by the Mortgagee in the sum of not less than EIGHT THOUSAND------($8,000.00)------------ Dollars as security for moneys secured by this Indenture, for the benefit of the said Mortgagee, and will pay all premiums and moneys necessary for that purpose as the same become due and payable in respect of such insurance, the loss if any to be payable to the said Mortgagee, and the production of this Indenture shall be sufficient authority for, and the said Insurance Company is hereby directed thereupon to pay such loss if any to the said Mortgagee; PROVIDED that if the said Insurance is not effected or kept duly renewed and default be made in payment of the said premiums or sums of money by the Mortgagor, the Mortgagee may pay the same and such sums of money shall be added to the debt hereby secured and shall bear interest at the same rate from the day of such payment and shall be repayable with the moneys next falling due under these Presents;

AND further the Mortgagor covenants with the Mortgagee that upon the issue of a writ of summons for a money demand against the Mortgagor, or upon the issue of any execution upon any judgment against the Mortgagor, or the issue of a warrant of distress for any rent or taxes, in respect of the premises, in or upon which the said goods and chattels or any part thereof may at any time during the currency of this Mortgage or any renewal thereof be situate; or upon the failure to insure or keep insured the said goods and chattels within the meaning of the provisions of this Indenture; or upon the abandonment of the said goods and chattels or any part thereof; or upon the making of any assignment for the benefit of creditors; or upon the arrest of the Mortgagor on any criminal charge or the issue of a writ of capias or a writ of attachment against the Mortgagor then so often as any of the said events may happen all the moneys secured by this Indenture shall immediately become due and payable and the Mortgagee shall forthwith be at liberty to take any and all proceedings for the better securing himself and for the enforcing and obtaining payment of the money secured hereby as though default had actually been made in the payment of the moneys hereby secured or any part thereof.

Figure 17.4. Chattel Mortgage – Page 2

65—Chattel Mortgage—p. 3
Dye & Durham

AND the Mortgagor covenants with the Mortgagee that he will during the continuance of this Mortgage and any renewal or renewals thereof keep up the amount of stock in trade in the said premises so that at no time will it be less than the actual cash value of (amount if applicable--see note above) Dollars if sold by public auction, and that should the same at any time during such period not be of such value (as to which the Mortgagee shall be sole judge) all the money secured by this Indenture shall immediately become due and payable and the Mortgagee shall thereupon have liberty forthwith to take any and all proceedings for the better securing himself and for the enforcing and obtaining payment of the moneys secured hereby as though default had actually been made in the payment of the moneys secured hereby or any part thereof.

AND the Mortgagor doth put the Mortgagee in full possession of said goods and chattels by delivering to him at the sealing and delivery hereof this Indenture in the name of all the said goods and chattels.

AND it is hereby further understood and agreed by and between the parties hereto that any and all payments hereafter made by the Mortgagor to the Mortgagee, whether the same be specially applied by the Mortgagor or not, may be applied by the Mortgagee to any portion or portions of the present or future indebtedness of the Mortgagor to the Mortgagee, and the Mortgagee may at any future time and as often as he shall see fit and either before or after any renewal hereof or any seizure or sale hereunder, apply, change the application of or re-apply any or all of such payment, whether such portion or portions of the present or future indebtedness be due or accruing due at the time of such application or any such re-application, and notwithstanding that entries of any previous application may be made in the books of the Mortgagee or in any receipts or statements furnished by him or otherwise.

AND the Mortgagor hereby covenants with the Mortgagee that he will pay the costs, charges and expenses of and incidental to the taking, preparation, execution and filing of these Presents and of every renewal thereof.

AND it is hereby understood that in case of withdrawal by death, voluntary act or otherwise from the said firm of Mortgagees, of any member or members thereof, or in case of the addition of any person or persons thereto, then these Presents shall be for the benefit of such new firm continuing to carry on the business of the present firm, and shall operate as security for all the then present and future indebtedness of the Mortgagor to such new firm, and all the provisions of these Presents shall apply to such new firm as fully and effectually as if such new firm were now in existence and as if these Presents were taken in the name of such new firm.

PROVIDED, and it is hereby agreed, that in construing these presents the words "Mortgagor" and "Mortgagee" and the personal pronoun "he" or "his" relating thereto and used therewith, shall be read and construed as "Mortgagor or Mortgagors", "Mortgagee or Mortgagees", and "his", "her" or "their", respectively, as the number and gender of the party or parties referred to in each case require, and the number of the verb agreeing therewith shall be construed as agreeing with the said word or pronoun so substituted; And that all rights, advantages, privileges, immunities, powers and things hereby secured to the Mortgagee or Mortgagees shall be equally secured to and exercisable by his, her, or their executors, administrators and assigns, or successors and assigns as the case may be; And that all covenants, liabilities and obligations entered into or imposed hereunder upon the Mortgagor or Mortgagors shall be equally binding upon his, her or their executors, administrators and assigns, or successors and assigns as the case may be.

IN WITNESS WHEREOF the said parties have hereunto set their hands and seals.

SIGNED, SEALED AND DELIVERED
    in the presence of

If the affidavit is made by an agent, or by the officer of a Corporation the following clause must be added at the end of the affidavit: "And that I am aware of the circumstances connected with the said Bill of Sale by way of Mortgage, and have personal knowledge of the facts herein deposed to."

ONTARIO

County of York

        To Wit:

I, ELIZABETH MAUD PETERSON

of the Borough   of   Etobicoke

in the County of York, Secretary

the Mortgagee   in the foregoing Mortgage named make oath and say: that Ronald Craig-------

Anderson-- the Mortgagor   in the foregoing
Mortgage named is   justly and truly indebted to Elizabeth Maud Peterson   this deponent the
Mortgagee   therein named in the sum of Eight Thousand ($8,000) Dollars mentioned therein.

THE said Mortgage was executed in good faith and for the express purpose of securing the payment of the money so justly due or accruing due as aforesaid, and not for the purpose of protecting the goods and chattels mentioned in the said Mortgage against the creditors of the said Mortgagor   therein named, or of preventing the creditors of the said Mortgagor   from obtaining payment of any claim against

SWORN before me at the   Borough

of   Etobicoke

in the County of York

this   day of October   19 70

A Commissioner for taking affidavits, etc.

Figure 17.4. Chattel Mortgage – Page 3   163

SCHEDULE "A" REFERRED TO IN THE WITHIN MORTGAGE

1969 International Tandem Truck, eight cylinder, Model VF190

serial number CW30074, licence number Y52191

1969 Ford Tractor Trailer truck, eight cylinder, Model MX9753,

serial number FU49875, licence number 255 4987.

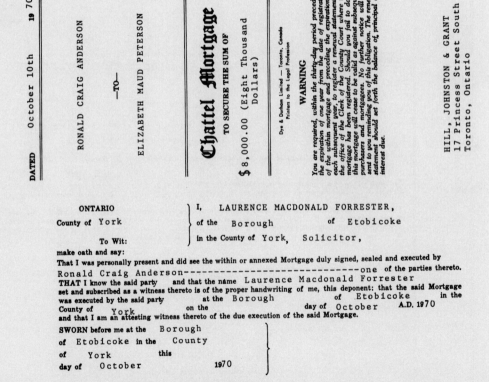

ONTARIO

County of York

To Wit:

I, LAURENCE MACDONALD FORRESTER,

of the Borough of Etobicoke

in the County of York, Solicitor,

make oath and say:

That I was personally present and did see the within or annexed Mortgage duly signed, sealed and executed by

Ronald Craig Anderson-----------------------------one of the parties thereto.

THAT I know the said party and that the name Laurence Macdonald Forrester

set and subscribed as a witness thereto is of the proper handwriting of me, this deponent: that the said Mortgage

was executed by the said party at the Borough of Etobicoke in the

County of York on the day of October A.D. 1970

and that I am an attesting witness thereto of the due execution of the said Mortgage.

SWORN before me at the Borough

of Etobicoke in the County

of York this

day of October 1970

A Commissioner for taking affidavits, etc.

Figure 17.4. Chattel Mortgage – Back

Revised, July, 1964

Dye & Durham Limited — Toronto, Canada
Printers to the Legal Profession
Form No. 72

RENEWAL STATEMENT

STATEMENT exhibiting the interest of   ELIZABETH MAUD PETERSON

in the property mentioned in the Mortgage dated the   18th   day of   October   19 65

made between

RONALD CRAIG ANDERSON
32 Dawson Street

of the   Borough   of   Etobicoke   in the   County of York

of the one part and

ELIZABETH MAUD PETERSON
301 Canmotor Boulevard

of the   Borough   of Etobicoke   in the   County of York,

of the other part and registered in the office of the Clerk of the   County   Court of the County   of

York   on the   23rd   day of   October   1965

and of the amount due for principal and interest thereon

The said   ELIZABETH MAUD PETERSON

is   still the Mortgagee   of the said property and has   not assigned the said Mortgage

~~The said~~

~~the assignee — — of the said Mortgage by virtue of an assignment thereof from the said~~

~~to h—————, dated the ——————————day of——————————————19——~~

THE amount still due for principal and interest on the said Mortgage is the sum of   TWO THOUSAND

FIVE HUNDRED ————————($2,500.00)————————————— Dollars.

Dated at the   Borough   of   Etobicoke

this   day of   October   A.D., 1970

Signature of Mortgagee or Assignee.

Figure 17.5.   Renewal of Chattel Mortgage –
Page 1

COUNTY OF YORK   I,   ELIZABETH MAUD PETERSON

of the   Borough   of   Etobicoke

TO WIT: in the County of   York,   Secretary

the Mortgagee named in the Mortgage mentioned in the within statement make oath and say:

1. THAT the within statement is true.

2. THAT the Mortgage mentioned in the said statement has not been kept on foot for any fraudulent purpose.

*Strike out if not an Agent or Officer of a Corporation.   *3. ~~THAT I am aware of all circumstances connected with the said Chattel Mortgage, and have personal knowledge of the facts herein deposed to.~~

SWORN before me at the   Borough

of   Etobicoke

in the   County

of   York

this

day of   October   1970

A Commissioner for taking Affidavits, etc.

Dated   October   1970

ELIZABETH MAUD PETERSON

—TO—

RONALD CRAIG ANDERSON

Renewal of Chattel Mortgage

STATEMENT AND AFFIDAVIT

Dye & Durham Limited — Toronto, Canada
Printers to the Legal Profession

HILL, JOHNSTON & GRANT
17 Princess Street S.
Toronto, Ontario

Figure 17.5. Renewal of Chattel Mortgage – Back

Dye & Durham Limited — Toronto, Canada
Printers to the Legal Profession
Form No. 189

Discharge of Chattel Mortgage.

𝕿𝕠 𝖙𝖍𝖊 𝕮𝖑𝖊𝖗𝖐 of the   COUNTY   𝕮𝖔𝖚𝖗𝖙 𝖔𝖋 𝖙𝖍𝖊 COUNTY OF YORK

I,   ELIZABETH MAUD PETERSON

of the   Borough   ofEtobicoke in the   County of York, Secretary,

𝕯𝖔 𝕮𝖊𝖗𝖙𝖎𝖋𝖞 𝖙𝖍𝖆𝖙 RONALD CRAIG ANDERSON, of the Borough of Etobicoke, in the County of York, Physician,   has satisfied all money due, or to grow due on a certain MORTGAGE, made by

RONALD CRAIG ANDERSON

to

ELIZABETH MAUD PETERSON

which Mortgage bears date the   20th   day of   October   19 65 and was registered in the Office of the Clerk of the   County   Court of the County of York

on the   23rd   day of   October   19 65.

as No. 23456 E.P.

THAT such Mortgage has   not   been assigned

AND that   I was   the person   entitled by law to receive the money, and that such Mortgage is therefore discharged.

WITNESS my hand this   day of December   1970

WITNESS

Figure 17.6. Discharge of Chattel Mortgage –
Page 1

COUNTY
of
YORK
To Wit:
} I, PETER THOMAS GRANT,
of the Borough of Etobicoke
in the County of York,
Solicitor, make oath and say:

1. That I was personally present and did see the within Discharge of Chattel Mortgage duly signed and executed by Elizabeth Maud Peterson--- --------------------------------one of the parties thereto.

2. That the said instrument was executed by the said parties at the Borough of Etobicoke in the County of York on the day of December 1970

3. That I know the said parties

4. That I am a subscribing witness to the said instrument.

Sworn before me at the Borough
of Etobicoke
in the County
of York
this
day of December 1970
}

A Commissioner, etc.

Dated December 1970

ELIZABETH MAUD PETERSON

to

RONALD CRAIG ANDERSON

DISCHARGE OF
Chattel Mortgage

Dye & Durham Limited — Toronto, Canada
Printers to the Legal Profession

HILL, JOHNSTON & GRANT
17 Princess Street S.
Toronto, Ontario

Figure 17.6. Discharge of Chattel Mortgage – Back

CHAPTER 18

Introduction to Civil Litigation

Many lawyers are involved in the area of legal practice known as "civil litigation", where disputes between parties are resolved in court trials, or applications are made for an order of the court that some specific thing be done.

There are many courts in a province. Surrogate Courts deal primarily with the handling of estates; Juvenile Courts deal with the problems of children under the age of sixteen; Family Courts deal with domestic problems; Provincial Courts deal with criminal and quasi-criminal matters; Division Courts deal with small civil claims; County and Supreme Courts deal with both civil and criminal matters.

There are two Federal courts. The Supreme Court of Canada is the highest court in Canada, and has exclusive final jurisdiction in civil and criminal matters within Canada. The second court is presently the Exchequer Court which deals with matters in which the Crown is concerned, but in March, 1970 a bill was introduced in the House of Commons to restructure and rename this court. It is proposed that the Exchequer Court become the Federal Court of Canada with trial and appeal divisions and increased jurisdiction.

We will be concerned first with the provincial courts having civil jurisdiction.

Division Courts

Division Courts are known as the "small claims" courts, since in the counties of Ontario they usually deal with small claims not in excess of $400.00; in the districts, they have jurisdiction up to $800.00.

There is at least one Division Court for each county, district, regional municipality,

or judicial district identified by the name of the area in which it is located. In the County of York there are twelve Division Courts located in various parts of the county, and identified by number as well as county; for example, Eleventh Division Court of the County of York.

The judgment of a Division Court judge may be appealed to the provincial Court of Appeal if the amount in dispute is over $200.00.

The clerk of the Division Court has a great deal of responsibility in administering the procedural steps necessary to bring a dispute before the court.

County Courts

County Courts usually deal with claims involving amounts in excess of $400.00, but not in excess of $3,000.00, as well as trying criminal matters.

Each county, district, regional municipality, or judicial district in the province has a County Court, situated in one town in the area. The court is identified by the name of the area in which it is located; for example, County Court of the County of Halton, County Court of the Regional Municipality of Ottawa – Carleton, County Court of the Judicial District of Niagara South.

An appeal from the judgment of this court may be made to the provincial Court of Appeal.

Supreme Court of Ontario

The Supreme Court of Ontario is the highest provincial court. The two divisions of this court are outlined below.

High Court of Justice
(Trial Division)

The High Court of Justice is the highest trial court in Ontario. This court usually deals with claims involving amounts in excess of $3,000.00, as well as trying criminal matters. Sittings of the court are held at set intervals each year in the Court House of each county or other area in the province.

In Toronto the courtrooms of the High Court of Justice are located in the County Court House of the County of York.

An appeal from the judgment of this court may be made to the provincial Court of Appeal if specified conditions are met by the *appellant*, the person bringing the appeal.

Court of Appeal

The Court of Appeal is the highest court in the province. This court hears both civil and criminal appeals from lower courts. An appeal from the judgment of the provincial Court of Appeal may be made to the Supreme Court of Canada if specified conditions are met by the appellant.

The Court of Appeal for Ontario sits at Osgoode Hall in Toronto, the capital city of Ontario.

Court Offices

There are many court offices with which you will be in contact in your work as a legal secretary. In most areas, all such offices are located in the County Court House: offices of the County Court, Sheriff's Office, Judges' Offices, Local Registrar of the Supreme Court, and courtrooms.

In Toronto many offices are also located in Osgoode Hall, the home of The Law Society of Upper Canada. At Osgoode Hall you will find the following offices: Central Office for the Supreme Court, Master's Office, Weekly Court Office for the Supreme Court, Court of Appeal Office, courtrooms for the Court of Appeal.

Court Officers

There are several officers of the courts whose official titles should be familiar to you.

Judges

Judges are the lawyers who are appointed by the Federal Government to hear cases in the courts. They are said to "sit", or to be "on the bench".

Registrar of the Supreme Court of Ontario

The *Registrar* is the chief administrative officer, and is responsible for receiving court documents and making the necessary entries in the records. Each county or other area has a local registrar responsible for performing these duties in his particular area.

Clerk of the County Court

The *clerk* is the chief administrative officer for the County Court, and performs similar duties in that court as are performed by the Registrar of the Supreme Court.

Sheriff

The *sheriff* is an important officer of the Crown in the county, and his duties include the execution of certain writs or orders issuing from the County and Supreme Courts and the summoning of jurors for cases being tried with a jury.

Master

The *Master* is an officer of the court who is a lawyer appointed to assist the judges. He does not try actions, but may hear and dispose of certain matters brought to him for determination, or referred to him by the judges.

Agent

Solicitors or individual lawyers who do not have their office for the practice of law in the county town, or in the City of Toronto, may appoint someone known as an agent to act on their behalf with respect to business carried on in the County or Supreme Court offices.

CHAPTER 19

Preparing Court Documents

In this chapter, discussion is limited to the preparation of court documents used in the County Courts and the Supreme Court of Ontario. A knowledge of the requirements of those courts will provide adequate information to assist a secretary in preparing all the necessary documents required for a claim brought in the Division Court.

The rules of practice and procedure applicable in the Supreme Court of Ontario are followed in the County Courts with exceptions which are noted where applicable.

Legal Proceedings

All documents prepared for court work are for use in some form of legal proceedings. Legal proceedings are also referred to as an *action*, a *cause*, a *matter*, or simply *proceedings*.

An action is a civil proceeding in the courts commenced by a *writ of summons*, or in the manner stipulated in the statutes or the rules of practice of the courts. In actual practice, actions are usually commenced by the issuance of a writ of summons. Under a writ, one party (the *plaintiff*) is suing another party (the *defendant*) in order to have a dispute between them settled by the courts. When the writ is issued, the court assigns a court file number to the action known as the *action number*.

Civil proceedings in the court which are not commenced by the issuance of a writ of summons are commenced by the issuance of an *originating notice of motion*. This notice makes application to the courts for direction that certain things be done.

While the term "action" correctly refers to legal proceedings commenced either by the issuance of a writ or an originating notice of motion, usually the term "action" refers to legal proceedings commenced by the issuance of a writ, and the term "proceedings" refers to legal proceedings commenced by an originating notice of motion.

The term "cause" refers to actions or other original proceedings between a plaintiff and a defendant. The term "matter" includes every proceeding in the court that is not a cause.

In the chapters which follow dealing with court documents and procedures, we will use the term "action" to refer to legal proceedings commenced by the issuance of a writ of summons, and the term "matter" to refer to all other legal proceedings commenced in the courts.

Types of Paper for Court Documents

Since 1965 all court documents in Ontario have been prepared on paper 8½ by 11 inches. Many law firms use plain, unruled paper of good quality, but others use a margin ruled paper printed with a wide margin of 1⅜ inches on the left, and a narrow margin of ⅝ inches on the right. All copies of a document are prepared on the same quality paper as the original.

Parts of Court Documents

Heading

As in legal instruments, the parts of court documents include a heading, a body or text, an ending, and a back.

The heading on a court document is called a style of cause, and gives the following information:

1. the name of the court in which the action or matter is to be tried or heard
2. the name of the party or parties to the action, identified by the descriptive label of plaintiff(s) and defendant(s), or a brief description of the matter to be determined
3. the name of the document
4. the action number if the document is for use in an action which has been commenced.

Once a style of cause has been established

in the document which commences the action or matter, that style is followed in preparing all other documents, unless the court gives permission to alter it.

Figures 19.1A, B, C, and D illustrate various forms of styles of cause for both actions and matters, which are typed following these guides:

1. Type the action number, if any, in the upper right-hand corner of the first page.
2. Type the name of the court in capital letters preceded by the words "IN THE", centred on the page, or between the rulings, approximately six lines, or one inch, from the top of the page.
3. Single space the description of the matter with a double space between paragraphs, and capitalize the introductory words of each paragraph; or single space the names of the parties in capital letters, centred on the page, or between the rulings, and follow each party or parties with the short descriptive label, in upper and lower case type, ending flush with the right-hand margin.
4. Type the name of the document in capital letters, underscored, centred on the page, or between the rulings.

Regardless of the length of the body of the document, the style of cause is always typed in the top portion of the page. Figure 19.1A illustrates the usual spacing between the parts. This spacing may be varied slightly to provide for better balance on the page when a short document is typed, or when only one or two lines of a long document could not be typed on the page.

Short Style of Cause

When referring to the style of cause of an action in correspondence or citations, use only the last name of the parties, or a shortened version of a company name, and separate the names by a "v." (versus), indicating the first-named party is suing the second-named party. If there are a great many plaintiffs or defendants, show the name of the first and then the words *et al* to indicate there are other parties involved.

<u>Williamson</u> v. <u>Misanthrope</u>
<u>Gold</u> v. <u>Bell et al</u>

If your client is the defendant, the lawyer may wish his name to appear first in referring to the parties. Instead of separating the names by a "v." use the words *ats* (at the suit of), indicating the second-named party is the one who commenced the action.

<u>Misanthrope</u> ats <u>Williamson</u>
<u>Bell et al</u> ats <u>Gold</u>

Body

A few court documents are prepared on printed forms in accordance with the requirements for completing forms set out on page 36. The majority of documents, however, are completely typed from dictated material in accordance with the requirements for typing legal papers set out on page 36.

The typing of court documents is so important that the rules of practice for the courts contain specific instructions regarding size of paper, margins, and line spacing! Briefly summarized, court documents should be typed following these requirements:

1. Use one side only of good quality paper 11 by 8½ inches.
2. On plain unruled paper, leave a left-hand margin of approximately 1½ inches, and a right-hand margin of approximately one inch.
3. On ruled margin paper, type within two spaces of the rulings.
4. Start the style of cause approximately one inch from the top of the page.
5. Double space the body of the document and triple space between paragraphs.
6. Indent paragraphs ten spaces.
7. Number each paragraph, or capitalize the first word or group of words.
8. Leave a bottom margin of no more than one inch.
9. Type at least two lines of the body of the document on the page with the ending.
10. Number each page after the first page. Centre the number approximately three lines from the top of the page.

Ending

The date of preparing the document, and frequently the city where it was drawn, appear in the ending as "DATED at . . . this . . . day of . . . , 197 ".

As each specific type of document is considered, any variation in the ending will be noted. Basically, however, in addition to the date, the ending includes the name and address of the law firm drawing the document, and on whose behalf the law firm is acting.

Back

All copies of court documents have a back (Figures 19.2A, B, C) known as a long back, since it is typed by inserting the paper in the normal fashion providing the 11-inch length of paper for typing purposes. The information contained on a back includes the name of the court in which the action or matter is being tried or heard, the style of cause, and the name of the document. In addition, if the document is for use in an action, the action number is also shown. If an action or matter is in the Supreme Court of Ontario, the county in which it was commenced must also be shown.

These guides for preparing backs should be noted:

1. Type only on the right-hand half of the page.
2. If margin ruled paper is used for the document, it is also used for the back. Type on the unruled side of the page ensuring that the wide margin is at the right when the back is typed, so that the rulings coincide when the back is affixed to the document.
3. Type the action number, if any, in the upper right-hand corner.
4. Type a description of the court approximately one inch from the top of the page, using the initials of the court rather than its full name. Space the initials out to occupy the whole half of the page, and underscore with a double line.
5. If the document is to be filed for use in the Supreme Court of Ontario, type in capital letters, two spaces beneath the underscored name of the court "ACTION COMMENCED IN THE COUNTY OF . . .", or "PROCEEDINGS COMMENCED IN THE COUNTY OF . . ." This information is obtained from the first document prepared in the action or matter. Some offices prefer that this information be enclosed in brackets.
6. Type the description of the matter, or the names of the parties (omitting descriptive labels and separated by a "v.") in capital letters and centred, approximately one inch from the name of the court or the "action or proceedings commenced" statement. Leave a double space between sections of a matter; leave approximately four spaces between names of parties and the "v."
7. Type the name of the document in capital letters halfway down the right-hand side of the page, centred, and a double space from typed horizontal bars. Short terms may be typed expanded (e.g., C O N S E N T). If the name of the document must carry over to a second line, single space your typing.
8. Type in capital letters, approximately one inch from the bottom of the page, the name and address of the law firm in whose office the document is prepared.

Special Terms

Before considering the preparation of court documents, a secretary must understand the significance of several special terms.

Service of a Document

Frequently, before a court document may be processed further after it has been typed, it must be *served* on the party on the other side, or upon his solicitors or their agent. Service is usually accomplished by leaving a copy of the document with an authorized person in the office of the solicitor for the party being served, and requiring the completion of an *admission of service* on the back of the original copy of the document, certifying that a true copy of the document has been received.

SERVICE OF A TRUE COPY HEREOF ADMITTED

THIS   DAY OF   19

SOLICITOR FOR

It is your responsibility to ensure that the admission of service is stamped on the back of the original of any document which you hand to a clerk in your office to serve.

If someone from another law office attends at your office to serve a copy of a document upon your law firm as solicitors for the other side, or as agents for another firm of solicitors, the secretary or a clerk in the office may admit service on behalf of your law firm. This is done by completing the date portion of the admission of service stamp, signing in ink the name of your law firm, and indicating for which party the law firm acts in an action or matter. If your law firm is admitting service as agent for an out-of-town law firm, indicate this by writing in after the name of your firm the words "Agents for (name of out-of-town firm)", and showing on behalf of which party service is admitted.

Most law offices maintain a record of documents served upon them, and before the document is given to the lawyer handling the action or matter to which it refers, or before it is sent on to the law firm for whom your firm is agent, the proper entry is made in any records established by the law office for that purpose.

In Ontario the rules of practice provide that service shall be effected before the hour of four o'clock in the afternoon. During *long vacation* (July and August), *short vacation* (December 24 to January 6), and on Saturdays, service shall be effected before one o'clock in the afternoon. Service effected after those hours is deemed to have been made on the next juridicial day.

Filing a Document

Filing is the term which describes the delivery of the original or a copy of a document to the appropriate court office for use by the court during the trial of the action, or hearing of the matter. The court office requires proof that a copy of the document has been provided to the other side, or to other interested parties. This is accomplished by having such parties admit service on the original of the document, and either showing this admission of service to the court officials when filing a copy of the document, or filing the original with the court. Sometimes this admission of service is insufficient and an affidavit of service is required. The form of this affidavit is discussed in Chapter 20.

With the exceptions noted in subsequent chapters, most documents are first served, then filed.

There is a charge for filing most court documents known as a fee or tariff. The amount of such a fee varies depending on the nature of the document filed. The amounts are set out in schedules included in THE RULES OF PRACTICE AND PROCEDURE, a copy of which the lawyer will usually have in his office. For most documents, no marking of any kind appears on the original to indicate payment of any tariff fee; on some others, a cancelled law stamp showing the amount of the fee is placed in the upper left-hand corner of the original.

Fees paid by the law firm to file documents with court offices are treated as disbursements, and subsequently charged to the client when the account is rendered.

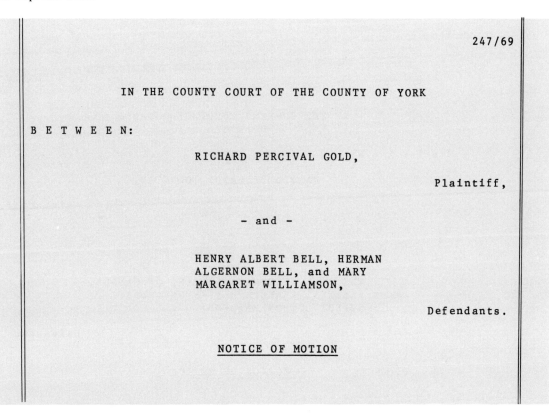

IN THE SUPREME COURT OF ONTARIO

B E T W E E N:

JOHN JOSEPH WILLIAMSON,

Double space

Plaintiff,

- and -

HENRY HORACE MISANTHROPE,

Double space

Defendant.

STATEMENT OF DEFENCE

1.

line from of page

ole space

able space

ole space

ole space

ole space

ple space

Figure 19.1A. Style of Cause for Action in the Supreme Court

247/69

IN THE COUNTY COURT OF THE COUNTY OF YORK

B E T W E E N:

RICHARD PERCIVAL GOLD,

Plaintiff,

- and -

HENRY ALBERT BELL, HERMAN
ALGERNON BELL, and MARY
MARGARET WILLIAMSON,

Defendants.

NOTICE OF MOTION

Figure 19.1B. Style of Cause for Action in the County Court

```
                    IN THE SUPREME COURT OF ONTARIO


                    IN THE MATTER OF Jennifer Anne Martin,
                    Infant;

                    AND IN THE MATTER OF The Infants Act,
                    R.S.O. 1960, c.187.


                            NOTICE OF MOTION
```

Figure 19.1C.   Style of Cause for Proceedings.


```
                                                        384/70


                    IN THE SUPREME COURT OF ONTARIO


        B E T W E E N:

                    HAROLD RICHARDS JOHNSTON,

                                                Plaintiff,


                            - and -


                    THE BELL TELEPHONE COMPANY OF CANADA,
                    PERCIVAL KENNETH BLACKSTONE, and
                    HUBERT LYNDON MacLEOD,

                                                Defendants.


                            NOTICE OF MOTION
```

*Figure 19.1D.   Style of Cause on Unruled
Paper Showing Alternate Way of
Centring Parties*

e of court, indicated by initials

Supreme Court, type
TION (PROCEEDINGS) COMMENCED
THE COUNTY OF . . ."

e of parties with "v." between names

ription of document

and address of law firm
1g document

S.   C.   O.

ACTION COMMENCED IN THE COUNTY
OF YORK

RONALD CRAIG ANDERSON

v.

PERCIVAL ANDREW PETERSON

A F F I D A V I T
of
PETER THOMAS GRANT

HILL, JOHNSTON & GRANT
17 Princess Street S.
Toronto, Ontario

Figure 19.2A. Back for Action in the Supreme Court

789/70

C. C. C. Y.

WILLIAM HUNT McLEAN

v.

LESLIE JOHN BROWN

STATEMENT OF DEFENCE

HILL, JOHNSTON & GRANT
17 Princess Street South
Toronto, Ontario

Figure 19.2B. Back for Action in the County Court

S. _____ C. _____ O.
_____

PROCEEDINGS COMMENCED IN THE COUNTY
OF YORK

IN THE MATTER OF Jennifer Annabel
Martin, Infant,

AND IN THE MATTER OF The Infants
Act, R.S.O. 1960, c.187.

_____

NOTICE OF MOTION

_____

HILL, JOHNSTON & GRANT
17 Princess Street South
Toronto, Ontario

Figure 19.2C.   Back for Matter

CHAPTER 20

Types of Court Documents

The court documents which must be typed fall largely within four main categories: affidavits, notices, pleadings, and orders and judgments.

Affidavits

As discussed earlier in Chapter 8, affidavits are used in all areas of legal practice to establish and prove facts. Affidavits are used frequently in court work. (See Figure 20.1.)

Heading

The style of cause of the action or matter determines the heading of an affidavit prepared for use in the courts.

Title of Document

An affidavit is one document in which it is not essential that the name of the document be shown following the style of cause. However, in practice, this title is frequently shown.

Body

The first sentence of the body of the affidavit begins with the name and general description of the person making it, and ends with the words "make oath and say as follows", or merely, "make oath and say". Numbered paragraphs follow setting out the facts to which the deponent will swear.

Ending

The jurat in affidavits used for court purposes is identical to that of other affidavits.

Back

Each copy of the affidavit has a back. In addition to identifying the document, it is usual to also indicate on the back the name of the deponent.

Number of Copies

The lawyer will indicate the number of copies of the affidavit required, which is determined by the purpose and nature of the affidavit.

Swearing an Affidavit

An affidavit prepared in the office for use in an action or matter in which that office is engaged is not acceptable to the courts if it is sworn before the solicitor of the party on whose behalf it is made, or before the clerk or partner of that solicitor. Therefore, it is necessary to take the deponent to another law office, and tell the receptionist in that office that you wish to have an affidavit sworn. She will usually arrange for this to be done.

Only the original of an affidavit is sworn and signed by the deponent. You should make true copies of all other copies of the affidavit.

Exhibits to an Affidavit

Frequently the person swearing the affidavit attaches to it material in support of the facts set out in the affidavit. Such material is known as an *exhibit*.

Marking Exhibits to an Affidavit

Each exhibit referred to in an affidavit is identified as Exhibit "A", Exhibit "B", Exhibit "C", and so on, depending on the number of exhibits referred to in the affidavit. Each exhibit is stamped with an exhibit stamp which is illustrated below.

THIS IS EXHIBIT "   " REFERRED TO IN THE
AFFIDAVIT OF
SWORN BEFORE ME THIS   DAY
OF   19

A Commissioner, etc.

In preparing the exhibits, the stamping is completed with the appropriate letter designation and the name of the deponent. The date line is not completed unless you know with certainty the date upon which the affidavit will be sworn.

At the time he completes his portion of the jurat, the Commissioner who takes the affidavit must also complete the exhibit stamp for each original exhibit as an indication that it is the exhibit referred to in the affidavit.

Attaching Exhibits

There are two ways of referring to exhibits in an affidavit. If in the affidavit it says: "Now shown to me and marked Exhibit "A" to this my affidavit . . ." the exhibits referred to are attached by a paper clip *outside* the back of the affidavit. Exhibits produced in this way are not filed with the court, but are left for the use of the court, and are returned when the action or matter has been resolved unless the court orders otherwise.

If in the affidavit it says: "Attached hereto and marked Exhibit "A" . . ." or "Annexed hereto and marked Exhibit "A" . . ." the exhibits referred to are stapled at the end of the affidavit *inside* the back. They are a permanent part of the affidavit and are not returned by the court when the action or matter has been resolved.

True Copies of Exhibits

Attached to each copy of the affidavit must be a copy of each exhibit to the affidavit, and each copy must bear the exhibit stamp. When the original affidavit with its exhibits has been sworn, you should make true copies not only of all copies of the affidavit itself, but also of all copies of the exhibits. If you are required to copy in a signature that you cannot read, and all attempts to ascertain the name prove useless, write in the word "Illegible" in place of the signature.

Disposition of Affidavit

A copy of the affidavit for use in court proceedings is first served on all parties on the other side, and the original affidavit with exhibits is then filed in the court office. The original of an affidavit is always filed with the court.

Affidavit of Service

As we have discussed, certain court documents must be served upon the other parties before the document may be filed with the appropriate court office. There is usually no problem if the other side will admit service of a copy of the document; however, this will not always be the case.

When it is not possible to secure an admission of service of a document, a copy is left with the law office where service was attempted. The person who attempted to serve the document will then complete an affidavit of service (Figure 20.1A), which sets out the facts and names the person with whom a copy of the document was left. Frequently this affidavit is typed; however, there is a printed form which may be used.

If the printed form is used, prepare two copies of the affidavit filling in the name of the court, the style of cause, and the necessary details. When the affidavit has been sworn, attach the signed original affidavit to the face of the document. When the document is being filed, present the signed affidavit to the court office to indicate proof of service.

An affidavit of service has no back, since it is attached to the face of the document to which it refers.

Notices

During the course of legal proceedings many *notices* may be served and filed to formally inform the court and the other parties concerned of some step or change which should be brought to their attention. Such notices include notice of motion, notice of trial, jury notice, notice of discontinuance, notice of change of solicitors, and so on, all of which are prepared in accordance with Figure 20.2.

Heading

The style of cause of the action or matter determines the heading of a notice.

NAME OF COURT

S T Y L E   O F   C A U S E

        I, PETER THOMAS GRANT, of the City of Toronto, in the
County of York, Solicitor, make oath and say as follows:

1.   _____

_____

_____.

2.   _____

_____

_____

_____.

3.   _____

_____

_____

_____.

                        etc.

SWORN before me at the City   )
)
of Toronto, in the County   )
)
of York, this   )
)
day of   , 19--   )
)
)
)
)
)
)
            A COMMISSIONER ETC.

Figure 20.1. Basic Format of Affidavit

Title of Document

Notices are identified by the special name of the document (e.g., NOTICE OF TRIAL).

Body

Notices begin with an unnumbered paragraph called the *preamble*, commencing with the words "TAKE NOTICE that". This paragraph frequently constitutes the entire text of the notice, but in some notices may be followed by numbered paragraphs.

Ending

Notices end with a "DATED at ..." line, followed by the typed signature of the law firm drawing the document, and addressed to the solicitors or parties on the other side.

Names of solicitors in the ending of notices are identified as "Solicitors for the plaintiff" or "Solicitors for the defendant". In matters, solicitors are identified by the name of the party whom they represent in the application to the courts.

Notices are addressed to the party or solicitors on the other side, or to other interested parties such as the Official Guardian.

AFFIDAVIT OF SERVICE

477/70

Dye & Durham Limited — Toronto, Canada
Printers to the Legal Profession
Form No. 283

In the COUNTY Court of THE COUNTY OF YORK

Between

RONALD CRAIG ANDERSON,

PLAINTIFF

AND

PERCIVAL ANDREW PETERSON,

DEFENDANT

I, HAROLD NORMAN GOOD,

of the   City   of   Toronto   in the
County   of   York

make oath and say:

1. THAT I did on   Mon day, the   15th   day of February, 1970 , personally serve Ross, Smith, Green, Williamson & Bell, solicitors for the above-named defendant,

with a true copy of the   statement of claim hereunto annexed, by delivering such copy to, and leaving the same with Helen May Glazier, the receptionist   at the offices of Ross, Smith, Green, Williamson & Bell, 75 Martindale Boulevard, Toronto.

SWORN before me at the   City
of   Toronto   in the   County
of   York   this
day of February   19 70

      A Commissioner, etc.

Figure 20.1A. Printed Affidavit of Service

183

If there are several people or firms to whom the notice is addressed, it is addressed to each in the order of interest in the action or matter.

Back

Each copy of the notice has a back which indicates the specific type of notice (e.g., NOTICE OF DISCONTINUANCE).

Number of Copies

A minimum of four copies of a notice is prepared; one each for the lawyer, the other side, the court, and the file. A further copy is required for each additional party to whom the notice is addressed.

Disposition of Notices

A copy of the notice is first served on the parties to whom it is addressed, and the original, with its admission of service, is filed in the appropriate court office.

Notice of Motion

The most common notice is a notice of motion by which an application is made to the courts for an order requiring that some particular thing be done or not done. There are three types of such notices which are outlined below.

Originating Notice of Motion

By this form of notice matters are originated in the courts. There is no action or file number. This form of notice is used, for example, to ask the courts to construe (interpret) the true intent of the will of a deceased person when there is doubt or dispute as to the meaning of a clause in his will.

The style of cause in an originating notice of motion is always headed by the name of the court, and paragraphs commencing with the words "IN THE MATTER OF". The style of cause usually contains only this reference to the matter to be considered. The style of cause may, however, after such

reference also show the names of the parties to the application (Figure 20.2A), usually identifying them as *applicant* – the party on whose behalf the application is made to the court, and *respondent* – the party whose position on the application is different from or opposed to that of the applicant.

In certain legal proceedings, however, such as an application for direction to partition or sell certain lands, the parties are described as "plaintiff" and "defendant".

Interlocutory Notice of Motion

This is a notice of motion which is made during the course of legal proceedings. The style of cause is the same as used in other documents in the action or matter.

Ex Parte Notice of Motion

An *ex parte* notice of motion is a motion brought without giving notice to the opposite party. Under certain circumstances it may be used during the course of legal proceedings. It is, however, usually brought in circumstances in which no proceedings have been commenced, and the style of cause commences with the words "IN THE MATTER OF", and shows the parties. An ex-parte notice of motion is not addressed to anyone.

Material Required With Notice of Motion

An affidavit setting out the facts which give rise to the application to the court is usually required on an originating or ex parte notice of motion.

Who Hears Motions

Motions are heard by a judge in court, a judge in Chambers, that is, his office, or in some cases by a Master of the Supreme Court.

Service of Notices of Motion

All interested parties, that is, all parties directly involved in the action or matter, must be served with a copy of the notice and

Action No. if
there is one

NAME OF COURT

STYLE OF CAUSE

TITLE OF DOCUMENT

TAKE NOTICE that_____

_____

_____

_____

_____

_____

_____

_____

_____

etc.

DATED at (city)   , this   day of   , 19--

NAME OF SOLICITORS
Address
Solicitors for the plaintiff (or defendant)

TO: NAME OF SOLICITORS
      Address
      Solicitors for the defendant (or plaintiff)

AND TO: _____)
          _____)   if required
          _____)

Figure 20.2. Basic Format for Notices   185

```
          IN THE SUPREME COURT OF ONTARIO


          IN THE MATTER OF the estate of Thomas
          Theodore Harrison, late of the City
          of Hamilton, in the County of Went-
          worth, deceased,


BETWEEN:

          THE NORTHERN BANK OF CANADA,

                                        Applicant,


               - and -


          HOWARD NORMAN GOOD, executor
          of the last will and testament
          of Thomas Theodore Harrison,
          deceased,

                                        Respondent.



                  NOTICE OF MOTION
```

Figure 20.2A. A Form of Style of Cause Sometimes Found in a Notice of Motion in a Matter

any accompanying affidavit before the original is filed with the appropriate court office. There must be at least seven days between the service of an originating notice of motion and the day for hearing, and at least two days between the service of an interlocutory notice of motion and the day of hearing. In calculating the number of days required, exclude the day of service and the day of hearing.

Decision on Motion

When a motion has been heard, the decision of the judge or Master is formally recorded in an order of the court. Orders are discussed later in the chapter.

Pleadings

Once an action has been commenced in the courts, each party prepares his *pleadings,* that is, his interpretation of the facts in dispute. The following are examples of pleadings: statement of claim, statement of defence, reply and joinder of issue, counter-claim, reply and defence to counter-claim. The basic format for pleadings is illustrated in Figure 20.3.

Only a statement of claim and defence *must* be served and filed in an action; other pleadings are used only if the facts of the case require that this be done.

A defendant may, in his statement of defence, include his *counter-claim,* which is a claim against the plaintiff and is separate and distinct from his defence to the plaintiff's claim. The plaintiff has a right to answer a statement of defence, and to put in a statement of defence to the counter-claim. Other pleadings which may be filed will be discussed in greater detail in Chapter 21.

Heading

The style of cause for a statement of claim, a statement of defence, or a statement of defence and counter-claim follows the form of the style of cause in the action. Replies follow the same form of the style of cause of the document which they answer.

If a counter-claim is prepared as a separate document, and is not included with the statement of defence, the style of cause reverses the parties. This new style is followed in the plaintiff's reply and defence to counter-claim. Figure 20.4 illustrates the form of style of cause used in these circumstances.

Title of Document

Pleadings are identified by the specific name of the document (e.g., STATEMENT OF DEFENCE).

When typing a statement of claim, two spaces beneath the title you must indicate, in brackets, the date of issuance of the writ which commenced the action:

(Writ issued the . . . day of . . . , 1970.)

Body

Numbered paragraphs set out the position of the party on whose behalf the document is prepared.

Two special exceptions must be noted when typing a statement of claim. The second last paragraph called the *prayer for relief* sets out the claim of the plaintiff against the defendant.

The last numbered paragraph in a statement of claim indicates the *venue*, that is, the city where it is proposed the action be tried:

10. The plaintiff proposes that this action be tried at the City of Toronto.

Ending

Pleadings end with an unnumbered paragraph beginning with the words "DELIVERED at", followed by the date of typing, the name and address of the solicitors, and the parties for whom they are acting.

Back

Each copy of a pleading has a back, which identifies the pleading by its proper designation (e.g., COUNTER-CLAIM).

Number of Copies

A minimum of four copies of pleadings is prepared; the original, one copy for the court, one copy for each firm of solicitors acting for the defendants, and a copy for the use of the lawyer.

Disposition of Pleadings

Pleadings are first served, and a copy (not the original) is then filed in the appropriate court office.

Judgments and Orders

When an action or matter has been tried or heard, a formal document recording the decision of the judge or Master is prepared – usually by the solicitors for the successful party. Such documents are known as *judgments* and *orders* (Figure 20.5).

Orders may be made in both actions and matters; judgments are usually handed down (made) following the trial of an action. Part of the transcript of the trial is a document known as the *reasons for judgment,* which sets out the judge's reasons for arriving at his decision. Many lawyers arrange to purchase a copy of these reasons when judgment has been given.

From the wording used in the document as it is dictated to you, you will be able to determine whether you are to prepare a judgment or an order, both of which follow a basically similar form.

Number of Copies

A minimum of four copies of a judgment or an order is prepared including the original, one copy for the court, one copy for the party on the other side, and a file copy.

Disposition of Copies

Before anything else is done after the order or judgment is typed, it is submitted to all interested parties for approval as to form and content.

Once approved, the original and a copy, together with the approved copy, are taken

Action No.

NAME OF COURT

S T Y L E   O F   C A U S E

TITLE OF DOCUMENT

    1**

1.   _____

_____

2.   _____

_____

3.   _____

_____

4.   _____

_____

_____

5.   _____

_____

_____

    2**

6.   _____

_____

DELIVERED at (city)   , this   day of
19--, by (name and address of solicitors), solicitors for the
plaintiff (or defendant as case may be).

**It is at these locations that two special statements are
included in a Statement of Claim.

*Figure 20.3. Basic Format for Pleadings
– County Court and Supreme Court,
Trial Division*

to the appropriate court office, so the original may be signed and "entered". When an order or judgment has been signed and entered, it is said to have been "issued".

Judgments and orders are entered in the records maintained in the court office either by inserting a copy of the document into a book kept for that purpose, or by microfilming the order or judgment and filing the negative. A notation of the appropriate entry book, or negative number, appears at the foot of the original document.

County Court judgments and orders are signed and entered in the local County Court office; Supreme Court judgments and orders are signed in the Supreme Court office located in the county in which the order was made, but entered in the Supreme Court office located in the county in which the action or matter was commenced.

Once the judgment or order has been issued, the original is returned to you, and a copy is retained in the court office. A true copy of the document is then delivered to the other side, or to the other interested parties. An admission of service is not usually required.

Heading

Immediately beneath the reference to the court on the face of the document, every judgment and order gives the name of the judge or Master who handed down (i.e., gave) the judgment, or made the order, and the day of the week and month on which it was given or made. The style of cause is set out below this information.

Title of Document

An order or judgment is not identified by name on the face of the document.

Body

Both an order and a judgment begin with an unnumbered paragraph known as the preamble, which gives a brief history of the matter or action to which the document relates. The judgment or order made is then set out in numbered paragraphs the first words of which are capitalized.

In a judgment, the paragraphs follow this guide:

```
                                          199/70


         IN THE SUPREME COURT OF ONTARIO

   B E T W E E N:

         HENRY HORACE MISANTHROPE,

                         Plaintiff by Counter-Claim,


               - and -


         JOHN JOSEPH WILLIAMSON,

                         Defendant by Counter-Claim.


         COUNTER-CLAIM
```

Figure 20.4. Style of Cause for a Separate Counter-Claim

1. THIS COURT DOTH ORDER AND ADJUDGE that . . .
2. AND THIS COURT DOTH FURTHER ORDER AND ADJUDGE that . . .

OR

1. IT IS ORDERED AND ADJUDGED that . . .
2. AND IT IS FURTHER ORDERED AND ADJUDGED that . . .

The words "AND DOTH ORDER AND ADJUDGE THE SAME ACCORDINGLY" may, in certain circumstances, come at the end of the numbered paragraph rather than at the beginning. You type exactly what is dictated by the lawyer, and you need only remember that the phrase containing the words "order and adjudge" is typed in capital letters.

In an order, the paragraphs follow this guide:

1. THIS COURT DOTH ORDER that . . .
2. AND THIS COURT DOTH FURTHER ORDER that . . .

OR

1. IT IS ORDERED that . . .
2. AND IT IS FURTHER ORDERED that . . .

Ending

On a judgment only, the following line is typed in the ending: "Judgment signed . . ." On both an order and a judgment, a line for the signature of the appropriate court official is typed four or five lines beneath the last line of typing.

Back

A back is prepared for all copies of the order or judgment in the usual way, but with one exception. Since the order or judgment must be entered in the county where the action or matter was commenced, the reference to "ACTION COMMENCED . . ." which must appear on the back of other Supreme Court documents, need not be typed on the back of a Supreme Court order or judgment.

Default Judgment

If the defendant in an action does not take any of the steps open to him to defend the action against him, the plaintiff may then get judgment against him by default. The form of the judgment then varies slightly from a regular judgment after trial (Figure 20.5A).

The style of cause is identical to that of the writ which commenced the action. No reference is made to any judge or date of judgment. The first line of the body of the judgment is the date the default judgment is prepared. Unnumbered paragraphs follow setting out the basis for seeking judgment in default. The default judgment is ended as a regular judgment.

Costs

In orders and judgments, references may be made to *costs*. This is a reference to money to which a party may be entitled in order to compensate him for the expense of being a party to a court action or matter.

Consent

A common legal document which does not fall into the four main categories we have just considered is a *consent* (Figure 20.6). This document formally puts into words an agreement reached by the solicitors or parties without a trial or outside the court.

Heading

The style of cause in a consent follows the form used in the action or matter to which it relates.

Title of Document

The document shows its name on its face.

Body

The body of the document commences with the phrase "WE HEREBY CONSENT . . ." and simply states the terms of the consent agreement.

Ending

Following the "DATED at . . ." line, sufficient lines for the signatures of the solicitors or interested parties are typed at the right-hand side of the page. Beneath each line is an indication of the capacity of the person who is to sign the consent.

Back

Each copy of the consent has a back.

Number of Copies

Sufficient copies are prepared to provide the original signed copy for the court, one copy for each firm of solicitors or interested parties, and a copy for your file.

Executing the Consent

Sufficient copies of the consent are signed to provide a signed copy for each firm of solicitors, each interested party, and the court.

Disposition of Copies

The original signed copy of the consent is filed with the appropriate court, and each firm of solicitors or other interested party receives a signed copy.

```
                                                  Action No. if
                                                  there is one
                        NAME OF COURT

THE HONOURABLE MR. JUSTICE JENKINS )   WEDNESDAY, THE 10th DAY OF
                                   )
                                   )   OCTOBER, 19--


            S T Y L E   O F   C A U S E


       UPON_____

       _____

       _____

       _____

       _____:


    1.      _____

       _____

       _____

    2.      _____

       _____

       _____

    3.      _____

       _____

       _____

    4.      _____

       _____
                                                      This line
       Judgment signed this      day of          , 19--  appears
                                                      only on a
                                                      Judgment.

            _____
```

Figure 20.5. Basic Format for Orders and Judgments

IN THE COUNTY COURT OF THE COUNTY OF YORK

B E T W E E N:

        ARMSTRONG, STAFFORD, MAYE,
        COLLINS, HARRIS & LITTLE,

                               Plaintiff,

               - and -

        GEORGE PHILLIP EDWARDS,
        BLAKE CHARLES WINTERS, and
        ALEXANDER GELON HEWITT,

                             Defendants.

Monday, the 22nd day of February, 1970.

NO APPEARANCE having been entered to the writ of summons herein:

IT IS THIS DAY ADJUDGED that the plaintiff do recover against the defendants damages to be assessed.

JUDGMENT signed this   day of   , 1970.

_____

Figure 20.5A. Form of Default Judgment

IN THE SUPREME COURT OF ONTARIO

B E T W E E N:

WILLIAM H. McLEAN,

Plaintiff,

- and -

LESLIE JOHN BROWN,

Defendant.

C O N S E N T

WE HEREBY CONSENT to the dismissal of this action and the counter-claim without costs.

DATED at Toronto this   day of April, 1970.

_____
Solicitors for the plaintiff

_____
Solicitors for the defendant

Figure 20.6. Consent

CHAPTER 21

Steps in a Civil Lawsuit

An action is frequently referred to as a *lawsuit,* and it is the steps which are taken in such a suit that we now consider. (See Figure 21.1.)

While other special factors may alter the basic guide, the court in which a lawsuit is brought depends on the amount of damages claimed. County Courts usually deal with claims up to $3,000.00; Supreme Court deals with claims over $3,000.00.

The practice and procedure is basically identical in both courts. These rules are contained in THE RULES OF PRACTICE AND PROCEDURE OF THE SUPREME COURT OF ONTARIO, obtainable from the Queen's Printer, Toronto. Each lawyer engaged in the practice of litigation will usually have his own copy of this book, which sets out the rules of procedure, and contains an appendix of forms used in civil matters, as well as a *tariff* of court fees and disbursements.

Commencement of an Action

When one party wishes to seek redress from another in the courts, his action is commenced by issuing a *writ of summons.* The parties to an action are the plaintiff(s) – the person or persons who are making a claim against another person or persons, and the defendant(s) – the person or persons against whom a claim is made.

Writs

A writ is a document in the Queen's name, issued at the request of the plaintiff for the purpose of giving the defendant notice of the claim made against him, and compelling him to defend the claim if he does not admit it. The issuance of a writ is the first step in an action. A writ is on a printed form.

The writ contains the names of the parties and the capacity in which they sue and are sued, and indicates the office in which, and the time within which, the defendant is to enter an *appearance*. An appearance indicates that the defendant intends to challenge the plaintiff's claim. The writ is endorsed on page 2 with a short, concise statement of the nature of the plaintiff's claim.

When the writ is issued, the style of cause for the action is established unless subsequently amended.

Types of Writs

A writ of summons may be either "generally endorsed" or "specially endorsed", and each of these two types may also be "out of jurisdiction", that is, the writ may name defendants who reside outside of Ontario.

Generally Endorsed Writ of Summons

A generally endorsed writ (Figure 21.2) is the most common type of writ and is used to commence most actions in the courts. The generally endorsed writ is used when there is uncertainty as to the amount in dispute.

Specially Endorsed Writ of Summons

A specially endorsed writ (Figure 21.3) "speeds up justice" and is used when there would seem to be no defence to the claim. The amount of the claim involved is clear and determinable, for example, as in a lease or a contract. There is either no uncertainty as to the amount in dispute, or the amount can easily be determined by reference to a fixed formula.

Writs "Out of Jurisdiction"

Writs *out of jurisdiction* may be either generally or specially endorsed. An order of the court must be obtained before a writ for service out of Ontario may be issued. The solicitors acting for the intended plaintiff will move ex parte for an order for service out of the jurisdiction. On hearing the matter, an affidavit is read which sets out the

Steps in a Civil Lawsuit

COUNTY COURT AND SUPREME COURT OF ONTARIO

WRIT OF SUMMONS   p.

This writ is either

A.

or

B.

and may also be out of the jurisdiction, in which event the steps vary

GENERALLY ENDORSED

SPECIALLY ENDORSED

APPEARANCE   d.

DEFAULT JUDGMENT   p.

APPEARANCE AND AFFIDAVIT OF MERITS   d.

STATEMENT OF CLAIM
(within one month after Appearance)   p.

(A & B are alternative ways of proceeding)

A.

B.

STATEMENT OF DEFENCE   d.

STATEMENT OF DEFENCE AND COUNTER-CLAIM   d.

REPLY AND JOINDER OF ISSUE   p.

REPLY AND DEFENCE TO COUNTER-CLAIM   p.

REPLY TO DEFENCE TO COUNTER-CLAIM   d.

NOTICE TO PRODUCE   p. & d.

AFFIDAVIT ON PRODUCTION   p. & d.

EXAMINATION FOR DISCOVERY   p. & d.

RECORD and NOTICE OF TRIAL

CERTIFICATE OF READINESS

TRIAL

JUDGMENT

BILL OF COSTS

TAXATION APPOINTMENT

TAXATION CERTIFICATE

Figure 21.1

facts in support of the intended plaintiff's contention that he has a claim against a person who resides outside Ontario. If the court is satisfied, an order will be granted. The order must accompany the writ before it can be issued.

Preparation of Writ

The solicitors for the plaintiff prepare a writ of summons on the printed forms of writ for the proper court.

Number of Copies

The number of copies prepared is determined by the number of defendants. A good rule to follow is: prepare a minimum of two copies, plus one for each defendant.

Style of Cause

Only the names of the parties are shown in the style of cause. However, if an infant is suing, he cannot do so personally, and does so through what is known as a *next friend,* that is, a person over the age of 21 who consents to have his name used as a next friend. Companies can sue and be sued in the company name.

Addressed to Defendants

In addressing the writ of summons, the full address of each defendant is shown, so that the defendant can be located in order to be served with a true copy of the writ.

Instructions to Defendant

The writ indicates the period of time in which the defendant must enter an appearance in order to defend the action, and the place where such an appearance is to be entered.

Endorsement

Following the lawyer's instructions, a concise statement of the plaintiff's claim is typed on page 2 of the writ. If the writ is specially endorsed, a blank on page 3 is completed to indicate the amount of costs claimed. The lawyer must personally sign the writ to certify that he believes the claim is properly the subject matter of a specially endorsed writ.

Back

The county in which the action is commenced is shown on the back of Supreme Court writs. The plaintiff's address is shown as well as the name and address of his solicitors.

Disposition of a Writ

After the writ has been prepared, the original and a copy are taken to the office of the appropriate court. Upon payment of the required fee, the writ is issued. The Registrar signs the original, affixes a large red seal, and writes in the action number on the face and the back of the writ in the appropriate blanks. Action number 195/70 indicates that this was the 195th writ issued in that court to date in 1970. This action number is typed on all subsequent documents filed with the court.

Effect of Issuing a Writ

The issuance of a writ only protects the rights of the plaintiff until he determines whether to proceed with the action. A writ is in force for twelve months from the date of issuance, but it may be renewed.

What Happens to the Issued Writ

Often the writ is issued and held, that is, it is not served on the defendant. It is issued in order to protect the rights of the plaintiff who must bring an action within a certain time limit or lose the right to do so.

More frequently, however, the writ is served on the defendant by the sheriff or a private process server. If the writ is to be "issued and served", the original and a copy for each defendant to be served are given to the sheriff after it has been issued by the appropriate court. The sheriff will then arrange to personally serve the defendant and return the original to the plaintiff's solicitors. He will also enclose an affidavit of service and his account.

AMENDED JUNE, 1965

Dye & Durham Limited — Law and Commercial Stationers
76 Richmond Street E., Toronto
Form No. 574-576

Writ of Summons S.C.O.—General   No.   A.D. 1970

In the Supreme Court of Ontario

Between

RONALD CRAIG ANDERSON, and
LUCILLE CAROLINE ANDERSON,

PLAINTIFF^S

(SEAL)   AND

BRUCE ANDREW McCLELLAND, and
HARVEY HERMAN BELL,

DEFENDANT^S

Elizabeth the Second, by the Grace of God, of the United Kingdom, Canada and Her other Realms and Territories Queen, Head of the Commonwealth, Defender of the Faith.

TO   Bruce Andrew McClelland,
1593 Danforth Avenue,
Toronto 19, Ontario.

AND TO: Harvey Herman Bell,
320 Guildwood Parkway,
Etobicoke, Ontario.

*sert Defendant's
me and Address*

We Command You, that within ten days after the service of this writ on you, inclusive of the day of such service, you do cause an appearance to be entered for you in this action; AND TAKE NOTICE, that, in default of your so doing, the plaintiffs may proceed therein and judgment may be given in your absence on the plaintiff's own showing, and you may be deemed to have admitted the plaintiff's claim and (subject to Rules of Court) will not be entitled to notice of any further proceedings herein.

In Witness Whereof this writ is signed for the Supreme Court of Ontario by GORDON
FRANK BEDDIS   Registrar of the said Court at Toronto
this   day of   January   1970

....
(signature of officer)

N.B.—This writ is to be served within twelve calendar months from the date thereof, or, if renewed, within twelve calendar months from the date of such renewal, including the day of such date, and not afterwards.

Appearance may be entered at the Registrar's   Office at Osgoode Hall
Queen Street West, Toronto 1, Ontario.

Figure 21.2.   Generally Endorsed Writ – Page 1   197

575—Writ of Summons—General S.C.O.—p. 2.
Dye & Durham Ltd.

~~The Plaintiff's claim is~~

The Plaintiffs' claim is for damages suffered as a result of the negligent operation of a motor vehicle owned by the defendant Bruce Andrew McClelland and operated by the defendant Harvey Herman Bell on or about the 3rd day of December, 1969, at Gerrard Street at or near the intersection of Berkeley Street in the City of Toronto in the County of York.

Figure 21.2. Generally Endorsed Writ – Page 2

No.   A.D. 19 70

𝔍𝔫 𝔱𝔥𝔢 𝔖𝔲𝔭𝔯𝔢𝔪𝔢 ℭ𝔬𝔲𝔯𝔱 𝔬𝔣 ℭ𝔫𝔱𝔞𝔯𝔦𝔬

ACTION COMMENCED IN THE COUNTY
OF YORK

RONALD CRAIG ANDERSON,
and LUCILLE CAROLINE
ANDERSON

VS.

BRUCE ANDREW McCLELLAND,
and HARVEY HERMAN BELL

𝔚𝔯𝔦𝔱 𝔬𝔣 𝔖𝔲𝔪𝔪𝔬𝔫𝔰

GENERAL FORM

Dye & Durham Limited, Toronto, Canada
Law and Commercial Stationers

This Writ was issued by HILL, JOHNSTON

& GRANT, 17 Princess Street South,

of the   City   of Toronto

in the   County   of   York

Solicitors for the said Plaintiffs

who reside   at 987 Helena Avenue,

Toronto, Ontario

HILL, JOHNSTON & GRANT
Plaintiffs' Solicitors
PLAINTIFF'S SOLICITOR

Figure 21.2. Generally Endorsed Writ – Back

EFFECTIVE JAN. 1968

Dye & Durham Limited — Law and Commercial Stationers
76 Richmond Street E., Toronto
Form No. 563-566

Writ of Summons S.C.O.—Special Endorsement　　　No.　　　　　　　A.D. 1970

In the Supreme Court of Ontario

Between

RONALD CRAIG ANDERSON,
and HENRY PETER MARTIN,

PLAINTIFF

(SEAL)　　　　　　　　　　　　　　　AND

BRUCE ANDREW McCLELLAND,

DEFENDANT

Elizabeth the Second, by the Grace of God, of the United Kingdom, Canada and Her other Realms
and Territories Queen, Head of the Commonwealth, Defender of the Faith.

TO　　Bruce Andrew McClelland,
　　　　1593 Danforth Boulevard,
　　　　Toronto 19, Ontario.

Insert Defendant's
Name and Address

We Command You that within 15 days after the service of this writ on you, inclusive of the day
of such service, if you desire to defend this action;
(1) you serve upon the plaintiffs　or　their　solicitors　a copy of an affidavit that you have
　　a good defence upon the merits and showing the nature of your defence, if any, to the plaintiff's
　　claim, with the facts and circumstances which you deem entitle you to defend the action; and
(2) you file such affidavit with proof of service thereof, together with an appearance, in the court
　　office from which this writ was issued.

And Take Notice that in default of your so doing, the plaintiffs　may sign judgment for the
relief claimed as endorsed on this writ, and execution will at once issue thereon.

In Witness Whereof this writ is signed for the Supreme Court of Ontario by　　GORDON
FRANK BEDDIS　　　　　Registrar of the said Court at　Toronto
this　　　　　　　　　　day of　January　　　　　1970

....
　　　　　　　　　　　　　　　　　　　(signature of officer)

　　N.B.—This writ is to be served within twelve calendar months from the date thereof, or, if
renewed, within twelve calendar months from the date of such renewal, including the day of such
date, and not afterwards.

　　Appearance may be entered at the　Registrar's　　Office at Osgoode Hall,
Queen Street West, Toronto 1, Ontario.

　　　　　　　　　Figure 21.3. Specially Endorsed Writ – Page 1

~~The plaintiff's claim is~~

The plaintiffs' claim is against the defendant for the price of goods sold and delivered to the defendant.

The following are the particulars :

September 23, 1968	25 Automobile Radios No. 5	$1,437.65
August 4, 1969	25 Automobile Radios No. 6	$2,957.28
		$4,394.93

Demand for payment of the said sum has been made on the defendant, which demand has not been satisfied in whole or in part.

Figure 21.3. Specially Endorsed Writ – Page 2

(This space may be used if the particulars of the claim require
more space than provided on page 2 of the writ)

I believe the above claim is one which comes within the provisions of rule 33.

....
SIGNATURE OF SOLICITOR ISSUING WRIT

And the Plaintiffs further claim $ 500.00 for costs.

WARNING TO DEFENDANT

This writ being specially endorsed, the defendant is warned that his failure
to comply with the requirements of this writ may result in a default judgment being
entered and an execution being issued against

If the amount of the plaintiff's claim is paid within the time limited for appearance,
further proceedings will be stayed. If the amount claimed for costs is deemed to be
excessive, the defendant may have them taxed.

Figure 21.3. Specially Endorsed Writ – Page 3

No.   A.D. 1970

In the Supreme Court of Ontario

ACTION COMMENCED IN THE COUNTY
OF YORK

RONALD CRAIG ANDERSON,
and HENRY PETER MARTIN

VS.

BRUCE ANDREW McCLELLAND

Writ of Summons

SPECIAL ENDORSEMENT

Dye & Durham Limited, Toronto, Canada
Law and Commercial Stationers

This Writ was issued by HILL, JOHNSTON
& GRANT, 17 Princess Street South,

of the   City   of   Toronto
in the   County   of   York
Solicitors for the said Plaintiffs
who reside   at 987 Helena Avenue,
Toronto, Ontario.

HILL, JOHNSTON & GRANT
Plaintiffs' Solicitors
~~PLAINTIFF'S SOLICITOR~~

Figure 21.3. Specially Endorsed Writ – Back

203

Acceptance of Service of Writs

In large cities like Toronto the solicitors issuing the writ quite frequently have been negotiating with the solicitors for the defendants, and rather than serving the defendants personally with the writ, may ask the defendants' solicitors to *accept service* of the writ on behalf of their clients. If the solicitors for the defendants will accept service of the writ, they thereby acknowledge receipt of a copy of the writ and undertake to appear on behalf of the defendants. Their acceptance of service is usually typed on the back of the original of the writ:

We hereby accept service of a true
copy of the within Writ of Summons
on behalf of the defendant(s) and
undertake to appear thereto in
accordance with the exigencies
thereof.

Dated this   day of   , 197-

_____
Solicitors for the defendant(s)

You should never accept service of a writ unless specifically authorized by the lawyer to do so.

Responses to Writs

Since writs out of the jurisdiction are not common, we shall limit our consideration to the procedures related to generally and specially endorsed writs served in Ontario.

Within ten days of service upon him of the generally endorsed writ (counting the day of service as one of such days), the defendant must file the original of an appearance at the appropriate court office to indicate he intends to dispute the plaintiff's claim. No copy is served upon the solicitors for the plaintiff.

Two copies of an appearance are typed setting it up in the style of a notice, but not addressing it to anyone. The wording of an appearance is:

ENTER AN APPEARANCE on behalf of the defendant(s) in this action.

DATED at . . .

If there is more than one defendant, and not all defendants are represented by the same law firm, then the wording of the appearance is:

ENTER AN APPEARANCE on behalf of John Boyd Williamson, one of the above-named defendants in this action.

DATED at . . .

Ten days after service of the writ, the plaintiff's solicitors will arrange to have a search made in the court office to determine whether an appearance has been entered. From this search the plaintiff's solicitors will learn (if it is not already known) what firm of solicitors is acting on behalf of the defendants.

Within fifteen days of service of a specially endorsed writ each defendant not only must enter an appearance, but also must serve and file an *affidavit of merits,* that is, an affidavit outlining any defence he may have to the plaintiff's claim. This affidavit is typed in the style of a regular court affidavit, and a minimum of four copies is prepared: the original with the admission of service for the court, a copy for the solicitors for the plaintiff, a copy for your lawyer, and a copy for the file.

If the defendant does not enter an appearance within the time specified, the solicitors for the plaintiff may proceed to have judgment signed for the claim outlined in the writ.

Pleadings

All pleadings are typed, and the contents will be dictated by the lawyer acting in the case.

After the appearance (and affidavit of merits, if required) has been filed, the plaintiff then has one month to serve and file his statement of claim, which is an outline of the facts of the case, and includes his prayer for relief.

The defendant has ten days after service of the statement of claim to serve and file his statement of defence, in which he gives his version of the facts, and his defence to the claim against him.

The plaintiff may then, if he so wishes, serve and file a reply to the statement of defence, called a reply and joinder of issue.

The defendant, however, may if he wishes counter-claim against the plaintiff. He may do this by including his counter-claim as part of his statement of defence, or by filing and serving a separate document. In the latter case, there is an alteration in the style of cause, as we have discussed in Chapter 20. In either event the original plaintiff has a right to reply in a document known as a reply and defence to counter-claim.

If the original defendant wishes, he may then file and serve a document known as a reply to defence to counter-claim.

With the filing of the final reply, the pleadings are said to be "closed" (completed).

Notice to Produce

Each party in an action has the right to require the other party to inform him, by means of an affidavit, what material he has or had in his possession which relates to the matter in dispute and upon which he is relying to prove his case, and which he will let the other side inspect if it wishes; in addition, what material he has which he will not produce for inspection.

This right is exercised by serving on the other party two *notices to produce*. These are notice to produce on discovery (Figure 21.4), and notice to produce at trial (Figure 21.5). These are both printed legal forms, suitable for use in both the County and Supreme Courts, requiring the insertion of the name of the court, the style of cause, the date, and the name of the solicitors to whom it is addressed.

Both sides in an action prepare these notices. A minimum of two copies of each is typed; the original of each notice is served at the same time on the solicitors for the other side. These notices are not filed with the court, and therefore the back of the notice need not show the county in which the action was commenced, or the action number. Many lawyers, however, feel it is wise to show this information in the event that the other party does not comply with the requirement to produce documents. It would then be necessary to ask the court to order them to do so.

Affidavits on Production

Upon being served with notices to produce, each plaintiff or each defendant must complete an affidavit setting out the material he has or had, the material he is willing to produce, as well as the material he will not produce. This affidavit is called an *affidavit on production*.

The affidavit is a printed form, again suitable for use in either the County or Supreme Court. There are two types of this affidavit; one for an individual (Figure 21.6), and one for an officer of a company (Figure 21.7). The action number is shown on the affidavit for production as well as the county in which the action was commenced.

Prepare a minimum of three copies of the affidavit; the original is filed in the court office, a copy is served upon the solicitors for the other side, and a copy is kept for the use of the lawyer.

Listing Material in the Affidavit

Dated material which is being produced and set out in the affidavit is listed in chronological order, commencing with the earliest date. Undated material is placed into logical groupings and follows the list of dated productions.

Actual copies of the material being produced are *not* attached to the affidavit when it is filed, or when it is served. Such material is retained by the solicitors, but the other side may arrange to inspect any production.

Examinations for Discovery

When the exchange of pleadings has been completed, notices to produce served, and affidavits on production filed, the next step is to hold *examinations for discovery*. The parties to the action are examined under oath at some time before the trial, and answer questions touching upon the matters in dispute. This provides each side with a great deal of information about the case to be presented by the other side. It is held in the office of reporters known as *special examiners*.

Revised June, 1965
Notice for Production and Discovery.

Dye & Durham Limited — Toronto, Canada
Law and Commercial Stationers
76 Richmond St. East, Toronto
Form No. 278

ONTARIO

In the COUNTY Court of THE COUNTY OF YORK

Between

RONALD CRAIG ANDERSON, and
LUCILLE CAROLINE ANDERSON,

Plaintiff s

and

BRUCE ANDREW McCLELLAND, and
HARVEY HERMAN BELL,

Defendant s

Take Notice that you are required within ten days from this date to make discovery on oath of the documents which are or have been in your possession or power relating to any matters in question in this action and to produce and deposit the same with the proper officer of this Court for the usual purposes, and that you are also required to serve a copy of the affidavit upon the undersigned forthwith after it has been filed.

DATED this 31st day of January 19 70

Hill, Johnston & Grant
Solicitors for the plaintiffs

To ROSS, SMITH, GREEN, WILLIAMSON & BELL,
75 Martindale Boulevard,
Toronto, Ontario.

Solicitor s for the defendants.

206

Figure 21.4. Notice to Produce on Discovery

In the COUNTY   **Court of**   THE COUNTY

OF YORK

RONALD CRAIG ANDERSON, and
LUCILLE CAROLINE ANDERSON,

—VS.—

BRUCE ANDREW McCLELLAND, and
HARVEY HERMAN BELL

Notice for Production and Discovery

Dye & Durham Limited — Toronto, Canada
Printers to the Legal Profession

HILL, JOHNSTON & GRANT
17 Princess Street South
Toronto, Ontario

*Figure 21.4. Notice to Produce on Discovery —
Back*

207

Revised June, 1965

NOTICE TO PRODUCE DOCUMENTS AT THE TRIAL

Dye & Durham Limited — Law and Commercial Stationers
76 Richmond Street E., Toronto
Form No. 278

In the SUPREME Court of ONTARIO
Between

SMITH MANUFACTURING COMPANY LIMITED,

Plaintiff

and

WILLIAM HENRY BELL,

Defendant

Take Notice that you are hereby required to produce and show to the court on the trial of this action all books, papers, letters, copies of letters, and other writings and documents in your custody, possession or power, containing any entry, memorandum or minute relating to the matters in question in this action, and particularly the following:

DESCRIPTION OF DOCUMENT	DATE

Dated this 31st day of January 1970

To the above named plaintiff
and to HILL, JOHNSTON & GRANT
17 Princess Street South
Toronto, Ontario

ROSS, SMITH, GREEN, WILLIAMSON
& BELL,
75 Martindale Boulevard
Toronto, Ontario

Solicitors for the plaintiff

Solicitors for the above-named defendant

Figure 21.5. Notice to Produce at Trial

In the SUPREME Court

of ONTARIO

ACTION COMMENCED IN THE COUNTY
OF YORK

SMITH MANUFACTURING COMPANY
LIMITED

VS.

WILLIAM HENRY BELL

Notice to Produce Documents At Trial

Dye & Durham Limited — Toronto, Canada
Printers to the Legal Profession

ROSS, SMITH, GREEN
WILLIAMSON & BELL
75 Martindale Boulevard
Toronto, Ontario

Figure 21.5. Notice to Produce at Trial —
Back

AMENDED JUNE, 1965

Affidavit as to Production of Documents.

DYE & DURHAM LIMITED — LAW & COMMERCIAL STATIONERS
76 RICHMOND ST. EAST, TORONTO
Form No. 378-381

In the COUNTY Court of THE COUNTY OF YORK

Between

RONALD CRAIG ANDERSON, and
LUCILLE CAROLINE ANDERSON,

PLAINTIFF

and

BRUCE ANDREW McCLELLAND, and
HARVEY HERMAN BELL,

DEFENDANT

I RONALD CRAIG ANDERSON, one of

the above-named plaintiffs,

make oath and say as follows:—

1.—I have in my possession or power the documents relating to the matters in question in this action set forth in the first and second parts of the first schedule hereto.

2.—I object to produce the said documents set forth in the second part of the said first schedule hereto.

3.—That the same are privileged.

Here state upon what grounds the objection is made, and verify the facts as far as may be.

4.—I have had, but have not now, in my possession or power the documents relating to the matters in question in this suit set forth in the second schedule hereto.

State when

5.—The last-mentioned documents were last in my possession or power on or about their respective dates.

Figure 21.6. Affidavit on Production,
Individual — Page 1

6.—That the same were mailed or delivered to the parties to whom they were respectively addressed and should be in their possession.

7.—According to the best of my knowledge, information and belief, I have not now, and never had in my possession, custody or power, or in the possession, custody or power of my solicitors or agents, or in the possession, custody or power of any other persons or person on my behalf, any deed, account, book of account, voucher, receipt, letter, memorandum, paper, or writing, or any copy of or extract from any such document, or any other document whatsoever relating to the matters in question in this action or any of them, or wherein any entry has been made relative to such matters, or any of them, other than and except the documents set forth in the said first and second schedules hereto, and the pleadings and other proceedings in the action.

Sworn before me at the   City

of   Toronto

in the   County   of York

this

day of   February   19 70

A Commissioner, etc.

_____

THE FIRST SCHEDULE HERETO.

The First Part thereof:— Showing documents in my possession which I do not object to produce.

1.   Copy of letter, February 7, 1969, from Harvey Herman Bell to Ronald Craig Anderson

2.   Copy of letter, February 17, 1969, from plaintiffs' solicitors to Harvey Herman Bell.

3.   Letter dated March 15, 1969, from defendants' solicitors to Ronald Craig Anderson. Envelope attached, bearing postmark March 15, 1969.

Figure 21.6. Affidavit on Production,
Individual – Page 2

The Second Part:—Showing documents in my possession which I object to produce.

Correspondence between the plaintiffs and their solicitors, correspondence between the plaintiffs and third persons for the purpose of giving or receiving information concerning this action, correspondence written without prejudice, and documents prepared for use in this litigation.

(NOTE: If the affidavit is on behalf of the defendant, then change "plaintiff" to "defendant" in this paragraph.)

THE SECOND SCHEDULE HERETO.

Showing documents which I have had, but have not now in my possession or power.

Letters and documents, copies of which are referred to in the first part of the first schedule as having been written by myself or my solicitors.

Figure 21.6.   Affidavit on Production, Individual – Page 3

In the COUNTY Court of THE COUNTY
OF YORK

RONALD CRAIG ANDERSON, and
LUCILLE CAROLINE ANDERSON

VS.

BRUCE ANDREW McCLELLAND,
and HARVEY HERMAN BELL

Affidavit
AS TO PRODUCTION OF DOCUMENTS

Dye & Durham Limited — Toronto, Canada
Printers to the Legal Profession

This affidavit is filed by HILL, JOHNSTON
& GRANT

of the City of Toronto

in the County of York

on behalf of the plaintiffs

HILL, JOHNSTON & GRANT
17 Princess Street South
Toronto, Ontario

AMENDED JUNE, 1965

Affidavit on Production, Officer

Dye & Durham Limited — Law & Commercial Stationers
76 Richmond St. East, Toronto
Form No. 628-681

In the SUPREME Court of ONTARIO

Between

LESLIE JAMES BROWN,

Plaintif

AND

PRINCIPAL MINES LIMITED,

Defendan

I, WILLIAM HOWARD McLEAN,

of the City of Toronto in the County of York

make oath and say as follows:

1.—I am the Secretary-Treasurer of Principal Mines Limited

Here state the name of the office held by the deponent in the service of the Company on whose behalf he makes the affidavit.

and as such have knowledge of all documents which are, or have been, in the custody or possessio of the said defendant relating to the matters in question in this action.

2.—I am cognizant of the matters in question in this action.

3.—The said defendant has in its possession or power the docu ments relating to the matters in question in this action set forth in the first and second parts c the first schedule hereto.

4.—The said defendant object s to produce the said documents set forth in th second part of the said first schedule thereto.

5.— That the same are privileged.

Here state on what grounds the objection is made, and verify the facts as far as may be.

6.—The said defendant has had, but has not now, in its possession or power, the documents relating to the matters in question in this action set forth i the second schedule hereto.

7.—The last-mentioned documents were last in the possession or power of the said defendant on or about their respective dates.

State when

8.—That the said documents are now in the possession of the plaintiff or his solicitors.

Here state what has become of the last mentioned documents, and in whose possession they now are.

9.—According to the best of my knowledge, information and belief, the said defendant has not now, and never had, in its possession, custody, or power, or in the posses sion, custody, or power of myself, or of any of its solicitors or agents, or of any person persons whomsoever, on its behalf any deed, account, book of account, voucher, receipt, lette memorandum, paper, or writing, or any copy of or extract from any such document, or any oth document whatsoever relating to the matters in question in this action or any of them, or where any entry has been made relative to such matters, or any of them, other than and except th documents set forth in the said first and second schedules hereto, and the pleadings and oth proceedings in the action.

Sworn before me at the City

of Toronto

in the County of York

this

day of February 1970

A Commissioner, etc.

Figure 21.7. Affidavit on Production, Officer of a Company – Page 1

THE FIRST SCHEDULE

THE FIRST PART THEREOF: showing documents in the possession of the said defendant which it does not object to produce.

1. Copy of agreement, August 30, 1967, between Leslie James Brown and Principal Mines Limited.

2. Letter, August 30, 1967, from Leslie John Brown to Principal Mines Limited.

3. Copies of Mining Recorders' Abstracts of Mining Claim for claims SSM 36807 to SSM 36824 inclusive, Sault Ste. Marie Division.

Figure 21.7. Affidavit on Production, Officer of a Company – Page 2

THE SECOND PART: showing documents in the possession of the said   defendant   which
it   objects   to produce.

Correspondence between the defendant and its solicitors, correspondence between the defendant and third persons for the
purpose of giving or receiving information concerning this
action, correspondence written without prejudice, and documents
prepared for use in this litigation.

THE SECOND SCHEDULE

SHOWING documents which the said   defendant   has   had but has   not now
in   its   possession or power.

Letters, copies of which are referred to in the first part of
the first schedule as having been written by it or its solicitors.

Figure 21.7. Affidavit on Production, Officer
of a Company – Page 3

In the SUPREME   Court of ONTARIO

ACTION COMMENCED IN THE COUNTY
OF YORK

LESLIE JAMES BROWN

VS.

PRINCIPAL MINES LIMITED

Affidavit on Production

BY

OFFICER OF CORPORATION

Dye & Durham Limited — Law & Commercial Stationers
76 Richmond St. East, Toronto

This affidavit is filed by HILL, JOHNSTON

& GRANT

of the   City   of   Toronto

in the   County   of   York

on behalf of the defendant.

HILL, JOHNSTON & GRANT
17 Princess Street South
Toronto, Ontario

Figure 21.7. Affidavit on Production, Officer of a Company – Back   217

Arranging an Appointment

When a suitable date for discovery has been determined by the solicitors, you may be asked to arrange the appointment with the special examiner selected. A telephone call is placed to the special examiner and the following information is given:

1. the date for the examination, and whether morning or afternoon. Indicate how long it is anticipated the examination will take.
2. the name of the parties, that is, the style of cause
3. the name of the firm of solicitors involved, and the name of the individual lawyer who will be attending on the discovery
4. the number of people to be examined – the plaintiff, or the defendant, or both
5. the type of examination to be held, since examinations may be held in other proceedings connected with a trial:

a. examination for discovery in an action
b. cross-examination of a person on an affidavit filed in support of or in defence of a claim
c. examination of a judgment debtor.

After arrangements have been made, two copies of the appointment form (Figure 21.8) are prepared, and the original is served upon the solicitors for the party to be examined seven days before the day appointed for the examination. Your law office will usually use one special examiner for all its examinations. The special examiner will provide you with a supply of signed appointment forms for completion.

The rules of practice require that a small sum of money, known as *conduct money,* be paid to the party being examined for expenses incurred in travelling to the examination.

What Happens on Examinations for Discovery

On an examination for discovery the party being examined is asked questions by the solicitor for the other side which deal with the matters in dispute. The solicitor for the party being examined is also present. Frequently questions are asked that the party being examined cannot immediately answer, and an undertaking (promise) is given to provide the required information by letter.

A shorthand reporter is present and records the entire examination. These notes are typed up to form a "transcript" of the examination, and a copy is sent to each solicitor together with an account. Questions and answers appearing in a transcript may be used as evidence at the trial.

Record

The next step in progressing to trial is to set the action down. This is done by preparing and "passing", that is, filing with the appropriate court office, a document known as a *record,* which contains an original of all the pleadings in the action, and any order containing directions respecting the trial. The record is for the use of the judge hearing the action and is normally prepared by the solicitors for the plaintiff.

Preparing the Record

Only one copy of the record is usually prepared. Carbon copies cannot be used. Therefore, one copy of all pleadings in the action is retyped or duplicated. No backs are required.

The pleadings are assembled in chronological order with the statement of claim first. The pages are numbered in the upper right-hand corner commencing with figure 1. An index (Figure 21.9) is prepared listing the first page at which each pleading may be found.

A front page is prepared for the record (Figure 21.10) indicating the names of the solicitors for both parties in the action.

A back is prepared for the record on heavy paper which will be available in your office's stationery supplies. A blue back is used for a Supreme Court record; a grey back for a County Court record. This back is typed as a regular court back, and the document is identified by name (i.e., RECORD).

The record is assembled in the following order: the front page, the index page, the pleadings, and the back. This material is stapled down the left-hand side so that the material forms a small booklet. The blue or grey back is approximately ½ inch longer and wider than a normal sheet; this edge will show at the top and bottom, and at the right-hand side of the booklet.

This record is then taken to the appropriate court office and filed.

If a notice has been filed and served indicating that either party wishes the action tried with a jury, a copy of that notice is clipped to the record, but does not form part of it.

Notice of Trial

Within ten days of filing the record, the solicitors must serve and file a notice of trial, the wording of which is:

TAKE NOTICE that this action was set down on the . . . day of . . . , 197-, for trial at the Toronto non-jury sittings.

DATED . . .

Proceeding to Trial

In both the County Courts and the Supreme Court of Ontario, a case (action) is said to be on the general list of cases awaiting trial when the action has been set down (i.e., the record passed), and notice of trial has been served and filed. In most areas of Ontario the case proceeds to trial in due course, without the necessity of serving or filing further documents.

However, in one County Court and in several cities where sittings of the Supreme Court are held, an additional document is required to get the case on the list of cases said to be ready for trial. This list is called the *ready list*.

In actions being tried in the County Court of the County of York, and actions being tried in the Supreme Court in the cities of Hamilton, London, Ottawa, Toronto, and Windsor, the solicitor on the record in the trial, who is ready for trial and has completed all proceedings necessary before trial, serves on all other parties a *certificate of readiness* (Figure 21.11) indicating he is ready to proceed to try the action.

When certificates of readiness have been served and filed by, or on behalf of, all parties in the action, or two months after certificates of readiness have been filed on behalf of one or more but not all of the parties in the action, the case is put on the ready list.

If a case is not removed from the general list to the ready list within one year of being set down for trial, the case may be taken off the list altogether. A special application must be made to the court to restore the case to the list.

On the day the action is placed on the ready list, the Registrar of the Supreme Court of Ontario notifies the solicitors of record. The weekly lists of actions to be heard are made up by the Registrar from the appropriate ready lists and are posted two weeks in advance. Once a list has been posted, no action may be added or withdrawn from it before trial without an order of the Chief Justice of the High Court, or the senior judge presiding in the appropriate court.

Certificate of Readiness

A certificate of readiness is a printed form and a minimum of three copies is prepared. After a copy has been served on the other side, the original is filed with the court and a copy is retained in your file.

The certificate is signed by the individual lawyer who will be appearing at the trial, and is addressed to the other solicitors involved. An indication is given of the length of time it is estimated the trial will take, and this information permits the Registrar to properly determine the number of cases that may be heard in a day or week.

A Brief

As the date for trial approaches, your lawyer may ask you to assemble his *brief* – the file of pleadings, documents, etc., relating to the action which he will take with him to court.

Each lawyer has his own individual preference as to the exact content of his brief, but it usually contains a copy of the writ of summons and of all pleadings, a copy of each affidavit on production, any memoranda of law prepared for use in the action, and copies of pertinent file memoranda and productions.

This material is assembled with the court documents, and inserted in a brief cover using accopress clips to secure the material. Alternatively, the lawyer may have a folder which folds back to permit the insertion of material into the folder while simultaneously securing the material. This is a very useful folder, since the material can be inserted and removed easily and the folder can be used on many different occasions.

Subpoena

A *subpoena* is a command issued in the name of the Sovereign requiring the person(s) to whom it is addressed to be present at a specified place and time for a specified purpose. Figure 21.12 illustrates a subpoena requiring the attendance of two witnesses at a trial to give evidence on behalf of one of the parties. When typed, the subpoena is served upon the witness or witnesses by the sheriff.

Your office will usually have a supply of blank subpoena forms, which have already been sealed and signed by the appropriate court officer. One subpoena form is completed and can then be used for any number of witnesses. When the subpoena form is prepared, it is duplicated (or typed on plain paper) to provide sufficient copies — one for each witness to whom it is addressed and a copy for your file. The original and the necessary copies are given to the sheriff for service upon the witnesses.

Trial

When the date for the trial or hearing is reached, the lawyer will attend in court, along with the lawyer for the other party. Witnesses will be called by each side to present evidence, and exhibits in support of that evidence will be filed with the court. These exhibits are numbered Exhibit 1, Exhibit 2, Exhibit 3, and so on, by the court official who receives them. When all the evidence has been given, each lawyer will present his "argument", that is, his final presentation to the court. Judgment may be given at once, but is usually reserved until the judge has had an opportunity to consider all the facts presented to him. After judgment is given, the solicitor for the successful party prepares and issues the formal judgment which usually takes the form of an order.

SPECIMEN ONLY

In the

ONTARIO

SUPREME **Court of** ONTARIO

Between

WILLIAM KENNETH WILLIAMSTONE **PLAINTIFF**

AND

SMITH MANUFACTURING COMPANY LTD. **DEFENDANT**

I hereby Appoint Tuesday the 21st day of

October 19 70 at the hour of two-thirty o'clock

in the after.noon, at my office, 360 Bay Street Toronto, Suite 401, for the

examination *viva voce* upon oath of R. J. Brown, an officer of the defendant,

touching his knowledge of the matters in question in this action, pursuant to the rules of

Court in that behalf

Dated at Toronto this 9th day of October 19 70.

(A.C. DEVENPORT)
Special Examiner

Figure 21.8. Appointment for Examination on Discovery

221

IN THE SUPREME COURT OF ONTARIO

B E T W E E N:

MARY WOODSTOCK,

Plaintiff,

- and -

GEORGE SMYTHE, HENRY SMYTHE,
PERCIVAL SMYTHE, and MARY-ANNE
SMYTHE,

Defendants.

I N D E X

	Page
Statement of Claim	1
Statement of Defence	3
Reply and Joinder of Issue	11

Figure 21.9. Index Page of Record

197/70

IN THE SUPREME COURT OF ONTARIO

B E T W E E N:

MARY WOODSTOCK,

Plaintiff,

- and -

GEORGE SMYTHE, HENRY SMYTHE,
PERCIVAL SMYTHE, and MARY-ANNE
SMYTHE,

Defendants.

R E C O R D

HILL, JOHNSTON & GRANT,
17 Princess Street South, Toronto,
Solicitors for the plaintiff.

ROSS, SMITH, GREEN, WILLIAMSON & BELL,
75 Martindale Boulevard, Toronto,
Solicitors for the defendants.

Figure 21.10. Face Page of Record   223

CERTIFICATE OF READINESS

Dye & Durham Limited
Law and Commercial Stationers
76 Richmond St. E., Toronto
Form No. 712

In the Supreme Court of Ontario

Between

RONALD CRAIG ANDERSON,

Plaintiff

- and -

PERCIVAL ANDREW PETERSON,

Defendant

CERTIFICATE OF READINESS

I, PETER THOMAS GRANT , solicitor for the above-named

plaintiff , DO HEREBY CERTIFY that to the best
(PLAINTIFF   OR DEFENDANT   )

of my belief all interlocutory proceedings and examinations on behalf of my client have been completed and that we are ready now to proceed to trial.

I estimate that this action will take   one-half day   at trial.
(HOURS OR DAYS)

DATED at   Toronto   this 26th day of February   1970.

Peter J Grant
(SIGNATURE OF SOLICITOR)

TO:

(ALL OTHER PARTIES)

ROSS, SMITH, GREEN, WILLIAMSON & BELL
75 Martindale Boulevard
Toronto, Ontario
Solicitors for the defendant

TAKE NOTICE that where a CERTIFICATE OF READINESS has been served and filed on behalf of one or more but not all of the parties to an action and two months have elapsed since the filing of the first CERTIFICATE OF READINESS therein, the action will be placed at that time on the READY LIST.

AND FURTHER TAKE NOTICE that if and when CERTIFICATES OF READINESS are served and filed on behalf of all parties, the action will be placed immediately on the READY LIST unless it has already been so placed.

Figure 21.11. Certificate of Readiness

In the Supreme Court of Ontario

ACTION COMMENCED IN THE COUNTY
OF YORK

RONALD CRAIG ANDERSON

vs.

PERCIVAL ANDREW PETERSON

CERTIFICATE OF READINESS

Service of a true copy hereof is
hereby admitted

this   day of February 1970

SOLICITOR FOR   the defendant

HILL, JOHNSTON & GRANT
17 Princess Street South
Toronto, Ontario

Figure 21.11.   Certificate of Readiness—Back

Dye & Durham Limited—Toronto
Printers to the Legal Profession
Form No. 265

CIVIL SUBPOENA
(For Trial)

In the Supreme Court of Ontario

Between:

JAMES WILLIAM SMITH,

PLAINTIFF(S)

AND

THE BLACK MANUFACTURING COMPANY LIMITED,
JOHN ARNOLD FRANKS, and ALBERT DOUGLAS SCOTT,

DEFENDANT(S)

Elizabeth the Second, by the Grace of God of the United Kingdom, Canada and Her other Realms and Territories QUEEN, Head of the Commonwealth, Defender of the Faith.

Greeting.

L.S.

To WAYNE PATRICK McLEOD,
19 Havergale Boulevard,
Toronto 18, Ontario.

AND TO: WILLIAM DOUGLAS PHILLIPS,
1500 Rexdale Crescent,
Scarborough, Ontario.

We Command You to attend at the sittings of the Supreme Court of Ontario in and for the County (*or* District) of __York__

to be holden at ____Toronto____ on ____Wednesday__day the __24th__ day of ____March____, 19__70__, at the hour of ____ten____ o'clock

in the ____fore__noon, and so from day to day during the said sittings until the above cause is tried, to give evidence on behalf of the __plaintiff__,

and also bring with you and produce at the time and place aforesaid all books, receipts, vouchers, letters, telegrams and

records in any way related or bearing upon the above-styled action.

In Witness Whereof this subpoena is signed for the Supreme Court of Ontario by ____Donald C. Saunders,____ Assistant Registrar

of the said Court at ____Toronto____ , this ____21st____ day of ____March____ 1970 .

226

Figure 21.12. Subpoena at Trial

In the Supreme Court of Ontario

JAMES WILLIAM SCOTT

v.

THE BLACK MANUFACTURING
COMPANY LIMITED, JOHN
ARNOLD FRANKS, and ALBERT
DOUGLAS SCOTT

Civil Subpoena

(For Trial)

This Subpoena was issued by:

HILL, JOHNSTON & GRANT

of the ____ City ____ of ____ Toronto ____

in the ____ County ____ of ____ York ____

Solicitor for the plaintiff.

HILL, JOHNSTON & GRANT
17 Princess Street South
Toronto, Ontario

Figure 21.12.   Subpoena at Trial – Back

CHAPTER 22

Bills of Costs and Taxation of Costs

When a trial of an action or the hearing of a matter or an appeal (discussed in Chapter 23) has been completed, the judgment or order which is made usually contains some provision concerning the payment of costs to the successful party. The successful party is entitled to be partially reimbursed for the expense he incurred in being a party to the action or matter. In some proceedings, for example, the interpretation of a will, all parties may receive costs.

When costs are allowed, the solicitors for the party concerned prepare what is known as a *bill of costs* (Figures 22.1, 22.2), which sets out the claim for costs being made. The amounts shown in this bill are then taxed (examined) by an official of the court known as the Taxing Officer, who determines exactly the costs allowed, and issues a certificate to this effect. THE RULES OF PRACTICE AND PROCEDURE set out the tariff of fees and disbursements allowed to solicitors; bills of costs are prepared with reference to these tariffs.

Bill of Costs

Heading

The form used in the style of cause of the legal proceedings to which the bill refers is followed in this document.

Title of Document

The document is identified as a bill of costs with additional identification to show whose bill it is:

BILL OF COSTS OF THE PLAINTIFF
OR
BILL OF COSTS OF THE DEFENDANTS
(APPELLANTS) ON APPEAL

Body

The body of the bill of costs contains the items for which fees are claimed or disbursements have been made. Frequently these two columns are referred to merely as "in" and "out". Disbursements appear in the "out" column, that is, the column nearest the right-hand margin, and the fees are shown in the column nearest the typed words describing the item, or the "in" column.

When all items have been listed, each column is totalled, the sum of the disbursement column is carried beneath the sum of the fee column, and a final total is typed.

Ending

A bill of costs is not signed by the solicitors who prepare it, nor is it addressed to anyone. It is ended by typing the following line commencing flush with the left-hand margin:

Taxed and allowed at $ . . . this . . . day of . . . , 197-.

When the bill has been considered by the Taxing Officer, he will insert the amount allowed and the date.

Back

Each copy of the bill has a back, and is identified for example as a BILL OF COSTS OF THE DEFENDANT.

Number of Copies and Disposition

A minimum of four copies of a bill of costs is prepared; the original is filed with the Taxing Officer, and a copy is prepared for the lawyer, each party on the other side, and the file.

Taxing the Costs

Securing an Appointment

When the bill of costs has been prepared, an appointment to tax the costs is arranged.

The original bill of costs and a true copy of the judgment or order is taken to the office of the Taxing Officer. A completed appointment form will then be received indicating the day and hour set to tax the costs.

Disposition of Appointment Form

Two copies of the appointment are made, and the other side is served with a copy of the appointment and a copy of the bill of costs. It is not necessary to serve them with another copy of the judgment; they have received this earlier.

While THE RULES OF PRACTICE AND PROCEDURE provide that one day's notice of a taxation is sufficient, in practice more time is usually given.

Day of Taxation

On the day appointed to tax the costs, the lawyer appearing on the taxation goes to the office of the Taxing Officer with the original of the appointment, on which service has been admitted by the other side. Solicitors for the other side will normally be present; they have the right to dispute items on the bill of costs. If solicitors for the other side fail to appear, the Taxing Officer will proceed to tax the costs in their absence.

After Taxation

After taxation, the Taxing Officer completes a form indicating the date of taxation and the amount of costs allowed. When the form is received, a copy is made for each party on the other side and is served upon them as official notice of the taxation.

In due course, your office receives a cheque in payment of "taxed costs". This cheque is deposited to the credit of the client, and the necessary accounting form is prepared to indicate the money has been received. This amount is usually deposited in the firm account to be credited against the account rendered to the client.

IN THE SUPREME COURT OF ONTARIO

B E T W E E N:

HUMBER TRUST COMPANY LIMITED,

Plaintiff,

- and -

ALEXANDER JAMES THOMPSON,

Defendant.

BILL OF COSTS OF THE PLAINTIFF

Institution of Action	$35.00	
Paid issue writ		$15.00
Paid Sheriff for service of writ		4.70
Signing Default Judgment	25.00	_____
	$60.00	$19.70
	19.70	
	$79.70	

Taxed and allowed at $ this   day of March, 1970

IN THE SUPREME COURT OF ONTARIO

B E T W E E N:

JAMES THOMAS (TOM) MARTIN,

Plaintiff (Respondent),

- and -

EDWARD PERCIVAL WILLIAMSON,
and MUTUAL UNDERWRITERS
INSURANCE ASSOCIATION,

Defendants (Appellants).

BILL OF COSTS OF THE DEFENDANTS (APPELLANTS) ON APPEAL

Counsel fee on appeal to the Court of Appeal, including all preliminary proceedings, notices, services etc., appeal book, statement of points of law and fact, preparation, counsel fee on appeal, and attendance to hear judgment	$750.00	
Paid to file notice of appeal		$ 25.00
Paid for reasons for judgment		6.50
Paid for evidence		113.00
Order	15.00	
Taxation of Costs	15.00	
	$780.00	$144.50
	144.50	
	$924.50	

Taxed and allowed at $ this   day of February, 1970

Figure 22.2. Bill of Costs on Appeal   231

CHAPTER 23

Appeals

Once judgment has been delivered in legal proceedings, either of the parties in the original proceedings may have a right to appeal the judgment. Usually it is the unsuccessful party who appeals, but in some circumstances an apparently successful party may appeal. For example, in an action to determine damages as a result of an automobile accident, the plaintiff may be awarded damages, but feel the amount of damages is not large enough. He may decide to appeal in an effort to have the amount increased. Alternatively, the defendant may also decide to appeal in an effort to have the amount of damages reduced.

The highest trial court in Ontario is the Supreme Court, which has two divisions: High Court of Justice (trial division) and Court of Appeal (appeal division).

It is to the appeal division of the Supreme Court of Ontario that a party in a trial may initially appeal the decision or judgment handed down by a lower court.

Following the hearing of the appeal, either party may have a right of appeal to the Supreme Court of Canada, the highest court in Canada and the court of last resort.

We are not concerned with the question of whether a party has or has not a ground of appeal – that is the lawyer's responsibility. We are concerned with what steps will be followed if a party does appeal a decision of a lower court (See Figure 23.1.)

Appeals to the Supreme Court of Ontario

Notice of Appeal

Within fifteen days (exclusive of specified vacation periods like long and short vacation) from the date of the judgment, the party appealing must serve and file a notice of appeal, which sets out the grounds of his appeal. The filing of this notice is known as "setting the appeal down".

There is a fee levied for filing the notice of appeal. The original notice of appeal with admissions of service from solicitors for the other party or parties must be presented as proof that notice has been given. In addition, proof must be furnished that the evidence of the proceedings at the trial has been ordered.

Notices of appeal are typed in the format of a general notice, but some special points should be noted:

1. Parties: In an appeal, either the plaintiff or defendant may appeal the decision. The party appealing is known as the *appellant*. The party defending the appeal is known as the *respondent*.

2. Style of Cause: In referring to the parties, the style of cause follows the form of that established when the action or matter was commenced. In other words, the plaintiff's name always appears first, the defendant's second. It does not matter whether the plaintiff is the appellant or the respondent in the appeal – his name still comes first in the style of cause (Figure 23.2).

   You do, however, indicate in the style of cause the capacity (i.e., the new designation) of each party in the appeal in addition to showing that they were plaintiff and defendant.

3. Court Appealed From: Unless the appeal is from a judgment handed down in the trial division of the Supreme Court of Ontario, it is necessary to show from what court the appeal is being made by typing beneath the name of the appeal court either "IN THE MATTER OF an Appeal from the County Court of the County of . . .", or "IN THE MATTER OF an Action pending in the County Court of the County of . . ." Both forms are correct, and the one used depends on the personal preference of the solicitor acting for the appellant.

4. Action Number: No action number is required on any document filed for use on an appeal.

Ordering Evidence

At the original trial, the evidence would have been taken down by a court reporter, but the evidence is not transcribed unless "the evidence is ordered". The number of copies ordered depends on the court from which the appeal is taken:

Appeal from Judgment of	Minimum Number of Copies Ordered
Division Court	3
County Court	5
Supreme Court	7

The cost of securing the evidence is borne entirely by the person appealing. He must provide a copy to each firm of solicitors on the other side, and to each judge sitting on the appeal.

Exhibits Secured Out of Court

It is necessary to secure from the appropriate court office the exhibits filed during the course of the trial so that the lawyers may decide which exhibits are to be submitted on the appeal.

The lawyers for the parties in the action sign a consent which is presented to the appropriate court office to obtain the release of the exhibits for use in preparing the appeal.

Appeal Books

On a trial it is necessary to provide for the use of the courts a record which contains the pertinent documents pertaining to the action. On appeal, the judge(s) must be given *appeal books* containing copies of the material relating to the matter under appeal.

Contents of Appeal Books

Appeal books must contain, in the order listed, the following material:

1. notice of appeal
2. the pleadings
3. the judgment or order appealed from
4. the reasons for judgment
5. any exhibits relevant to the hearing of the appeal arranged in chronological order.

No backs are required for court documents appearing in an appeal book.

Number of Copies

The number of judges sitting to hear an appeal is determined by the court from which the appeal is brought. The number of judges also determines the number of copies of an appeal book which must be prepared and filed for use of the judge or judges.

Basically, the number of copies prepared includes the number required for the Court of Appeal plus one copy for each firm of solicitors involved. The table below may be useful.

Covers of Appeal Books

The contents of appeal books are bound front and back in buff-coloured covers, which must be of 130M weight cover stock. Appeal books were at one time punched and tied with pink ribbon, but cirlox binding is now generally used.

The back cover is left plain, but the front cover (Figure 23.3) shows the style of cause, identifies the book as an appeal book, and shows the firms of solicitors involved in the appeal. Each cover may be typed individually, or run off on a Xerox machine which has been adjusted for the heavier type of paper which must be used.

Preparation of Contents of Appeal Books

Once it is known which exhibits are to be included, and the exhibits have been obtained from the court on consent, the

Appeal from Judgment of	Number of Appeal Books Required to be Filed	Minimum Number of Appeal Books to be Prepared
Division Court	1	3
County Court	3	5
Supreme Court	5	7

Steps on Appeal to the Supreme Court of Ontario

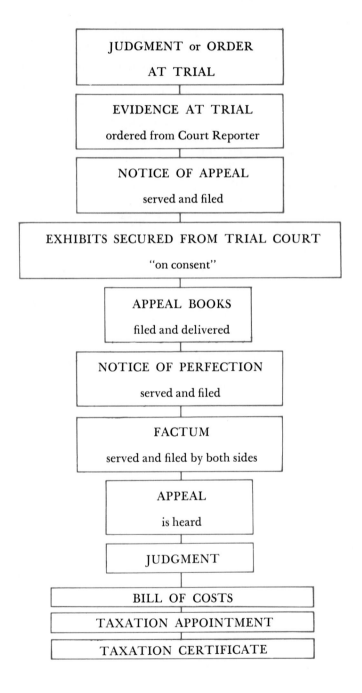

| JUDGMENT or ORDER AT TRIAL |
| EVIDENCE AT TRIAL ordered from Court Reporter |
| NOTICE OF APPEAL served and filed |
| EXHIBITS SECURED FROM TRIAL COURT "on consent" |
| APPEAL BOOKS filed and delivered |
| NOTICE OF PERFECTION served and filed |
| FACTUM served and filed by both sides |
| APPEAL is heard |
| JUDGMENT |
| BILL OF COSTS |
| TAXATION APPOINTMENT |
| TAXATION CERTIFICATE |

Figure 23.1

required number of copies of the appeal books are prepared.

With the advent of Xerox and similar systems of copying equipment, typing of material for an appeal book is no longer absolutely necessary. The required number of copies of as much of the material as possible is reproduced omitting backs on any court documents.

Material which is too large to be reproduced in your office (e.g., a map), or material (e.g., photographs) which requires that all copies be secured from the person with whom it originated, require special attention.

From the back of the photograph, the photographer and his file number are ascertained. The required number of copies of each photograph are ordered from him, giving him the file number to facilitate location of the negative, and specifying the size of print required. When the copies have been received, each photograph is mounted on a sheet of paper, showing in the centre top of each page the appropriate exhibit number.

Large, bulky material, such as maps, is sent to commercial duplicating firms for reproduction. When the copies are received, instead of binding the map itself into the appeal book, a letter-size brown envelope is inserted in the place where the map, for example, will come in the contents of the appeal book. The envelope is placed flap-side up, and approximately one inch of the left-hand portion of the flap is cut off so that the flap will not be caught in the binding. Before inserting into the appeal book, the appropriate exhibit number is typed on the envelope just beneath the flap. When the appeal book is bound, the map is folded and inserted into the envelope, which is treated as one page in the appeal book. In this way the map or other bulky material can be removed, unfolded, and easily referred to.

```
                IN THE SUPREME COURT OF ONTARIO


B E T W E E N:

                    MARGARET ELIZABETH WEST,

                                        Plaintiff (Appellant),


                        - and -


                    THE HAMILTON LIFE INSURANCE
                    COMPANY OF CANADA,

                                        Defendant (Respondent).


                        NOTICE OF APPEAL
```

Figure 23.2. Style of Cause in Appeal from Supreme Court

IN THE SUPREME COURT OF ONTARIO

B E T W E E N:

xxxxxxxxxxxxxxxxxxxxxxxxxxxxxxxxxxxx
xxxxxxxxxxxxxxxxxxxxxxxxxxxxxxxxx
xxxxxxxxxxxxxxxxxxxxxxxxxxxxxxxxxxxx
xxxxxxxxxxxxxxxxxxxx,

                              PLAINTIFFS (APPELLANTS),

                  - and -

xxxxxxxxxxxxxxxxxxxxxxxxxxxxxxxxxx
xxxxxxxxxxxxxxxxxxxxxx,

                              DEFENDANT (RESPONDENT).

                  ===========================

            A P P E A L   B O O K

                  ===========================

        HILL, JOHNSTON & GRANT,
        17 Princess Street S., Toronto, Ontario,
        Solicitors for the Plaintiffs (Appellants).

        THOMAS, CARSWELL, MAXTON & WILLIAMSON,
        45 Queen Street North, Toronto, Ontario,
        Solicitors for the Defendant (Respondent).

Figure 23.3. Cover for Appeal Book Showing Form of Heading in Appeal from the Supreme Court

Numbering the Pages

All pages in an appeal book, with the exception of the index page, are consecutively numbered. One set of the material is assembled and the pages are numbered in the upper right-hand corner. The index is then prepared. The other sets of material are then numbered. Many offices have numbering machines which facilitate this process.

Index

The first page inside the front cover of an appeal book is the index (Figure 23.4). This page is not numbered. The notice of appeal, pleadings, judgment, and reasons for judgment are listed in order of appearance in the appeal book with the page number at which they commence.

Exhibits are listed in numerical order (as numbered in the initial legal proceedings), not in their chronological order of appearance in the appeal book. For example, the exhibits may read Exhibit 1, Exhibit 5, Exhibit 11, and so on. Unless they are listed in numerical order you are preparing only a table of contents, which is not of much assistance in locating a specific exhibit – particularly if there are a large number of exhibits included in the appeal book.

Perfecting an Appeal

When the appeal books have been prepared, and the necessary number of copies of the appeal book and the evidence are filed with the Registrar of the Court of Appeal, the appeal is said to have been "perfected". The date of perfection is the date of filing.

Within five days of filing, a copy of the appeal book and the evidence must be delivered to each firm of solicitors acting for the respondent(s), and a notice of perfection served and filed. This notice is typed in the same style as ordinary notices and the wording is:

TAKE NOTICE that the appeal herein has been perfected this . . . day of . . . , 197-.

DATED . . .

Factums

Each party to an appeal must file with the court, and exchange with each other, a document formally known as a "statement of points of law and fact", but informally called a *factum*.

Figures 23.5 and 23.6 illustrate the first and last pages of a factum. Note that:

1. Factums are divided into sections which bear Roman numerals, that is, I, II, III. Paragraphs, beginning with figure 1, are numbered consecutively from beginning to end.
2. The ending of a factum differs from that of pleadings. It is not delivered, but submitted. The name of the law firm does not appear on the factum. The factum is "signed" by typing in the name of the individual lawyer(s) who is appearing on the appeal, and who is identified as "Of counsel for the . . ."
3. A factum is *not* dated.
4. The back of the factum (Figure 23.7) must indicate the county in which the original action was commenced if the appeal is from the Supreme Court of Ontario. The short name of the document is used to identify it, indicating which party's factum it is. The name of the law firm, *not* of the individual lawyers, appears on the back.

Time Limits

Lawyers may determine with some degree of precision the month in which an appeal is to be heard. In order to have an appeal on the list of appeals to be heard in the following month, certain time limits must be met in the current month. By the fifteenth of the current month appeal books and evidence must be filed, and notice of perfection served and filed. By the twenty-fifth of the current month a copy of the factum of both sides must be filed and delivered to the other side.

Reference to Evidence and Cases in Factums

In preparing factums it is usual to refer to passages of the evidence at trial, and to decided cases which support the client's case. The references are indented five spaces and double spaced.

IN THE SUPREME COURT OF ONTARIO

IN THE MATTER OF an Appeal from the County
Court of the County of York,

B E T W E E N:

THE ONTARIO BRIDGES AND
WATERWAYS COMMISSION,

Plaintiff (Respondent),

- and -

HENRY PERCIVAL CRAIGLAND,
GEOFFREY KENNETH WOOD,
and PETER BLAIR SMITHE,

Defendants (Appellants).

I N D E X

Page

Notice of Appeal. 1

Statement of Claim. 3

Statement of Defence. 8

Judgment. 12

Reasons for Judgment. 15

Exhibit 1--Photograph, Peterborough Main Canal. 57

Exhibit 2--Photograph, Welland Bridge 48

Exhibit 4--Plan of Toronto River, 19th October, 1963. 39

Exhibit 10--Order-in-Council, 20th February, 1962 31

Exhibit 15--Order-in-Council, 27th March, 1962. 33

Exhibit 19--Map of the Province of Ontario. 59

and so on, listing all exhibits contained
in the appeal book, in numerical order.

Figure 23.4. Index Page for Appeal Book
Showing Form of Heading in Appeal from a
County Court

IN THE SUPREME COURT OF ONTARIO

IN THE MATTER OF an Appeal from the County
Court of the County of York,

B E T W E E N:

THE ONTARIO BRIDGES AND
WATERWAYS COMMISSION,

Plaintiff (Respondent),

- and -

HENRY PERCIVAL CRAIGLAND,
GEOFFREY KENNETH WOOD,
and PETER BLAIR SMITHE,

Defendants (Appellants).

STATEMENT OF POINTS OF LAW AND FACT
intended to be argued on behalf of
the plaintiff (RESPONDENT)

aces

I

aces

1. _____

_____

_____

2. _____

_____

_____

ces

II

ces

3. _____

_____

*Figure 23.5. First Page of Factum Showing
Form of Heading in Appeal from a
County Court*

References to Evidence at Trial

References to evidence indicate the name of the witness whose evidence is referred to, and give the page and exact line at which the pertinent evidence begins and concludes (Figure 23.6).

In typing page and line references, use "p." for page, but write "line" in full in order to avoid confusion with the figure 1.

If at all possible, do not carry evidence references over from the bottom of one page to the top of the next page.

Citing Cases

Citations are typed in proper form immediately following the paragraph to which they refer. Endeavour to have all citations completed on one page. It is better to have almost no bottom margin on a page than to break a list of citations.

Appeals to the Supreme Court of Canada

Once judgment has been delivered on an appeal to the highest court in a province, either of the parties may have a right to appeal the judgment on appeal to the Supreme Court of Canada, which has the exclusive ultimate appeal jurisdiction within Canada, and whose judgment is final and conclusive.

Appeals to the Supreme Court of Canada must be brought within sixty days from the signing or entry of pronouncing of the judgment appealed from, but long vacation is excluded in computing the sixty days.

Ottawa Agent

In order to facilitate filing notices and material for use on the appeal, each side on an appeal appoints an Ottawa firm of solicitors to act as "Ottawa agents" on the appeal. That firm files material, and once the sittings of the Supreme Court of Canada begins, keeps in touch with the progress of the cases on the list to provide information as to when the appeal may be reached.

Notice of Appeal

To bring an appeal to the Supreme Court of Canada, the appellant in that appeal must serve a notice of appeal upon all parties directly affected, and file the notice with the Supreme Court of Canada, and also with the court appealed from. In addition, the appellant must deposit with the Registrar of the Supreme Court of Canada an amount of money known as "security" to be applied against the costs of the respondent if the appellant is not successful on the appeal.

Notices of appeal are typed in the format of general notices with the following points of difference:

1. Court Appealed From: It is necessary to show beneath the court in which the appeal is to be heard, the court from which the appeal is made.
2. Parties: In referring to the parties in the headings of a document for use in the Supreme Court of Canada, the regular style of cause is not followed. The name of the party who is the appellant is shown first, and then the name of the party who is the respondent in the appeal to the Supreme Court of Canada.

Figure 23.8 illustrates the heading of a document prepared for use on appeal to the Supreme Court of Canada.

Appeal Case

A bound booklet, known as the *appeal case* is prepared on an appeal to the Supreme Court of Canada. This is not typed in the law office; it is printed by a firm like Canada Law Book Limited from material furnished by the solicitors for the appellant.

The appeal case may contain the original pleadings, the notice of appeal to the Supreme Court, the judgment at trial and on appeal, the reasons for judgment, the evidence at trial, and the exhibits.

A legal secretary herself does not generally have responsibility for many of the details involved in an appeal to the Supreme Court of Canada. A solicitor must sign a certificate in the appeal case verifying the authenticity of its contents. The judge who pronounced the order of the Court of Appeal must sign the judgment as it is to

7.

_____

_____.

    Evidence of plaintiff,   p. 56, line 29 to p. 63, line 7

                                p.127, line 47 to p.135, line 19

                                p.164, line 58 to p.165, line 46

    Evidence of Wyand,   p.197, line 4 to p.204, line 12

                                p.218, line 17 to p.226, line 25

                                p.219, lines 7-21

  Report, Exhibit 1, Appeal Book p.15

VIII

21.   _____

_____

_____.

3 spaces

      All of which is respectfully submitted,

                  PETER T. GRANT

         Of counsel for the plaintiff (RESPONDENT).

This document is *not* dated. This is an exception to the rule that
all legal instruments and documents are dated.

Figure 23.6. *Ending of Factum*

If appeal is from trial division of Supreme Court of Ontario, this information is required.

If appeal is not from trial division of the S.C.O., then information must appear as to the court from which appeal is sought.

S.   C.
_____

ACTION COMMENCED IN THE COUNTY OF YO
O R
IN THE MATTER OF an Appeal from th
County Court of the County of York

THE ONTARIO BRIDGES AND
WATERWAYS COMMISSION

v.

HENRY PERCIVAL CRAIGLAND,
GEOFFREY KENNETH WOOD,
and PETER BLAIR SMITHE

_____

On back, "Statement of Points of Law etc." is simply called "Factum".

RESPONDENT'S FACTUM

_____

HILL, JOHNSTON & GRANT,
17 Princess Street,

Name of law firm, *not* individual lawyer who "signs" factum

Toronto, Ontario.

Figure 23.7. Back of Factum

IN THE SUPREME COURT OF CANADA

ON APPEAL FROM THE COURT OF APPEAL FOR ONTARIO

B E T W E E N:

CANADIAN WINDOWLEDGE COMPANY
LIMITED,

(Defendant) Appellant,

- and -

H. W. McLEOD & CO. INC.

(Plaintiff) Respondent.

*Figure 23.8. Style of Cause in
Appeal to the Supreme Court of Canada*

appear in the appeal case. You may be requested to check the galley proofs received from the printer, but the lawyer assisting the counsel who is to appear on the hearing of the appeal normally supervises preparation of the appeal case and takes any other necessary steps.

Factum

Each side in the appeal must file with the Court, and provide to each other, a document known as a factum, similar in form and content to that used in the Court of Appeal.

This factum is typed in the office and then sent to the law printer for reproduction in a bound booklet. The citation of cases and authorities which appear throughout the factum are summarized on a separate sheet headed "List of Authorities", which is inserted at the end of the factum.

Inscribing on List

When the appeal case has been filed with the court, and the factums have also been filed, the appeal is *inscribed* on the list of appeals to be heard at a sittings of the Supreme Court of Canada.

The sittings of that court commences at various times during the year, and solicitors are provided each year with dates by which appeals must be inscribed if they are to be heard at a specified sittings.

Judgment

When the judgment of the Supreme Court of Canada is given, the Ottawa agents notify the lawyer concerned, and send copies of the reasons for judgment and the judgment itself.

The judgment of that court is final and there is no right of further appeal except under very exceptional circumstance, when the court may be directed by the Minister of Justice to reconsider its judgment.

CHAPTER 24

Wills

A *will* is an individual's written statement of how he intends his real and personal property, called his *estate*, to be distributed after his death. The Wills Act of each province sets out certain requirements which must be followed to make a valid will. In the provinces of Alberta, Manitoba, Newfoundland, Quebec, and Saskatchewan, a handwritten will, called a *holographic* will, written by and signed by only the person making it without any witness, is valid. In the other provinces, including Ontario, it must be signed in the presence of two witnesses.

A will is more formally known as a last will and testament. Originally, a will disposed of real property; a testament, personal property. Today the single word "will" covers the disposition of both real and personal property.

Many other terms used in connection with estate are derived from the word *testament*: *testate* – the state of having a will; *intestate* – the state of having no will; *testator* – a man who has made a will; *testatrix* – a woman who has made a will.

In his will the testator designates and appoints the person or persons who will carry out the terms of his will after his death; he may name one or more individuals, or a trust company. These persons are referred to as *executor(s)* – male(s) or a trust company, or *executrix (rices)* – female(s). If all or part of the estate is to be held in trust, the executor is also known as a *trustee*.

In many offices wills are now prepared on the Magnetic Tape Selectric Typewriter which produces standard material in usable form from pre-typed magnetic tapes. Basic will clauses are prepared on tape, and any necessary additions or corrections are made by the lawyer in accordance with the particular circumstances of each case. These additions or corrections are then inserted by the operator. The introduction of this equipment has vastly reduced the amount of repetitious typing required of a legal secretary.

In some law offices wills are still completely typed by the secretary. Frequently a draft is prepared, and when the lawyer is satisfied with its contents, the final will is then typed.

Parts of a Will

Heading

The heading of the will states exactly what the document is, the name of the testator, his general address and occupation.

THIS IS THE LAST WILL AND TESTAMENT of me, RONALD CRAIG ANDERSON, of the Borough of Etobicoke, in the County of York, Physician.

Body

The body of a will contains clauses dealing with the intentions of the testator as to the disposition of his estate after his death. The first clause is the revocation clause, cancelling any previous will made by the testator. This is followed by clauses outlining specific gifts to individuals or groups who are known as *beneficiaries,* clauses dealing with the payment of debts, death duties and taxes on the estate, clauses dealing with the disposition of the balance (residue) of the estate, and other clauses which may be required under the particular circumstances involved. For example, if an infant is a beneficiary, special clauses are necessary to authorize payment to the parent or guardian before the infant becomes twenty-one.

Many of the clauses used in the body of a will are standard, and are used by lawyers in almost all of the wills they prepare. Normally, you will be instructed to copy in such clauses, ensuring that the necessary changes in gender and case are made.

The second edition of CANADIAN FORMS OF WILLS by Terence Sheard, The Carswell Company, Limited, Toronto, is a source of reference for forms of wills, and you may be instructed to copy into a will clauses from specimen wills in that book, which is usually maintained in the office law library.

Ending

The ending of a will as illustrated in Figure 24.1 contains a testimonium and attestation clause. The ending varies to show whether a man or woman is executing the will. The initial wording of the testimonium clause may be either "IN TESTIMONY WHERE-OF...", or "IN WITNESS WHEREOF ...", depending on the preference of the lawyer, and may be followed by a reference to the number of pages (exclusive of the back) in the completed will.

Back

Each copy of a will has a short back showing the date, the name of the document, and the name and address of the law firm. Figure 24.2 illustrates the back for a will.

Preparing a Will

Types of Paper

Since forms used in the Surrogate Court are on 8½ by 11-inch paper, most wills are prepared on paper of that size. The paper may be plain, or may be ruled in a variety of ways. Figures 24.3 and 24.4 illustrate a common form of will paper – margin rulings (blue) on all four edges.

Some law offices prefer to prepare wills on 14-inch paper. The length of paper you will use will depend on the practice of the office in which you are employed.

Date of Will

Wills are dated the day of execution. When preparing the will, the day of the month is left blank unless you know with certainty that it will be executed on a specific day.

Number of Copies

In most law offices, three copies of a will are prepared, and the original is executed. In some law offices, however, additional copies of the will are typed, and the will is executed in duplicate. Your lawyer will instruct you if more than one copy of the will is to be executed. If you receive no instructions, follow the traditional practice of typing three copies of the will, and having only the original executed.

Typing Guide

1. If plain unruled paper is used, leave a margin of approximately 1½ inches on the left, and one inch on the right.
2. If ruled margin paper is used, type within two spaces of all rulings.
3. Commence the heading of the will approximately six lines, or one inch, from the top of plain paper.
4. Double space the heading and the body of the will; triple space between paragraphs.
5. Number each paragraph in the body of the will. Type the initial words of each paragraph in either upper and lower case, or in capitals, depending on the practice of the office.
6. Number each page after the first (beginning with figure 2), centring the figures on the third line from the top of the page.
7. Single space the attestation clause.
8. Type at least two lines of the body of the will on the page with the testimonium and attestation clauses.

Erasures

In many offices *no* erasures are permitted in a will. Other offices permit only erasures which do not involve names or amounts, and which, of course, are not visible to the eye. Where erasures are permitted, frequently the testator and witnesses must initial each one as an indication that the correction was made prior to the execution of the will.

Execution of a Will

Testator

When the will has been prepared, the testator reads it over carefully, and if he approves

IN TESTIMONY WHEREOF I have to this my last will and

testament, written upon this and five preceding pages of paper,

subscribed my name this   day of March, 1970.

SIGNED, PUBLISHED AND DECLARED)
by the said testator, RONALD   )
CRAIG ANDERSON, as and for his)
last will and testament, in the)
presence of us, both present
at the same time, who at his
request, in his presence and
in the presence of each other,
have hereunto subscribed our
names as witnesses.

Figure 24.1. Ending of Will Prepared on

it, will then execute it. While it is not obligatory, many offices also have the testator initial the bottom corner of each page of the will except the last.

Witnesses

In Ontario a testator must execute the will in the presence of two witnesses, who in the presence of each other sign in the space to the left of his signature beneath the attestation clause. It is usual for each witness to write his full address beneath his signature to facilitate locating the witnesses when it becomes necessary to prove the authenticity of the will following the death of the testator. If the testator initialled each page of the will, each witness also does so.

A witness is required to witness only the signature of the testator; he does not read the will itself, nor is he aware of its contents. No person who is to benefit under a will, or who is married to a beneficiary named in the will, can act as a witness. If he does, both he and his wife will be unable to benefit from the testator's estate.

True Copies

When the will has been executed, true copies of all unsigned copies of the will are made.

Disposition of Copies of Will

A signed will is a very valuable document. It must be treated with the utmost care, and immediately put in safekeeping in accordance with the instructions of the testator. The signed will may be:
1. kept in the vault of the office of the lawyer who drew the will.
2. deposited with the Registrar of the Surrogate Court.
3. deposited with a trust company named as executor in the will.
4. taken by the testator to be kept by him.
   If the signed will is not retained in your

office, make a note on your file copy of its location.

Safekeeping of Wills

Each law office has its own particular system of maintaining signed wills. Some offices place all wills in envelopes marked "LAST WILL AND TESTAMENT OF ..." Others place wills in special covers similarly identified. Others insert them in labelled file folders. These wills may then be deposited in locked drawers in the office vault, special filing cabinets, or bank safety deposit boxes.

An alphabetical card index is usually maintained under the name of the testator showing the date of the will, and the names of witnesses and executor(s).

As soon as possible after the will has been executed, follow the procedures of your office to ensure its safekeeping.

Destruction of Previous Will

When a new will has been executed, any previous will is revoked, and the signed earlier will is burned, torn, or otherwise destroyed by the testator, or by someone else in his presence and upon his instructions.

Codicil

A testator may change the terms of an existing will by executing a document known as a *codicil* (Figure 24.5). This document usually contains only a minor change to the will. If a major change is required, the lawyer will usually recommend that the testator execute a new will.

A codicil is prepared in the same way as a will, and is also executed and witnessed in the same manner. Each copy of the codicil has a short back identified as "CODICIL TO THE LAST WILL AND TESTAMENT OF ..."

The signed codicil is filed with the executed will to which it refers, and must be treated with the same degree of care as the will itself.

DATED: _____ MARCH, 1970

LAST WILL AND TESTAMENT

OF

RONALD CRAIG ANDERSON

HILL, JOHNSTON & GRANT
17 Princess Street S.
Toronto, Ontario

Figure 24.2.   Back of a Will

THIS IS THE LAST WILL AND TESTAMENT of me, RONALD CRAIG ANDERSON, of the Borough of Etobicoke, in the County of York, Physician.

1.   I HEREBY REVOKE all wills and testamentary dispositions of every nature and kind whatsoever by me heretofore made.

2.   I GIVE, DEVISE AND BEQUEATH all my property of every nature and kind and wheresoever situate, including any property over which I may have a general power of appointment, to my wife, LUCILLE CAROLINE ANDERSON, for her own use absolutely, and I appoint her sole executrix of this my will.

        IN TESTIMONY WHEREOF I have to this my last will and testament, written upon this single page of paper, subscribed my name this   day of March, 1970.

```
SIGNED, PUBLISHED AND DECLARED )
by the said Testator, RONALD    )
CRAIG ANDERSON, as and for his  )
last will and testament, in     )
the presence of us, both        )
present at the same time, who   )
at his request, in his presence )
and in the presence of each     )
other, have hereunto subscribed )
our names as witnesses.         )
                                )
                                )
                                )
                                )
                                )
                                )
                                )
                                )
                                )
                                )
```

Figure 24.3. One-page Will on Ruled Paper   249

THIS IS THE LAST WILL AND TESTAMENT of me, RONALD CRAIG ANDERSON, of the Borough of Etobicoke, in the County of York, Physician.

1.   I HEREBY REVOKE all former wills and codicils by me at any time heretofore made.

2.   I NOMINATE, CONSTITUTE AND APPOINT Lucille Caroline Anderson, and Percival Andrew Peterson to be the Executors and Trustees of this my will. The expression "my Trustees" hereinafter used shall mean the Executors and Trustees or the Executor and Trustee for the time being of this my will.

3.   I GIVE, DEVISE, BEQUEATH AND APPOINT all my estate, both real and personal, of whatever kind and wheresoever situate, including all monies which may become payable to my estate by reason of my death under any policies of insurance, and also any real or personal property over which I may have a general power of appointment, unto my Trustees to hold the same upon the following trusts:

(a)   To pay out of and charge to the capital of my general estate my just debts, funeral and testamentary expenses and all estate and inheritance and succession duties or taxes, whether imposed by or pursuant to the law of this or any other jurisdiction whatsoever, that may be payable in connection with any property

Figure 24.4. First Page of Longer Will on Ruled Paper

THIS IS A CODICIL TO THE LAST WILL AND TESTAMENT of me, RONALD CRAIG ANDERSON, of the Borough of Etobicoke, in the County of York, Physician, which last will and testament bears the date the 27th day of March, 1970.

1.   I REVOKE the appointment of Percival Andrew Peterson as an Executor and Trustee contained in paragraph 2. of my said last will and testament, and I appoint Howard Albert East to be an Executor and Trustee of my said last will and testament in the place and stead of the said Percival Andrew Peterson.

2.   In all other respects I confirm my said will.

IN TESTIMONY WHEREOF I have to this codicil to my last will and testament, written upon this single page of paper, subscribed my name this   day of November, 1970.

SIGNED, PUBLISHED AND DECLARED   )
by the said RONALD CRAIG   )
ANDERSON, as and for a codicil   )
to his last will and testament,)
in the presence of us, both   )
present at the same time, who,   )
at his request, in his presence)
and in the presence of each   )
other, have hereunto subscribed)
our names as witnesses.   )
)
)
)
)
)
)
)
)

Figure 24.5. Codicil to Will   251

CHAPTER 25

Probate and Administration of Estates

When an individual dies, the property he leaves is known as his estate, and the laws of each province set out the conditions which must be fulfilled prior to distributing the estate.

It is the Surrogate Court of a province which deals with estate matters. In Ontario each county or other judicial area has a local Surrogate Court administered by a Registrar, and identified as the Surrogate Court of the particular area it serves.

If the deceased died testate, his will usually names the executor(s) appointed to carry out his intentions; if he died intestate, the Surrogate Court, upon application, appoints someone to carry out administration of the estate according to the laws of the province. Printed forms are used for almost all documents required in the Surrogate Court, and that court has also adopted the practice of using paper 8½ by 11 inches.

First Steps on the Death of a Client

When a solicitor first learns of the death of a client, he will ascertain whether there is a signed will, and where it is located. Any special instructions contained in the will are noted, and the executors named in the will are notified. The executors are not obliged to have the solicitors who drew the will act in the processing of the estate, but in practice they usually do.

The executors, or *next of kin* of the deceased if the deceased died intestate, provide the solicitor processing the estate with certain basic information. This information is necessary in order to complete the documentation required before the estate can be distributed. The information provided by the executors or next of kin includes the following:

1. the full name of the deceased, his occupation or marital status
2. the date and place of death
3. the date of birth of the deceased
4. the name, address, birth date, and blood relationship of each beneficiary
5. the location and number of safety deposit boxes, and whether the safety deposit boxes are held jointly with another
6. the location and number of bank accounts, and whether the bank accounts are held jointly with another
7. details of all policies of insurance
8. the location and manner of holding title to real estate
9. other details of assets – mortgages, pension, group insurance, stocks, bonds, car or household goods
10. details of gifts made within the previous five years
11. details of debts such as funeral, medical
12. the name, full address, and occupation of executors
13. the name, full address, and occupation of witnesses to the will, and to any codicils thereto.

Safety Deposit Box

Before proceeding with any applications to the court, the solicitor arranges an appointment with the bank to open any safety deposit boxes of the deceased. The boxes are sealed by the bank upon notification of the testator's death, and before inspection for Succession Duty Branch purposes, may be opened only in the presence of an officer of the bank to search for an executed original will or the deed to the burial plot. The bank acts as agent for both the Provincial Succession Duty Department and the Federal Estate Tax Department. Each bank is provided by the Succession Duty Branch with a supply of forms for the purpose of the listing of safety deposit box contents. When the listing has been completed, the bank sends the original to the Succession Duty Branch and a copy to the Estate Tax Branch. The listing is done in the presence of a representative of the estate.

When the provincial and federal authorities have received the list of contents, a consent to withdraw the contents is usually granted. The list of contents is kept by the federal and provincial authorities to verify returns that are subsequently made by the executors which set out the assets of the estate.

Administering the Estate

If the deceased died testate, an application will be made on behalf of the executor(s) for a grant of *letters probate*. If the deceased died intestate, an application will be made by the next of kin for a grant of *letters of administration*. If the deceased died testate, but the executor(s) named in the will is unable or unwilling to act, or no executor was named in the will, an application will be made for a grant of *letters of administration with will annexed*. There are other special ways of granting administration, but the three named above are those most frequently encountered.

Letters Probate

A will usually names the person(s) the deceased appointed to be executor(s) of his estate. The executor(s) presents the original signed will to the Surrogate Court to have it "proved" to be the last will and testament of the deceased, and the court will grant letters probate (Figure 25.1), a document under the seal of the court certifying that the will, a copy of which is attached, has been proven and registered in the court, and that administration of the estate of the testator is given by the court to the executor(s) described therein.

Preparation for Applying for Probate

The first step in applying for probate is to secure the original signed copy of the will (and any codicils) of the deceased. This must be filed with the court when application for letters probate is made. If only a signed carbon copy of the will (and any codicil) is available, then subject to proof that the original has been lost and that the carbon copy is a true copy of the *last* will and testament of the deceased, it may be used in place of the original.

From the information secured from the executors, two copies of each of the following forms are prepared: application for probate, affidavit of executor(s), affidavit of execution of will, affidavit of execution of codicil (if applicable), inventory of estate.

Two copies of each form are typed; the original is filed with the Registrar of the appropriate Surrogate Court, and the carbon copy remains in the office file.

Application for Probate

The application for probate is completed by the executor, or jointly by the executors if more than one. The full name, the full address, and the occupation of each executor must be shown. Figure 25.2 illustrates this form.

The application need not be signed personally by the executors; it may be signed by their solicitors.

If the deceased was divorced, full particulars of the divorce are given in paragraph 2 of the application. If there is a codicil to the will, information as to its date is shown in paragraph 3.

Affidavit of Executor(s)

Each executor must complete an affidavit stating that he will faithfully administer the property of the deceased; two or more executors cannot join in a single affidavit. Figure 25.3 illustrates this affidavit.

The original will is Exhibit "A", and the inventory of the property that belonged to the deceased at the time of his death is Exhibit "B" to each affidavit. If there is a codicil which is also produced, reference is made to it in paragraph 1 of the affidavit, and it becomes Exhibit "C". If there are several codicils, they are known as Exhibit "C", "D", "E", and so on.

Affidavit of Execution of Will

Either witness to the will completes an affidavit of execution of will (Figure 25.4) which certifies that the deponent did see the will executed. It provides details as to time and place, and identifies the second witness. The original will is Exhibit "A" to this affidavit.

Canada: SPECIMEN ONLY **Province of Ontario**

In Her Majesty's Surrogate Court of the County of York

No.

BE IT KNOWN that on the   1st   day of   March   19 69   , the LAST WILL AND TESTAMENT   of   <u>JOHN DOE</u>   , Labourer

late of the   City   of   Toronto   in the   County   of

York,   who died on or about the   1st   of   February   , 19 69

at   the City of Toronto, in the County of York,   and who at the time of   his   death

had a fixed place of abode at   the City of Toronto   in the said   County   of   York,

was proved and registered in the said Surrogate Court, a true copy of which said LAST WILL AND

TESTAMENT   is hereunto annexed, and that the   administration of All

and Singular the property of the said deceased and in any way concerning   his   Will   was

granted by the aforesaid Court to   MARY DOE, Widow, of the City of Toronto, in the

County of York, the

Execut rix   named in the said Will   she   having been first sworn well and
faithfully to administer the same by paying the just debts of the deceased and the legacies contained in
    his   Will   so far as   she is   thereunto bound by law and by
distributing the residue (if any) of the property according to law and to exhibit under oath a true and
perfect inventory of All and Singular the said property, and to render a just and full account of   her
Executorship when thereunto lawfully required.

WITNESS HIS HONOUR   IAN McLEAN MACDONELL,   Judge of the said Surrogate Court at
the City of Toronto, in the County of York, the day and year first above written.

By the Court

(L. S.)   H.B.Ridout
                            REGISTRAR OF THE SURROGATE COURT
                            OF THE COUNTY OF YORK

100

254   *Figure 25.1.   Specimen Letters Probate*

Dye & Durham Limited — Law and Commercial Stationers
76 Richmond Street E., Toronto
Form No. 235

In describing the Court, insert County, United Counties, District, Regional Municipality or Judicial District where appropriate. For place of residence, insert appropriate County, District, Regional Municipality, etc.

To the Surrogate Court of the COUNTY OF YORK

In the Estate of HENRY JAMES EAST
deceased

Name, address and occupation, or if none, give marital status of both deponent and deceased.

The petition of HOWARD ALBERT EAST, of 19 King Street,

of the City of Toronto, in the County of York,

Professor, and of MARY ANN EAST, of 135 William Street, in the

City of Toronto, in the County of York, Widow,

Showeth,

1. HENRY JAMES EAST,

Name, address and occupation, or if none, give marital status.

Or had no fixed place of abode in Ontario or resided out of Ontario but had at such time property in the county of

late of 135 William Street, in the City of Toronto, in the County of York, Retired Dentist, , deceased, died on or about January 31, 1970 , at the City of Toronto, in the County of York, and the deceased at the time of death had a fixed place of abode at the City of Toronto, in the County of York.

Or as the case may be ; here give particulars as required by rule 5.

2. The deceased was at the time of death (unmarried, married, a widower or divorced) and the marriage of the deceased or any person with whom he went through a form of marriage has never been dissolved or annulled.

Add codicils, if any.

3. The last will of the deceased was dated November 7, 1963, and at that time the deceased was of the full age of twenty-one years.

A codicil to the last will of the deceased was dated April 19, 1968, and at that time the deceased was of the full age of twenty-one years.

4. The deceased did not marry subsequent to the last mentioned date .

5. Neither witness to the will or the codicil is a beneficiary or the husband or wife of a beneficiary named therein.

6. Your petitioners are the executors named in the will

7. The value of the whole property of which the deceased died possessed or entitled to

is $ 95,829.00.

Wherefore it is prayed that probate of the will and the codicil of the deceased may be granted to your petitioners .

Dated March 1 1970

Hill, Johnston & Grant
....
Signature of applicant or solicitors

Figure 25.2. Application for Probate

AFFIDAVIT OF EXECUTOR
Revised June, 1966

Dye & Durham Limited — Law and Commercial Stationers
76 Richmond Street E., Toronto
Form No. 211

In the Surrogate Court of the COUNTY OF YORK

In the Estate of HENRY JAMES EAST

deceased

In describing the Court, insert County, United Counties, District, Regional Municipality or Judicial District where appropriate. For place of residence, insert appropriate County, District, Regional Municipality, etc.

I, HOWARD ALBERT EAST of 19 King Street, in the City of Toronto, in the County of York, Professor,

Name, address and occupation, or if none, give marital status.

make oath and say:

1. The document now produced and shown to me and marked as Exhibit "A" to this my affidavit is to the best of my knowledge and belief the last will of the deceased.

If codicils, produce and identify them as "C", "D" etc.

The document now produced and shown to me and marked as Exhibit "C" to this my affidavit is to the best of my knowledge and belief a codicil to the last will of the deceased.

2. I am one of the executors named in the will and am of the full age of twenty-one year and my name, place of residence and occupation are above correctly stated.

3. I have read over carefully the annexed petition and the statements therein are true.

4. Now shown to me and marked as Exhibit "B" to this my affidavit is the true and perfec inventory and valuation of the property of the deceased.

5. I will faithfully administer the property of the deceased by paying the just debts an legacies, so far as the same will thereunto extend and the law bind me and by distributing the residue, if any, of the property according to law; and I will exhibit under oath a true an perfect inventory of all the property of the deceased and render a just, full and true account of my administration when lawfully required.

SWORN before me at the City

of Toronto

in the County

of York

this   day of March   1970

A Commissioner, etc.

This affidavit is filed on behalf of the applicant   by HILL, JOHNSTON & GRANT, 17 Princess Street South, Toronto, Ontario.

Solicitor s   for the applicant s

Figure 25.3. Affidavit of Executor

AFFIDAVIT OF EXECUTION OF WILL
Revised June, 1966

Dye & Durham Limited — Law and Commercial Stationers
76 Richmond Street E., Toronto
Form No. 213

In the Surrogate Court of the COUNTY OF YORK

In the Estate of HENRY JAMES EAST   deceased

I,   MARGARET LESLIE FOX   of 160 Jardinierre Avenue, in the

City of Toronto   in the York, Secretary,

make oath and say:

1. I knew Henry James East,

late of the City of Toronto,

in the   County of York, Retired Dentist,   deceased.

2. On or about   November 7   19 63, I was personally present and did see the paper writing
hereunto annexed and marked as exhibit "A" to this my affidavit, executed by the deceased as
it now appears,
as and for   his   last will and testament, by signing   his   name Henry James
East,   at the foot or end thereof.

3. The deceased was on that date of the full age of twenty-one years to the best of my knowledge
and belief.

4. The will was so executed by the deceased in the presence of myself and Peter Thomas
Grant,   , of the City   of Toronto
in the County of York, Solicitor,
                                , who were both present at the same time;
whereupon the said Peter Thomas Grant
and I did, in the presence of the deceased, attest and subscribe the will as witnesses.

5. ~~Previous to the execution of the will the same was read over to the deceased by me (or by~~
~~in my presence), and the deceased at such time seemed~~
~~thoroughly to understand it (or had full knowledge of its contents)~~.

SWORN before me at the   City

of Toronto

in the County of York

this   day of   March,   1970

A Commissioner, etc.

This affidavit is filed on behalf of the applicants   by HILL, JOHNSTON & GRANT,
17 Princess Street South, Toronto, Ontario,
                                    Solicitor s   for the applicant s

Figure 25.4. Affidavit of Execution of Will

Affidavit of Execution of Codicil

If there is a codicil to the will, one of the witnesses to it completes an affidavit (Figure 25.5) similar to the affidavit of execution of will. The original codicil is an exhibit to this affidavit, and is known as Exhibit "C"; there are no Exhibits "A" and "B" produced with this affidavit.

Inventory of Estate

The executor(s) applying for a grant of probate submit an inventory (Figure 25.6) of all the property that belonged to the deceased at the time of his death. Insurance payable to a named beneficiary, assets held as joint tenants which pass by survivorship, or real property situated outside of Ontario are not considered in this inventory.

Since the total value of the estate which appears in this form also appears on other documents used on the application, it is usual to complete this inventory form first.

Exhibits Filed

Regardless of the number of affidavits to which they are produced as exhibits, only the original signed copy of the will, any codicil, and the original of the inventory form are filed with the Registrar of the Surrogate Court.

Inventory Form, Exhibit "B"

This inventory is Exhibit "B" to the affidavit of each executor, and the majority of law stationers have printed the form accordingly, providing sufficient space to allow for the insertion of the names of each executor in accord with the affidavit to which it is shown as an exhibit.

Regardless of whether there are any other exhibits to an affidavit, this inventory form is always Exhibit "B".

Will, Exhibit "A"

The original signed copy of the will is produced as Exhibit "A" to the affidavit of each executor, and to the affidavit of execution of the will. Certain formalities must be followed. The will must be stamped with the exhibit stamp; one stamping for each affidavit to which it is an exhibit. Each executor must endorse the will. Stampings and the endorsement appear on the last page of the will beneath the attestation clause as illustrated in Figure 25.7. If there is not sufficient room on the page, the reverse side may be used.

Codicil, Exhibit "C"

The original signed codicil, or codicils, must be endorsed and stamped in the same manner as the original signed will.

Grant of Probate

When all the original probate forms have been considered by the Surrogate Court, the original grant of letters probate is obtained. The original signed will remains in the custody of the court; a true copy is affixed to the letters probate.

The lawyer will then instruct you as to the number of notarial copies of the letters probate to prepare. These are either typed or duplicated, and a special notarial certificate (Figure 25.8) is completed by the lawyer.

Letters of Administration

When a person dies intestate, he has not appointed anyone to distribute his estate, and the Surrogate Court considers applications for appointment of administrator(s) of the estate.

It is the practice of the court that those, such as a widow of the deceased, who have a prior right to administration must renounce that right before administration will be granted to anyone else. When a person dies intestate and leaves neither a husband nor wife, there is a prescribed order of preference among the next of kin for the appointment of the administrator. The children of the deceased are usually the first ones eligible for the appointment, but this will be indicated by the lawyer.

Preparation for Applying for Administration

The Surrogate Court Act requires that before an application for letters of administration is considered, a search must be made for an executed will in all places where the deceased usually kept his papers, and a certificate provided by the Registrar of the Surrogate Court stating that no will has been deposited with the Surrogate Court office.

When there is no will, the following forms are prepared from the information obtained from the deceased's next of kin by the solicitor acting for the estate: application for administration, affidavit of administrator, inventory of estate.

Two copies of each form are typed. The original is filed with the Registrar of the appropriate Surrogate Court, and the carbon copy remains in the office file.

Application for Administration

The application for administration as illustrated in Figure 25.9 is completed on behalf of the individual(s) applying to the court for appointment as administrator(s) of the estate. The full name, address, and occupation of each applicant is shown. Paragraph 5 of the application requires each applicant to state the grounds upon which his right to be appointed administrator is based.

If the applicant is not the next of kin first entitled to apply for letters of administration, the first ranked next of kin must formally renounce his or their right to apply for administration in a document (Figure 25.10) which is executed under seal, and is accompanied by an affidavit of execution. Then the first ranked next of kin will complete a nomination (Figure 25.11), which is also executed under seal, and accompanied by an affidavit of execution.

An application for administration need not be signed personally by the applicants; it may be signed by their solicitors.

Affidavit of Administrator

Each applicant must complete an affidavit of administrator (Figure 25.12); two or more applicants cannot join in a single affidavit.

The inventory of the estate is Exhibit "B" to each affidavit; there is no Exhibit "A".

Inventory of Estate

The form for the inventory of the estate (Figure 25.6) is completed in the same manner as in an application for letters probate.

Grant of Letters of Administration

When all the original application for administration documents have been considered by the Surrogate Court, the original grant of letters of administration (Figure 25.13) is obtained. You will then be instructed by the lawyer as to the number of notarial copies to prepare.

Letters of Administration with Will Annexed

Though a person dies testate, it sometimes happens that (1) the testator omits to appoint an executor; (2) the executor may die prior to the testator; (3) the executor may die after the death of the testator but before application for probate of the will has been made; (4) the executor may renounce his right to apply for probate; (5) the executor may be incapable of acting; (6) a number of other contingencies may occur which will leave the testator without an executor. In any of these circumstances the court appoints some person to administer the estate by grant of letters of administration with will annexed.

Preparation for Applying for Letters of Administration with Will Annexed

When applying for letters of administration with will annexed, the first step in preparation is to secure the original signed copy of the will and any codicils of the testator. The following forms will be prepared in accordance with information obtained from the testator's next of kin: an application for grant of administration with will annexed, an affidavit of administrator, a renunciation (if any), an affidavit of execution of will, an affidavit of execution of codicil (if any), and an inventory of estate.

Two copies of each form are typed. The original is filed with the Registrar of the appropriate Surrogate Court, and the carbon copy remains in the office file.

Application for Grant of Administration with Will Annexed

The application for grant of administration with will annexed is similar to Figure 25.2, and is completed in the same manner. There is an additional paragraph which sets out the circumstances under which the application is made, and gives the reasons why there is no executor.

Affidavit of Administrator

The affidavit of administrator is similar in content to the affidavit of an executor in an application for probate (Figure 25.3), and each person applying for appointment as an administrator must complete a separate affidavit.

The original will and any codicils are exhibits to this affidavit, as is the statement setting out the inventory of the estate.

Affidavit of Execution of Will and Codicils

Affidavits of execution of will and codicils are completed in the same manner as an application for grant of letters probate (Figures 25.4 and 25.5).

Inventory of Estate

The inventory of estate is completed in the same manner as in other applications to the Surrogate Court, and is Exhibit "B" to the affidavit to which it refers.

Renunciation

If an executor named in a will is renouncing his right, or if the next of kin first entitled to apply for administration with will annexed does not wish to do so, then a renunciation form is completed (Figure 25.14). This is executed under seal, and is accompanied by an affidavit of execution.

Exhibits

As in an application for letters probate, only the original signed copy of the will and of any codicils are filed with the application. The applicant must endorse the will and codicils in the same manner as an executor, and the will must be stamped as an exhibit to the appropriate affidavits.

Grant of Letters of Administration with Will Annexed

When all the original material filed with the application has been considered by the Surrogate Court, the original grant of letters of administration with will annexed is obtained. This is similar to other grants, but sets out the particular circumstances of the application.

Administration Bonds

The Surrogate Court Act provides that every person to whom a grant of administration, including administration with will annexed, is given shall provide a bond payable to the judge of the Surrogate Court of the county or judicial area in which the application is made, to ensure faithful administration of the estate. Such a bond is not required of a trust company whose charter provides that it may act as executor or administrator of an estate.

The amount of the bond is double the gross amount of the estate if those guaranteeing "faithful administration" are individuals; it may be only the amount of the estate if the bond is furnished by a *surety*, that is, a person or company who promises to satisfy the obligation of another in the event of default of the other.

The form of bond is determined by the form of administration sought, and care should be taken to ensure that the proper form is used. (See Figures 25.15 and 25.16.)

The full names, addresses, and occupations of the sureties are given, and the bond is signed by the sureties and the applicant(s) for administration. The bond is signed under seal and witnessed. The witness executes an affidavit of execution swearing to the signatures of all individuals to the bond. If a company is the surety and executed the bond under its corporate seal, no affidavit of execution is required for the signature of its officer(s).

If individuals are sureties, the bond is accompanied by an affidavit of justification in which the sureties swear that they possess assets sufficient to cover the amount of the bond, and are of the age of twenty-one. This affidavit is not required of a bonding company.

It should be noted that a judge of the Surrogate Court may, under special circumstances, reduce the amount of a bond, or dispense with it entirely.

Release of Bond

When the administration of the estate is completed, the following material is filed with the Registrar of the appropriate Surrogate Court: a draft order; affidavit or affidavits in support of the order, setting out the facts proving the completed administration of the estate; releases from the next of kin or beneficiaries; and an affidavit proving advertisement for creditors.

If the material presented is satisfactory, the judge signs the order, and it and the bond are returned to the solicitors acting for the estate.

Documents prepared for use in the Surrogate Court, such as an affidavit or order, are typed following the requirements for Supreme or County Court documents.

Execution of Affidavits in Estate Practice

Unlike affidavits for use in litigation in the County or Supreme Courts, affidavits prepared for use in applications to the courts for probate or administration may be sworn before a solicitor in the office in which such documents are prepared. However, no affidavit of execution of a will or codicil may be sworn by a witness to the will before any lawyer who was the second witness to the will or codicil.

Surrogate Court Fees

The Surrogate Court in Ontario levies a fee for grants of probate or administration the amount of which depends on the value of the estate. These fees are outlined in an appendix to The Surrogate Court Act.

AFFIDAVIT OF EXECUTION OF CODICIL
Revised June, 1966

Dye & Durham Limited — Law and Commercial Stationers
76 Richmond Street E., Toronto
Form No. 214

In the Surrogate Court of the COUNTY OF YORK

In describing the Court, insert County, United Counties, District, Regional Municipality or Judicial District where appropriate. For place of residence, insert appropriate County, District, Regional Municipality, etc.

In the Estate of HENRY JAMES EAST   deceased

I, KATHLEEN PATRICIA WOLFE,   of 17 Hillsdale Court, in the

Borough of Etobicoke in the County of York, Secretary,

make oath and say:

Name, address and occupation, or if none, give marital status of both deponent and deceased.

1. I knew Henry James East
late of the   City of Toronto,
in the County of York, Retired Dentist,   deceased

If deceased was a marksman or blind, delete "signing his name" and add "making his mark"

2. On or about April 19,   1968, I was personally present and did see the paper
writing hereunto annexed and marked as exhibit "C" to this my affidavit, executed by the deceased
as it now appears,
as and for a codicil, to   his   will by signing   his   name Henry James East,
at the foot or end thereof.

3. The deceased was on that date of the full age of twenty-one years to the best of my knowledge
and belief.

4. The codicil was so executed by the deceased in the presence of myself and Peter Thomas
Grant   , of the City of Toronto,
in the County of York, Solicitor,
who were both present at the same time
whereupon the said Peter Thomas Grant
and I did, in the presence of the deceased, attest and subscribe the codicil as witnesses.

If deceased was a marksman or blind, delete if not applicable.

5. - Previous to the execution of the codicil the same was read over to the deceased by me (or by
in my presence), and the deceased at
such time seemed thoroughly to understand it (or had full knowledge of its contents).

SWORN before me at the   City

of   Toronto

in the   County

of   York

this   day of March   1970

A Commissioner, etc.

This affidavit is filed on behalf of the applicant s   by HILL, JOHNSTON & GRANT

17 Princess Street S., Toronto,   Solicitor s   for the applicants

Figure 25.5. Affidavit of Execution of Codicil

INVENTORY OF ESTATE
Revised June, 1966

Dye & Durham Limited — Law and Commercial Stationers
76 Richmond Street E., Toronto
Form No. 233

In the Surrogate Court of the COUNTY OF YORK

In the Estate of HENRY JAMES EAST   deceased

Inventory and Valuation of the property of the deceased. GENERAL DESCRIPTION OF PROPERTY	VALUE OR AMOUNT INSERT NIL WHERE APPLICABLE
	$
Clothing, Jewellery, Household Goods and Furniture	2,000.00
Stock-in-Trade at fair market value	nil
Book Debts, Promissory Notes, Mortgages and other monies on loan	3,109.00
Bonds, Debentures, Stocks & other securities	50,187.00
Life insurance payable to the estate	10,000.00
Cash on Deposit without right of survivorship and cash on hand	457.00
Farming implements, Animals, Poultry and Produce	nil
Interest of the deceased in trusts or estates	nil
Other Personal property not before mentioned (itemize)	76.00
Old Age Security Cheque--uncashed	
Real estate at fair market value less encumbrances (itemize)	30,000.00
135 William Street, Lot 30,	
Plan 4666, Toronto	
	TOTAL $ 95,829.00

This is exhibit "B" to the affidavit of HOWARD ALBERT EAST and MARY ANN EAST

Sworn before me this   day of   March   1970

A Commissioner, etc.

Figure 25.6. Inventory of Estate   263

10.   In case my wife shall not survive me for thirty days, this will shall be read and construed as if she had predeceased me, except as to her appointment as executrix.

IN TESTIMONY WHEREOF I have to this my last will and testament, written upon this and eight preceding pages of paper, subscribed my name this 7th day of November, 1963.

SIGNED, PUBLISHED AND DECLARED)
by the said testator, HENRY)
JAMES EAST, as and for his)
last will and testament, in the)
presence of us, both present at)
the same time, who at his)
request, in his presence and in)   *Henry James East*
the presence of each other, have)
hereunder subscribed our names)
as witnesses.)
)
Margaret Leslie Fox)
160 Jardiniere Ave.)
Toronto)
)
Peter T. Grant, Q.C.)
Toronto)
)

This is the last will and testament of Henry James East.

THIS IS EXHIBIT " A " REFERRED TO IN THE
AFFIDAVIT OF   HOWARD ALBERT EAST
SWORN BEFORE ME THIS   DAY
OF   March   19 70

_____
                    A Commissioner, etc.

_____
                    Executor

_____
                    Executrix

THIS IS EXHIBIT " A " REFERRED TO IN THE
AFFIDAVIT OF   MARY ANN EAST
SWORN BEFORE ME THIS   DAY
OF   March   19 70

_____
                    A Commissioner, etc.

THIS IS EXHIBIT " A " REFERRED TO IN THE
AFFIDAVIT OF   MARGARET LESLIE FOX
SWORN BEFORE ME THIS   DAY
OF   March   19 70

_____
                    A Commissioner, etc.

Figure 25.7. Endorsement and Stampings on
Last Page of Will

Dye & Durham Limited, 76 Richmond Street East, Toronto
Law and Commercial Stationers
Form No. 165

CANADA

Province of Ontario

To Wit

To all whom these Presents

may come, be seen or known

I, PETER THOMAS GRANT,

a Notary Public, in and for the Province of Ontario, by Royal Authority duly appointed, residing

at the City of Toronto, in the County of York, in said Province,

Do Certify and Attest that the paper-writing hereto annexed is a true copy of a document produced

and shown to me and purporting to be the original Letters Probate

of the estate of HENRY JAMES EAST,

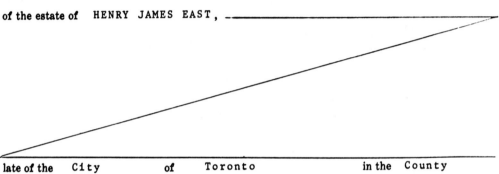

late of the City of Toronto in the County

of York, deceased, issued out of the Surrogate Court of the

County of York dated May 17th, 1970

and numbered 1756/70 the said copy having been compared by me with the

said original document, an act whereof being requested I have granted under my Notarial Form

and Seal of Office to serve and avail as occasion shall or may require.

In Testimony Whereof I have hereto subscribed my name and affixed my Notarial Seal of Office at

Toronto.

this 19th day of May 1970.

SEAL

A Notary Public in and for the Province of Ontario.

Figure 25.8. Notarial Certificate, Probate or Administration

Dye & Durham`Limited — Law and Commercial Stationers
76 Richmond Street E., Toronto
Form No. 236

To the Surrogate Court of the COUNTY OF YORK

In describing the Court, insert County, United Counties, District, Regional Municipality or Judicial District where appropriate. For place of residence, insert appropriate County, District, Regional Municipality, etc.

In the Estate of HENRY JAMES EAST   decease

The Petition of HOWARD ALBERT EAST, 19 King Street,

of the City of Toronto,   in the County of York,

Professor,

Name, address and occupation, or if none, give marital status of both deponent and deceased.

Showeth,

1. Henry James East,
late of 135 William St., in the City of Toronto, in the County of
York, Retired Dentist,   , deceased, died on
about   January 31   1970 , at the City of Toronto,
in the County of York,
and the deceased at the time of death had a fixed place of abode at the City of Toront
in the County of York

Or had no fixed place of abode in Ontario or resided out of Ontario but had at such time property in the county of

2. The deceased left no will, codicil or testamentary paper.

3. The deceased was at the time of death (~~unmarried,~~ married, ~~a widower or divorced~~) and th
marriage of the deceased or any person with whom he went through a form of marriage has nev
been dissolved or annulled.

Or as the case may be; here give particulars as required by rule 5.

4. The following next-of-kin and heirs-at-law survived the deceased

Here give names, addresses and relationship of relatives of deceased with ages of those under 21 and show if any under legal disability.

Name	Address	Relationship	age if under 2
Mary Ann East	135 William St. Toronto	Widow	
Howard Albert East	19 King Street Toronto	Son	

Here state grounds of applicant's right.

5. Your petitioner claims to be entitled to administration of the estate as son of the
deceased and nominee of the lawful widow.

6. The value of the whole property of which the deceased died possessed or entitled to
is $ 95,829.00.

Wherefore it is prayed that administration of the property of the deceased may be granted to you
petitioner

Dated March   19 70

....
Signature of applicant   or solicitor

Figure 25.9. Application for Administration

Dye & Durham Limited — Law and Commercial Stationers
76 Richmond Street E., Toronto
Form No. 239

In the Surrogate Court of the COUNTY OF YORK

In the Estate of HENRY JAMES EAST   deceased

WHEREAS   HENRY JAMES EAST

late of the   City   of   Toronto

in the County of York, Retired Dentist,   deceased

died on or about January 31,   1970

intestate, and had at the time of death a fixed place of abode

at the   City   of   Toronto

in the County of York

AND WHEREAS I,   MARY ANN EAST

of the   City of Toronto

in the County of York

To be varied
according to the
facts   am the lawful   widow   and the only next of kin

NOW I, do hereby expressly renounce all right and title to letters of administration of the property

of the deceased.

IN WITNESS WHEREOF   I   have hereunto set   my

hand   and seal   on March   ,   1970

SIGNED, SEALED AND DELIVERED
     In the Presence of

                                                   LS

Figure 25.10.   Renunciation of Administration
Accompanied by Affidavit of Execution

Dye & Durham Limited — Law and Commercial Stationers
76 Richmond Street E., Toronto
Form No. 78

In the Surrogate Court of the COUNTY OF YORK

In the Estate of HENRY JAMES EAST   decease~~d~~

Whereas, the above-named died on   January 31   , 19 70

Or as the case may be.

intestate, and the undersigned ~~are~~ is his   lawful widow   ~~and h ------ next of kin~~.

I   do nominate and appoint   HOWARD ALBERT EAST

to apply for a grant of administration of the property of the deceased.

Dated   March   1970

SIGNED IN THE PRESENCE OF

In the Surrogate Court of the COUNTY OF YORK

In the Estate of   HENRY JAMES EAST   decease~~d~~

I,   PETER THOMAS GRANT   of the   City   of Toronto

in the County of   York, Solicitor,   make oath and say:

1. THAT I was personally present and did see the above Nomination duly signed, an~~d~~
executed by Mary Ann East---

the party   thereto.

2. THAT the said Nomination was executed by the said party

at the   City   of   Toronto.

3. THAT I know the said party.

4. THAT I am a subscribing witness to the said Nomination.

SWORN before me at the   City
of   Toronto
in the   County
of   York
this   day of March   1970

A Commissioner, etc.

Figure 25.11. Nomination of Administrator

AFFIDAVIT OF ADMINISTRATOR
Revised June, 1966

Dye & Durham Limited — Law and Commercial Stationers
76 Richmond Street E., Toronto
Form No. 209

In the Surrogate Court of the COUNTY OF YORK

In the Estate of HENRY JAMES EAST   deceased

I,   HOWARD ALBERT EAST   **of**   19 King Street,

in the City of Toronto,

       in the County of   York, Professor,

Name address and occupation, or if none, give marital status.

make oath and say:

1. I am of the full age of twenty-one years and my name, place of residence and occupation are above correctly stated.

2. I am the petitioner for administration herein.

Or cause to be made.

3. I have made   or caused to be made a   diligent and careful search in all places where the papers of the deceased were usually kept, in order to ascertain whether the deceased had or had not left any will but I have been unable to discover any will, codicil or other testamentary paper and I verily believe that the deceased died without leaving any will, codicil or other testamentary paper whatsoever.

4. I have read over carefully the annexed petition and the statements therein are true.

5. Now shown to me and marked as Exhibit "B" to this my affidavit is the true and perfect inventory and valuation of the property of the deceased.

6. I will faithfully administer the property of the deceased by paying the just debts and distributing the residue, if any, of the property according to law and I will exhibit under oath a true and perfect inventory of all the property of the deceased and render a just, full and true account of my administration when lawfully required.

SWORN before me at the   City

of   Toronto

in the   County

of   York

this   day of March   1970

         A Commissioner, etc.

This affidavit is filed on behalf of the applicant   by HILL, JOHNSTON & GRANT, 17 Princess Street South, Toronto, Ontario.

                             Solicitors   for the applicant

Figure 25.12. Affidavit of Administrator

Canada: SPECIMEN ONLY

Province of Ontario

In Her Majesty's Surrogate Court of the County of York

No.

BE IT KNOWN that on the 1st day of March , 19 69 Letters of Administration of All and Singular the property of JOHN DOE , Labourer

late of the City of Toronto in the County of York,

who died on or about the 1st day of February 19 69 at the City of Toronto,

in the County of York,

Intestate, and had at the time of his death a fixed place of abode at the City of

Toronto in the said County of York, were granted

by the Surrogate Court of the County of York to MARY DOE, Widow, of the City of Toronto,

in the County of York, the lawful widow

of the Intestate she having been first sworn faithfully to administer the same by paying his just debts and distributing the residue (if any) of his property according to law, and to exhibit under oath a true and perfect inventory of All and Singular the said property and to render a just and full account of her administration whenever thereunto lawfully required.

WITNESS HIS HONOUR IAN McLEAN MACDONELL, Judge of the said Surrogate Court at the City of Toronto, in the County of York, the day and year first above written.

By the Court

(L.S.)

H.B.Ridout

Registrar of the Surrogate Court of
the County of York.

100

Figure 25.13. Specimen Letters of Administration

RENUNCIATION OF PROBATE OR ADMINISTRATION WITH WILL
Revised June, 1966

Dye & Durham Limited — Law and Commercial Stationers
76 Richmond Street E., Toronto
Form No. 238

In the Surrogate Court of the COUNTY OF YORK

In the Estate of HENRY JAMES EAST   deceased

WHEREAS HENRY JAMES EAST,

late of the   City   of   Toronto

in the County of York, Retired Dentist,   deceased,

died on or about January 31,   19 70

and had at the time of death a fixed place of abode at the City of Toronto,

in the County of York,   ,

And codicil,
if any.   And whereas, I am informed and believe that by a last will and testament,

dated   November 7,   1963

the deceased appointed Mary Ann East

as execut rix.

Now I,   Mary Ann East

And codicil,
if any.   do hereby expressly renounce all my right and title to the probate and execution of the

will------------of the deceased.

In witness whereof I have hereunto set my hand and seal this   1st day of

March,   19 70

SIGNED, SEALED AND DELIVERED

in the presence of

                                                    LS

Figure 25.14. Renunciation of Probate or   271
Administration with Will Annexed
Accompanied by Affidavit of Execution

Dye & Durham Limited — Law and Commercial Stationers
76 Richmond Street E., Toronto
Form No. 231

Know all Men by these Presents

That we   HOWARD ALBERT EAST, 19 King Street, in the City of
Toronto, in the County of York, Professor,

Administrator   ,

— and —
TORONTO INDEMNITY COMPANY LTD., 95 Adelaide
Street N., in the City of Toronto, in
the County of York,

Surety,

—Surety,

Full names, residences and occupations of all parties.

are jointly and severally bound unto the Judge of the Surrogate Court of the County of York

in the sum of $ 95,000.00 -------------------------- to be paid to the said Judge;
for which payment, well and truly to be made, we bind ourselves and each of us for the whole,
our and each of our heirs, executors and administrators, firmly by these presents., and the
said Company for itself, its successors and assigns, binds itself
for the whole firmly by these presents.

For Company surety, add after presents, "and the said Company for itself, its successors and assigns, binds itself for the whole firmly by these presents." And add after seals, "And the said Company affixes its Corporate Seal and the hand of its President" or other proper officers."

Sealed with our seals.   And the said Company affixes its Corporate Seal and
the hand of its President and Secretary.

The condition of this obligation is such that, if the above named administrator   of all the property
of Henry James East
late of the   City   of   Toronto
in the County of York, Retired Dentist,   deceased, who died on or about
the 31st day of January   1970, do, when lawfully called on in that behalf,
make or cause to be made a true and perfect inventory of all the property of the said deceased, which
has or shall come into the hands, possession or knowledge of the said administrator   , or into the
hands or possession of any other person or persons for   him   and the same so made do exhibit
or cause to be exhibited into the Registry of the said Surrogate Court, when thereunto lawfully
required, and the same property, and all other property of the deceased at the time of death, which
at any time after shall come into the hands or possession of the said administrator   , or into the
hands or possession of any other person or persons for   him   , do well and truly administer
according to law: that is to say, do pay the debts that the deceased owed at death, and then the
legacies contained in the will annexed to the letters of administration so far as such property shall
thereunto extend and the law bind   him   and further do make or cause to be made, a just, full
and true account of the said administration when lawfully required, and all the rest and residue of
the property, shall deliver and pay unto such person or persons as are by law entitled thereto then
this obligation to be void and of no effect, or else to remain in full force and virtue.

Dated   March   1970

SIGNED, SEALED AND DELIVERED
in the presence of

_____ LS

HOWARD ALBERT EAST

TORONTO INDEMNITY COMPANY LTD.

By: _____

_____

Figure 25.15.   Administration Bond Will Annexed

Dye & Durham Limited — Law and Commercial Stationers
76 Richmond Street E., Toronto
Form No. 285

Know all Men by these Presents

That we HOWARD ALBERT EAST, 19 King Street, in the City of
Toronto, in the County of York, Professor, Administrator ,

-and-

TORONTO INDEMNITY COMPANY LTD., 95 Adelaide Surety,
Street North, in the City of Toronto, in
the County of York,

Surety,

are jointly and severally bound unto the Judge of the Surrogate Court of the County of
York--
in the sum of $ 95,000.00-------------------------------to be paid to the said judge;
for which payment, well and truly to be made, we bind ourselves and each of us for the whole,
our and each of our heirs, executors and administrators, firmly by these presents, and the
said Company for itself, its successors and assigns, binds itself
for the whole firmly by these presents.

Sealed with our seals. And the said Company affixes its Corporate Seal
and the hand of its President and Secretary.

The condition of this obligation is such that, if the above-named administrator   of all the property
of Henry James East
late of the   City   of   Toronto
in the County of York, Retired Dentist,   deceased, who died on or about
the 31st day of January   1970 , do, when lawfully called on in that behalf,
make or cause to be made a true and perfect inventory of all the property of the said deceased, which
has or shall come into the hands, possession or knowledge of the said administrator   , or into the
hands or possession of any other person or persons for   him   and the same so made do exhibit
or cause to be exhibited into the Registry of the said Surrogate Court, when thereunto lawfully
required, and the same property, and all other property of the deceased at the time of death, which
at any time after shall come into the hands or possession of the administrator   , or into the hands
or possession of any other person or persons for   him   , do well and truly administer according
to law: that is to say, do pay the debts that the deceased owed at death, and further, do make, or
cause to be made, a just, full and true account of the said administration, when thereunto lawfully
required, and all the rest and residue of the property do deliver and pay unto such person or persons
respectively, as are entitled thereto; and if it hereafter appears that any last will or testament
was made by the deceased, and the executor or executors therein named do exhibit the same unto
the said Court, making request to have it allowed and approved accordingly, if the administrator   ,
being thereunto required, do render and deliver the said letters of administration to the said Court;
then this obligation to be void and of no effect, or else to remain in full force and virtue.

Dated   March   1970

SIGNED, SEALED AND DELIVERED
in the presence of

_____ LS
HOWARD ALBERT EAST
TORONTO INDEMNITY COMPANY LTD.
By:_____
President

_____
Secretary

Figure 25.16. Administration Bond – No Will

CHAPTER 26

Succession Duty and Estate Tax

The tax levied by the Provincial Government on persons entitled to property from the estate of a deceased person is known as *succession duty*.

The tax levied by the Federal Government on the estate of deceased persons is known as *estate tax*.

Before the executors or administrators of an estate may distribute assets of the estate, they first secure releases from the Provincial and Federal Governments certifying that all the taxes have been paid. Such releases are obtained after filing with the Provincial and Federal Governments an inventory of the estate, giving detailed particulars of the assets. Any tax payable is then levied, and upon payment of the succession duty and estate tax, releases are issued by the Provincial and Federal Governments respectively.

Not all estates are taxed. The amount of tax payable is usually determined by the value of the estate and the person(s) to whom it is left. Many estates are so small that no taxes are payable at all.

Property of Estate for Succession Duty and Estate Tax Purposes

For purposes of calculating succession duty and estate tax, the inventory of the property passing on the death of the deceased varies from that included in the inventory of estate for the purpose of applying for probate or administration.

In those applications, property which automatically passed to a survivor by reason of a joint tenancy, or life insurance payable to a named beneficiary, were excluded in computing the value of the estate. In a succession duty or estate tax application, property passing on the death of the deceased usually *includes* that property, unless it can be shown that the deceased did not really own the property or a portion of it. Accordingly, the inventory value of the assets of the estate prepared for a succession duty or estate tax return may be higher than that prepared for a probate or administration application.

Succession Duty

In Ontario succession duty may be imposed on gifts made under the terms of a will. You may recall that there is usually a clause in a will which provides that the executors are to pay all inheritance and estate taxes, so that persons receiving gifts do not pay the duty or tax personally.

The Ontario Succession Duty Department requires that within three months of the death of the deceased the executors or administrators of his estate file a document known as an *affidavit of value and relationship*. Two or more executors may severally swear this affidavit. It may be sworn before a solicitor in the office in which it was prepared.

For the purposes of this affidavit, each executor or administrator of the estate must provide detailed information regarding the assets of the estate. This information is similar to that required for the inventory filed on an application for probate or administration, with the exception we have already noted, but is described in greater detail.

There are three variations in the style of the affidavit, and which style is used depends on the size of the estate, where the deceased died, and whether application is made for probate or administration. Figure 26.1 illustrates the most frequently used style; it is the longest and most detailed. The other variations require similar information, which is presented in a condensed version of the longer form.

Preparation of Affidavit

The affidavit of value and relationship is prepared in duplicate, and executed jointly by the executors or administrators. The lawyer will usually draft the items to be included, and you will then prepare the affidavit.

The original signed affidavit is filed with

the provincial Succession Duty Branch of the Treasury Department; the carbon copy remains in the file. The solicitors filing the affidavit are shown, and the affidavit is personally signed by the individual solicitor acting for the estate.

When filed, the affidavit is accompanied by three schedules or exhibits.

Schedule "A"

Schedule "A" sets out the inventory of the assets of the estate giving specific detail as to the valuation of each category of assets.

The schedule consists of eight pages of information as to the various assets of the estate, and there are instructions on the printed form stating how the schedule should be completed. Much of the information required is furnished to the lawyer by the executors or administrators. However, the lawyer is required to ascertain some details such as accrued bank interest on bank accounts of the deceased, and the valuation of bonds, debentures, stocks and shares, which are set out as two separate categories on succession duty and estate tax forms.

The lawyer may request you to obtain valuations on bonds, debentures, or stocks as of the date of death of the deceased. This information can be obtained by telephone from a reputable stockbroker, and is usually checked by the Succession Duty Department when verifying contents of the affidavit filed with them.

Schedule "B"

Schedule "B" provides particulars of all gifts and dispositions made by the deceased during his lifetime, and shows the monetary value of any such gifts or dispositions at the date of death.

Gifts made within three years (for purposes of federal taxation) or five years (for purposes of provincial (Ontario) taxation) prior to the death of the deceased are included in computing the value of the estate, and if the recipient of such a gift is also a beneficiary under the will, the value of the gift is considered to be part of his bequest. It is customary, therefore, to have each beneficiary under the will complete a statu-tory declaration stating what, if any, special gifts he received from the deceased during the deceased's lifetime.

Schedule "C"

Schedule "C" outlines the name, address, and degree of relationship to the deceased of each person to whom or for whose benefit property passes on the death of the deceased.

If a beneficiary under the will is to receive the benefit only during his lifetime, he is known as a *life tenant,* and his age must be set out in the schedule.

Affidavit of Debts

An affidavit of debts (Figure 26.2), stating, for example, the amount of funeral expenses and debts incurred by the deceased and unpaid at the time of his death, is completed in duplicate, executed by the executors or administrators, and filed with the Succession Duty Branch. It usually does not accompany the affidavit of value and relationship, since information as to debts of the deceased may not be completely known at the time the affidavit of value and relationship is filed.

Creditors

In order to ascertain all the debts of the deceased, a notice to creditors is usually placed in one of the newspapers in the area in which the deceased normally resided or carried on business. This notice is published three times within a one-month period. This notice may be in a variety of styles, as reference to the legal column of your local newspaper will illustrate. One style which may be used appears in Figure 26.3.

Estate Tax

In Canada estate tax may be levied on the estate of a deceased. Within six months of the death of the deceased, the executors or administrators file an *estate tax return.* Two or more executors may jointly complete this return.

The return requires detailed information on the assets of the estate, similar to that provided in an affidavit of value and relationship.

There are three forms of estate tax returns. If the deceased died domiciled in Canada, form ET60 is used if the total value of his estate passing on his death is over $40,000, and form ET61 is used if the estate does not exceed that figure. Form ET62 is used if the deceased died domiciled outside of Canada, but had property situated in Canada.

Preparation of Return

The estate tax return (Figure 26.4) is prepared in triplicate, and two executed copies are filed with the District Taxation Office where the deceased filed his last income tax return, or the tax office in the district in which he resided at death. If the deceased lived outside of Canada, the return is filed with the Income Tax Office in Ottawa.

The return must be accompanied by a notarial and office copy of the will, and any marriage contract in existence at the date of death.

Summary of Property and Deductions

Page 2 of the estate tax return is a summary of the inventory of the property in the estate, similar to that appearing in the affidavit of value and relationship, but with several additional categories, such as interest in businesses or settlements under marriage contracts, which are included in the affidavit under the heading "other assets".

Following the net valuation of the estate, deductions are shown for debts of the deceased, and for *quick succession*. This term refers to tax which is payable upon property of the deceased which passed to him on the death of another within the previous five years, providing the property was taxed in the first estate. Such property is subject to a reduced rate of estate tax.

After calculating the net value of the estate, deductions are then made for survivors of the deceased, and the taxable value of the estate is determined.

Particulars of Property

Details of the inventory of the property passing on the death of the deceased are shown on page 3 of the form. If the space provided is not sufficient, supplementary statements may be obtained from the District Taxation Office. Alternatively, many lawyers submit duplicated copies of the supporting sheets attached to the inventory in the affidavit of value and relationship.

General Debts

Information regarding general debts is the same as that required for the affidavit of debts filed with the Succession Duty Department. If the space provided is insufficient, attach a typed statement which is prepared with headings identical to those in the printed form. Note, however, that under a federal return, no amount is allowed for solicitor's fees, but a reasonable amount is allowed for a grave marker.

Distribution of Property

Information regarding the distribution of property is the same as that provided to the Succession Duty Department. If the space provided is inadequate, attach a typed statement.

Calculation of Estate Tax

A portion of the estate tax return shows the calculations as to the amount of tax payable. These calculations will usually be worked out by the lawyer processing the estate. The calculations are the responsibility of the solicitors for the executors, but, if complicated, the Estate Tax Department will provide an estimate of the tax in the first instance. The amount of such tax depends on the taxable value of the estate, and increases in accordance with the size of the taxable value of the estate.

Releases

When the affidavit of value and relationship and the estate tax return have been filed, and the tax (if any) has been paid or satisfactory arrangements have been made to pay the tax in the future, succession duty and estate tax releases will be issued by the Provincial and Federal Governments. The executors or administrators require these releases in order to distribute or sell the assets in the estate.

Dye & Durham Limited, 76 Richmond Street East, Toronto
Law and Commercial Stationers
Form No. 246

FORM 1

AFFIDAVIT OF VALUE AND RELATIONSHIP

Section 13 (2)

THE SUCCESSION DUTY ACT, 1960

CANADA:
PROVINCE OF ONTARIO

IN THE MATTER OF THE ESTATE OF   HENRY JAMES EAST

late of the   City   of   Toronto

in the   County   of   York   Retired Dentist   , deceased.
                                                        (Occupation)

K̶X̶X̶X̶X̶X̶ WE, HOWARD ALBERT EAST, 19 King Street,

of the   City   of   Toronto

in the   County   of York, Professor

and   MARY ANN EAST, 135 William Street,

of the   City   of   Toronto,

in the   County   of   York, Widow,

and

the   of the   Company

(severally) make oath and say:

1. **THAT** Howard Albert East and Mary Ann East

are the applicants   for letters probate (or administration if applicable)

in the Estate of the above deceased who died on or about the   31st

day of   January   1970 , domiciled in Ontario.

2. That to the best of   our   knowledge, information and belief, the schedule hereto annexed and marked Schedule "A" contains an inventory of all property passing on the death of the above named deceased and such inventory shows the value of such property.

3. That to the best of   our   knowledge, information and belief, the schedule hereto annexed and marked Schedule "B" contains particulars of all gifts and dispositions made during the lifetime of the above named deceased and shows the value of such gifts and dispositions.

4. That to the best of   our   knowledge, information and belief, the schedule hereto annexed and marked Schedule "C" contains the name, place of residence and degree of relationship to the deceased of every person to whom or for whose benefit any property passes on the death of the above named deceased and such other information as is required by Schedule "C".

5. That the value at the date of the death of the deceased of all property passing on his death, wherever situate, was $ 98,829.00.

SEVERALLY SWORN BEFORE ME

at the   City   of Toronto

in the   County   of York

this   day

of   March   , 19 70

A Commissioner, etc., or Notary Public, etc.

This affidavit is filed by   HILL, JOHNSTON & GRANT, 17 Princess Street South, Toronto, Ontario.

Solicitor

17 Princess Street, Toronto

Address

NOTE:—If the deceased died domiciled outside Ontario give full particulars of the Ontario assets in the space applicable in Schedule "A" but totals only of assets situate outside Ontario.

Figure 26.1. Affidavit of Value and Relationship

Dye & Durham Limited — Toronto, Canada
Printers to the Legal Profession

Form No. 594

FORM 1—SCHEDULE A

Inventory in Detail of Property Wheresoever Situate

THE SUCCESSION DUTY ACT, 1960

In the Matter of the Estate of HENRY JAMES EAST

late of the   City   of Toronto   in the County

of York   Retired Dentist   deceased.
                                        (Occupation)

SUMMARY

The total of each class of assets must be carried to the proper place in this summary, and the summary totalled.

	Total	
	$	c.
Real Estate	30,000	00
Land Mortgages and Agreements for Sale	3,109	00
Chattel Mortgages and Lien Notes	Nil	
Book Debts and Promissory Notes	Nil	
Insurance and Annuities	13,000	00
Cash on Hand and Money on Deposit	457	00
Bonds and Debentures	25,187	00
Stocks and Shares	25,000	00
Other Assets	2,076	00
TOTAL	98,829	00

This is Schedule "A" referred to in the Affidavit of Value and Relationship of Howard Albert East

and Mary Ann East

Sworn before me on the   day of   March   1970

_____

A Commissioner, etc., or a Notary Public, etc.

*Figure 26.1.   Affidavit of Value and
Relationship, Schedule A – Sheet 1*

Dye & Durham Limited — Toronto, Canada
Printers to the Legal Profession
Form No. 595

REAL ESTATE

Date of Death: January 31, 1970

Give the registered description of each parcel in Ontario. If the registered description is long, the parcel may be identified by giving the lot and plan or concession number and the number of a registered instrument containing the description, and the place of registration and, in the case of property under the Land Titles System, the parcel number should also be given. In either case, the area or dimensions of the property must be shown. *The street and number must be given where possible.*

Foreign realty must be included on this sheet.

In the outside column, give the value as at time of death of the deceased's interest in the property less the amount of any lien, encumbrance, mortgage or balance owing under purchase agreement.

If the space reserved for any class of assets is not large enough, use additional pages.

Particulars	Assessed Value		Value of Equity	
	$	c.	$	c.

135 William Street, Toronto, Ontario
 	
The whole of Lot 30, according to a plan registered in the Registry Office for the Registry Division of Toronto as No. 4666, and more particularly described in a deed registered in the Registry Office for the Registry Division of Toronto as No. 56321
 	
  Frontage   60 ft.
  Depth   125 ft.
 	
No encumbrances.
 	
Assessment: Land $ 3,000.00
           Buildings   9,000.00
                  $12,000.00
	12,000	00	30,000	00

TOTAL	12,000	00	30,000	00

Figure 26.1. Affidavit of Value and
Relationship, Schedule A – Sheet 2

279

Dye & Durham Limited — Toronto, Canada
Printers to the Legal Profession
Form No. 596

LAND MORTGAGES AND AGREEMENTS FOR SALE

Mortgages and agreements for sale covering both Ontario parcels and foreign parcels, will be included. The instructions under the heading of Real Estate regarding descriptions will apply here.

Give, in each case, the name of mortgagor, or purchaser, as the case may be.

Give also the date of the instrument, the original amount, rate of interest and date from which interest has been accruing.

Extend to proper columns in each case the balance of principal and interest as at death and extend the total.

Particulars	Principal		Interest Accrued		Total	
	$	c.	$	c.	$	c.
Mortgagor: John Jacob Jones Mortgage on 19 Hill Heights Crescent, in the Borough of Etobicoke, more particularly described as the whole of Lot 16 according to a plan registered in the Registry Office for the Registry Division of the East and West Riding of the County of York as Number 4138. Mortgage dated March 29, 1966, and registered in the Registry Office for the Registry Division of the East and West Riding of the County of York as No. 85128 Principal: $9,000.00, at 6%, Interest accrued from September 29, 1969,	3,000	00	109	00	3,109	00
TOTAL	3,000	00	109	00	3,109	00

CHATTEL MORTGAGES AND LIEN NOTES

Extend to proper columns, in each case, the balance of principal and interest as at death and extend the total.

Name of Mortgagor	Address	Particulars, including date of instrument, original amount, rate of interest and date from which interest has been accruing.	Principal		Interest Accrued		Total	
			$	c.	$	c.	$	c.
	N I L							
		TOTAL						

Figure 26.1.   Affidavit of Value and Relationship, Schedule A – Sheet 3

Dye & Durham Limited — Toronto, Canada
Printers to the Legal Profession

Form No. 597

BOOK DEBTS AND PROMISSORY NOTES

Name of Deceased .... HENRY JAMES EAST .... Date of Death .... January 31, 1970 ....

Extend to the proper columns in each case, the balance of principal and interest as at death and extend the total.

Debtor Name and Address	Particulars Including date debt was incurred, or date of note, original amount, rate of interest, date from which interest has been accruing.	Principal or balance of principal	Interest accrued	Total	For use of Department only.
		$	$	$	
	N I L				
	TOTAL	$	$	$	

Figure 26.1. Affidavit of Value and
Relationship, Schedule A – Sheet 4

281

Dye & Durham Limited — Toronto, Canada
Printers to the Legal Profession
Form No. 598

INSURANCE AND ANNUITIES

It is essential that full particulars be given as indicated in the columns below.

No. of Policy or Contract	Issued by	Name of Beneficiaries	Relationship to Deceased	Other particulars including face value, bonuses, dividends and earned profits, loans against policy, accrued interest to date of death or number and amount of annuity payments	Amount	
					$	c.
468475	Windsor Life Insurance Company	Estate	N.A.	Face value of $10,000.00 with accumulated dividends of $752.64 to July 27, 1969. Accrued interest of $82.53 from July 27, 1969 to January 31, 1970	10,835.	17
M102013	The Prudential Insurance Company of America	Mary Ann East	Widow	Face value of $2,000.00 fully paid up, with earned profits to January 31, 1970 of $164.83	2,164.	83
				Total	13,000.	00

Figure 26.1. Affidavit of Value and Relationship, Schedule A – Sheet 5

Dye & Durham Limited — Toronto, Canada
Printers to the Legal Profession
Form No. 599

CASH ON HAND AND MONEY ON DEPOSIT

Give particulars of joint accounts.

Account Number	Name of Bank or Depository	Address or Branch	Principal		Interest		Total	
			$	c.	$	c.	$	c.
150	Bank of Montreal Account in name of Henry James East	Queen & University, Toronto	297	63	2	27	300	00
1900	Royal Bank of Canada Account in name of Henry James East	Stephen & Berry Rd., Etobicoke	108	51	0	49	109	00
	Cash on hand		48	00			48	00
		Total	454	14	2	76	457	00

Figure 26.1. Affidavit of Value and Relationship, Schedule A — Sheet 6

283

Dye & Durham Limited — Toronto, Canada
Printers to the Legal Profession
Form No. 600

BONDS AND DEBENTURES

Name of Deceased HENRY JAMES EAST   Date of Death January 31, 1970

Serial Numbers	Face Value	Description — Name and Head Office of Issuing Authority, Interest Rate, Maturity and Interest Dates, Special Privileges of the Issue, etc.	Value — Per Unit	Value — Interest Accrued to date of death	Value — Total	For Use of Department only — Consent	For Use of Department only — Increase or Decrease
	$		$	$	$		$
98851	25,000	$25,000 The Bell Telephone Company of Canada 5% 1st Mortgage Bond, Series O, due March 15, 1972. F/R Henry James East. Accrued interest from January 1, 1970--31 days	25,000	187.00	25,187.00		
		Total		$187.00	$25,187.00		$

*Figure 26.1. Affidavit of Value and
Relationship, Schedule A – Sheet 7*

Dye & Durham Limited — Toronto, Canada
Printers to the Legal Profession
Form No. 601

STOCK AND SHARES

Name of Deceased_____HENRY JAMES EAST_____   Date of Death_____January 31, 1970_____

Numbers Certificate	Number of Shares	Description Name and Head Office of Issuing Authority, *Class of Stock*, Par Value, Rate of Preferred Dividend, Privileges of Conversion, Redemption, etc.	Value		For Use of Department Only	
			Per Unit	Total	Consent	Increase or Decrease
			$	$		$
DC 2511	250	Great Lakes Power Corporation Limited, Com. N.P.V. and registered Henry James East, T.A. Montreal Trust Co., Toronto. Head Office: Ontario T.S.E.	32.00	8,000.00		
TC4385	340	Noranda Mines Limited Com. N.P.V., registered Henry James East T.A. Eastern & Chartered Trust Co., Toronto Head Office: Ontario	50.00	17,000.00		
		Total		$ 25,000.00		$

*Figure 26.1. Affidavit of Value and
Relationship, Schedule A – Sheet 8*

285

Dye & Durham Limited — Toronto, Canada
Printers to the Legal Profession
Form No. 602

OTHER ASSETS	VALUE	
	$	c.
Household goods and furniture..	1,200	00
Pictures, plate and jewelry...	800	00
Farm implements, produce and stock..	nil	
Automobiles and other vehicles (make, model, year and serial number)................	nil	
Interests in Trusts and other Estates (attach full particulars)........................	nil	
Interest in partnership or unincorporated business......................................	nil	
Any other property............Uncashed Old Age Security Cheque........................	76	00

JEWELRY

Masonic Ring set with diamond	$200.00
Set of onyx cuff links	$100.00
Set of jade cuff links	$200.00

PICTURE

| Oil Painting by Carson,
"Autumn Wind" | $300.00 |

Total................................	2,076	00

Figure 26.1.   Affidavit of Value and
Relationship, Schedule A – Sheet 9

Dye & Durham Limited — Toronto, Canada
Printers to the Legal Profession
Form No. 249

Form 1—Schedule B

DISPOSITIONS OR GIFTS INTER VIVOS

THE SUCCESSION DUTY ACT, 1960

In the Matter of the Estate of HENRY JAMES EAST,

late of the   City   of Toronto   in the County   of York   , deceased

NOTE.—Trace exact relationship of other than those in direct line or brothers or sisters, e.g., nephew, child of sister.

Date of Disposition or Gift	To Whom Made	Address	Relationship
	N I L		

Description of Property	Amount or Value	(Within Ontario) (Outside Ontario) Where made—	Other particulars. See Sec. 1, clauses f, m, o and p (Pars. IX and X); Sec. 2 S.S. 1, Clause d and S.S. 3. See also Sec. 5, clauses c and d.

This is Schedule "B" referred to in the Affidavit of Value and Relationship of Howard Albert East and Mary Ann East
Sworn before me on the   day of   March   19 70.

A Commissioner or Notary Public, etc.

Figure 26.1. Affidavit of Value and Relationship, Schedule B

Dye & Durham Limited — Toronto, Canada
Printers to the Legal Profession
Form No. 250

Form 1—Schedule C

DISTRIBUTION OF ESTATE

THE SUCCESSION DUTY ACT, 1960

In the Matter of the Estate of   HENRY JAMES EAST

late of the   City   of   Toronto   in the   County

of   York, Retired Dentist   , deceased

NOTE.—Trace exact relationship of beneficiaries other than those in direct line, or brothers or sisters, e.g., nephew, child of sister.

Name	Relationship	Address	Age of Life Tenant or Annuitant	Nature of Bequest or Property Passing	Value
Mary Ann East	Widow	135 William St., Toronto		Household goods	1,200.00
				Real Estate at 135 William St., Toronto	30,000.00
				Prudential Insurance Policy M102013	2,164.83
				Half of residue	
Howard Albert East	Son	19 King Street, Toronto		Set of jade cuff links	200.00
				Half of residue	
Grace Genevieve East	Niece-- daughter of brother	36 Kendale Road, Toronto		Oil Painting by Carson "Autumn Wind"	300.00
Peter Paul Palmer	Nephew-- son of sister	17 Highgate Road Toronto		Masonic Ring set with diamond	200.00
Henry Herbert Hall	Cousin-- son of sister of father	135 Glenedan Road, Toronto		Set of onyx cuff links	100.00

This is Schedule "C" referred to in the Affidavit of Value and Relationship of   Howard Albert East

and Mary Ann East

Sworn before me on the   day of   March   1970

A Commissioner or Notary Public, etc.

Figure 26.1. Affidavit of Value and Relationship, Schedule C

THE SUCCESSION DUTY ACT,
1960

IN THE MATTER OF THE ESTATE
OF
HENRY JAMES EAST

late of the City of Toronto
in the County of York
deceased

AFFIDAVIT OF VALUE
AND
RELATIONSHIP
(Form 1)

Dye & Durham Limited, 76 Richmond Street East, Toronto
Law and Commercial Stationers

HILL, JOHNSTON & GRANT
17 Princess Street South,
Toronto, Ontario.
Solicitors for Applicants

Figure 26.1. Affidavit of Value and
Relationship – Back

Dye & Durham Limited — Toronto, Canada
Printers to the Legal Profession
Form No. 295

THE SUCCESSION DUTY ACT, 1960

SECTION 3 (5)

_____

IN THE MATTER OF THE ESTATE OF HENRY JAMES EAST

late of 135 William Street, in the City of Toronto, in the

County of York, Retired Dentist,

, deceased.

I, WE, HOWARD ALBERT EAST, Professor, and MARY ANN EAST, Widow,

both
of the   City   of   Toronto   in the   County

of   York,   , make oath and say:

                  WE
That I have in the first part of the within Schedule, marked "A", set forth
full and true particulars of the debts, encumbrances and other allowances
authorized by and in accordance with subsection 5 of section 3 of The
Succession Duty Act, 1960.

                  WE
That I have in the second part of such Schedule set forth full and true
particulars of such debts, encumbrances and other allowances which are in
dispute or which have not yet been paid.

SEVERALLY

SWORN before me

at the   City   of   Toronto

in the   County   of   York

this   day of   April   1970

A Commissioner or Notary Public, etc.

Figure 26.2. Affidavit of Debts – Page 1

Dye & Durham Limited — Toronto, Canada
Printers to the Legal Profession
Form No. 251

THE SUCCESSION DUTY ACT (Ontario)

IN THE MATTER OF THE ESTATE OF HENRY JAMES EAST

deceased

late of the City of Toronto in the County of York

FIRST PART

Name of Creditor	Address	Nature of Claim	Amount Paid or Payable $	c.
Turner & Brown	2498 Bloor St. West, Toronto	Funeral services	824	00
Dr. Percy Blantyre	Medical Arts Building, Toronto	Medical services not covered by insurance	175	00
Toronto Western Hospital	1900 Bathurst Street, Toronto	Hospital expenses not covered by insurance	16	00
Surrogate Court of the County of York	Toronto	Fees on Probate	218	50
Trustees of the Toronto General Burying Grounds	Toronto	Preparation of grave	53	50
Department of National Revenue	Ottawa	1969 Income Tax	204	83
		Total	1,491	83

SECOND PART

Name of Creditor	Address	Nature of Claim	Amount $	c.	Reason for Non-Payment
Hill, Johnston & Grant	17 Princess Street South Toronto	Allowance for solicitors' fees	100	00	Account not yet rendered
		Total	100	00	

THIS IS SCHEDULE MARKED "A" referred to in the AFFIDAVIT OF DEBTS of Howard Albert East and Mary Ann East,

Sworn before me on the   day of April   1970

_____

A Commissioner, etc.

Figure 26.2. Affidavit of Debts – Page 2

NOTICE TO CREDITORS AND OTHERS

In the Estate of HENRY JAMES EAST, of the
City of Toronto, in the County of York,
Retired Dentist, deceased.

All persons having claims against the Estate of

Henry James East, late of the City of Toronto, in the County

of York, Retired Dentist, who died on or about the 31st day

of January, 1970, are hereby notified to send particulars of

same to the undersigned on or before the 30th day of April,

1970, after which date the Estate will be distributed with

regard only to the claims of which the undersigned shall

then have notice and the undersigned will not be liable to

any person of whose claim they shall not then have notice.

DATED at Toronto this 29th day of March, 1970.

HILL, JOHNSTON & GRANT,
17 Princess Street South,
Toronto, Ontario,
Solicitors for the Executors.

Figure 26.3. One Form of Notice to Creditors

CANADA

ET60
REV. 3-69

DEPARTMENT OF NATIONAL REVENUE, TAXATION

Estate Tax Return

- To be completed by the Executor or Administrator of the Estate, or a Successor to property passing on the death, of a person:
    - (a) who died, domiciled in Canada, on or after 23rd October, 1968, and
    - (b) where the total value of the property passing on the death exceeds $40,000.
- If the total value of the property passing on death is $40,000 or less use form ET61.
- Two completed copies of this return, together with one certified copy and one office copy of:
    - (a) the Last Will and Testament, if any, and
    - (b) the Marriage Contract, if any,

    are to be mailed or delivered within six months after the date of death of the deceased to the Taxation Office for the District in which the deceased resided at death. (The period for filing the return is extended by ninety days where the return is filed by a Successor.)

Particulars of the Deceased

Name						
HENRY JAMES EAST					Married	☒
Last Address						
135 William Street, Toronto, Ontario					Widow(er)	☐

Age	Date of Death	Province of Domicile	Separate as to, or in Community of, Property	Testate or Intestate	Last Income Tax Return filed for	Single
70	31 Jan. 1970	Ontario	Separate	Testate	1968	☐

Former active occupation, and, if retired, date of retirement	Address shown on last Income Tax Return
Dentist--Retired 1966	135 William Street, Toronto, Ontario

Name and address of person to whom communications should be sent
Messrs. Hill, Johnston & Grant 17 Princess Street South Toronto

Particulars of any Spouse(s) (Deceased or Living)

Name and last address (Attach list if space insufficient)	Date of Death (if deceased)
1. Mary Ann East, 135 William Street, Toronto, Ontario	–
2.	
3.	

Name(s) and address(es) of Trustee(s) of any property included in a trust created by any spouse (see Class Q Page 2)

1.

2.

3.

Instructions and Information

Estate Tax Guide—As this form does not contain the Rates of Estate Tax or other information essential for the completion of the return, reference should be made to the Estate Tax Guide. This Guide may be obtained from the District Taxation Office.

Penalty —The penalty for failure to file this return within the prescribed period is $10 per day.

Interest —Estate Tax not paid when due bears interest.

Remittance —Make payment by cheque or money order payable to the Receiver General of Canada.

Certification

I/We, __MARY ANN EAST and HOWARD ALBERT EAST__ in the capacity of __Executors__
(Print Name(s))   (Executor, Administrator, Successor)

Hereby Certify that the information given in this Return and in any documents attached hereto is true, correct and complete in every respect, and fully discloses all property of every kind wherever situated which passed, or is deemed by the Estate Tax Act to have passed, on the death of the deceased, and that the said property has been valued as required by the Act.

Signature	Signature	Signature
135 William Street, Toronto	19 King Street, Toronto	
Address	Address	Address
April 1970	April 1970	
Date	Date	Date

It is a serious offence to make a false Estate Tax Return

The material on this form is condensed from the Estate Tax Act and Regulations which contain the terms of the law on which the tax is determined
Form authorized and prescribed by the Minister of National Revenue

Figure 26.4. Estate Tax Return – Page 1

2
Summary of Property and Deductions

Summary of Property (Enter the total value of each class of property described on the "Particulars of Property" statement. If there is no property in a class enter "Nil")

Class	Value
A —Real Estate	$ 30,000.00
B —Mortgages, Hypothecs and Agreements for Sale Secured by Property	3,109.00
C —Stocks and Shares	25,000.00
D —Bonds and Debentures	25,187.00
E —Cash on Hand, Bank Accounts and other Deposits	457.00
F —Promissory Notes and Book Debts	Nil
G —Interest in Business	Nil
H —Interest of Deceased in other Estates or Trusts	Nil
I —Other Property not Included above	2,076.00
J —Life Insurance	13,000.00
K —Annuities, Pensions, Superannuation, Death Benefits, Gratuities and other Benefits.	Nil
* L —Settlements, Trusts and Transfers under Marriage Contracts	Nil
* M—Gifts Outright within Three Years of Death or at Any Time with Reservation of Benefit	Nil
* N —Transfers of Property for Less than Full Consideration; Property Transferred in Consideration of an Annuity; Property Transferable on Death Pursuant to Agreement	Nil
* O —Gifts by Way of Creation of Burden, Release of Rights or Extinguishment of Debts or Rights	Nil
P —Property over which the Deceased had a General Power of Appointment or Disposal	Nil
Q —A trust or other settlement created by a spouse of the deceased in which the deceased had the right to income or periodic payments therefrom and which trust or settlement is included in the property passing on the death of the deceased by Section 3(1a) of the Estate Tax Act where such trust or settlement was exempt from estate tax or gift tax by:	
(i) Section 7(1)(b)(i) A of the Estate Tax Act or Section 112(1)(e) of the Income Tax Act	Nil
(ii) Section 7(1)(b)(i) B of the Estate Tax Act	Nil
R —Any other Beneficial Interests Passing on the Death	Nil

* Section 32A of the Estate Tax Act provides that value declared includes any gift tax paid or payable thereon in respect of gifts made after 22nd October, 1968.

Total Value $ 98,829.00

Deductions

Quick Succession (See Guide and attach details)	$ —	
General Debts (See Guide and attach completed form ET60A)	1,956.83	$ 1,956.83
		Aggregate Net Value $ 96,872.17
Exempt Property (See Guide and attach details)		Nil
		Net Value $ 96,872.17

Exemptions for Spouse and Children—See Guide

[X] 1. Spouse

Name **Mary Ann East**   Date of Birth **Oct. 28 1910**

Address **135 William Street, Toronto**

Claim the value of any property passing on the death of the deceased in respect of which the surviving spouse succeeded to an indefeasible interest therein:

(i) outright . . . . $ 64,718.50

(ii) by trust or settlement (Section 7(1)(b)(i) A of Estate Tax Act or Section 112(1)(e) of Income Tax Act) . . . ▶ Nil

(iii) by trust or settlement (Section 7(1)(b)(i) B of Estate Tax Act) . . . ▶ Nil

[X] 2. Children age 26 and over (other than a child claimed in 4 below)

Claim the lesser of (a) the value of any property vesting indefeasibly in the child, OR (b) $10,000.

Name and Address (Attach list if space insufficient) | Date of Birth

Howard Albert East   **April 3 1930** ▶ 10,000.00

19 King Street, Toronto

[ ] 3. Children under age 26 (other than a child claimed in 4 below)

Claim the lesser of (a) the value of any property vesting indefeasibly in the child, OR (b) $10,000 plus the amount, if any, by which the product of $1,000 multiplied by the number of full years from the day of death to the day of the child's 26th birthday exceeds one-third of the amount, if any, by which the child's income, for the past three years, exceeds $15,000. (See example in Estate Tax Guide and attach statement in equivalent detail in respect of each child claimed.)

Name and Address (Attach list if space insufficient) | Date of Birth ▶ Nil

[ ] 4. Children of any age dependent because of infirmity

Claim the lesser of (a) the value of any property vesting indefeasibly in the child, OR (b) $10,000 plus the product of $1,000 multiplied by the number of full years from the day of death to the day of the child's 71st birthday. (See example in Estate Tax Guide and attach statement in equivalent detail in respect of each child claimed.)

Name and Address (Attach list if space insufficient) | Date of Birth ▶ Nil

$ 74,718.50

Aggregate Taxable Value $ 22,153.67

Figure 26.4. Estate Tax Return – Page 2

Particulars of Property

3

- Read carefully the Estate Tax Guide for classification, description, situs and valuation of property before completing. Total the value of each class and enter in the Summary of Property on page 2.
- If space below is insufficient attach a statement in like form, preferably form ET60 Supplementary Statement which is obtainable at the District Taxation Office.

Class	Description	Situs (Province, foreign country)	Value
			$
A	The whole of Lot 30, south side of William Street, Plan 4666 registered in the Registry Office of the Registry Division of Toronto, and more particularly described in a deed registered in the Registry Office for the Registry Division of Toronto as No. 56321. Assessed Value: Land--$3,000; Buildings--$9,000. Market Value--$30,000. No encumbrances	Ontario	30,000.00
B	19 Hill Heights Crescent, Etobicoke. Described in Instrument No. 85128, John Jacob Jones to Henry James East; $9,000, interest 6%; matures 29th March, 1971. Balance owing for Principal $3,000.00 Interest from Sept.29, 1969 109.00	Ontario	3,109.00
C	Great Lakes Power Corporation Limited, Certificate No. DC 2511 for 250 shares at $32.00, registered Henry James East H.O. Toronto T.A. Toronto	Ontario	8,000.00
	Noranda Mines Limited, Certificate TC4385, for 340 shares at $50.00, registered Henry James East H.O. Toronto T.A. Toronto	Ontario	17,000.00
D	The Bell Telephone Company of Canada 5% 1st Mortgage Bond, Series O, due March 15, 1972, fully registered Henry James East. Interest payable June 30th and December 31st. Principal--$25,000.00; Accrued interest from January 1st, 1970--31 days--$187.00	Ontario	25,187.00
E	Bank of Montreal, Account No. 150, Queen and University Branch, Toronto Principal $297.63 Interest to Jan. 31, 1970 2.27	Ontario	300.00
	Royal Bank of Canada, Account No. 1900, Stephen & Berry Road, Etobicoke Principal $108.51 Interest to Jan. 31,1970 0.49	Ontario	109.00
	Cash on hand	Ontario	48.00
I	Household Goods and Furniture	Ontario	1,200.00
	Personal effects and jewellery	Ontario	800.00
	Uncashed Old Age Security Cheque for January, 1970	Ontario	76.00
J	Windsor Life Insurance Company Policy No. 468475--Beneficiary: Estate Face Value $10,000.00 Additions 835.17	Ontario	10,835.17
	The Prudential Insurance Company of America Policy No. M102013. Beneficiary: Mary Ann East Face Value $ 2,000.00 Additions 164.83	Ontario	2,164.83

Figure 26.4. Estate Tax Return – Page 3

295

4

Distribution of Property

Name and Address of Successor			Age†	Amount of Benefit
				$
Mary Ann East	135 William St. Toronto	Household & personal goods Real Estate Insurance Half of Residue		1,200.00 30,000.00 2,164.83
Howard Albert East	19 King Street Toronto	Jewellery Half of Residue		200.00
Grace Genevieve East	36 Kendale Rd. Toronto	Painting		300.00
Peter Paul Palmer	17 Highgate Rd. Toronto	Jewellery		200.00
Henry Herbert Hall	135 Glenedan Rd. Toronto	Jewellery		100.00
Attach statement if space is insufficient				

†Age of successor need only be given where life interest, annuity or similar benefit is involved.

Calculation of Estate Tax
The Department on request will provide an estimate of the calucation, or the lawyer will work it out.

• If "Aggregate Net Value" is $50,000 or less, or if "Aggregate Taxable Value" is $20,000 or less, this calculation area need not be completed.

Estate Sum Calculation

A. Aggregate Taxable Value (as determined on Page 2) . . . . ▶ $_____

B. Add: Amount by which deceased's cumulative gift sum for his year of death exceeds the lesser of;
    (1) Value of gifts included in computing the cumulative gift sum for year of death and included in Aggregate Net Value, OR
    (2) the value included in computing the Aggregate Net Value and included in cumulative gift sum. ▶ $_____

C. Add: Gift Tax on amount included in item B that would be payable in year of death . . . . . . ▶ $_____

D. Estate Sum . . . . ▶ $_____

E. Tax on Estate Sum (See Guide for Rates of Tax) . . . . $_____

Gift Sum Calculation (if applicable)

Basic Amount . . . . $ 20,000.00
Amount included in item B above . . . . $_____
Amount included in item C above . . . . $_____
Gift Sum . . . . $_____

F. Tax on Gift Sum (See Guide for Rates of Tax) . . . . $_____

Estate Tax (before abatement and credits)—Item E minus Item F . . . . $_____

Less: **Provincial Tax Abatement** . . . . $_____
    (1) 50% of Estate Tax applicable to:
        (a) Property with a situs in Ontario or Quebec, and
        (b) Property (other than real property) with a situs outside Canada and passing to a successor other than as a trustee domiciled in or resident in the province of domicile of the deceased where the deceased died domiciled in Ontario or Quebec.
    (2) 75% of Estate Tax applicable to:
        (a) Property with a situs in British Columbia, and
        (b) Property (other than real property) with a situs outside Canada and passing to a successor other than as a trustee domiciled in or resident in British Columbia where the deceased died domiciled in British Columbia.

Gift Tax Credit . . . . $_____
The lesser of:
    (a) Estate Tax applicable to property included in "Total Value" on page 2 on which Gift Tax was payable or paid, OR
    (b) the amount of Gift Tax payable or paid on such property.

Foreign Tax Credit . . . . $_____
The lesser of:
    (a) Estate, legacy, succession or inheritance duties paid to the Government of a foreign country on property included in "Total Value" on page 2, OR
    (b) Estate Tax applicable to such property.
        (No credit where item Q property on page 2 is involved unless taxed by a foreign country by virtue of death of deceased.)

Notch Credit . . . . $_____
The amount by which the tax otherwise payable exceeds one-half the difference between the "Aggregate Net Value" and $50,000.

Total Tax Abatement and Credits $_____ $_____

Estate Tax Payable* $_____

*Where Estate Tax is less than $25.00 no amount is payable.

Interest $_____
Estate Tax and Interest Payable $_____
Payment Enclosed $_____

Figure 26.4. Estate Tax Return—Page 4

GENERAL DEBTS

● See Estate Tax Guide.
● For use in conjuction with Estate Tax Return—form ET 60

Name and Address of Creditor	Nature of Debt	Amount	If not paid, state reason
		$	
Turner & Brown
2498 Bloor Street West, Toronto	Funeral Services	824.00	
Dr. Percy Blantyre
Medical Arts Building, Toronto	Medical expenses not covered by insurance	175.00	
Toronto Western Hospital
1900 Bathurst Street, Toronto	Hospital expenses not covered by insurance	16.00	
Surrogate Court of the County of York, Toronto	Fees on probate	218.50	
Trustees of the Toronto General Burying Grounds, Toronto	Preparation of Grave	53.50	
Department of National Revenue, Ottawa	1969 Income Tax	204.83	
Quality Memorials, Malton, Ontario	Tombstone	465.00	Invoice not yet received and stone not yet installed
	Total	$1,956.83	◄ Enter on page 2 of ET60

FRANÇAIS AU VERSO

Figure 26.4. Estate Tax Return – Page 5

CHAPTER 27

Incorporating a Company

What is a Company?

The terms "company" or "corporation" are commonly used in the area of corporation law, but what is really meant by those terms is a particular type of company, the limited liability company. A company is created by law. It is basically an association of individuals, each of whom subscribes money or the equivalent of money to a common fund or "stock" to be used for some common purpose, and each of whom shares in proportion to his contribution in any profits which may be earned by the company. By incorporating a company, the individuals joining together to form the company restrict their liability to the amount of the full subscription price of their shares in the company. Once they have paid that amount into the treasury of the company, no additional claim for money may be made upon them. They can lose all they invested in the company, but no more.

It is mainly in this limitation of liability that a company differs from a partnership; each partner is responsible to the full extent of his personal assets for all and any partnership debts.

The contributions individuals make to the common fund or stock of a company is known as the *capital* of the company. Each individual's proportion of such capital is his *share* in the company. The record of ownership of such a share is contained in a paper known as a *share certificate,* and the individual is then known as a *shareholder.* The return he receives on profits earned by the company and paid to him is called a *dividend.*

The shareholders in fact "own" the company, and have a voice in its management. The shareholders elect directors from among themselves who supervise the operation of the company. Regular meetings of shareholders are held at which the directors report on the activities of the company, and submit reports and recommendations for approval by the shareholders.

Special Terms Relating to Companies

Before considering how a company is incorporated, you should understand certain terms which are used in corporate secretarial work.

Public and Private Companies

There are two types of limited liability companies: public and private. The main differences between the two are the number of shareholders, and whether or not shares in the company can be offered for sale to the public.

A public company:
1. offers shares for sale to the public
2. has no limitation on the number of shareholders
3. has no restrictions on transfer of shares
4. files its annual financial statement with the appropriate government.

A private company:
1. cannot offer its shares for sale to the public
2. has no more than fifty shareholders
3. has restrictions on the right to transfer shares
4. does not file a financial statement.

Capital of a Company

The capital of a company is the amount of money which the owners have invested or intend to invest in the company. "Authorized capital" is the maximum amount which the company may receive by selling all its shares at their face value; "subscribed capital" is the amount of authorized capital that has been subscribed for by the sale of shares, and "paid-up capital" is the actual amount of money received by the company on the sale of shares.

Shares of a Company

A company is owned by its shareholders, and the amount paid for the shares by the shareholders constitutes the paid-up capital of the company. The face value of a share is known as its *par value* (P.V.), and the P.V. of the shares is usually set out in the charter of the company at the time of its creation. The actual market value of a share is usually different from its par value. Companies may, if the charter so permits, issue shares with no par value (N.P.V.) or no face value.

Types of Shares

Shares in a company are either *common* or *preferred*. Preferred shares may have attached to them a variety of special rights, limitations, restrictions, or conditions.

1. *Common Shares*

   Common shares are also known as "ordinary" shares, and have no conditions attached to them. Holders of common shares have full voting rights, and subject to the rights of other shareholders, control the company through their elected representatives, the directors of the company. Holders of common shares, unlike holders of other shares, are not entitled to a fixed dividend, and any dividends they receive are declared by the directors of the company in accordance with the company's financial position.

2. *Preferred Shares*

   Preferred shares have special rights and conditions attached to them, and these rights and conditions protect the holders of such shares, and place them in a "preferred" position over holders of common shares. These rights and conditions usually call for a fixed dividend to be paid at a predetermined time and rate, and protect the capital contributed by the preferred shareholders in case the company runs into financial difficulties. Preferred shareholders usually do not have voting rights and therefore do not control the management of the company.

   There are many types of preferred shares, some of which are as follows:

   Participating: After payment of the regular dividends on the common and preferred shares, a participating preferred shareholder is entitled to share in any extra dividends declared by the Board of Directors.

   Non-participating: Only a fixed dividend at a fixed rate and time is paid to the holders of non-participating preferred shares.

   Cumulative: Unpaid dividends accumulate from year to year, and all such unpaid dividends are paid to the holders of cumulative preferred shares before any dividend is paid to the holders of common shares.

   Non-cumulative: If dividends are not paid for a given period, the right to such dividends is not absolute or cumulative, and is therefore lost.

   Redeemable: The company has the privilege of redeeming the redeemable preferred shares at any time upon payment of a premium plus the value of the share, after giving due notice to the holder of the share of its intention to redeem the share.

   Convertible: At the option of the holder, this type of preferred share may be exchanged for common shares of the company.

   Preferred shares may have a combination of the rights or conditions outlined above attached to them (e.g., a participating cumulative redeemable preferred share).

Prospectus

If the capital of the proposed company is to be derived from the sale of shares to other than the individuals involved in forming and operating the company, it is necessary to file with the Minister of Financial and Commercial Affairs in Ontario or his federal counterpart, a *prospectus*, which outlines all the pertinent information a prospective shareholder should have before investing in the company. The preparation of the prospectus is usually the responsibility of the brokerage company underwriting the sale of the shares to the public.

How Companies are Created

Under the provisions of the British North America Act, companies may be incorporated under federal jurisdiction to conduct business throughout Canada, or under provincial jurisdiction to conduct business mainly in the province where the company is incorporated. A provincial company may operate in another province by obtaining a licence from that province, and the company is then known as an "extra-provincial" or "foreign" company.

Some types of companies, such as insurance and trust companies, as well as banks, must follow special procedures when applying for incorporation. Other companies are incorporated in one of the ways outlined below.

1. Royal Charter

This method of the Crown granting a charter is extremely rare today. However, The Hudson's Bay Company, a Canadian company incorporated by Royal Charter in 1670, is still in existence.

2. Special Act of Parliament or Provincial Legislature

This method is not common. However, a number of companies such as Air Canada and the Canadian National Railways were incorporated by special acts of the Federal Parliament. Several crown corporations were set up in Ontario by acts of the provincial legislature.

3. Memorandum of Association

This method is followed in the provinces of Alberta, British Columbia, Newfoundland, Nova Scotia, and Saskatchewan.

⁋ A memorandum setting out the name and purpose of the proposed company, the amount of its capital, and any other necessary information is registered with the Registrar of Joint Stock Companies of the appropriate province, and if approved, in due course a Certificate of Registration is received.

4. Letters Patent

This method is presently followed in the provinces of Manitoba, New Brunswick, Ontario, Prince Edward Island, Quebec, and by the Federal Government. It is the one we shall consider in detail.

Letters Patent

Application for Letters Patent

In Ontario most companies are incorporated by the issuance of *letters patent,* which grant a company its charter of incorporation. This charter sets out, among other things, the purpose for which the company was incorporated, its powers, and its share structure. In the spring of 1969, it was announced that The Corporations Act of Ontario would be revised. It is anticipated that by late 1970 or early 1971 The Business Corporations Act will be the law in Ontario, and under this Act, a registration system requiring the filing of articles of incorporation substituted for the existing letters patent system. However, until that new act comes into force, companies will continue to be incorporated by letters patent. The application for incorporation is by petition to His Honour The Lieutenant Governor through the provincial Minister of Financial and Commercial Affairs (Figure 27.1). This petition is filed by no less than three shareholders of the proposed company, each of whom must be over twenty-one years of age.

It is not unusual for members of the lawyer's office staff to be the shareholders who make the application for incorporation. They become the directors of the new company, but once it has been incorporated, they usually resign in favour of the actual directors. This is not done in an attempt to evade any legal responsibilities; it is to facilitate the execution of the many documents which are required to incorporate and organize a new company.

The application for the issue of letters patent contains the following information:
1. the full name, address, and occupation of each applicant shareholder, of whom there must be a minimum of three
2. the names of the first directors of the company
3. the proposed corporate name of the company, which must end with "Limited" or "Ltd."
4. the objects of the company. A company can only do what it is empowered by law to do, and upon applying for incorporation, it must state the purpose or "objects" of the company.

5. the location of the head office of the company, which must be located in the province under whose jurisdiction the application for incorporation is made
6. the type, number, and par value of shares of the company, and any restrictions, limitations, or other conditions attaching to such shares.

Execution of Application

The application for letters patent is signed by each of the applicants in person in the presence of a witness, who may not be one of such applicants.

If an applicant finds it impossible to sign in person, he may execute the application through his attorney, but the original or notarial copy of the power of attorney must be produced when the application is filed.

Affidavits Required

The application for letters patent must be accompanied by an affidavit of execution, and an affidavit of bona fides completed by one of the applicants, or his attorney or agent, swearing to the truth of the facts set forth in the application.

Incorporation Fee

A fee is payable upon an application for incorporation, and the amount is determined by the amount of authorized capital of the proposed company.

Issuance of Letters Patent

If the application submitted to the provincial Minister of Financial and Commercial Affairs is in order, the incorporation fee is paid, and the name of the company as proposed is acceptable, the provincial Minister of Financial and Commercial Affairs will issue letters patent known as the "charter" of the company. The company legally comes into existence as of the date of the issuance of the letters patent.

While Awaiting Receipt of Letters Patent

When the application for letters patent has been filed, the secretary to the lawyer acting for the company should discuss with him the eventual requirements of a company seal, share certificates, and a minute book, all of which may be secured through a legal stationery firm.

However, these requirements should never be ordered until an indication has been given as to the date the charter will bear, or the charter itself has been received. Until the charter is actually received, there is a possibility that the application for incorporation may be refused.

What Happens Upon Receipt of Letters Patent

When the letters patent have been issued and received, the directors named call a meeting to pass the by-laws of the company, and elect the officers of the company. The letters patent are reviewed, and are usually copied into the minute book of the company.

Usually, immediately following the first meeting of directors, a meeting of shareholders is held to approve the actions of the directors.

In Chapter 28 we shall consider how the minutes of such meetings are prepared, the typing of by-laws, and other matters related to legal secretarial corporation work.

Form 1

The Corporations Act

APPLICATION FOR INCORPORATION
OF A COMPANY

To His Honour The Lieutenant Governor:

Application of:

RONALD CRAIG ANDERSON				of the	City	of
(names in full)						
Toronto	in the	County	of	York,	Physician	
(county or district)					*(calling)*	
HOWARD ALBERT EAST				of the	City	of
(names in full)						
Toronto	in the	County	of	York	Professor	
(county or district)					*(calling)*	
PERCIVAL ANDREW PETERSON				of the	City	of
(names in full)						
Toronto	in the	County	of	York	Merchant	
(county or district)					*(calling)*	
				of the		of
(names in full)						
	in the		of			
(county or district)					*(calling)*	
				of the		of
(names in full)						
	in the		of			
(county or district)					*(calling)*	

We, the applicants, hereby apply to Your Honour to issue, by letters patent, a charter under *The Corporations Act* constituting us and any others who become shareholders of the company thereby created a company and in support thereof state the following:

1. **Each** of the applicants is twenty-one or more years of age.

•2. **The name** of the company to be incorporated is PETERSON OFFICE SUPPLIES
.... Limited.

3. **The objects** for which the company is to be incorporated are

(a) To carry on the business of an office supply company.

(b) To furnish and decorate commercial and residential accommodations.

(c) To purchase or otherwise acquire and to hold, for investment

only, any shares, stocks, bonds, debentures, and other securities

issued or guaranteed by any government, public body or authority,

whether municipal, provincial, state or federal, and whether

Canada or in any other country, and any right, title or interest

therein.

67-5312

*Figure 27.1. Application for
Incorporation of a Company – Page 1*

4. **The head office** of the company is to be situate........... in the City .... of

.... *(status of municipality)*

Toronto ....in the ....County ....of ....York ....
.... *(name of municipality)* .... *(county or district)*

in the Province of Ontario.

5. **The authorized capital** of the company is to be............ THIRTY-FIVE THOUSAND--------

------------------------($35,000.00)-----------------------------------
.... *(if all shares are with par value, state amount of authorized capital in dollars or other currency)*

divided into   three thousand (3,000) preference shares with a par value
of Ten ($10.00) Dollars each, and five thousand (5,000) common
** shares with a par value of One ($1.00) each.

The preference shares and the common shares shall have
attached thereto the following:

1.   The holders of the preference shares shall in each year
in the discretion of the directors, but always in preference and
priority to any payment of dividends on the common shares for
such year, be entitled, out of any or all profits or surplus
available for dividends, to non-cumulative dividends at the rate
of six per cent (6%) per annum on the amount paid up thereon;
if in any year, after providing for the full dividend on the
preference shares, there shall remain any profits or surplus
available for dividends, such profits or surplus or any part
thereof may, in the discretion of the directors, be applied
to dividends on the common shares; the holders of the
preference shares shall not be entitled to any dividend other
than or in excess of the non-cumulative dividends at the rate
of six per cent (6%) per annum hereinbefore provided for.

2.   The preference shares shall rank, both as regards dividends
and return of capital, in priority to all other shares of the
company but shall not confer any further right to participate in
profits or assets.

(And continuing with further special rights, restrictions,
conditions or limitations attaching to the shares.
If there is not sufficient room on this page, a blank
sheet may be used to continue this item 5.)

Figure 27.1. Application for
Incorporation of a Company – Page 2

6. **The names** of the applicants who are to be the first directors of the company are

Residence
address
giving
street
and
number

Ronald Craig Anderson, 74 Prince William Street, Toronto

Howard Albert East, 19 King Street, Toronto

Percival Andrew Peterson, 936 Hillsdale Blvd., Toronto

•••7. **The class and number of shares** to be taken by each applicant and the amount to be paid therefor are as follows:

Applicants	Class and number of shares to be taken	Amount to be paid
Ronald C. Anderson	2 Common	$2.00
Howard Albert East	2 Common	$2.00
Percival A. Peterson	2 Common	$2.00

Dated this .... day of .... April ...., 19 70 ....

Signature of witness	Signatures of applicants

*Section 8 of the Act is as follows:

8. On an application for letters patent, supplementary letters patent or an order, the Lieutenant Governor may give the corporation a name different from its proposed or existing name, may vary the objects or other provisions of the application and may impose such conditions as he deems proper.

**Paragraphs 5, 6, 7 and 10 of subsection 1 of section 18 of the Act are as follows:

5. The authorized capital, the classes of shares, if any, into which it is to be divided, the number of shares of each class, and the par value of each share, or, where the shares are to be without par value, the consideration, if any, exceeding which each share or the aggregate consideration, if any, exceeding which all the shares of each class may not be issued.

6. Where there are to be preference shares, the preferences, rights, conditions, restrictions, limitations or prohibitions attaching to them or each class of them.

7. Where the company is to be a private company, a statement to that effect and the restrictions to be placed on the transfer of its shares.

10. Any other matters that the applicants desire to have included in the letters patent.

If the company is to be subject to Part IV, V or VI of the Act, set out a statement to that effect.

***Section 19 of the Act is as follows:

19. Upon incorporation of a company, each applicant becomes a shareholder holding the class and number of shares stated in the application to be taken by him and is liable to the company for the amount to be paid therefor.

Figure 27.1. Application for Incorporation of a Company – Page 3

AFFIDAVIT OF WITNESS

Probince of Ontario

COUNTY of YORK

TO WIT:

In the matter of *The Corporations Act* and of the application

of ...Ronald Craig Anderson, Howard Albert

East, and Percival Andrew Peterson,

and others for incorporation as ....

..............PETERSON OFFICE SUPPLIES...Limited

I, ...DOREEN JOYCE SPRING..
(names in full)

of the ....Borough........... of ....Etobicoke....... in the ......County....................... of

.......York.................................in the Province of Ontario,......Secretary.........,
(calling)

make oath and say that:

1. I was personally present and did see the within application duly signed and executed by

.........Ronald Craig Anderson, Howard Albert East, and

.........Percival Andrew Peterson, all of ------------------------------

....

....

....

the applicants thereto.

2. I know the applicants.

3. I am a subscribing witness to the application.

Sworn before me at the ....City........

of ....Toronto....... in the ......County......

of ....York..........this ....

day of ....April............, A.D. 19..70...

....
(signature of witness)

A Commissioner, etc.

Figure 27.1. Application for Incorporation of a Company – Page 4   305

AFFIDAVIT OF BONA FIDES

Province of Ontario

COUNTY of YORK

TO WIT:

In the matter of *The Corporations Act* and of the application

of ....Ronald Craig Anderson........

and others for incorporation as ....

........PETERSON OFFICE SUPPLIES........ Limited

I, ...RONALD CRAIG ANDERSON........

(names in full)

of the ....City........ of ....Toronto........ in the ....County........ of

........York........in the Province of Ontario,....Physician........,

(calling)

make oath and say that:

1.   I am one of the applicants herein.

2.   I have a knowledge of the matter and the statements in the annexed application contained are, to the best of my knowledge and belief, true in substance and in fact.

3.   Each of the applicants signing the application is of twenty-one or more years of age and his name and description have been accurately set out in the application.

4.   I have satisfied myself that no public or private interest will be prejudicially affected by the incorporation of the company aforesaid.

5.   To the best of my knowledge and belief, the proposed name of the company is not objectionable on any public grounds and is not the same as or similar to the name of any known corporation, association, partnership, individual or business so as to be likely to deceive.

6.   The application is made in good faith and is not made for any improper purpose.

Sworn before me at the ....City........

of ....Toronto........ in the ....County........

of ....York........ this ....

day of ....April........, A.D. 19.70.

....

(signature of applicant)

A Commissioner, etc.

Figure 27.1.   Application for Incorporation of a Company – Page 5

CHAPTER 28

Company Practice

Once a company comes into existence, the legislation of the provincial or federal act under which it was incorporated prescribes that certain books be maintained to record specified details of the company's activities. One of such books is the "minute book", in which are recorded the minutes of meetings of directors and shareholders. Other books record the names and addresses of past and present directors and shareholders, and the number and kinds of shares held by the shareholders.

Large companies usually keep these books of record in their head office. For smaller companies it is not unusual for these books of record to be kept in the office of their lawyers. Most of the company's records are contained in the minute book, which is divided into sections relating to the different subject matters to be recorded.

If the books of record are kept in the lawyer's office, a legal secretary will of necessity have certain responsibilities in keeping the books up-to-date and performing other duties.

Minute-book Paper

Material which is typed for inclusion in the minute book is prepared on special paper slightly wider and longer than normal 11-inch paper, and pre-punched for easy insertion in the proper section of the minute book.

Margins on Minute-book Paper

When typing material on minute-book paper, allow a margin of 1½ inches on the left, and one inch on the right. It is essential to have the wider margin on the left since this is the edge which is inserted into the minute book, and if the typed material is too close to the edge, it will not always be possible to read it.

Letters Patent

Upon receipt of the letters patent (or charter), the first meetings of the directors and shareholders are held. One of the first resolutions passed by the directors is to order that the letters patent be copied into the minute book. This is typed with great care on minute-book paper, and then inserted in the appropriate section of the minute book.

Errors in wording or spelling which may appear in the charter are not corrected; they are copied exactly as they appear.

Figure 28.1 illustrates an extract from a typed copy of letters patent.

By-laws

By-laws are the permanent rules for the operation and management of the company. They set out, among other things, the company's financial year; the procedures to be followed in calling and holding meetings of directors and shareholders; the number, qualifications, election and term of office of directors; the officers of the company, their duties, and authority to sign on behalf of the company.

At the first meeting of the directors of the company, the general by-laws are approved. The first meeting of shareholders usually follows immediately after the first meeting of the directors, and the by-laws passed by the directors are ratified and approved by the shareholders.

The general by-laws of any new company are available in printed form, and specific by-laws peculiar to the particular company will usually be drafted by the lawyer acting for the company and added to the printed form. Some lawyers will not accept the printed forms even for the general by-laws, and will require that all the by-laws be typed in full.

Copies of all the by-laws must be retained in the appropriate record book.

(COAT OF ARMS)

PROVINCE OF ONTARIO

By the HONOURABLE (name)

Minister of Financial and Commercial Affairs

TO ALL TO WHOM THESE PRESENTS SHALL COME, GREETING

(S E A L)

WHEREAS The Corporations Act provides that with the exceptions therein mentioned the Lieutenant Governor may in his discretion, by Letters Patent, issue a Charter to any number of persons, not fewer than three, of twenty-one or more years of age, who apply therefor, constituting them and any others who become shareholders or members of the corporation thereby created a corporation for any of the objects to which the authority of the Legislature extends;

AND WHEREAS by the said Act it is further provided that the

Figure 28.1. Extract from a Typed Copy of Letters Patent

Typing By-laws

Heading

By-laws are headed with the name of the company and the by-law number (Figure 28.2). As each by-law is drafted, passed, and enacted, it is usually identified by number and referred to as By-law Number 1, By-Law Number 2, and so on. By-laws may be general and contain a number of clauses, or they may be specific and limited to achieving one specific purpose.

Body

A by-law is usually divided into a number of sections, each of which has a general heading. Each section may be further divided into a number of related sections, each of which is numbered. If there are several numbered sections within one section, each sub-section is identified by a sub-heading. (See Figure 28.3.)

Ending

When all the various sections in the particular by-law number have been typed, and the by-laws have been passed and enacted at a meeting of the shareholders, the by-laws are then dated and signed by the chairman and secretary of the meeting. (See Figure 28.4.) No back is required for by-laws.

Typing Guide for By-Laws

1. Type the heading in capital letters, centred, and underscore the by-law number.
2. Double space the body of the by-laws.
3. Capitalize the first word or group of words of an unnumbered paragraph.
4. Type section headings in capital letters, centred, and underscored.
5. Number each item in a section.
6. Type each item heading in regular type, underscored, on the same line as the item number, and commencing at the normal paragraph indentation.
7. Leave spaces as follows:
a. two spaces between a section heading and an item in that section
b. three spaces between items of a section
c. three spaces between the end of an item and the heading of a new section.

Meetings and Minutes

A fully organized and active company usually holds three types of meetings during the business year: the annual meeting of shareholders, special general meetings of shareholders, and directors' meetings.

Each meeting held is governed procedurally by the by-laws of the company which set out, among other things, the requirements as to how notices of meetings are to be given, how the chairman is to be elected, and what number of shareholders or directors are needed to constitute a *quorum*.

Notice of Meetings

The by-laws outline the number of days' notice a shareholder must receive of the time and place of a meeting, and the circumstances under which all shareholders may waive such notice.

The notice of meeting (Figure 28.5) is sent to the shareholders, and outlines the nature of the matters to be considered at the meeting.

Proxy

If a shareholder will be unable to be present at a meeting, the by-laws of the company usually provide that he may appoint someone as his *proxy* to exercise his voting rights at the meeting. A proxy is appointed when the shareholder executes the proxy form which usually accompanies the notice of meeting. The shareholder indicates on the proxy form the number of shares he holds in the company. The person appointed as his proxy is then authorized to exercise the voting rights attached to these shares.

The proxy form illustrated (Figure 28.6) does not require that the shareholder's signature be witnessed. The by-laws of the company specify the form of proxy, and may require that a proxy form be witnessed. Usually however, this requirement is not necessary.

PETERSON OFFICE SUPPLIES LIMITED

BY-LAW NUMBER 1

WHEREAS it is deemed advisable and in the interests of the Company to pass a general by-law for regulating its affairs;

BE IT THEREFORE ENACTED AND IT IS HEREBY ENACTED as a by-law of PETERSON OFFICE SUPPLIES LIMITED (hereinafter called the "Company") as follows:

HEAD OFFICE

1.   The head office of the Company shall be in the City of Toronto, in the County of York, in the Province of Ontario, and at the place therein where the affairs of the Company are from time to time carried on.

Figure 28.2.   Heading on By-laws

FINANCIAL YEAR

2.   The financial year of the Company shall end on the 30th day of April in each year.

MEETINGS OF SHAREHOLDERS

3.   Annual Meeting. The annual meeting of the shareholders shall be held at such place within Ontario, at such time and on such day in each year as the board, or the president, or a vice-president who is a director may from time to time determine.

4.   Notices. Notice of the time and place of each meeting of shareholders shall be given not less than ten days before the day on which the meeting is to be held to the auditor of the Company and to each shareholder of record....

Figure 28.3.   Extract from Body of By-laws

```
PASSED AND ENACTED this        day of            , 19--


                                   _____
                                          Chairman


                                   _____
                                          Secretary
```

Figure 28.4.   Ending of By-laws

```
                  PETERSON OFFICE SUPPLIES LIMITED

                    NOTICE OF ANNUAL MEETING


          NOTICE IS HEREBY GIVEN that the Annual Meet-
     ing of shareholders of PETERSON OFFICE SUPPLIES LIMITED
     will be held at 17 Princess Street South, in the City
     of Toronto, on Monday, the 15th day of June, 1970, at
     3:00 p.m., for the following purposes:

          1.  To receive the report of the Directors,
              together with the audited financial
              statement.

          2.  To elect directors for the ensuing year.

          3.  To appoint auditors for the ensuing year.

          4.  To transact such other business as may
              properly come before the meeting.

          By order of the Board.

                                   Percival A. Peterson
                                   Secretary

     Toronto,
     May 31, 1970
```

Figure 28.5.   Notice of Meeting

311

PETERSON OFFICE SUPPLIES LIMITED

P R O X Y

I,_____(name of shareholder)_____, of

_____(address)_____, a shareholder in

PETERSON OFFICE SUPPLIES LIMITED, hereby appoint

___(name)_____, of____(address)_____, or

failing him___(name)_____, of___(address)_____,

as my proxy to vote for me and on my behalf at the

meeting of shareholders of the company to be held on

the___(date)_____, and at any adjournment

thereof.

DATED this   day of   , 197-.

_____

_____
Number of Shares

Figure 28.6. Proxy Form

ANNUAL MEETING OF SHAREHOLDERS
PETERSON OFFICE SUPPLIES LIMITED

MINUTES of the Annual General Meeting of Shareholders of PETERSON
OFFICE SUPPLIES LIMITED held at 17 Princess Street South, Toronto,
Ontario, on Monday, the 15th day of June, 1970, at the hour of
3:00 p.m.

Figure 28.7. Heading on Minutes Showing
Time and Place of Meeting as
Part of the Heading

Minutes

A summary of how and what decisions were made at a directors' or shareholders' meeting is prepared and is known as the *minutes* of the meeting. Quite frequently the lawyer is the secretary of the company, and his legal secretary types the minutes recording what was done, rather than what was said. Minutes include the following information: date, time, place, and nature of the meeting; the names of persons present, or number present if the meeting was a very large one; name of the chairman and secretary; and all resolutions or motions passed at the meeting.

If minutes are being typed for a meeting of a company which has been incorporated for some time, you should consult the minute book and follow the format used for minutes of earlier meetings. If, however, minutes are being prepared for a meeting of a newly-incorporated company, it is usually up to the secretary typing the minutes to establish the format to be followed.

Number of Copies

It is common to prepare two copies of the minutes, but the practice will vary depending upon the lawyer involved. The original is on minute-book paper which is inserted into the appropriate section of the minute book; the carbon is on plain white paper of 11-inch size, and is kept in the file.

Heading

The heading (Figure 28.7) of the minutes sets out the type of meeting and the name of the company. Information as to the time and place of the meeting may appear either in the heading, or as the first item in the body of the minutes.

Body

The format of minutes will usually follow one of the following:
1. margin headings in either capital or regular type (Figure 28.8)
2. shoulder headings in capital letters (Figure 28.9)
3. centred headings in capital letters (Figure 28.10).

When information as to the time and place of the meeting appears in the heading, the body of the minutes may follow any of the formats illustrated.

Typing Guide for Minutes

1. Single space minutes unless instructed otherwise.
2. Triple space between each item in the minutes; double space between individual paragraphs of an item.
3. Indent paragraphs when shoulder or centred headings are used; do not indent paragraphs when margin headings are used.
4. Underscore shoulder or centred headings; do not underscore margin headings.
5. When using margin headings, commence typing the text of an item approximately fifteen spaces from the margin.

Ending

Minutes are ended by typing the statement that the meeting was officially adjourned, and then typing lines for the signatures of the chairman and secretary of the meeting.

These lines may be side by side, approximately eight spaces apart, and five or six spaces beneath the last line of the body of the minutes. If margin headings are used, the lines for signatures are frequently typed one beneath the other on the right-hand side of the page. (See Figures 28.11A, B.)

The name of the office of the person signing the minutes is shown beneath each line.

Signing and Approval of Minutes

The secretary of the company whose responsibility includes preparing minutes of meetings (this is not the secretary who *types* them, but the officer of the company who holds the position of secretary) usually signs the minutes as soon as they have been typed.

The minutes of the meeting are then presented at the next meeting for approval, and when approved, are signed by the chairman to indicate that they have correctly recorded the decisions made at the meeting.

```
PLACE             The meeting was held at 17 Princess Street South,
AND TIME          Toronto, on Monday, the 15th day of June, 1970, at
                  3:00 p.m.


PRESENT                   Ronald C. Anderson
                          Howard Albert East
                          Percival C. Peterson

                  being all of the Directors of the company.


CHAIRMAN          Mr. Anderson took the Chair and Mr. Peterson acted
AND SECRETARY     as Secretary of the meeting.
```

Figure 28.8. Body of Minutes with Margin Headings Showing Time and Place of Meeting as Part of the Body

```
RESIGNATIONS AND ELECTION OF DIRECTORS

        Mr. Anderson presented his resignation as a Director, which
was accepted.

        Upon motion, duly proposed and seconded, it was unanimously
resolved:

        That Mr. Peter T. Grant be and he is hereby elected a
Director of the company.  Mr. Peter T. Grant then took his place at
the Board.
```

Figure 28.9. Body of Minutes with Shoulder Headings

```
                          BANK ACCOUNT

        Upon motion, duly proposed and seconded, it was unanimously
resolved:

        (a)  That the company's bank account be kept with The Royal
Bank of Canada.

        (b)  That all bills of exchange, promissory notes, cheques
and other negotiable instruments which require to be made, drawn,
endorsed or accepted by the company....
```

Figure 28.10. Body of Minutes with Centred Headings

```
        There being no further business to transact, on motion the
meeting was adjourned.



_____          _____
        Secretary                         Chairman
```

Figure 28.11A. Ending of Minutes with Lines for Signatures Side by Side

There being no further business to transact, on
motion the meeting was adjourned.

_____

Chairman

_____

Secretary

*Figure 28.11B.   Ending of Minutes with
Lines for Signatures One Beneath the Other*

PETERSON OFFICE SUPPLIES LIMITED

CERTIFIED EXTRACT FROM MINUTES

I, the undersigned, Secretary of Peterson Office
Supplies Limited, hereby certify that the following resolution
was duly passed at a meeting of the Board of Directors of
Peterson Office Supplies Limited duly held on the 15th day of
June, 1970, pursuant to the by-laws of the company and the
laws governing the company, and that the said resolution is in
full force and effect:

RESOLVED:

THAT.... (stating the resolution being certified,
copying it from the appropriate minutes)

WITNESS my hand and the seal of the company at
Toronto this   day of June, 1970.

(COMPANY SEAL)   _____

Secretary

*Figure 28.12A.   Typed Certified Extract
from Minutes*

Correction of Minutes

Signed minutes cannot be altered even to correct errors without the corrections being authorized at a subsequent meeting. The page is not removed from the minute book, nor is the error erased when corrections are made. The errors are neatly struck out in ink, and the corrections made in ink. The corrections are then initialled by the person who signed as chairman when the original minutes were approved.

Numbering Pages of Minutes

In addition to numbering the individual pages which comprise each set of minutes of meetings of the shareholders, it is common practice to number *all* pages of the minute book in a consecutive numbering pattern. This permits reference to other records and to the exact page of the shareholders' minutes in the minute book where some specific point has been recorded.

Let us suppose that page 4. of the minutes of a shareholders' meeting is being typed, and the pages have been numbered consecutively. The page being typed is the 67th page of the minutes in the shareholders' minute book.

To number this page, type "4." centred four or five spaces from the top of the page. In the upper right-hand corner, approximately one space from the top of the page and flush with the right-hand margin, type "67." The figure in the upper right-hand corner, that is, "67.", is what is meant when reference is made to the "Minute-book Folio" or "M.B. Folio".

Certified Copy of Extract from Minutes

The secretary of the company may be required to certify the passing of a resolution, which has been duly recorded in the minutes. This certificate may be typed for his signature (Figure 28.12A), or it may be a printed form (Figure 28.12B) such as that used to certify the resolutions regarding banking and the authority of the officers of the company.

Share Certificates

When a company is incorporated, each shareholder usually receives a certificate showing the number and class of shares which he holds in the company (Figure 28.13).

A large company usually employs a transfer agent, such as a trust company, to issue and transfer its shares of stock. For a small company the lawyer may act in this capacity, and his secretary will be instructed to issue a share certificate for a definite number and class of shares to each shareholder.

When the company's application for letters patent is submitted, the secretary, on instructions from the lawyer, should order a bound book of blank stock certificates for each kind of stock issued by the company. Each book will contain a number of share certificates and a perforated portion known as the "stub". The certificates and the stub are numbered with the same number, and all certificates in the book are numbered consecutively. The space for the number of shares represented by the certificate is usually left blank so that certificates may be issued for any number of shares.

Original Issue

An "original issue" of stock refers to a share of stock that has never before been issued. The certificate of incorporation authorizes the company to issue a stated number of shares. All of these shares need not be issued immediately, but as each is issued it is considered an original issue.

Issuance of a Share Certificate

To issue a share certificate, follow these steps:
1. Obtain the appropriate book of blank share certificates, that is, common or preferred.
2. On the stub of the certificate, enter the name and address of the person to whom the certificate is to be issued, and the number of shares represented by the certificate.
3. If the certificates have not been pre-numbered, enter the appropriate number on both the stub and the certificate.

(To be used in cases of companies incorporated under the Canada Corporations Act and the Companies Act of Manitoba, New Brunswick, Ontario, Prince Edward Island or Quebec: in cases of companies incorporated by Special Act of Canada or any such Province this form may require amendment. Special forms are provided for companies incorporated under the Companies Act of Alberta, British Columbia, Nova Scotia or Saskatchewan.)

COMPANIES

BY-LAW TO AUTHORIZE THE DIRECTORS TO BORROW AND GIVE SECURITY

PETERSON OFFICE SUPPLIES LIMITED
(Name of Company)

Head Office: _____Toronto, Ontario._____

INCORPORATED UNDER_____The Companies Act of Ontario_____

BY-LAW No._____2_____

Be it Enacted as a By-law of the Company as follows:—

The Directors of the Company are hereby authorized from time to time

(a) to borrow money upon the credit of the Company in such amounts and on such terms as may be deemed expedient by obtaining loans or advances or by way of overdraft or otherwise;

(b) to issue debentures or other securities of the Company;

(c) to pledge or sell such debentures or other securities for such sums and at such prices as may be deemed expedient;

(d) to mortgage, hypothecate, charge or pledge, or give security in any manner whatever upon, all or any of the property, real and personal, immoveable and moveable, undertaking and rights of the Company, present and future, to secure any debentures or other securities of the Company, present or future, or any money borrowed or to be borrowed or any obligation or liability of the Company, present or future;

(e) to delegate to such officer(s) or Director(s) of the Company as the Directors may designate all or any of the foregoing powers to such extent and in such manner as the Directors may determine.

This By-law shall remain in force and be binding upon the Company as regards any party acting on the faith thereof, until a copy, certified by the Secretary of the Company under the Company's seal, of a By-law repealing or replacing this By-law shall have been received by such party and duly acknowledged in writing.

ENACTED this_____27th_____day of_____June_____19 70

AS WITNESS the corporate seal of the Company.

President
(Corporate Seal)
Secretary

CERTIFICATE
(This must be completed in all cases)

It is hereby certified by the undersigned that the foregoing By-law was duly enacted by the Board of Directors of the above-named Company at a meeting of the Directors duly held and was duly sanctioned and confirmed by the shareholders/members of the Company in accordance with the Charter and By-laws or the Memorandum and Articles of Association of the Company and the laws governing the Company and that the said By-law is in full force and effect.

AS WITNESS the corporate seal of the Company this_____27th_____day of_____June_____1970

(Corporate Seal)
(Secretary)

Figure 28.12B. Printed Form of Certified Extract from Minutes

This number will be the next consecutive number following that shown on the preceding stub in the certificate book.

4. Remove the certificate from the share certificate book.
5. If the information has not been printed on the certificate, type in the name of the company and its authorized capital.
6. Type on the face of the certificate the name of the person to whom it is issued, the number of shares it represents, and the date.
7. Have the certificate signed by the proper signing officers of the company.
8. Affix the company seal in the space indicated in the lower left-hand corner of the certificate.
9. If possible, have the receipt of the stub of the certificate signed. If the person to whom the certificate is issued is not present to sign, type a receipt on a slip of paper the same size as the receipt portion of the stub, send it with the certificate, and ask that it be signed and returned. When the receipt is returned, paste it over the receipt portion of the stub.
10. If a share certificate must be sent through the mail, it should be sent by registered mail.

Transfer of Certificate

When a shareholder wishes to transfer his shares, or a part of his shares, he must complete the form (Figure 28.14) on the back of his original certificate. When shares are transferred, the company issues a new certificate to the new shareholder. The holder of a 25-share certificate might wish to transfer all of his shares, in which case a new share certificate for 25 shares is made out to the transferee (the new shareholder). If, however, the original shareholder wishes to transfer only 10 shares and retain the other 15, two new certificates would be issued; one to the transferee for 10 shares, and one to the original shareholder for 15 shares.

Figure 28.13. Share Certificate and Stub

When a certificate is transferred, the procedure outlined for the original issuance of a certificate is followed. The stub of a certificate for transferred shares requires more information than the stub for an original issue. It is necessary to show from whom the shares are transferred, the original certificate number, and the name of the transferor.

When certificates have been prepared, write in ink across the face of the old certificate the word "Cancelled". Date and initial the cancelled certificate and either retain it in a special file, or paste it to the stub in the bound book of certificates as nearly as possible in the original position.

Security Transfer Tax

In Ontario The Security Transfer Tax Act imposes a small tax on the change of ownership by sale, transfer, or assignment of securities. For shares, the tax is graduated depending on the amount paid for them when they are sold. For example, the tax is one cent per share on shares selling at a price of between $5.00 and $25.00 per share.

The tax is payable in cash, but is usually paid by transfer tax stamps which may be obtained from certain banks, the Provincial Treasurer's Office, or from the Stamp Office in Osgoode Hall. The stamp is affixed to the certificate to be cancelled.

Every company is required to make an annual return to the Provincial Treasurer showing every transfer of securities, together with the amount of tax collected.

Registers and Records

By law, a company is required to maintain a record of the names, addresses, and other pertinent information for all past and present shareholders and directors.

In a large company where the number of shareholders may be in the thousands, and where there are large numbers of directors as well as many changes in the ownership of shares, this record keeping is very detailed and may involve the use of computers and other electronic equipment. We are not concerned with the details of that aspect of corporation practice.

For Value Received,_____ hereby sell, assign, and transfer unto_____

_____Shares of the Preferred Stock represented by the within Certificate, and do hereby irrevocably constitute and appoint

_____Attorney to transfer the said Stock on the books of the within named Corporation with full power of substitution in the premises.

Dated_____ 19___

In presence of

_____   _____

Figure 28.14. Form on Back of Share Certificate – Completed When Shares Transferred

In a small company, however, where the number of shareholders is small, and where records may be maintained in the minute book, this procedure is much simpler.

Three types of records must be maintained: Shareholders', Directors' and Transfer Registers.

As share certificates are issued or transferred, or as directors are appointed or retire, the appropriate register is completed in order that the records of the company are at all times up-to-date and accurate.

These records are cross-indexed one to the other, and the forms used refer to the appropriate page or "folio" in the minute book, or to the number of the register sheet on which the original entry concerning the sale or transfer is recorded.

Shareholders' Register

Individual shareholders of a company are first listed in the general shareholders' register (Figure 28.15), which shows the date of acquisition of the shares, the name and address of the shareholder, and the class and number of shares held. Each sheet in this register is numbered consecutively.

Shareholders' Ledger Sheet

A separate ledger (Figure 28.16) may be kept for each class of share. This contains in alphabetical order individual ledger sheets for each present shareholder and past shareholders from the previous ten years, recording the number of shares held.

Directors' Register

A record (Figure 20.17) is maintained of past and present directors, indicating the page in the minutes of the appropriate meeting of shareholders at which the appointment or retirement of a director was ratified by the shareholders.

Transfer Register

When shares are transferred, the appropriate information is recorded (Figure 28.18) to show the transfer number, the certificate covering the shares being transferred, the name of the present shareholder, that is, the "transferor", the name of the new shareholder, that is, the "transferee", and the number of shares covered by each new certificate issued.

SHAREHOLDERS' REGISTER

DYE & DURHAM LTD. NO. 8312 SHAREHOLDERS	DATE 1970		NAME	ADDRESS	SHARES HELD	
					PREFERRED	COMMON
	June	15	ANDERSON, Ronald C.	74 Prince William Street Toronto		2
	June	15	PETERSON, Percival C.	936 Hillsdale Blvd. Toronto		2
	June	15	EAST, Howard Albert	19 King Street Toronto		2
	June	17	BATTERSLEA, Henry G.	135 Howard St., Guelph		3
	July	8	MATTHEWS, John Robert	34 Goodale Crescent S. Kitchener		2

Figure 28.15. Shareholders' Register Sheet

SHAREHOLDERS' LEDGER

NAME **ANDERSON, Ronald Craig**

ADDRESS **74 Prince William Street, Toronto, Ontario.**

OCCUPATION **Physician**

PHONE Nos. - OFFICE: **322 9999** RESIDENCE **364 0000** COMMON OR PREFERRED **Common**

DYE & DURHAM LTD. NO. 8312 LEDGER	DATE		CERT. No.	TRANS. No.	TO OR FROM WHOM	FOLIO	SHARES		
							TRANS. FERRED	ACQUIRED	BAL. HELD
	1970								
	June	15	3		Original issue	1		2	2
	July	8	3	1	Matthews, John David	1	2		0

Figure 28.16. Shareholders' Ledger Sheet

DIRECTORS' REGISTER

DYE & DURHAM LTD. NO 8312 DIRECTORS	NAME	ADDRESS	ELECTED		RETIRED		OFFICE HELD
			DATE	M. B. FOLIO	DATE	M. B. FOLIO	
	ANDERSON, R.C.	74 Prince William St. T.	1970 June 15	1	Sept. 10	4	President
	PETERSON, P.A.	936 Hillsdale Blvd., Toronto	June 15	1			Secretary
	WILLIAMSON, G.D.	7 Avar Road, Toronto	Sept. 10	5			President

Figure 28.17. Directors' Register

TRANSFER REGISTER

TRANSFER NUMBER	DATE	COM. OR PFD.	CERTIFICATES SURRENDERED		TRANSFEROR		TRANSFEREE		NEW CERTIFICATES ISSUED		ATTORNEY
			NO.	SHARES	TRANSFERRED FROM	LEDGER FOLIO	TRANSFERRED TO	LEDGER FOLIO	NO.	SHARES	
1	1970 July 8	Com.	3	2	Anderson, Ronald Craig	1	Matthews, John David	5	9	2	

Figure 28.18. Transfer Register

CHAPTER 29

Separation Agreements and Divorce Procedure

In Canada married persons rarely enter into a formal marriage contract, yet married persons are in a certain contractual relationship in the eyes of the law. This contractual relationship can in certain circumstances be terminated by an order of the court, and such an order is commonly known as a *divorce*.

Under the provisions of the British North America Act, exclusive legislative jurisdiction for "Marriage and Divorce" was given to the Federal Government. For many years however, each province except Quebec and Newfoundland had its own divorce law, and in some provinces, including Ontario, the main ground for divorce was adultery. In July, 1968, however, the new Divorce Act (Canada) came into force. This act provided a standard divorce law for all Canadians, and there are now a number of grounds which will support an action for divorce. The right to hear divorce proceedings was given to specified provincial courts; in Ontario this right was given to the trial division of the Supreme Court, but it is anticipated that concurrent jurisdiction may be given to County Courts.

The new act permits a "petition" for divorce to be brought on grounds other than adultery: physical and mental cruelty, marriage breakdown because of drug or alcohol addiction, imprisonment for certain periods, desertion by the *respondent* (the person from whom a divorce is sought) for a period of three years, or desertion by the *petitioner* (the person who files the petition for divorce) for a period of five years.

In many cases, however, married persons may mutually agree to separate. Before considering the steps that may be taken to legally terminate the marriage, we will consider what steps might be taken when the parties first agree to separate.

Separation Agreement

Prior to divorce proceedings being commenced, married persons may enter into an agreement called a *separation agreement* (Figure 29.1). This agreement will usually be drawn up by a lawyer and it will set out, among other things, how jointly-owned property is to be divided, which party will have the custody of any children of the marriage, and what amount will be paid for the support of the children or the wife.

These agreements are made in duplicate, and a copy will be made for the solicitor for each party. They are typed as a regular legal instrument in accordance with the requirements set out in Chapter 7. They are executed in the presence of a witness and are under seal. An affidavit of execution is required for each witness. It is uncommon for a person to witness the signature of both parties to a separation agreement; however, under certain circumstances this may be done.

Divorce

In divorce proceedings several of the papers required to be completed are in printed form; others must be typed in full. The requirements for typing court documents as set out in Chapter 19 should be followed. When the proceedings are commenced, the Registrar of the Supreme Court assigns a file number to the proceedings; the number is preceded by the letter "D" to avoid confusion with an action number. This file number must appear on all documents to be filed in the course of the proceedings.

Special Terms

petitioner: the person who files the petition for divorce.

respondent: the person from whom a divorce is sought.

co-respondent: if adultery is the ground upon which the divorce is sought, the person with whom adultery is alleged to have been committed.

In papers used in divorce proceedings, the respondent and any co-respondent are referred to jointly as the "respondents".

decree nisi: the interim grant of divorce.
decree absolute: the final grant of divorce.

Commencing a Divorce Proceeding

Number of Copies

The steps in obtaining a divorce commence with the preparation of a petition for divorce and a notice of petition.

A minimum of four copies of these printed forms is prepared; the original, a copy for the court, a copy for service on the respondent, and a copy for the lawyer's use. An extra copy is required for any co-respondent(s), and if children are involved, for the Official Guardian.

Petition for Divorce

A petition for divorce (Figure 29.2) consists of six pages and a back, and requires detailed information as to the grounds upon which the divorce is being sought; the particulars of any possibility of reconciliation; the efforts made to effect the reconciliation of the parties; particulars of the marriage; the place of residence; the *domicile* of the parties; information as to any parties who are under twenty-one years of age; information as to the children of the marriage; whether other proceedings have been instituted with reference to the marriage or any children of the marriage; details of any separation agreements and financial arrangements; and an outline of the relief sought.

The petitioner must sign the petition to verify the accuracy of the facts set out in the petition. The solicitor for the petitioner also signs a statement in the petition to certify that he has complied with the requirements of the act in connection with the steps taken to effect any possible reconciliation of the parties.

It is possible that an additional page will be required to include all the pertinent information required on pages 1 and 4 of this form. In such cases, blank sheets may be used, and should be numbered 1A and 4A respectively.

Notice of Petition for Divorce

A notice of petition for divorce (Figure 29.3) consists of three pages and a back. It is addressed to the respondent(s), and sets out the number of days within which an "answer" may be filed to the petition (twenty days if served in Ontario, or forty days if served elsewhere in Canada or the United States), the place for filing an answer, and the place of trial in default of filing an answer.

The notice sets out the address of the petitioner, and the name and address of the solicitors acting on his or her behalf.

The third page of the notice is an acknowledgement which will be completed by the respondent(s) when he is served with the notice.

Filing of Petition and Notice

The original and one copy of each document are taken to the office of the local registrar of the Supreme Court. The local registrar issues the petition, just as a writ is issued, and assigns a file number to the proceedings. The local registrar signs the notice of petition addressed to the respondent(s). One copy of each document is then filed with the appropriate court office.

Serving Petition and Notice

Within sixty days of filing the notice, it must be served by someone other than the petitioner upon the respondent(s), who signs the acknowledgement of service set out in the notice in the presence of the person effecting service. Each respondent is then asked to provide his current mailing address to expedite service of any future documents required to be served.

If it is not possible to effect personal service on the respondent(s), an order of the court may be obtained allowing "substitutional service". Substitutional service is sometimes allowed by publishing the notice in the legal column of a newspaper serving the area where it is believed the respondent(s) resides.

An affidavit of service is then completed by the person who served the respondent(s).

Reply to Petition for Divorce

If the respondent wishes to "contest", that is, dispute the divorce, he must serve and file an "answer" within the time stipulated in the notice of petition. If the respondent wishes to make a claim similar to a counter-claim in a civil action, he serves and files an answer and counter-petition.

Figure 29.4 illustrates what documents the petitioner and respondent may serve and file if an answer or an answer and counter-petition are required. An answer and counter-petition are usually typed.

Special Steps if There are Children Involved

If there are children of the marriage within the meaning of the Divorce Act, a copy of the petition or counter-petition must be served on the Official Guardian within thirty days after service on the respondent(s). Other pleadings which may be served and filed in the proceedings are served on the Official Guardian within the same time limits as on the other parties.

Within thirty days of service upon him of the petition, the Official Guardian serves on the parties, and files with the court, a copy of a report concerning the welfare and custody of the children.

Setting Divorce Proceedings Down for Hearing

Record

As in the actions for trial in the County and Supreme Courts, a record containing an original of all pleadings must be filed with the court. The record is prepared in the same way as the record in any other civil proceedings.

If the Official Guardian has served and filed a report, this is attached to the record, but the report is not part of the record.

Notice of Hearing

When the record has been filed, and an answer has been filed, a notice of hearing is filed and served. If the proceeding is to be set down for hearing other than at Toronto, it must be set down at least ten days before the commencement of the sittings at which it is to be heard, and the form of notice reads:

TAKE NOTICE that this proceeding has been set down for hearing at the sittings of this Court at . . . commencing on the . . . day of . . . , 197-.

If the proceeding is to be set down for hearing at Toronto, the wording is:

TAKE NOTICE that this proceeding has been set down on the . . . day of . . . , 197-, for hearing at the Toronto Non-Jury Sittings.

If the respondent has not filed an answer, the petition can be set down for hearing without serving and filing a notice of hearing.

Certificate of Registrar

Under the Divorce Act, it is possible for both a wife and a husband to file divorce petitions against each other in two different jurisdictions. The first of such petitions filed takes precedence. If, for example, a court in Manitoba had no notice of a previous petition filed in Ontario, and the Manitoba court granted a divorce, the filing of the first petition would nullify that divorce.

In order to avoid this possibility, a Central Divorce Registry has been established at the Department of Justice in Ottawa. Court officials each week complete a Registration of Divorce form which is filed with the Central Registry, and records the details of age, name, address, and birth place of the parties in a divorce action commenced in that jurisdiction. This information is compiled using a computer, and any conflicting claims are quickly discovered and appropriate steps are taken to resolve any problems created by conflicting claims.

Before a petition for divorce will be put on the list to be heard, a certificate must be obtained from the Central Divorce Registry and filed with the Registrar or local registrar. The certificate verifies that no prior or other petitions for divorce are pending in other jurisdictions.

Decree Nisi

When a claim for divorce is allowed, a decree nisi is usually granted (Figure 29.5). This decree is an interim one, and is usually made final after three months providing certain conditions have been fulfilled within that period.

This decree is a judgment of the court. After the judgment has been issued, it is served on the respondent(s) unless such service has been dispensed with by the trial judge.

Decree Absolute

After the expiration of the required period from the granting of the decree nisi, the petitioner may file with the office of the Registrar or local registrar the following documents: a notice of application for decree absolute (Figure 29.6), an original or certified copy of decree nisi with proof of service on respondent(s), an affidavit setting out facts to indicate there is no bar to granting the decree absolute (Figure 29.7).

If everything is in order, the Registrar will present the application for decree absolute to a judge for signature. When the decree absolute has been signed, the parties are then divorced, and the marriage contract is terminated.

THIS AGREEMENT made in duplicate this 10th day of June, 1970.

B E T W E E N:

CUTHBERT DUNSTAN BLACKSTONE, of the City of Toronto, in the County of York, Engineer,

hereinafter called "the husband"

OF THE FIRST PART,

- and -

BLANCHE AGATHA BLACKSTONE, of the City of Toronto, in the County of York, wife of the said Cuthbert Dunstan Blackstone,

hereinafter called "the wife"

OF THE SECOND PART.

WHEREAS the husband and the wife were married at the City of Toronto, in the County of York, on the 10th day of April, 1956;

AND WHEREAS the husband and the wife have two surviving children, namely Ashley Julian Blackstone, born on the 25th day of September, 1959, and Rosamund Cordelia Blackstone, born on the 1st day of March, 1961, hereinafter called "the children";

NOW THEREFORE THIS AGREEMENT WITNESSETH that in consideration of the premises and the covenants hereinafter expressed and contained, the husband and wife do covenant, undertake and agree, the one with the other as follows:

1.   The husband and the wife will continue to live separate and apart from each other and neither of them will molest or disturb or annoy or interfere with the other in any manner whatsoever and neither of them will take or cause to be taken any proceedings against the other of them for any cause or matter whatsoever arising out of or in any way connected with their marriage; provided that nothing herein contained shall constitute a bar to any proceedings which may be taken by either the husband or the wife for dissolution of their marriage or to enforce any of the terms of this agreement. The wife shall be free from the control and authority of her husband as if she were a femme sole.

Figure 29.1. Extract from Separation Agreement

Dye & Durham Limited, 76 Richmond Street East, Toronto
Law and Commercial Stationers
Form No. 717 - 728

Registrar's File No.   19 70

In the Supreme Court of Ontario

Between

LUCILLE CAROLINE ANDERSON,

PETITIONER

and

RONALD CRAIG ANDERSON,

RESPONDENT(S)

PETITION FOR DIVORCE

(To be completed according to Form 140 as the same appears in the Rules of Practice)

To this Honourable Court:

See Form 140.   I hereby petition for a decree of divorce from the Respondent spouse

Ronald Craig Anderson, and for costs,

on the grounds and in the circumstances following:

1. GROUNDS:

See Form 140.   A. My Petition is under the DIVORCE ACT (Canada), section   4   , subsection (1)(e)(i)

See Form 140.   B. The particulars of my grounds for divorce are:

    1.   Separation for three years, Section 4 (1)(e)(i)

    2.   There has been a permanent breakdown of my marriage to the Respondent by reason of the following circumstances:

       I have not deserted the Respondent and from on or about the 31st day of December, 1966 I have lived and continue to live separate and apart from the Respondent.

Use additional
page if
necessary.

Figure 29.2. Petition for Divorce – Page 1

2. RECONCILIATION:

A. The particulars of the circumstances which may assist the Court in ascertaining whether there is a possibility of reconciliation or resumption of cohabitation are:

1. The Respondent has no desire and has never had any desire to continue the marriage since the separation.

2. For the past two years I have had no desire to continue to be married to the Respondent and presently do not wish any reconciliation with him.

3. For approximately six months prior to our said separation the Respondent, although living in the same house as myself, rarely communicated with me and refused to have normal sexual relations with me for approximately five months prior to the said separation, and in fact the marriage had broken down for several months prior to the said separation.

4. In the month prior to our said separation the Respondent admitted keeping company with another female person.

state "no efforts
to reconcile
have been made"
if such be the
case.

B. The following efforts to reconcile have been made:

1. I broached the subject of reconciliation with the Respondent on at least three occasions after we separated, but he was very definite in not wishing to discuss the matter and in not wishing to consider reconciliation, and has in fact since the time of the said separation always made it very clear that he is not interested in any reconciliation.

2. In January, 1967 my mother raised the question of a reconciliation with the Respondent, with the same result--i.e. complete disinterest on his part.

3. When I again approached the subject of reconciliation with the Respondent in July, 1967, he indicated he was leaving for the United States of America, and that his reason was to avoid supporting me.

4. I wrote to the Respondent two or three times in or about the months of February or March, 1968 on the subject of reconciliation and received no reply at all on this subject.

5. I telephoned my husband in June, 1969 to again suggest reconciliation, and he indicated that if further calls of this nature were made by me he would consider them to be a breach of the Separation Agreement and would therefore stop paying the alimony.

Figure 29.2. Petition for Divorce – Page 2

3. PARTICULARS OF MARRIAGE:

(Where possible, set out the particulars from the marriage certificate to be produced at the hearing)

A. The date of the marriage was: October 28, 1960

B. The place of the marriage was: Toronto, Ontario

C. The surname of the wife before marriage was: Black

D. The maiden surname of the wife was: Black

E. The marital status of the spouses at the time of the marriage was,

wife: Spinster   husband: Bachelor

F. The wife was born at   Ontario   on   February 14   19 39
(province or country)   (month, day)

G. The husband was born at   Ontario   on   June 18   19 38
(province or country)   (month, day)

4. DOMICILE AND JURISDICTION:

A. My residence is: 17 Prince William Avenue, Islington, Ontario.

B. My spouse's residence is: 502 St. Clair Avenue South, Welland, Ontario

C. I ceased to cohabit with my spouse on or about: December 31, 1966

D. My domicile is: Canada

E. Such domicile has subsisted since: date of birth

See Form 140.   F. I have   been ordinarily resident in Ontario

since   date of birth, Feb. 14   , 1939   and actually resided in the said Province

for   36   months of that period at: 17 Prince William Avenue,
Islington, Ontario.

5. AGE AND DISABILITY:

State "No party to these proceedings is under 21 years of age" if such be the case.   A. The names of any of the parties under 21 years of age and the ages of such parties are:

No party to these proceedings is under 21 years of age.

State "No party to these proceedings is under any other legal disability" if such be the case.   B. The names of the parties suffering any other legal disability and the nature thereof are:

No party to these proceedings is under any other legal disability.

Figure 29.2. Petition for Divorce – Page 3

6. CHILDREN:

A. The names and dates of birth of all living children of the marriage as defined by the DIVORCE ACT (Canada) are:

State "there are no such children of the marriage" if such be the case.

There are no such children of the marriage.

B. The particulars of the past, present and proposed custody, care, upbringing and education of the said child(ren) are as follows:

State "not applicable" where no children are shown in para. A.

Not applicable.

C. I claim custody of the following child(ren):

State "not applicable" where no children are shown in para. A, or "no claim for custody is being made" if such be the case.

Not applicable.

D. The facts on which such claim for custody is founded are:

State "not applicable" if no claim for custody is being made.

Not applicable.

Use additional page if necessary

Figure 29.2. Petition for Divorce – Page 4

7. OTHER PROCEEDINGS:

State "there have been no such petitions or proceedings instituted" if such be the case.

A. The particulars and status of all other petitions or proceedings instituted with reference to the marriage or any child thereof, including applications to the Parliament of Canada or actions for alimony or applications under any statute, are:

There have been no such petitions or proceedings instituted.

8. SEPARATION AGREEMENTS AND FINANCIAL ARRANGEMENTS:

State "there have been no such written or oral agreements between the parties" if such be the case.

A. The dates of any written or oral separation or financial agreements between the parties are:

Written Separation Agreement dated February 15, 1967.

Complete where a claim for corollary relief is made or state "not applicable" if no such claim is made.

B. The financial position, both income and capital, of the respective spouses is:

Not applicable.

9. COLLUSION, CONDONATION AND CONNIVANCE:

A. There has been no collusion in relation to this Petition.

Where the facts are otherwise, see Form 140.

B. There has been no condonation of or connivance at the grounds for divorce set forth in this Petition.

Figure 29.2. Petition for Divorce – Page 5

10. RELIEF ASKED:

I therefore ask this Honourable Court for the following relief:

A. A decree that I be divorced from the respondent, Ronald Craig Anderson.

B. Costs of this petition.

C.

11. DECLARATION OF PETITIONER:

I have read and understand this Petition. Those statements contained therein of which I have personal knowledge are true, and those of which I do not have personal knowledge I believe to be true.

DATED at   Toronto   , this   day of   June   , 1970

....
(signature of petitioner)

17 Prince William Avenue
....
(address of petitioner)
Islington, Ontario.

....

PLACE OF HEARING

See Rule 245.   I propose that this Petition be heard at the sittings of this Court at   Toronto, Ontario.

STATEMENT OF SOLICITOR

See Form 140.   I,   PETER THOMAS GRANT------------------------------- the solicitor for
Lucille Caroline Anderson   , the Petitioner herein certify to this Court that I have complied with the requirements of section 7 of the DIVORCE ACT (Canada).

DATED at   Toronto   , this   day of   June   , 1970

....
(signature of solicitor)

Figure 29.2.   Petition for Divorce – Page 6

Registrar's File No.   19 70

In the Supreme Court of Ontario

PROCEEDINGS COMMENCED IN THE
COUNTY OF YORK

LUCILLE CAROLINE ANDERSON

Petitioner

and

RONALD CRAIG ANDERSON

Respondent(s)

Petition for Divorce

Dye & Durham Limited, 76 Richmond Street East, Toronto
Law and Commercial Stationers

Solicitor for Petitioner:

HILL, JOHNSTON & GRANT
17 Princess Street South,
Toronto, Ontario.

Figure 29.2. Petition for Divorce – Back

Dye & Durham Limited, 76 Richmond Street East, Toronto
Law and Commercial Stationers
Form No. 724 - 727

Registrar's File No.   19 70

In the Supreme Court of Ontario

Between

LUCILLE CAROLINE ANDERSON,

PETITIONER

and

(seal)

RONALD CRAIG ANDERSON,

RESPONDENT(S)

NOTICE OF PETITION FOR DIVORCE

To: RONALD CRAIG ANDERSON,
       502 St. Clair Avenue South,
       Welland, Ontario.

See Form 141.   **And to:**

Take Notice that a Petition for a Decree of Divorce has been presented to this Court by the Petitioner. A copy of it is attached to this notice.

And Further Take Notice that if you wish to oppose the said Petition or if you wish other relief you must cause your Answer to be served on the Petitioner and filed with proof of service in the office of the undersigned registrar within the time hereinafter stated:

Where you are served within Ontario, within twenty days after service on you of this Notice, inclusive of the day of such service;

Where you are served elsewhere in Canada or within one of the United States of America, within forty days after service on you of this Notice, inclusive of the day of such service; or

Where you are served elsewhere than within Canada or within one of the United States of America, within   days after service on you of this Notice, inclusive of the day of such service, as provided in the order of the Court authorizing such service to be made.

Figure 29.3. Notice of Petition for Divorce –
Page 1

335

And Further Take Notice that in default of your serving and filing such Answer within the time prescribed above the Petitioner may proceed herein and (subject to the Rules of Court) you will not be entitled to notice of any further proceedings and a decree and other relief may be given in your absence.

See Rules 799 & 245.

And Further Take Notice that in default of Answer this proceeding may be set down within thirty days of such default for hearing at the sittings of this Court at Toronto and where so set down and subject to the Rules of Court, you will not be entitled to any further notice of the hearing.

And Further Take Notice that you may ascertain the approximate date of the hearing of the said Petition and the date and details of any decree from the office of the said registrar.

And Further Take Notice that any decree given at such hearing may become final after the expiration of such time from the granting thereof as the decree may provide unless in the meantime you deliver to the undersigned and to the Petitioner and to Her Majesty's Proctor at Toronto, a written Notice that you wish to show cause why the decree should not become final and the grounds therefor.

And Further Take Notice that neither spouse is free to remarry as a result of these proceedings until a decree of divorce has been granted and such decree has been made final.

DATED at Toronto , the day of June , 1970

....
Registrar, S.C.O.

....
(full address)

....

The Petitioner's address is:.......17 Prince William Avenue, Islington, Ontario

....

This Notice of Petition was issued on behalf of the Petitioner

by: HILL, JOHNSTON & GRANT   solicitor(s)

whose address is: 17 Princess Street South, Toronto, Ontario.

Figure 29.3. Notice of Petition for Divorce –
Page 2

NOTE 1: This Notice is to be served upon the respondent spouse within sixty days from the date on which it was issued, unless otherwise ordered.

NOTE 2: The person who serves this notice shall at the time of service request each respondent to complete and sign in his presence the following form of acknowledgement of service and shall sign his name as a witness to any signature thereto.

I am the person named as   Ronald Craig Anderson   a Respondent in this Notice of Petition. I have this day received a copy of the within Notice and attached Petition and my mailing address for further service of documents is

....

....

WITNESS:

....
                                          (signature)

I am the person named as   a Respondent in this Notice of Petition. I have this day received a copy of the within Notice and attached Petition and my mailing address for further service of documents is

....

....

WITNESS:

....
                                          (signature)

Figure 29.3. Notice of Petition for Divorce –
Page 3

Registrar's File No.   1970

In the Supreme Court of Ontario

PROCEEDINGS COMMENCED IN THE
COUNTY OF YORK

LUCILLE CAROLINE ANDERSON

Petitioner

and

RONALD CRAIG ANDERSON

Respondent(s)

Notice of Petition for Divorce

Dye & Durham Limited, 76 Richmond Street East, Toronto
Law and Commercial Stationers

Solicitor for Petitioner:

HILL, JOHNSTON & GRANT
17 Princess Street,
Toronto 1, Ontario.

Figure 29.3. Notice of Petition for Divorce –
Back

Basic Steps in a Petition for Divorce (No Children)

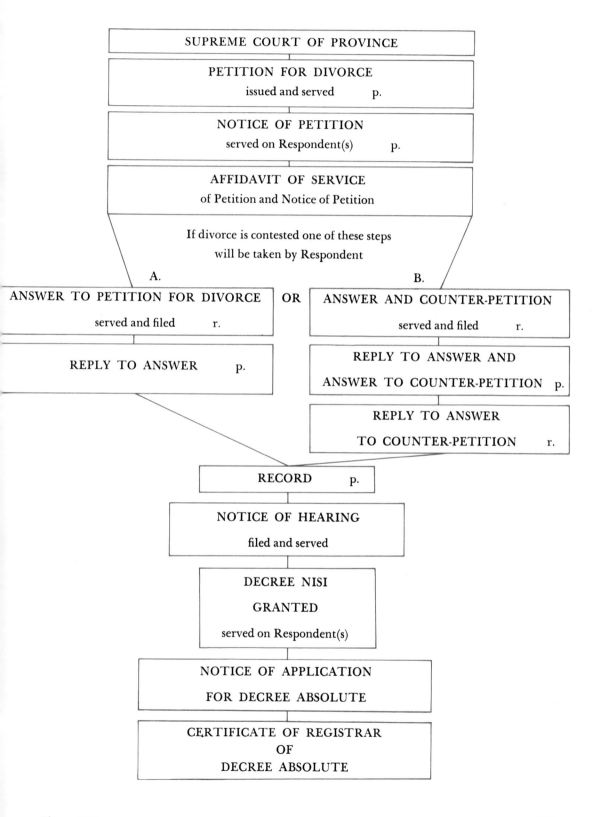

SUPREME COURT OF PROVINCE

PETITION FOR DIVORCE
issued and served   p.

NOTICE OF PETITION
served on Respondent(s)   p.

AFFIDAVIT OF SERVICE
of Petition and Notice of Petition

If divorce is contested one of these steps
will be taken by Respondent

A.

ANSWER TO PETITION FOR DIVORCE
served and filed   r.

OR

B.

ANSWER AND COUNTER-PETITION
served and filed   r.

REPLY TO ANSWER   p.

REPLY TO ANSWER AND
ANSWER TO COUNTER-PETITION p.

REPLY TO ANSWER
TO COUNTER-PETITION   r.

RECORD   p.

NOTICE OF HEARING
filed and served

DECREE NISI
GRANTED
served on Respondent(s)

NOTICE OF APPLICATION
FOR DECREE ABSOLUTE

CERTIFICATE OF REGISTRAR
OF
DECREE ABSOLUTE

Figure 29.4

339

No. D 58895/70

IN THE SUPREME COURT OF ONTARIO

THE HONOURABLE MR. JUSTICE DOE) TUESDAY, THE 24th DAY OF
)
) SEPTEMBER, 1970

B E T W E E N:

      LUCILLE CAROLINE ANDERSON,

                 Petitioner,

       - and -

      RONALD CRAIG ANDERSON,

                 Respondent.

DECREE NISI

    THIS proceeding coming on this day for hearing at the sittings of this court at Toronto, in the presence of counsel for the petitioner, no one appearing for the respondent, although duly served with the notice of petition, the petition, and with the notice of hearing, upon hearing read the pleadings and hearing the evidence adduced, and what was alleged by counsel aforesaid:

1.   THIS COURT DOTH DECREE AND ADJUDGE that the petitioner Lucille Caroline Anderson, whose marriage to the respondent Ronald Craig Anderson was solemnized at the City of Toronto, in the County of York, on the 28th day of October, 1960, be divorced from the said respondent Ronald Craig Anderson, unless sufficient cause be shown to this court within three months from the date hereof why this decree should not be absolute.

Figure 29.5. Decree Nisi in Divorce Proceedings – Page 1

2.

2.   AND THIS COURT DOTH ORDER AND ADJUDGE that service of
a copy of this decree nisi upon the said respondent, Ronald Craig
Anderson, be dispensed with.

        JUDGMENT signed this   day of September, 1970

                            _____
                                  Registrar, S.C.O.

Figure 29.5. Decree Nisi in Divorce
Proceedings – Page 2   341

IN THE SUPREME COURT OF ONTARIO

B E T W E E N:

LUCILLE CAROLINE ANDERSON,

Petitioner,

- and -

RONALD CRAIG ANDERSON,

Respondent.

APPLICATION FOR DECREE ABSOLUTE
BY THE PETITIONER

I, PETER THOMAS GRANT, the solicitor in this proceeding for the petitioner Lucille Caroline Anderson, give
notice that application is hereby made for a decree absolute
in this proceeding, and I hereby certify to this Honourable
Court that:

1.   No appeal from the decree nisi herein has been served
upon me or upon my firm.

2.   No notice of desire to show cause why the decree
should not be made absolute has been served upon me or upon my
firm.

DATED at Toronto this   day of December, 1970.

_____
Solicitor for the Petitioner.

*Figure 29.6. Application for Judgment
Absolute*

No. D 58895/70

IN THE SUPREME COURT OF ONTARIO

B E T W E E N:

LUCILLE CAROLINE ANDERSON,

Petitioner,

- and -

RONALD CRAIG ANDERSON,

Respondent.

I, LUCILLE CAROLINE ANDERSON, of the Borough of Etobicoke, in the County of York, Secretary, make oath and say as follows:

1.   I am the above-named petitioner.

2.   No appeal to the Court of Appeal for Ontario, or to the Supreme Court of Canada is pending in this proceeding.

3.   No petition for divorce has been served on me by the respondent Ronald Craig Anderson.

4.   I have not been reconciled with the respondent Ronald Craig Anderson.

SWORN before me at the   )
)
City of Toronto, in the   )
)
County of York, this   )
)
      day of December,   )
)
1970.   )
)
)
)
)
)
                A COMMISSIONER ETC.

Figure 29.7. Petitioner's Affidavit on Application for Judgment Absolute

Summary of Civil Courts in Other Provinces
Equivalent to Those of Ontario

Ontario	Division Court	County and District Court
Alberta	Magistrates Court	District Court
British Columbia	Provincial Court of British Columbia	County Court
Manitoba	Magistrates Court	County Court
New Brunswick	Provincial Court	County Court
Newfoundland	Magistrates Court	District Court
Northwest Territories	Small Debts Court	Police Magistrates Court
Nova Scotia	Municipal Court	County Court
Prince Edward Island	County Court	County Court
Quebec		Provincial Court
Saskatchewan	Magistrates Court	District Court
Yukon	Small Debts Court	

Supreme Court of Ontario
  High Court of Justice
	Supreme Court of Ontario
	  Court of Appeal

Supreme Court of Alberta
  Trial Division
	Supreme Court of Alberta
	  Appellate Division

Supreme Court of British Columbia	Court of Appeal of British Columbia
Court of Queen's Bench for Manitoba	Court of Appeal of Manitoba

Supreme Court of New Brunswick
  Queen's Bench Division
	Supreme Court of New Brunswick
	  Appeal Division

Supreme Court of Newfoundland	Supreme Court of Newfoundland [1]
Territorial Court of the Northwest Territories	Northwest Territories Court of Appeal [2]

Supreme Court of Nova Scotia
  Trial Division
	Supreme Court of Nova Scotia
	  Appeal Division

Supreme Court of Prince Edward Island	Supreme Court of Prince Edward Island [1]
Superior Court	Court of Queen's Bench of Quebec
Court of Queen's Bench for Saskatchewan	Court of Appeal of Saskatchewan
Territorial Court of the Territory of Yukon	Court of Appeal [3]

[1] Appeals are heard by a court composed of three Supreme Court judges.

[2] Court consists of the justices of appeal of the Alberta Court of Appeal, and the judges of the Yukon Territory and the Northwest Territories Territorial Courts.

[3] In practice the Court of Appeal of British Columbia serves as the Court of Appeal.

Glossary

A legal secretary requires an understanding of many special words and phrases, some of which have already been mentioned. There are many additional expressions which may be encountered, some of which are in Latin. While the following list does not, of course, contain all such expressions, it is hoped it will widen your knowledge of the special vocabulary associated with legal secretarial work.

a priori: from the cause to the effect.

abatement: the act of reducing or mitigating an amount.

abstract of title: a chronological statement of the registered legal instruments relating to real property.

accept service: to accept service of a writ of summons on behalf of a defendant, and undertake to enter an appearance in order to defend the action. (See *admission of service*.)

act: laws passed by the Provincial or Federal Government.

action: legal proceedings commenced either by the issuance of a writ of summons, or in the manner stipulated in the statutes or rules of practice of the courts.

action number: a court file number which is assigned when an action is commenced in the courts.

ad hoc: for this special purpose.

adjourn: to suspend a sittings of a court, for resumption at another time or place.

adjudication: a judgment or decision of the court.

administrator (male): see *administratrix*.

administratrix (female): a person appointed to manage the property of another during his lifetime; a person appointed by the courts to administer the estate of a deceased who died intestate or without an executor.

admission of service: to acknowledge receipt of a true copy of a legal document prepared for use in legal proceedings.

admit to probate: an act of the court authenticating a will so as to give it legal effect.

affidavit: a written statement of facts in the name of a person, by whom it is voluntarily signed and sworn to under oath.

affidavit of bona fides: the sworn statement of a party to a legal instrument as to the genuineness of the transaction covered by the instrument.

affidavit of execution: the sworn statement of a witness to the execution of a legal instrument certifying that he actually saw the instrument signed.

affidavit of legal age: the sworn statement of a party or parties executing a legal instrument that he was of the age of twenty-one. This affidavit is usually combined with an affidavit of marital status.

affidavit of marital status: the sworn statement of a party or parties executing a legal instrument certifying his or their marital status.

affidavit of merits: a court document filed by a defendant in response to a specially endorsed writ of summons, if he wishes to dispute the claim against him.

affidavit on production: an affidavit completed by each party in an action outlining material the party has or had relating to the matter in dispute.

affidavit of value and relationship: an affidavit filed with the Ontario Succession Duty Department by the executors or administrators of an estate, giving information on the assets, debts and distribution of the estate, for the purpose of determining the amount of succession duty payable.

agenda: a list of items of business to be transacted at a meeting.

agreement of purchase and sale: an accepted offer to purchase.

alimony: monies paid by a husband to his wife for support while separated or prior to divorce.

amendment: a proposed change to a proposed motion.

amortize: to provide for the gradual payment of a debt by periodical, set payments, at a rate calculated to repay the debt in a given number of years.

ancillary: auxiliary.

ante: before.

appeal book: a book prepared for use on an appeal, containing material relating to the issues in dispute on the appeal.

appeal case: printed material prepared for use in an appeal to the Supreme Court of Canada.

appearance: a court document by which a defendant initially indicates he will defend an action commenced against him.

appellant: the party who brings an appeal from the judgment of a lower court.

applicant: the party on whose behalf an application is made to the court in a matter.

arbitration: the settling of a dispute by a party or parties appointed or chosen by the disputing parties.

arms' length: genuine, open and above-board.

articling: the period a student lawyer spends working under the direction of a practising lawyer to gain practical experience before being called to the bar.

assignee: the party to whom a contract is assigned.

assignor: the party who assigns a contract.

ats: at the suit of.

attest: to witness an act or event; for example, the execution of a legal instrument.

attestation clause: a clause in a legal instrument which indicates the instrument was executed in the presence of a witness.

attorney: the American term to refer to a lawyer. In Canada this term refers to a person who receives authority under a power of attorney. (See *donee.*)

authority: a case which is cited in support of a legal theory in another case.

back: the last page of a legal paper, which identifies the nature of the legal paper to which it is affixed. (See *long back* and *short back.*)

Bar Admission Course: in Ontario the six-month course taken by a student lawyer following completion of his law school training and his period of articling, and following the successful completion of which he is called to the bar.

bar of dower: the giving up by a wife of her inchoate one-third life interest in the real property of her husband.

bargainee: the party buying personal property under a bill of sale.

bargainor: the party selling personal property under a bill of sale.

barrister: a lawyer who appears in the courts. In Canada a lawyer is both a barrister and a solicitor.

Bencher: a lawyer elected to serve as a member of his provincial Law Society.

beneficiary: a person who receives a benefit under a will, or from a policy of insurance.

bequest: a gift of personal property by will.

bill of costs: a document in legal proceedings which sets out the claim for costs in an action or matter.

bill of sale: a legal instrument covering the sale of personal property when title to but not physical possession of the property is conveyed.

blended payment: a payment on a loan (usually a mortgage) of a set amount of money regularly. The monies so paid are applied first as against accrued interest on the loan, and second as against the unpaid principal balance of the loan.

bona fide: in good faith; honestly; without fraud.

brief: a file of pleadings, documents and other memoranda prepared for the use of the lawyer appearing at a trial or other hearing.

by-law: a rule or requirement made by a public or private corporation for the regulation of its own affairs or its dealings with others.

capacity: the legal competency to enter into a contract.

capital: the contribution of each shareholder to the common fund or stock of a company.

case law: the decisions of judges which establish the law in a given set of circumstances. (See *precedent.*)

cause: actions or other original legal proceedings between a plaintiff and a defendant.

cause of action: facts which give rise to a right of action.

caveat: a warning.

certificate of readiness: a document filed by one or both parties in an action to indicate that they are ready for trial.

certiorari: a writ quashing a decision of an inferior court.

cessation of charge: a legal instrument which formally acknowledges that the claim against real property contained in a charge has been discharged.

cestui que trust: he who benefits by the trust.

chains and links: a term used when the description of the perimeter of a parcel of land is by a chain measuring 66', and by links of the chain.

charge: a legal instrument under the Land Titles system which formalizes the claim upon title to real property as security for a debt or loan.

charges: see entry.

chattel mortgage: a mortgage of personal property as security for a loan or debt.

chose in action: a right of proceeding in a court of law.

citation: a reference to a decided case or matter.

cite, citing: to refer to a decided case in support of a legal theory.

Clerk of the County Court: the chief administrative officer of a County Court, whose responsibilities include supervision of all County Court records and court papers filed by litigants for use in County Court proceedings.

client: an individual or company who comes to a lawyer for assistance.

closing: a meeting of the solicitors representing the vendor and the purchaser in a real estate transaction to finalize the transaction.

codicil: a legal instrument which adds to or amends a will made previously by the same person.

Commissioner: one who may administer oaths to persons coming before him to swear to the truth of statements.

committee: a person to whom the custody of the estate or person of an individual of unsound mind is committed.

common shares: shares having no special privileges attached to them and which usually convey full voting rights.

conditional sales agreement: an agreement covering the sale of personal property where title to the property will only pass to the purchaser when certain conditions (usually the payment in full of the purchase price) have been fulfilled.

conduct money: money given to a person who will be examined for discovery, or to a witness at a trial, to defray his expenses in attending at the discovery or the trial.

conjugal rights: the right of a married person to the society and cohabitation of his or her spouse.

consent: a document filed with the court in which parties to legal proceedings mutually agree to do or not to do something.

consideration: the return given for the act or promise of another.

constitutional law: the area of law dealing with the distribution and exercise of power between the Federal Government and the provinces.

construction: the process of ascertaining the meaning of a written document.

contra: against.

convey: to transfer or pass title to real property to another.

conveyancing: the act of transferring or passing title from one party to another.

co-respondent: the party in a divorce action named in the petition as being the person with whom the respondent committed adultery.

corner: a diamond-shaped pocket into which the left-hand corner of pages may be inserted before stapling.

corpus: the capital amount of a fund.

corroboration: evidence which confirms a fact in a material particular.

costs: money to which a party may be entitled in order to partially compensate him for the expense of being a party in legal proceedings.

counsel: a lawyer whose practice largely involves court work.

counter-claim: a separate and distinct claim of the defendant against the plaintiff, having nothing to do with the defendant's defence to the plaintiff's claim.

courses: a term used when the description of the perimeter of a parcel of land is by minutes and degrees.

covenant: an agreement creating an obligation.

cy-près: the doctrine related to the carrying out of the intention of a testator in a manner as nearly as possible to the way stipulated by the testator.

damages: an amount of money claimed or awarded to a party in legal proceedings as a result of damage done to or suffered by that party because of the actions of another party.

de bene esse: to act in anticipation of a future occasion.

de facto: in fact, actually.

de jure: by right.

de novo: anew.

declarant: a person who voluntarily declares a statutory declaration.

decree absolute: an order of the court terminating a marriage.

decree nisi: an order of the court terminating a marriage subject to obtaining a decree absolute.

deed: a legal instrument under the Registry Office system by which title to real property is conveyed from one party to another.

defendant: the party who is being sued in a civil lawsuit.

demise: to grant a lease of lands.

deponent: a person who voluntarily signs an affidavit.

deposed: to swear under oath.

devise: a gift of real property by will.

disbursement: an item of expense, other than for work performed, paid for by the law firm on behalf of a client.

discharge of mortgage: a legal instrument which formally acknowledges that the debt covered by a mortgage has been discharged.

distance: a term used when the description of the perimeter of a parcel of land is by feet and inches.

distinguish: to differ from.

dividend: a payment made to a shareholder out of profits earned by a company.

divorce: an order of the court terminating a marriage.

docket: a record of time spent on a case, or matter, and the disbursements incurred.

domicile: the place in which a person has his permanent home and to which, whenever he is absent, he has the intention of returning.

donatio mortis causa: a gift of personal property in anticipation of death.

donee: the party who receives a power of attorney; also known as the *attorney.*

donor: the party who gives a power of attorney.

dower: the interest of the widow in one-third of her late husband's real property, or the rents or profits therefrom, for her life.

duces tecum: bring with you, as in a *subpoena duces tecum,* by which a witness is ordered to appear and bring certain material with him.

duplicate original: the first carbon copy of a legal instrument which has been executed as if it were also the original.

E. & O. E.: errors and omissions excepted.

easement: a right enjoyed by the owner of real property over the lands of another.

eleemosynary corporation: a charitable organization.

en ventre sa mere: a child not yet born.

encumbrance: a claim or lien upon real property.

endorsement: a concise statement in a writ of summons which sets out the claim of the plaintiff against the defendant.

engross: to do a final copy of a legal paper, usually after such a paper has been first done in draft.

entry: a lawyer's day-by-day record of time spent and/or work performed for a client.

enure: to operate or take effect.

equity of redemption: a right which a mortgagor has upon payment of the total mortgage debt and all accrued interest, to redeem the mortgaged property after the mortgagor has gone into default and breached the terms of the mortgage.

erratum, errata (pl.): error(s).

escheat: the reversion of land to the Crown.

escrow: the holding in trust of a written agreement or material by a third party until certain conditions are fulfilled.

estate: the real and personal property owned by a person as of the date of his death.

estate tax: a tax levied by the Federal Government on the estate of deceased persons.

estate tax return: a return filed with the Federal Government by the executors or administrators of an estate, giving information on the assets, debts and distribution of the estate for purposes of determining the amount of estate tax payable.

estoppel: the doctrine which precludes a person from denying the truth of some statement made by him, or the existence of facts which he has by words or conduct led others to believe.

et al: and others.

et seq.: and those following.

et ux: and wife.

ex officio: by virtue of his office.

ex parte: on one side only; by or for one party.

examination for discovery: an examination under oath of parties to an action, held before the trial and touching upon the matters in dispute.

execution: doing what is required to give validity to the legal instrument including signing, sealing and delivering the instrument.

executor (male): see *executrix.*

executrix (female): a person designated in a will to administer the estate of a testator in accordance with the terms of the testator's will.

exhibit: an article or material filed in the course of legal proceedings; written material referred to and forming part of an affidavit.

expropriation: compulsorily depriving a person of the right to property belonging to him, in return for compensation.

factum: an informal term for the statement of points of law and fact filed by each party in an appeal.

feme sole: an unmarried woman including one who has been divorced or widowed.

fiduciary: one who is placed in a position of trust.

fieri facias (fi fa): cause to be made. A writ directed to the Sheriff to reduce a judgment debtor's property to money in the amount of the judgment.

file: to deliver to the appropriate court office the original or a copy of a document prepared for use in legal proceedings.

file memorandum: a memorandum which records for the file information relevant to the matter being looked after for a client.

firm account: a bank account of the law firm in which it may deposit monies belonging to the firm itself.

foreclosure: the act of the mortgagee requiring the mortgagor of real property to pay off the mortgage upon its maturity, or relinquish his interest in the real property.

grantee: the party in a deed who receives title to real property.

grantor: the party in a deed who gives title to real property.

guaranty: a promise to answer for the debt or default of another.

guardian ad litem: a person appointed to defend an action or other proceedings on behalf of an infant.

habeas corpus: writ directed to a person who detains another in custody, commanding him to "produce the body" before a court.

habendum clause: a clause in a legal instrument dealing with real property which indicates the estate to be taken by the grantee.

holographic: an instrument wholly in the handwriting of the purported author.

ibid: in the same place.

idem: the same.

in camera: any judicial, quasi-judicial, or administrative hearing conducted in private.

in esse: in being.

in fee simple: a term used to describe absolute ownership of real property.

in loco parentis: in the place of a parent.

in re: in the matter of.

in toto: entirely.

inchoate: begun but not completed.

indenture: an agreement in writing, usually in duplicate.

infant: an individual under the age of twenty-one years.

infra: below.

injunction: an order or decree by which a party to an action is required to refrain from doing, or to do some particular thing.

inscribe: to enter an appeal to the Supreme Court of Canada on the list of appeals to be heard by that court.

inter alia: among others.

inter vivos: during a lifetime.

interlocutory: a term describing an act or decision of a court which is made after legal proceedings have been commenced and which act or decision is complete in itself before the legal proceedings are final and complete.

intestate: the state of having no will.

intestacy: the state of dying without a will.

intra vires: within the power.

ipso facto: by the mere fact.

issue: a person's children, grandchildren, and all other lineal descendants.

joint tenants: the holding of title to real property by two or more parties, where each holds the same interest as the other. Upon the death of one party, the surviving co-owner acquires the interest of the deceased tenant.

judge: a person (usually a lawyer) appointed by either a Provincial or Federal Government to adjudicate on matters within the jurisdiction of the court to which he is appointed.

judgment: the final decision of a court in legal proceedings.

judgment creditor: a person to whom a judgment of the court orders that payment be made.

judgment debtor: a person ordered by the court in a judgment to make payment to another person.

judicial area: in Ontario, a County, United County, Provisional County, District, Regional Municipality, or Judicial District.

jurat: the ending of an affidavit or statutory declaration, beginning with the words "SWORN" or "DECLARED", which attests when, where and before whom the affidavit was sworn.

jurisprudence: the science of law.

King's Counsel (K.C.): the equivalent designation to Queen's Counsel (Q.C.), when the reigning monarch is a King.

laches: negligent or unreasonable delay in putting forward legal rights.

land transfer tax affidavit: a sworn statement as to the actual consideration paid, required in a legal instrument transferring title of real property.

law reports: the written, published reports of legal decisions in cases of interest before the courts.

lawsuit: legal proceedings in a court.

lease: a legal instrument under which one party conveys possession of property to another in return for monetary or other consideration.

ledger statement: a statement attached to an account which indicates the actual amount due after deducting from the account any monies paid in advance or on account of services rendered.

legal instrument: formally written documents such as wills, deeds, or contracts, which give formal expression to a legal act or agreement.

legal proceedings: an action or matter being tried or heard in a court.

legal seal (locus sigilii): a small, red gummed sticker which is affixed following the name of the signing parties in an instrument; or the seal of a company which is stamped over or beside the signatures of the officers of a company.

lessee: the party renting real or personal property for monetary or other consideration.

lessor: the party owning real or personal property which he rents out to another party (lessee).

letter book: a chronological file of all outgoing correspondence.

letters of administration: the formal instrument of authority and appointment granted by the appropriate court (e.g. in Ontario the Surrogate Court) to an administrator of an estate of a deceased person who died intestate.

letters of administration with will annexed: the formal instrument of authority and appointment granted by the appropriate court (in Ontario the Surrogate Court) to an administrator of an estate of a deceased person who died testate, when the executor or executors named in the will are unable or unwilling to serve, or when there is a will but no executor has been named in the will.

letters patent: the official document issued by the appropriate government, certifying the existence, purpose and financial structure of a company.

letters probate: the formal instrument of authority granted by the appropriate court (e.g., the Surrogate Court in Ontario) to an executor to carry out the provisions of the will of the deceased.

lien: the right to hold the property of another as security for an obligation.

life tenant: a person in possession of real property during the term of his lifetime only.

liquidated damages: a fixed or readily ascertained amount of money owed by one person to another as the measure of damages accruing as a result of a breach of a contractual obligation.

lis pendens: notice of a pending suit, action, or matter.

locus sigilli: the place of the seal.

long back: a back on a legal paper, which is typed down the length of the paper.

long vacation: the period during the months of July and August when the courts do not normally sit.

lot: a small parcel of land forming part of a larger area covered by a registered plan.

maintenance: monies paid after divorce by a man to his former wife.

mala fides: bad faith.

mandamus: we command. A writ directed to an inferior tribunal directing it to act on a matter.

Master: a person (usually a lawyer) appointed by the Ontario Government to assist Ontario Supreme Court judges in carrying out their administrative and judicial duties.

Master of Titles: a person appointed by the Ontario Government whose main responsibility is to supervise and administer the registration of all documents affecting the ownership of real property registered under the Land Titles system in Ontario.

matter: every legal proceeding in a court which is not a cause.

maturity: the date upon which a mortgage or charge is due.

mechanics' lien: a claim against property for satisfaction of a debt incurred as a result of work done or materials supplied to improve the property.

memorandum of law: a memorandum which in some detail refers to decided cases on some point at issue, and which may quote from the decisions made in such cases.

mens rea: the state of a man's mind.

metes and bounds: a description of real property which commences with a determinable point, and outlines the perimeter of the parcel in directions and distances.

minutes: the formal, permanent record of decisions made and business conducted at a shareholders' or directors' meeting.

mitigate: to make or become less severe. The term "mitigation of damages" is descriptive of the legal obligation on a party to legal proceedings to take all reasonable steps to minimize the damages resulting from another party's action.

mortgage: a legal instrument under the Registry Office system which formalizes the conveyance of title to the mortgagee as security for a debt or loan owed to the mortgagee by the mortgagor.

mortgage, to: to convey property, upon certain terms and conditions, as security for the payment of a debt.

mortgagee: the party to whom property is mortgaged.

mortgagor: the party who gives a mortgage on property.

mutatis mutandis: the necessary changes being made.

next friend: a person over the age of 21 who consents to let an infant bring an action in the courts in his name.

next of kin: the closest blood relatives of a deceased person.

nolle prosequi: an agreement to proceed no further with an action or matter in the courts.

non compos mentis: not of sound mind.

non sequitur: it does not follow.

non sui juris: without capacity to manage his own affairs.

nonsuit: a judgment given against a plaintiff for failure to establish his case.

notarial certificate: a legal instrument which certifies the authenticity of the copy of the legal paper to which it is affixed.

Notary Public: one who may affirm under notarial seal the execution of certain legal writings, or the authenticity of a copy of a document or writing.

notice: a court document by which advice is given of some step or application in an action or matter before the court. Notices may be "interlocutory" (during the course of an action or matter), or may be "originating" (commencing a matter), or "ex parte".

notice to produce: a document in an action served by both parties on the other, requiring disclosure of material relating to the matter in dispute.

nulla bona: no goods; the wording of a return to a writ of fieri facias.

nunc pro tunc: now for then.

352

obiter dictum: an opinion by a judge on collateral issues.

offer to purchase: an offer signed by a party seeking to purchase the real property of another.

Official Guardian: a person appointed by the Ontario Government whose main responsibility is to ensure that the rights and interests of infants are protected when they become involved in legal proceedings.

order: a decision of the court in a legal proceeding, usually involving some direction to the disputing parties to do or not to do some particular thing.

originating notice of motion: a notice issued to commence legal proceedings in the courts in a matter.

par value: the fixed monetary value of a share as stated on the share certificate and in the letters patent.

parcel: parts or portions of land.

pari passu: equally, without preference.

parol: verbal, not in writing or under seal.

partition: the act of dividing real property in certain proportions amongst persons who previously owned the property as joint tenants or as tenants in common.

pendente lite: while litigation is pending.

per annum: by the year.

per autre vie: for another's life.

per capita: by head or individual.

per diem: by the day.

per se: by itself, taken alone.

per stirpes: by family stock or branches.

personal property: movable property; all rights or interests which are not land or anything permanently attached to land.

petitioner: the person who commences a divorce action against the respondent.

plaintiff: the party who is suing another party in a civil law suit.

plan: a design covering the division of an area of real property into smaller parcels or lots.

pleadings: statements delivered alternately by the parties to an action. For example: a statement of claim, or a statement of defence.

power of attorney: a legal instrument by which one person empowers another to represent him, or to act in his place.

praecipe: a simple order directed to the clerk of a court.

prayer for relief: a paragraph in a pleading which sets out the claim or remedy sought by one party from another party.

preamble: an introductory paragraph in judgments, orders and notices, setting out the events leading up to or the reasons for the document.

precedent: a judgment or decision of a court of law which is cited as an authority as to what decision should be made by a judge in an analogous fact situation.

preferred shares: shares having special privileges attached, such as the payment of a fixed dividend, and which usually carry no voting rights.

prima facie: at first sight, on the face of it.

principal: the amount of the mortgage or charge, upon payment of which, together with any accrued interest, the mortgage or charge is discharged or cancelled.

pro forma: as a matter of form.

pro rata: according to the rate or proportion.

proceedings: legal proceedings commenced in the courts, either in an action or matter.

prospectus: a document setting out the objectives and financial structure of a company, designed to facilitate the sale of the company's shares to the public.

proxy: in company practice the person appointed to represent a shareholder of the company at a shareholders' meeting; the paper by which such an appointment is confirmed.

Public Trustee: a person appointed by the Ontario Government, whose main responsibility is to ensure that mentally incompetent persons' estates are administered and distributed in a competent and proper manner.

quaere: query or question.

quantum: the amount.

quantum meruit: as much as he has earned or deserved.

quash: to discharge or set aside.

quasi: as if, as it were.

Queen's Counsel: a lawyer who has been appointed counsel to Her Majesty on the recommendation of the Attorney General or

Minister of Justice of his province, or of the Federal Government.

Queen's Proctor: a representative of the Crown who may intervene in divorce proceedings.

quick succession: succession to title of property inherited by the deceased within the five years prior to his death from the taxed estate of another.

quid pro quo: something for something.

quit claim: to relinquish a claim to real property.

quorum: the minimum number of persons who must be present in order to hold a valid meeting of shareholders or directors of a company.

ratio decidendi: the decision of a judge on the main issue in dispute.

ready list: the list of actions in the County Courts and the Supreme Court of Ontario, said to be ready for trial.

real property: also known as "realty" or immovable property; the land, buildings, and all permanent attachments thereto. For example, a tree is "real property", but branches cut from the tree are "personal property".

realty: see *real property*.

reasons for judgment: a document in which a judge sets out his reasons for arriving at his decision.

record: the copy of pleadings provided for the use of a judge in legal proceedings.

register: to file notice of an interest in real or personal property at the appropriate Registry Office or Land Titles Office.

release: a legal instrument, or a clause in a legal instrument, relinquishing rights or interests.

rent: the consideration paid for the use of the real or personal property of another.

replevin: the remedy of a person whose chattels are unlawfully taken from him.

res ipsa loquitur: the thing speaks for itself.

res judicata: a thing adjudicated.

rescission: the revocation of a contract.

residuary clause: a clause in a will which sets out how all the remaining property in an estate will be distributed after all the special devises have been made.

residue: the remaining real or personal property in an estate after all succession duties, estate taxes, debts of the deceased and specific legacies and bequests have been paid or distributed.

respondeat superior: the master is liable for his servant's or agent's acts.

respondent: the party holding a different or opposing position to that of the party on an application to the courts in a matter; the party against whom an appeal is brought in an action; the party against whom a divorce action is commenced.

retainer: a sum of money received by a law firm from a client at the time the client engages the firm to act for or advise him.

satisfaction piece: a formal written acknowledgment filed with the court, certifying that a judgment creditor has been paid in full by a judgment debtor.

search: an examination by a purchaser of real property of records and registers, for the purpose of checking the state of the title to the property.

security for costs: an amount of money which may be required to be paid into court by a party making a claim against another party in legal proceedings, to protect such other party against his costs of disputing the claim.

separation agreement: a contract signed by a man and his wife, setting out the terms under which they agree to live separate and apart from each other. Such terms usually include provision for the custody and maintenance of the children, division of property, and alimony.

serve: to leave a copy of a legal document with the party on the other side, or a person not a party to the action but who has an interest in the proceedings.

set off: a claim by the defendant in an action to set off against the claim of the plaintiff an amount owed by the plaintiff to the defendant.

share: a definite portion of the capital of a company; shares are either "common" or "preferred".

share certificate: an instrument under seal recording ownership of a stated number and type of shares of a company.

shareholder: a person who holds shares in a company.

sheriff: a person appointed by the Ontario Government as the chief administrator of the Crown's business in a particular county within the province. His duties include serving writs and other court documents, as well as being responsible for keeping records of persons against whom there are outstanding unpaid judgments.

short back: a back on a legal paper which is typed across the length of the paper.

short vacation: the period at Christmas, from the 24th of December to the 6th day of the following January, both days inclusive, when the courts do not sit.

sine die: indefinitely.

solicitor: a lawyer who conducts legal proceedings, or who advises on legal matters. In Canada a lawyer is both a barrister and a solicitor.

special examiner: a person appointed by the Provincial Government to record the questions and answers at an examination for discovery.

specific performance: an order of the court compelling a person to do that which he had previously agreed to do in accordance with a contractual obligation.

stare decisis: to abide by decided cases.

statement of adjustments: a detailed statement prepared in a real estate transaction, outlining the exact amount of money which the purchaser must pay when the transaction is closed.

status quo: the existing state of things at any given time.

statute: a law enacted by the legislative branch of a government.

statute law: the written law as set out in Acts of the Federal Government, or a Provincial Legislature.

Statute of Limitations, The: the provincial statute which sets out time limits within which a legal proceeding must be commenced in order to protect a cause of action.

statutory declaration: a written statement of facts in the name of one or more persons, by whom it is voluntarily signed and declared under oath before a Commissioner.

stipulation: an undertaking in writing to do a certain thing, usually made when litigation is pending.

style of cause: the heading on court documents, which sets out the names of the parties in an action, or describes the nature of the matter before the courts.

subpoena: a command issued in the name of the Sovereign to require the person to whom it is addressed to be present at a specified time and place, and for a specified purpose.

subrogation: substitution of one person or thing for another.

succession duty: a tax levied by the Provincial Government on persons receiving property from the estate of a deceased person.

sui juris: of his own right.

supra: above.

surety: a guarantor, who binds himself to satisfy the obligation of another.

tariff: a schedule of fees which may be charged to perform specified legal services.

tax: to assess the amount of money to be paid as costs to the successful party, or to interested parties in legal proceedings.

tenants in common: the holding of title to property by two or more persons, under which each tenant may dispose of his interest independently of the other by deed or will. There is no right of survivorship.

tenure: the mode of holding or occupying land or an office.

terms: the conditions of repayment of a mortgage or charge.

testament: originally, an individual's written statement of how he intended his personal property to be distributed after his death. The term *will* is now commonly used to refer to disposition of both real and personal property, but the formal instrument begins "THIS IS THE LAST WILL AND TESTAMENT OF . . ."

testate: the state of having a will.

testator (male): see *testatrix.*

testatrix (female): a person who has a will.

testimonium clause: a clause by which the body of a legal instrument concludes. The clause commences with either "IN WITNESS WHEREOF . . ." or "IN TESTIMONY WHEREOF . . ."

title: the right to ownership of property.

transfer: a legal instrument under the Land Titles system by which title to real property is conveyed from one party to another.

transferee: the party who receives title to real property under a transfer.

transferor: the party who transfers title to real property under a transfer.

true copy: a carbon copy of an executed legal instrument, on which the names of the executing parties have been written, in ink, and in quotation marks, and upon which all other insertions or corrections made at the time of execution have been noted.

trust account: a bank account of the law firm in which are deposited all monies received in trust for someone else, or to which the law firm has no claim as payment for services rendered.

trustee: a person who holds real and/or personal property in trust for another.

ultra vires: beyond the power.

vacation: a period during which the courts do not normally sit. (See *long vacation* and *short vacation*.)

venue: the place where legal proceedings are to be tried or heard.

versus (v.): against.

via: by way of.

vice versa: on the contrary.

viva voce: by word of mouth.

void: of no legal effect.

voir dire: the part of a hearing in a criminal case to determine the admissibility of a confession or statement.

waive: to renounce or give up a benefit or right.

will: an individual's written statement of how he intends his estate to be distributed after his death.

winding-up: a final settlement of the accounts and affairs of a company.

without prejudice: a term used in correspondence dealing with legal proceedings to indicate that statements made in such correspondence cannot be used as evidence in the proceedings, or cannot be deemed an admission of liability.

writ of summons: a court document by which actions are commenced in the County and Supreme Courts in Ontario.

writs "out of jurisdiction": writs prepared for use in an action where the defendant does not reside in Ontario.

Index

A

abbreviations
judges   20
law reports   17
revised statutes   16

abstract of title   125

acceptance of service   204

account
back of   29
information in   29
ledger statement with   29
monies received prior to   24, 29
paper for   28
payment of   29

accounting forms
account   28-29
credit slip   24
disbursements   28
dockets   22
entries   24

action number
assigned   171
on appeals   232

Acts
see Statutes
name of   16
typing reference to   17

address
barristers and solicitors   8
esquire   8
heading, legal instrument   36
mesdames   7
messrs.   7
Queen's Counsel   8

administration bonds
affidavit of justification with   261
amount of   260
form of   261
release of   261

administration, letters of   258
administration bond   260
affidavit of administrator   259
application for   259
grant of   259
inventory of estate   259

administration, letters of with will annexed
administration bond   260
affidavit of administrator   260
affidavit of execution of witness   260
application for   260
grant of   260

inventory of estate   260

administrator
affidavit of   259, 260
appointment of   259
bond of   260-261
nomination of   259

admission of service
as agent   174
form of   174
stamping for   173
steps on   174
times for   174

affidavit
administrator   259
company, on behalf of   54, 71-72
ending of   49-50
executor   253
gift   275
heading of, legal instruments   49
in assignment of mortgage   103
in bill of sale   152
in cessation of charge   105
in chattel mortgage   152
in deeds   65
in discharge of chattel mortgage   153
in discharge of mortgage   105
in leases   145
in legal instruments   50
in mortgage   87-88
in power of attorney   151
in quit claim deed   72
in renewal of chattel mortgage   153
in renewal of mortgage   104
in separation agreement   324
jurat   49-50
land transfer tax   65, 71
swearing of   49, 180, 261

affidavit, court
back of   180
body of   180
ending   180
exhibits in   180-181
filing of   181
form of   182
heading of   180
number of copies   180
service of   181
swearing of   180

affidavit of bona fides   152

affidavit of debt
filing of   275
number of copies   275

affidavit of execution
of codicil   258, 260
of will   253, 260
purpose of   50
wording of   50

affidavit of justification   261

affidavit of legal age   50

affidavit of legal age and marital status
by agent   54
by married couple   65
by two people   65
in charge   88
in deed   65
in mortgage   87-88
in transfer   71

affidavit of marital status   50

affidavit of merits   204
filing of   204
number of copies   204
service of   204
style of   204
time limit for   204

affidavit of service
number of copies   181
when used   181

affidavit of value and relationship
execution of   274
filing of   274-275
form of   274
number of copies   274
schedules to   275
swearing of   274
time limit for   274

affidavit on production
filing of   205
general   205
listing material in   205
number of copies   205
officer   205
service of   205

agent
admitting service as   174
appointment of   170
Ottawa   240

agreement extending mortgage
see renewal of mortgage   103

agreement of purchase and sale   124

amortized mortgage   87

amounts   36

appeal
courts of   169, 170, 232, 240
Division Court   169
parties on   232

appeal books
contents of   233
cover of   233
date for filing   237
index in   237
number of copies   233
numbering pages of   237
preparation of   233, 235

appeal case
contents of   240
preparation of   240-243

appeals to Supreme Court of Canada
appeal case   240-243
factum   243
inscribing of   243
notice of appeal   240
Ottawa agent   240
style of cause   240
time limits for   240

appeals to Supreme Court of Ontario
appeal book   233-237
determining date for   237
factum   237
ordering evidence   233
parties to   232
perfection of   237
setting down   232
style of cause   232
time limit for   232

appearance
filing of   204
form of   204
number of copies   204
time limit for   204

application
letters of administration   259
letters of administration with will annexed
260
letters patent   300-301
letters probate   253
mortgage   83

assignment of mortgage
affidavits in   103
consideration clause in   103
date of   103
direction re payment of   103
execution of   103
mortgage statement for   103
number of copies   103
parties to   103
registration of   103

attention line   9

attestation
legal instrument, generally   37
officer of corporation   37
wills   245

B

back
see specific legal paper
accounts   29

court documents   173
legal instruments   44
long   44
short   44

bank accounts
firm   24
trust   24-25

barristers and solicitors
defined   2
in inside address   8

bill of costs
body of   228
ending of   228
heading of   228
number of copies   228
serving and filing of   228
title of   228

bill of sale
affidavits in   152
date of   152
execution of   152
information to complete   152
number of copies   152
parties to   152
registration of   152-153

body
see specific legal paper
court documents   172
legal instruments generally   36
typing guides for   36

brief   219-220

buying and selling real property
see real property, buying and selling of

by-laws
approval of   309
body of   309
ending of   309
heading of   309
scope of   309
typing of   309

C

call to the bar   2

Canadian Bar Association   2

capitalization
in correspondence   9
in legal descriptions   60
in legal papers   33, 36, 172, 189-190

carbon copies
blind copy   11
duplicate original   33

case law   17

Central Divorce Registry   326

certificate of readiness
filing of   219
number of copies   219
purpose of   219
service of   219

cessation of charge
date of   104
execution of   104
information required to complete   104
number of copies   104
partial   105
registration of   105

charge
affidavits in   83, 88
cessation of   104
date of   88
distinguished from mortgage   83
filing of   88
number of copies   83
parties to   83, 88
points similar to mortgage   88
registration of   88
with dower   83
without dower   83

chattel mortgage
affidavits in   152
date of   152
discharge of   153
execution of   152
information required for   152
number of copies   152
parties to   152
registration of   153
renewal of   153
uses of   152

cheque
closing real estate transaction   132
requisition for   28

citations
brackets in   18
date essential in   18
date not essential in   18
in factums   237, 240
in law reports   17
typing of   18

closing
cheques required on   132
exchange by parties at   133
searches on   133
steps on   133

codicil
affidavit of execution of   258

witness to   247

codicil to will   247

Commissioner   4

common shares   299

company
affidavit by officer of   54, 71
affidavit in legal instruments   54
books of record of   307
by-laws of   307
capital of   298
creation of   299-301
defined   298
first meetings of   301
incorporating of   298-301
incorporation fee   301
letters patent of   307
liability of   298
meetings of   309
minutes of   313, 316
mortgage with   131
private   298
prospectus of   299
public   298
seal of   301
shares of   298-299

comparing   5

complimentary close   9-10

conduct money   218

consent
back of   191
body of   190
ending of   190-191
execution of   191
filing of   191
heading of   190
number of copies   191
transfer of insurance   141

consideration clause
in assignment of mortgage   103
in deed   63-64
in mortgage   86
in transfer   71

constitutional law   16

corner   44

corporation taxes   125

correspondence
see letters

costs
bills of   228
defined   190
taxation of   228-229

counter-claim   205

County Courts
appeals from   169

jurisdiction of   169
names of   169
rules of practice of   194

county law associations   2

court documents
backs of   173
body of   172
ending of   172-173
filing of   174
heading of   171-172
paper for   171
service of   173
types of   180

courts
appeal   169, 170, 232, 240
capitalization of   9
divorce   324
federal   169
juvenile   169
officers of   170
offices of   170
probate   252
provincial   169, 170
table of   344-345

credit slip   24

creditors, notice to   275

D

date
assignment of mortgage   103
bill of sale   152
cessation of charge   104
charge   88
chattel mortgage   152
deed   62
discharge of mortgage   104
essential in citation   18
leases   145
legal papers   33
letter   7
mortgage   83
non-essential in citation   18
power of attorney   151
renewal of mortgage   104
transfer   71
will   245

decree absolute
application for   327
grant of   327

decree nisi   326-327

deed
affidavit of execution in   65

affidavit of legal age and marital status
in   65
affidavits in   62
approval of   131
back of   65
compared with transfer   71
consideration clause in   63-64
covenants and release in   64
date of   62
deed to uses   62-63
ending of   65
execution of   65, 133
executor's deed   63
granting clause in   64
habendum clause in   64
heading of   63
joint tenancy deed   62
legal description in   64
legal seals in   62
number of copies   62
parties to   62
quit claim deed   63, 72
registration of   65, 133
signatures to   65
with dower   62
without dower   62

deed to uses   62-63

deed with dower   62

deed without dower   62

default judgment   190

destruction of will   247

diary, entries re real estate
transaction   124, 132

direction
re mortgage payments   103
re payment to vendor   133
re taking title   124

directors' register   321

disbursements
cheque requisition   28
petty cash expenditure   28
telegram   28
telephone call   28

discharge of chattel mortgage
affidavits in   153
execution of   153
information required   153
number of copies   153
registration of   153

discharge of mortgage
execution of   104
information required for   104
number of copies   104
partial   105
parties to   104
registration of   105

Division Courts   169

divorce
certificate of registrar   326
counter-petition   326
court hearing   324
decree absolute   327
decree nisi   326
file number of   324
grounds for   324
notice of hearing   326
notice of petition for divorce   325
Official Guardian   326
parties to   324
petition for divorce   325
record   326
registration of   326
reply to petition   325-326
steps on   339
when children   326

dockets   22
alphabetical system of   22
contents of   22
lawyer's docket sheet   22
numerical system of   22
opening of   24

dower   57, 59

duplicate original   33

E

E. & O. E.   136

ending
see specific legal paper
attestation clause   37
court documents   172-173
jurat   49-50
testimonium clause   36

endorsement
back   44
writ of summons   196

entries
contents of   24
information for   24
preparation of   24

envelopes   11

esquire   8

estate, administration of
see administration with will
annexed, letters of   259-260
administration, letters of   258-259
nomination of administrator   259
renunciation by next of kin   259

estate tax
calculation of   276
defined   274
estate tax return   275-276
quick succession   276
release of   274, 276
time limit for return   275

estate tax return
debts   276
filing of   276
inventory of estate   276
material with   276
number of copies   276

estates
administration of   258-261
distribution of   275, 276
information on death of client   252
for estate tax purposes   274
for succession duty purposes   274
inventory of   259
probate of   252, 253-258
safety deposit box   252-253
Surrogate Court fees   261
testate or intestate   252

evidence
cost of   233
ordered on appeal   233
typing references to   240

ex parte notice of motion   184

examination for discovery
appointment for   218
conduct money   218
described   205
transcript of   218

Exchequer Court   169

execution
see also specific legal paper
legal instruments generally   44-45

executor
affidavit of   253
appointment of   244
deed of   63
renunciation by   260

exhibits
at trial   220
marking of   180-181
to administration application   260
to affidavit   180-181
to probate application   258
true copies of   181

F

factum
back of   237

citations in   237, 240
ending of   237
filing of   237
form of   237, 243
list of authorities in   243
Supreme Court of Canada   243

Federal Court of Canada   169

Figures
account
  back of   31
  two page   31
  with ledger statement   32
administration bond
  no will   273
  will annexed   272
affidavit
  back of   177
  basic format   182
  of administrator   269
  of debts   290-291
  of executor   256
  of legal age and marital status   53
  of officer of company   78
  of service   183
  of value and relationship   277-289
affidavit of execution   53
  of codicil   262
  of will   257
*affidavit on application for judgment
absolute*   343
affidavit on production
  individual   210-213
  officer   214-217
agreement extending mortgage   111-114
agreement of purchase and sale   126-127
amortization schedule   97
amortized payment page of mortgage   96
appeal book
  cover of   236
  index in   238
appeal to S.C.O., steps on   234
application
  for administration   266
  for incorporation   302-306
  for mortgage   84-85
  for probate   255
*appointment for examination for
discovery*   221
assignment of mortgage   106-110
attention line
  envelope   15
  letter   13
back
  account   31
  action, County Court   178
  action, Supreme Court   177
  factum   242
  legal instruments   46-47
  matter   179

share certificate   320
will   248
bill of costs   230, 231
bill of sale   157-160
by-laws
    ending of   311
    extract from   310
    heading of   310
carbon copy notation   14
certificate of readiness   224-225
cessation of charge   118-120
charge   98-102
chattel mortgage   161-164
cheque requisition   29
citations
    printed   19
    typed   19
codicil to will   251
company, affidavit by officer of   78
complimentary close   12, 13, 14
consent   193
cover for appeal book   236
credit slip   27
deed   66-70
deed, quit claim   79-82
default judgment   192
direction
    on taking title   129
    payment of proceeds   135
directors' register   322
disbursement forms   29-30
discharge of chattel mortgage   167-168
discharge of mortgage   115-117
divorce
    affidavit on application for judgment
    absolute   343
    application for judgment absolute   342
    decree nisi   340-341
    notice of petition   335-338
    petition for   328-334
    steps on   339
docket, opening entries for   25
docket sheet, lawyer's   23
dower, bar of in deed   66
ending
    company   43
    individual   43
    printed instruments   42
    typed instruments   43
entries
    alphabetical system   26
    numerical system   27
envelopes   15
estate tax return   293-297
factum
    back of   242
    ending of   241
    heading of   239
file folder, real estate transaction   128
generally endorsed writ   197-199
governing bodies of legal profession
in Canada   3

headings
    company   38
    individuals   37
    married couple   38
    number of parties   39
    printed instrument   37
    typed instrument   38
    wife barring dower   66
index
    appeal book   238
    record   222
inside address   12, 13, 14
insurance, transfer of   142
introductory words, legal instruments   35
inventory of estate   263
judgment
    basic format of   191
    default   192
land registration systems in Ontario,
comparison of   58
Land Titles system   58
land transfer tax affidavit   69
lawsuit, steps on   195
lawyer's docket sheet   23
lease, house   147-150
ledger statement   32
legal description, extract from   61
legal instruments
    backs of   46-47
    endings of   42-43
    extracts from   40-41, 61, 154, 327
    headings of   37-39
    introductory words   35
legal letterhead   4
letter
    indented   12
    semi-block   13, 14
letters of administration   270
letters patent, typed extract from   308
letters probate   254
mailing notation
    envelope   15
    letter   12
margin headings   314
margin ruled paper   34
memoranda of law   21
minutes
    centred headings   314
    certified extract from, printed   317
    certified extract from, typed   315
    ending of   314, 315
    heading of   312
    margin headings in   314
    shoulder headings in   314
mortgage
    agreement extending   111-114
    amortized payment page   96
    application for   84-85
    assignment of   106-110
    chattel   163-164
    discharge of   115-117
    discharge of chattel   167-168

guide for completing repayment clause
95
    married couple as mortgagors 94
    partial discharge of 121-123
    renewal of chattel 165-166
    with dower 89-93
new docket memo 25
new matter entry 25
nomination of administrator 268
notarial certificate
    administration 265
    printed 51
    probate 265
    typed 52
notice, basic format of 185
notice of meeting 311
notice to creditors 292
notice to produce
    at trial 208-209
    on discovery 206-207
offer to purchase 126-127
opening entries 25
order, basic format of 191
paper, ruled 34
partial discharge of mortgage 121-123
personal notation
    envelope 15
    letter 12
petition for divorce 328-334
petty cash voucher 30
pleadings, basic format of 188
power of attorney, general, extract from
154
power of attorney, short 155-156
proxy 312
quit claim deed 79-82
real estate file folder 128
record
    face page of 223
    index for 222
register
    directors' 322
    shareholders' 321
    transfer 323
Registry Office system 58
release 48
renewal of chattel mortgage 165-166
renunciation
    of administration 267
    of administration, will annexed 271
    of probate 271
reporting letter 143, 144
request for amortization schedule 97
requisition for docket 26
salutations 12, 13, 14
separation agreement, extract from 327
share certificate 318, 320
shareholders' ledger sheet 322
shareholders' register sheet 321
short back
    11" paper 47
    14" paper 46

special notations
    envelope 15
    letter 12, 14
specially endorsed writ 200-203
statement of adjustments 139-140
statutory declaration 55-56
steps on appeal to S.C.O. 234
steps on divorce proceedings 339
steps on a lawsuit 195
style of cause
    action, County Court 175
    action, Supreme Court 175
    appeal from County Court 238, 239
    appeal to Supreme Court 235, 236
    appeal to Supreme Court of Canada
    243
    counter-claim 189
    matter 176, 186
    unruled paper 176
subject line 11, 12, 13
subpoena 226-227
tax certificate 130
telephone call record 30
transfer 73-77
transfer of insurance 142
transfer register 323
will
    affidavit of execution of 257
    back of 248
    codicil to 251
    ending of 246
    endorsement and stamping of 264
    first page of 250
    one-page 249
writs of summons
    generally endorsed 197-199
    specially endorsed 200-203

filing
see specific legal paper
court documents 174
fee on 174

firm bank account 24

G

gift affidavit 275

Glossary 346-356

H

habendum clause 64

headings
see specific legal paper
company as party   36
court documents   171-172
husband and wife as party   36
individual as party   36
legal instruments   33
wife party to bar dower   62

holographic will   244

I

Illustrations
see Figures

in escrow   44

incorporating a company
application for   300
letters patent   300-301
memorandum of association   300
prospectus   299
royal charter   300
special act   300

index
appeal books   237
names and terms   6
record   218

insurance
consent to transfer   141
in statement of adjustments   137-138
transfer of   134, 141

interlocutory notice of motion   184

inventory of estate   258, 259

J

joint tenancy deed   62

joint tenants   59

judges
defined   170
references to   20

judgment
back of   190
body of   189-190
default   190
ending of   190

entry of   187, 189
form of   191
heading of   189
number of copies   187
on appeal   243
signing of   189

jurat   49-50

Juvenile Court   169

K

King's Counsel
see Queen's Counsel

L

Land Titles system
administration of   57
filing under   57
offices of   45

land transfer tax
affidavit re   65, 71
cheque to pay   132
computation of   65

law firms
composition of   4
inside address of   8
letterhead of   4
name of   4
salutations for   8

law reports
abbreviations of   17
citations in   17
defined   17
identification of   17
names of   17, 18

Law Societies
governing body of   2
head of   2
list of   3
membership in   2
rules of   2

lawsuits
parties to   171
steps on   194-220

lawyers
admission to practice   2

advertising by 7
areas of service for 2
barrister and solicitor 2
Canadian 2
Commissioner 4
counsel 2
educational background of 2
English 2
fiduciary 5
governing body of 2
Notary Public 4
Queen's Counsel 2
references to 2
salutation for 8

lease
affidavits in 145
back of 145
body of 145
date of 145
ending of 145
forms of 145
heading of 145
leaseback 146
number of copies 145
parties to 145
preparation of 145
term of 145
typed form of 146

ledger statement 29

legal descriptions
checking 60
copying of 60
in deeds 64
in mortgage 86
in partial cessation of charge 105
in partial discharge of mortgage 105
in transfer 71
lot and plan 59
metes and bounds 59
township and concession 59
typing guide for 60

legal directories
Canada 4
local 4

legal instruments
see also specific instrument and court
papers
affidavits in 50
assembly of 44
attestation clause in 37
backs of 44
body of 36
date of 33
disposition of 44
divided in sections 146
duplicate original of 33
endings of 36
execution of
   company 37
     individual 37

headings of 33
number of copies 33
parties to 36
registration of 45
sealing of 37
testimonium clause in 36
typing of 36

legal papers
capitalization of words in 9
classification of 33
numbers in 36
paper for 33
printed forms 36
true copy of 45
types of 33
typing guides 36

legal proceedings
commencement of 171
parties to 171
types of 171

legal profession
governing body of 2
rules of conduct for 2

legal seal
see seal

legal secretary
characteristics of 5
performance of 5
qualifications for 5
role of 6

letter book 11

letters
attention line 9
blind carbon copy 11
body of 9
capitalization in 9
carbon copies 10
complimentary close 9
date line 7
enclosures 10
inside address 7
number of copies 11
opinion letters 9
punctuation 7, 9
reference line 10
salutations 8
second pages 10
signature of 9-10
special notations 11
subject lines 9

letters of administration 258-259

letter of administration with will annexed
259-260

letters patent
application for 300
copy of 307
errors in 307

issuance of   301
receipt of   307

letters probate   253, 258

list of authorities   243

long distance telephone calls   28

M

Magnetic Tape Selectric typewriter   244

mailing notations   11

margins
court documents   172
legal instruments   36
minute book paper   307
quoted material   20
ruled paper   36
unruled paper   36
wills   245

meeting
minutes of   309, 313
notice of   309
proxy for   309
types of   309

memorandum
form of   20
number of copies   21
of law   20
purpose of   20
quoted material in   20

mesdames   7

messrs.   7

metes and bounds description   59

minute book
ordering of   301
paper for   307
registers and records in   321

minutes
approval of   313
body of   313
certified extract from   316
content of   313
correction of   316
ending of   313
heading of   313
number of copies   313
numbering pages of   316
signing of   313
typing guide for   313

mortgage
affidavits in   83, 87-88

amortized   86, 87
application for   83
assigned   103
assumed   131, 132
back   131, 134
consideration clause in   86
covenants in   87
date of   83
discharged   104, 132
disposition of   88
distinguished from charge   83
execution of   87
foreclosed   83
heading of   83
legal description in   86
notices re   134
number of copies of   83
parties to   83
registration of   88, 134
renewed   103-104
repayment clause   87
repayment of   86
seals on   87
second   83
signature to   87
special clauses   87
statement   131
statement of adjustments in   137
with dower   83
with mortgage company   131
without dower   83

mortgage statement   103, 131

Municipal Board   45

N

nomination of administrator   259

notarial certificate
form of   49
number of copies   49
purpose of   49
signing of   49

notarial copies
letters of administration   259
letters probate   258

Notary Public   4

notice
back of   184
body of   183
ending of   183-184
filing of   184
form of   185
heading of   181
mortgage, payment of   134

number of copies   184
of appeal   232, 240
of meeting   309
of motion   184
of taxes   134
service of   184

notice of appeal
service and filing of   232, 240
to Court of Appeal   232
to Supreme Court of Canada   240

notice of hearing   326

notice of motion   184
ex parte   184
filing of   186
interlocutory   184
material required   184
originating   184
service of   184-185
times for service of   186

notice of perfection
form of   237
serving and filing of   237
time limit for   237

notice of petition   325

notice of trial
form of   219
time limit for   219

notice to creditors   275

notice to produce
at trial   205
number of copies   205
on discovery   205
service of   205

number of copies
see also specific legal paper
administration forms   259
affidavit   180
affidavit of debts   275
affidavit of value and relationship   274
affidavit on production   205
appeal books   233
appearance   204
assignment of mortgage   103
bill of costs   228
bill of sale   152
certificate of readiness   219
cessation of charge   104
charge   83
chattel mortgage   152
consent   191
deed   62
discharge of chattel mortgage   153
discharge of mortgage   153
entries   24
estate tax return   276
evidence   233
judgment   187

lease   145
legal papers   33
letters   11
memorandum   21
minutes   313
mortgage   83
notarial certificate   49
notice to produce   205
notices   184
order   187
petition for divorce   325
pleadings   187
probate forms   253
release   44
renewal of chattel mortgage   153
renewal of mortgage   104
transfer   71
transfer of insurance   141
will   245
writ of summons   196

numbering
pages   36, 146, 172
   appeal book   237
   court documents   172
   legal instruments   36
   long instrument   146
   minutes   316
   record   218
   sections of long instrument   146
   two numbers   146
paragraphs   36

numbers
in legal descriptions   60
in legal papers   36

O

offer to purchase
acceptance of   124
information in   124
terms and conditions in   124

Official Guardian
defined   45
in divorce   326

order
back of   190
body of   189-190
ending of   190
entry of   187, 189
form of   191
heading of   189
issuing of   187, 189
number of copies   187

originating notice of motion   184

P

paper
for account 28
for court documents 171
for legal papers 33
for minute-book 307
for wills 245

paragraphs
indentation of 36
numbering of 36

partial cessation of charge 105

partial discharge of mortgage 105

parties
company 36
husband and wife 36
in legal instrument 36
individual 36
to appeals 232
to assignment of mortgage 103
to bill of sale 152
to cessation of charge 105
to charge 83
to chattel mortgage 152
to deed 62
to discharge of mortgage 104
to divorce 324
to lease 145
to legal proceedings 171
to mortgage 83
to power of attorney 151
to renewal of mortgage 104
to transfer 71
to will 244

personal notations 11

petition for divorce
answer to 325-326
filing of 325
information in 325
issuance of 325
notice of 325
number of copies 325
serving of 325

pleadings
back of 187
body of 187
closed 205
ending of 187
filing of 187
format of 188
heading of 186-187
in lawsuit 204-205
number of copies of 187
service of 187
time limits for 204
types of 186, 204-205

power of attorney
affidavits in 151
date of 151
execution of 151
forms of 151
general 151
parties to 151
short 151

precedents, set of 6

preferred shares 299

printed forms
date in 33
ruling on 36
typing of 36

private company 298

probate, letters of
affidavit of execution of codicil 258
affidavit of execution of will 253
affidavit of executor 253
application for 253
exhibits filed 258
forms for 253
grant of 258
inventory of estate 258
preparation for 253

proofreading 5

provincial courts 169

proxy 309

public company 298

Public Trustee 45

punctuation
closed 7
letters 9
mixed 7
quoted material 20

Q

Queen's Counsel 2

quick succession 276

quit claim deed 63, 72

quotations
margins for 20
omissions from 20
spacing 20

R

ready list 219

real property
buying and selling of
acting for the purchaser 124-132,
133-134
acting for the vendor 132-133, 134
agreement of purchase and sale 124
closing 132-134
existing mortgage re 132
file folder re 124
information from vendor 132
mortgage back 132
offer to purchase 124
reporting letters re 134, 141, 142
statement of adjustments 133, 136-138
tax certificates 125
lease of 145

realty taxes
notice re change of ownership 134
search of 125
statement of adjustments 137

reasons for judgment 187

record
assembly of 218-219
back of 218
contents of 218
divorce proceedings 326
index for 218
jury notice with 219
passing 218, 219

reference line 10

registration
see specific instrument
defined 45
of divorce 326
systems of land registration 57

Registry Office system
administration of 57
buying and selling real property under
124-134
deeds 62
mortgages 83
offices of 45

release
back of 44
defined 44
number of copies 44

renewal of chattel mortgage
affidavits in 153
execution of 153
filing of 153
information required for 153
number of copies 153
time limits for 153

renewal of mortgage
affidavits in 104
date of 104
execution of 104
information for 104
number of copies 104
parties to 104

renunciation
by executor 260
by next of kin 259

repayment clause
mortgage 86
renewal of mortgage 104

reporting letter
contents of 141, 142
to purchaser 134, 141-142
to vendor 134, 142

requisitions on title 124, 125

retail sales tax, search of 125

S

safekeeping of will 247

safety deposit box of client 252

salutations 8

seal
attestation of 37
company 37
individual 37
ordering of 301
typed notation for 37

search
building restrictions 131
corporation tax 125
liens generally 131
on closing 133
retail sales tax 125
tax certificates 125
title 125

second mortgage 83

security transfer tax 319

separation agreement
affidavit of execution in 324
contents of 324
execution of 324
typing of 324

service
see specific court paper
admission of 173-174
affidavit of 181

during vacation   174
substitutional   325

share certificate
issuance of   316, 319
numbering of   316
ordering of   301, 316
tax on transfer of   319
transfer agent for   316
transfer of   319

shareholders
ledger sheet for   321
proxy of   309
register of   321

sharheolders' ledger sheet   321

shareholders' register   321

shares
common   299
original issue   316
preferred   299

sheriff   170

signature
see specific instrument
illegible   181
in letters   9-10

sources of law   16

spacing
legal descriptions   36
legal papers   36
quotations   20
styles of cause   172

special notations
envelopes   11, 15
letters   11, 12, 14

statement of adjustments
approval of   131
balance due   138
body of   136
computation of   136, 137
ending of   136
heading of   136
insurance   137
mortgage assumed   136
mortgage back   137
oil tank   138
preparation of   133, 136
realty taxes   137
rent   138
set-up of   136
water rates, hydro, telephone and gas   138

statement of claim   186, 204
see also pleadings

statement of defence   204

statement of points of law and fact
see factum

statute law   16

Statutes
identification of   16
name of   16
publications of   16
revised   16

statutory declarations
back of   54
body of   54
by beneficiary   275
by two people   54
declaration of   54
ending of   54
heading of   54
purpose of   54

style of cause
affidavit   180
appeal to Supreme Court of Canada   240
appeal to Supreme Court of Ontario   232
counter-claim   187
default judgment   190
ex parte notice of motion   184
information on   171-172
notices   181
originating notice of motion   184
pleadings   186-187
short form   172
typing guides   171-172

subject line   9

subpoena
preparation of   220
service of   220

succession duty
affidavit of debts   275
affidavit of value and relationship   274-275
defined   274
estate included for   274
release of   274, 276
time limit for   274

Supreme Court of Canada
appeals to   240, 243
described   169

Supreme Court of Ontario
court of appeal   170
rules of practice of   194
trial division of   169-170

Surrogate Court
described   169, 252
fees of   261

swearing
affidavits   49
court affidavits   180
estate affidavits   261

T

tables
appeal books, number of copies 233
comparison of land registration systems in Ontario 58
evidence, copy ordered 233
governing bodies of the legal profession in Canada 3
provincial courts 344-345
wording for affidavit of execution 50

tax certificate 125

taxation of costs
appointment for 228-229
certificate of 229
payment of 229
steps on 229

telegrams
charging for 28

tenants in common 59

testimonium clause
date in 36
in instruments 36

time limit
affidavit of merits 204
affidavit of value and relationship 274
appeals 232, 240
appearance 204
estate tax return 275
gifts 275
notice of motion 186
notice of perfection 237
notice of trial 219
perfecting appeal 237
pleadings 204
renewal of chattel mortgage 153
service of documents 174
taxation appointment 229

title
abstract of 125
direction re taking 124
encumbrance on 125
joint tenants 59
requisition re 125
search of 125
Statutes 16
tenants in common 59

transfer
affidavit of execution 71
affidavit of legal age and marital status 71
affidavit of officer of company 71-72
back of 72
comparison with deed 71
consideration clause in 71
date of 71
execution of 71
land transfer tax affidavit 71
legal description in 71
number of copies of 71
parties to 71
signature to 71

transfer of insurance
consent to 141
execution of 141
mortgage clause 141
number of copies 141

transfer register 321

true copies 45

trust bank account 24-25

typing
see specific legal paper
accounts 29
Acts, reference to 17
backs 44
backs, court documents 173
body
  court documents 172
  legal papers 36
brackets in citations 18
by-laws 309
citations 18
court names 172, 173
evidence, references to 240
headings, legal instruments 36
legal descriptions 60
long instrument 146
minutes 313
numbers 36, 60
printed legal forms 36
quotations 20
styles of cause 171-172
wills 244-245

W

will
administration of 259-260
attestation clause 245
back of 245
body of 244-245
codicil to 247
date of 245
defined 244
destruction of 247
disposition of 247
ending of 245
erasures in 245
execution of 245-246
executor, appointment of 244
heading of 244
holographic 244
number of copies 245

paper for   245
parties to   244
probate of   252-258
safekeeping of   247
search for   259
testimonium clause   245
typing of   245
witnesses to   247

without prejudice   11

witness
affidavit of execution   50
affidavit of execution of codicil   258
affidavit of execution of will   253, 260
to will   247

writs of summons
acceptance of service   204
back of   196
defined   194

endorsement in   196
generally endorsed   194
holding of   196
issuance of   196
number of copies   196
out of jurisdiction   194-195
preparation of   196
responses to   204
service of   196
specially endorsed   194
style of cause   196

Z

Z ruling   36

Notes